FINLAND

Helsinki

slo

Stockholm

SWEDEN

Copenhagen

BALTIC
SEA

Berlin

AST
ERMANY

P O L A N D

Warsaw

Prague

CZECHOSLOVAKIA

Vienna

USTRIA

Budapest

HUNGARY

YUGOSLAVIA

ADRIATIC
SEA

Belgrade

ALBANIA

Tirana

GREECE

Athens

Moscow

S O V I E T

U N I O N

ROMANIA

Bucharest

Sofia

BULGARIA

BLACK SEA

Ankara

T U R K E Y

TIMOTHY GARTON ASH

History of the Present

ESSAYS, SKETCHES AND DESPATCHES FROM
EUROPE IN THE 1990S

ALLEN LANE
THE PENGUIN PRESS

ALLEN LANE
THE PENGUIN PRESS

Published by the Penguin Group
Penguin Books Ltd, 27 Wrights Lane, London W8 5TZ, England
Penguin Putnam Inc., 375 Hudson Street, New York, New York 10014, USA
Penguin Books Australia Ltd, Ringwood, Victoria, Australia
Penguin Books Canada Ltd, 10 Alcorn Avenue, Toronto, Ontario, Canada M4V 3B2
Penguin Books (NZ) Ltd, Private Bag 102902, NSMC, Auckland, New Zealand

Penguin Books Ltd, Registered Offices: Harmondsworth, Middlesex, England

First published 1999
3 5 7 9 10 8 6 4

Set in 11/14 pt Monotype Sabon
Typeset by Rowland Phototypesetting Ltd, Bury St Edmunds, Suffolk
Printed in Great Britain by The Bath Press, Bath

A CIP catalogue record for this book is available from the British Library

ISBN 0-713-99323-5

To Robert Silvers

Contents

Introduction

Even at one minute past midnight on 1 January 1990 we already knew that this would be a formative decade in Europe. A forty-year-old European order had just collapsed with the Berlin Wall. Everything seemed possible. Everyone was hailing a 'new Europe'. But no one knew what it would look like.

Now we know: in Western Europe, in Germany, in Central Europe and in the Balkans. Of course, in all these parts, the future will be full of surprises. It always is. But at the end of the decade we can see the broad outline of the new European order that we have already ceased to call 'new'. Only in the vast, ethnically chequered territory of the former Soviet Union is even the basic direction of states such as Russia and Ukraine still hidden in the fog. And perhaps also, at Europe's other end, that of the decreasingly United Kingdom.

This book does not pretend to be a comprehensive account of the 1990s in Europe. It is a collection of what are rightly called pieces – in other words, fragments – that reflect my own interests, expertise and travels. However, a chronology running through the book not only supplies missing links between the pieces but also records significant European developments not covered in any of them. Into this time-line I have inserted some short diary-like sketches, mainly drawn from my own notebooks and recollections. There are also several longer sketches in the main text. The largest part of the book consists of analytical reportages, mostly published in the *New York Review of Books*, after the skilled attentions of the editor to whom this book is dedicated. Finally, there are a few essays in which I attempt an interim synthesis on a larger subject, such as the development of the European

Union, Britain's troubled relationship with Europe, or the way countries deal with the legacy of a dictatorship.

As befits 'history of the present', everything in the main text was written at or shortly after the time it describes. The pieces have been lightly edited, mainly to eliminate repetition, but nothing of substance has been added or changed. I compiled the chronology and short sketches more recently. Occasionally I have also added a comment at the end of a piece.

Here I want to reflect on writing 'history of the present'. The phrase is not mine. It was, so far as I know, coined by the veteran American diplomatist and historian George Kennan, in a review of my book about Central Europe in the 1980s, *The Uses of Adversity*. It is, for me, the best possible description of what I have been trying to write for twenty years, combining the crafts of historian and journalist.

Yet it immediately invites dissent. History of the present? Surely that's a contradiction in terms. Surely history is by definition about the past. History is books on Caesar, the Thirty Years War or the Russian revolution. It is discoveries and new interpretations based on years of studying documents in the archives.

Let's put aside straightaway the objection that 'the present' is but a line, scarcely a millisecond wide, between past and future. We know what we mean here by 'the present', even if the chronological boundaries are always disputed. Call it 'the very recent past' or 'current affairs' if you would rather. The important point is this: not just professional historians but most arbiters of our intellectual life feel that a certain minimum period of time needs to have passed, and that certain canonical kinds of archival source should be available, before anything written about this immediate past qualifies as History.

It was not ever thus. As the formidably learned German intellectual historian Reinhart Koselleck has observed, from the time of Thucydides until well into the eighteenth century, to have been an eyewitness to the events described, or, even better, to have been a participant in them, was considered to be a major advantage in the writing of history.[1] Contemporary history was thought to be the best history. It is only since the emergence of the idea of progress, the growth of critical philology and the work of Leopold von Ranke that historians have come to believe that you understand events better if you are further away from them. If you stop to think about it, this is actually a very odd idea: that the person who wasn't there knows better than the person who was.

Even the most ascetic neo-Rankean depends upon the witnesses who make the first record of the past. If they do not make a record, there is no history. If they do it badly, or in pursuit of a quite different agenda (religious, say, or astrological, or scatological), the historian will not find answers to the questions he wants to ask. It's therefore best to have a witness who is himself interested in finding answers to the historian's questions about sources and causes, structure and process, the individual and the mass. Hence, for example, Alexis de Tocqueville's personal memoir of the 1848 revolution in France is worth twenty others.

Now this need for the historically minded witness has become more acute in recent times, for a simple reason. In Ranke's day, politics was put on paper. Diplomacy was conducted or immediately noted down in correspondence. Politicians, generals and diplomats wrote extensive diaries, letters and memoranda. Even then, of course, much that was vital was not written down – murmured private understandings in the corridors of the Congress of Vienna, the pillow talk of queens. Then, as now, most of human experience was never recorded at all. But most of politics was.

Today, however, high politics is more and more pursued in personal meetings (thanks to the jet airplane), or by telephone (increasingly by mobile phone), or by other forms of electronic communication. Certainly, minutes of meetings are made afterwards and, at the highest levels, also transcripts of phone conversations. But the proportion of important business actually put on paper has diminished. And who writes narrative letters or detailed diaries any more? A dwindling minority.

To be sure, researchers can watch television footage. Sometimes, they can listen to the telephone tapes – or taps – of those conversations. Perhaps in future they will also read the e-mails. The point is not that there are fewer sources than there were. Quite the reverse. Where the ancient historian has to reconstruct a whole epoch from a single papyrus, the contemporary historian has a roomful of sources for a single day. It is the ratio of quantity to quality that has changed for the worse.

On the other hand, politicians, diplomats, soldiers and businessmen have never been so eager to give their own version of what has just happened. Iraqi crises famously unfold in 'real time' on CNN. European ministers tumble out of EU meetings to brief journalists from their own countries. Naturally, each gives his own twist and spin. But, if you put the different versions together, you have a pretty good instant picture of what occurred.

In short, what you can know soon after the event has increased, and what you can know long after the event has diminished. This is particularly the case with extraordinary events. During some of the dramatic debates between the leaders of Czechoslovakia's 'velvet revolution', in the Magic Lantern theatre in Prague in November 1989, I was the only person present taking notes. I remember thinking, 'If I don't write this down, nobody will. It will be gone for ever, like bathwater down the drain.' So much recent history has disappeared like that, never to be recovered, for want of the present recorder.

Two objections remain strong. First, since what governments and individuals try to keep secret is often the most important things, the eventual release of new sources will change the picture substantially. This is not a conclusive argument for waiting – in the meantime, other equally important things, well understood at the moment, may be forgotten – but it is a major hazard of the genre. In the preface to my first 'history of the present', an account of the Solidarity revolution in Poland, I observed that I would not have attempted to write the book had it seemed likely that the official papers of the Soviet and Polish communist regimes would become available in the foreseeable future. That, I blithely continued, seemed 'as probable as the restoration of the monarchy in Warsaw or Moscow'. Eight years later, the Soviet bloc had collapsed and many of those papers were available. Fortunately I also quoted Walter Raleigh's warning, in the preface to his *History of the World*, that 'who-so-euer in writing a modern Historie shall follow truth too neare the heeles, it may happily strike out his teeth'.

The second strong objection is that we don't know the consequences of current developments, so our understanding of their historical significance is much more speculative and liable to revision. Again, this is patently true. Every sixth-former studying ancient history knows that the Roman empire declined and fell. Writing about the Soviet empire in the 1980s, none of us knew the end of the story. In 1988 I published an essay entitled 'The Empire in Decay', but I still thought the empire's fall was a long way off. In January 1989 I wrote an article pooh-poohing suggestions that the Berlin Wall might soon be breached.

Yet there is also an advantage here. You record what people did not know at the time – for instance, that the Wall was about to come down. You dwell on developments that seemed terribly important then but would otherwise be quite forgotten now, because they led nowhere. You thus avoid perhaps the most powerful of all the optical illusions of historical writing.

One of the real pleasures of immersing yourself in the archives of a closed period is that you gradually, over months and years, see a pattern slowly emerging through the vast piles of paper, like a message written in invisible ink. But then you start wondering, Is this pattern really in the past itself? Or is it just in your own head? Or perhaps it is a pattern from the fabric of your own times. Each generation has its own Cromwell, its own French revolution, its own Napoleon. Where contemporaries saw only a darkling plain, you discern a tidy park, a well-lit square, or most often a road leading to the next historical milestone. The French philosopher Henri Bergson talks of the 'illusions of retrospective determinism'.

American journalists writing books of recent history sometimes modestly refer to them as 'the first draft of history'. This implies that the scholar's second or third draft will always be an improvement. Well, in some ways it may be, having more sources and a longer perspective. But in others it may not be, because the scholar will not know, and therefore will find it more difficult to re-create, what it was really like at the time. How places looked and smelled, how people felt, what they didn't know. Writers work in different ways, but I can sum up my own experience in a doggerel line: there is nothing to compare with being there.

Kennan observed that history of the present lies 'in that small and rarely visited field of literary effort where journalism, history and literature . . . come together'. Again, this seems to me exactly right. The corner of Europe where Germany, France and Switzerland meet is known in German as the *Dreiländereck*, or Three Country Corner. 'History of the present' lies in a Three Country Corner between journalism, history and literature. Such frontier areas are always interesting, but often tense. Sometimes working in this one feels like walking in no man's land.

The shortest and best marked frontier is that between history and journalism, on the one side, and literature, on the other. Both good journalism and good history have some of the qualities of good fiction: imaginative sympathy with the characters involved, literary powers of selection, description and evocation. Reportage or historical narrative is always an individual writer's story, shaped by his or her unique perception and arrangement of words on the page. It requires an effort not just of research but of imagination to get inside the experience of the people you are writing about. To this extent, the historian or journalist does work like a novelist. We implicitly acknowledge this when we talk of 'Michelet's Napoleon' as opposed to 'Taine's Napoleon' or 'Carlyle's Napoleon'.

Yet there is a sharp and fundamental difference, which concerns the kind of truth being sought. The novelist Jerzy Kosinski, who played fast and loose with all facts, including those about his own life, defended himself aggressively. 'I'm interested in truth not facts,' he said, 'and I'm old enough to know the difference.' In a sense, every novelist can say that. No journalist or historian should. In this we also differ from the father of contemporary history. Thucydides felt free to put words into Pericles' mouth, like a novelist. We are not. Our 'characters' are real people, and the larger truths we seek have to be made from the bricks and mortar of facts. What did the prime minister say *exactly*? Was it before or after the explosion in the Sarajevo market place, and whose mortar actually fired the fatal shell?

Some postmodernists disagree. They suggest that the work of historians should be judged like that of fiction writers, for its rhetorical power and capacity of imaginative conviction, not for some illusory factual truth. Eric Hobsbawm gives a finely measured response. 'It is essential', he writes, 'for historians to defend the foundation of their discipline: the supremacy of evidence. If their texts are fictions, as in some sense they are, being literary compositions, the raw material of those fictions is verifiable fact.'[2]

That applies equally to journalism. We all know about fabrications at the bottom end of journalism, in the gutter press. Unfortunately, the frontier with fiction is also violated at the top end of journalism, especially in reportage that aspires to be literature. Any reportage worth reading involves rearrangement of material, highlighting and, to some extent, the turning of real people into characters in a drama. But the line is crossed when quotations are invented or the order of events is changed. There is one genre of modern journalism, the 'drama-documentary' or 'faction', which does this avowedly. Faction is, so to speak, honestly dishonest. But more often this is done behind a mask of spare authenticity.

The precedents are distinguished. John Reed's account of the Russian revolution, *Ten Days that Shook the World*, is probably one of the most influential pieces of reportage ever written. Yet he spoke virtually no Russian, regularly made up dialogue, offered second-hand accounts as first-hand, mixed up dates, and added imaginative detail. As Neal Ascherson observes, in a fine essay on his work, Reed 'gives a thrilling account of Lenin's appearance at a closed Bolshevik meeting in Smolny on 3 November, allegedly communicated to him outside the door by Volodarsky as the meeting went on. No such meeting took place . . .'[3]

To save us from Reed's Disease, and to spoil our best stories, great American journals like *The New Yorker* employ 'fact-checkers'. As they drag their nit-combs through your text, it is horrible to find how many small errors of fact have slipped into your notebook, or intruded on the path from notebook to text. But sooner or later you come to the passages, often the most important ones, that they annotate in the margin, 'On author'. This means you are the only source for the fact (if fact it be) that, say, a church door in the Krajina was stained with blood, or a Kosovo rebel leader said what your notebook says he said. Then you are alone with your notebook and your conscience. Did he really say that?

Ideally, I suppose, one should be permanently wired for sound, like a superspy. Or, even better, have a miniature video camera implanted in one's skull. And certainly some of the very best contemporary history has been done on television. I think of documentary series such as 'The Death of Yugoslavia'. Although the television camera can also be made to lie, by tendentious selection and manipulative editing, at best it brings you closer than any other medium to how things really were.

For the writer, however, the conventional, hand-held, visible tape recorder and television camera have major disadvantages. They are cumbersome, even in their latest, slimmed-down, high-tech versions. Try using one at the same time as taking notes during a fast-moving demonstration. It is, in practice, very difficult to see simultaneously with both the camera's and the writer's eye. You're always liable to miss the telling detail that is vital to good reportage because you're fiddling with a tape or lens. And then you keep worrying about whether and what they are recording. Also, tape recorders and cameras put people off. Politicians and so-called ordinary people speak less naturally and freely as soon as the machines come out. Worse still, cameras and microphones turn people on. Demonstrators or soldiers strike heroic poses and make portentous statements they would not otherwise make. So these apparently neutral, mindless recorders of reality actually change it by their mere presence. Yet even the visible notebook does that.

I occasionally use a tape recorder for an important conversation, but my inseparable companion is a pocket notebook. The notebook is often open when the person is speaking, but sometimes, when I think they will talk more freely, or simply when walking or eating or whatever, it is not. Then I write the conversation down as soon as possible afterwards. I am obsessed with accuracy and, after twenty years, rather well practised in this kind of remembering. But as I look back through my notebooks there is always this nagging concern: Did he really say that?

Take the opening passage of my reportage from Serbia in March 1997 (see p. 254): the student called Momčilo exclaiming 'I just want to live in a normal country', and so on. Now Momčilo said this, in his imperfect English, as we hurried through the streets of Belgrade towards a students' meeting. I wrote it down as soon as we got there. If I had a tape recording of what he actually told me, it would probably be slightly different – a bit more awkward and less sharp.

But I don't have a tape recording. The verifiable historical truth of that fragment of the past is gone for good. You just have to trust me. A little later I record excited exchanges at the student meeting. These I scribbled down as they happened. But I don't speak Serbian, so what you read is my interpreter's version – and we both have to trust her.

Altogether, the business of language is crucial. Most of what is quoted in this book was said or written in languages I understand. But some, especially from Albanian and the south Slav languages now bewilderingly called Serbian, Croatian, Bosnian and Macedonian, was translated for me by an interpreter, with the inevitable loss of accuracy and nuance. The first thing to ask of anyone writing about anywhere is, Does he or she know the language?

Finally, it seems to me, the key to trust is not the technical apparatus of audio-visual recording and sourcing and fact-checking, invaluable though that is. It is a quality that may best be described as veracity. No one will ever be completely accurate. There is a margin of unavoidable error and, so to speak, necessary licence, if cacophonous, Babel-like reality is to be turned into readable prose. But the reader must be convinced that an author has a habit of accuracy, that he is genuinely trying to get at all the relevant facts, and that he will not play fast and loose with them for literary effect. He should feel that, while the author may not actually have a video recording of what he is describing, he would always like to.

George Orwell's *Homage to Catalonia* is a model of this kind of veracity. The book is a piece of literature. It is inaccurate in many details, not least because his notebooks were stolen by the communist goons who came to arrest him as a Trotskyist.[4] Yet you don't doubt for a single moment that he is striving for the greatest possible accuracy, for the fact-based truth that must always set apart the plains of history and journalism from the magic mountains of fiction.

The frontier between journalism and history is the longest in our Three Country Corner. It is also the least well marked, and therefore the most tense and disputed. I can testify to this, having lived on both sides and in-between. In journalism, to describe a piece as 'rather academic' – meaning boring, jargon-heavy, unreadable – is the surest path to the spike. In academe, it's a put-down to say that somebody's work is 'journalistic', meaning superficial, racy and generally not serious. 'Contemporary history?' sniffed an elderly don, when I returned to my Oxford college from a job in journalism at the end of the 1980s. 'You mean journalism with footnotes?'[5]

I think it's important to understand that the reasons why so much is made of the differences between journalism and academic or professional history have at least as much to do with the practical exigencies, self-images and neuroses of the two professions as they have with the real intellectual substance of the two crafts. Granted, the qualities of bad journalism and bad history are very different: sensationalist, intrusive, populist tosh with millions of readers on the one side; overspecialized, badly argued, ill-written doctorates with no readers on the other. But the virtues of good journalism and good history are very similar: exhaustive, scrupulous research, a sophisticated, critical approach to the sources, a strong sense of time and place, imaginative sympathy with all sides, logical argument, clear and vivid prose. Was Macaulay, in his essays for the *Edinburgh Review*, a historian or a journalist? Both, of course.

Yet, in modern Western societies, profession is a defining feature of personal identity, and the professions that are closest together take most pains to distinguish themselves. I say modern *Western* societies, incidentally, because this was not so true in the communist world, where the most important social identification was with a broad class: intelligentsia, workers or peasants. One of the interesting experiences of the last decade in formerly communist parts of Europe has been to see friends rapidly becoming differentiated by profession, Western-style. Where once they were all fellow members of the intelligentsia, now they are academics, lawyers, publishers, journalists, doctors, bankers, with diverging ways of life, styles of dress, homes, incomes and attitudes.

Now, because of the ways in which the professions of journalism and history have developed, and the edginess between them, the writing of 'history of the present' has tended to fall between the two. That no man's land is perhaps wider and more tense than it was when Lewis Namier put aside eighteenth-century English politics to chart the European diplomatic history of his own times and Hugh Trevor-Roper turned from Archbishop Laud to write *The Last Days of Hitler*.

Every profession has its characteristic fault. If I had to summarize in a word, I would say that the characteristic fault of journalistic writing is superficiality and that of academic writing is unreality. Journalists have to write so much, and they are so pressed for time. Sometimes they are 'parachuted' into countries or situations about which they know nothing and expected to report on them within hours. Hence the famous, horrible line 'Anyone here been raped and speak English?' Then their copy is cut and rewritten by editors and sub-editors who are working to even tighter deadlines. And, anyway, tomorrow is another day, another piece.

Academics, by contrast, can take years to finish a single article. They can (and sometimes do) take infinite pains to check facts, names, quotations, texts and contexts, to consider and reconsider the validity of an interpretation. But they can also spend a life describing war without ever seeing a shot fired in anger. Witnessing real life is not what they are supposed – or funded – to do. Methodology, footnotes and positioning in some ongoing academic debate can seem as important as working out what really happened and why. Participants in the worlds they describe sometimes throw up their hands in laughter and despair at the unreality of what comes out.

Of course, I could equally dwell on the characteristic virtue of each side, which is the opposite of the other's characteristic fault: depth in scholarship, realism in journalism. The interesting question is, Has it got worse or better? Well, some things have improved. If you read what passed for contemporary history in Britain in the 1920s, you find a bluff amateurism unthinkable today. In journalism, the growth of world television news services like CNN, Reuters and BBC World Television, and that of documentation on the Internet, offers wonderfully rich new sources for present history. But, on the whole, I think it has got worse.

There is still a handful of great international newspapers of record: the *New York Times*, the *Washington Post* and the *International Herald Tribune*, the *Financial Times*, *Le Monde* in France, the *Neue Zürcher Zeitung* and the *Frankfurter Allgemeine Zeitung* in the German-speaking world. You can generally believe what you read in these papers. Yet, even with this select group, it is astonishing how many discrepancies you find if you buy them all and compare their accounts of the same event. By and large, they do still separate fact and opinion, although there are exceptions. For example, the coverage of the wars of the Yugoslav succession in the *Frankfurter Allgemeine Zeitung* was for years distorted by the pro-Croat views of one of that paper's publishers.

Standards are much lower in national newspapers – particularly in Britain, where competition for readers is so fierce. I'm not just talking about the quite astonishing levels of routine inaccuracy and distortion, for reasons of both sensationalism and ideology – although in Britain this is especially apparent in anything to do with the European Union. As important are two other traits: featurism and futurism.

A large part of our newspapers is now taken up not, as their name would suggest, with news, but with features: lifestyle, beauty, fashion, medicine, food, holidays etc. This is what readers are held to want. Meanwhile, in what remains of the news pages, there is the more subtle disease of futurism. More and more space is devoted to speculating about what may happen tomorrow rather than describing what happened yesterday – the original mission of journalism. When read any time after today, this stuff is useless, except as an illustration of what people did not know at the time. Reading my own pieces for this book, I am again reminded that nothing ages more quickly than prophecy – even when it was prescient.

For all these reasons, the history of the present gets written less in its first natural home, the newspapers. But there are also problems on the academic side of the frontier. Some professional historians do tackle subjects in recent history. Even the Oxford history faculty, long accounted conservative (with a small c), now has a syllabus in British history that is open-ended towards the present. Yet, in my experience, most academic historians are still reluctant to venture much closer to the present than the canonical thirty years after which official papers are released in most democracies. They still incline to leave this territory to colleagues who have made it their own in subjects such as International Relations, Political Science, Security Studies, European Studies or Refugee Studies.

Yet these relatively new specialisms often feel the need to establish their academic credentials, their claim to the high name of Science (in the German sense of *Wissenschaft*), by a heavy dose of theory, jargon, abstraction or quantification. Otherwise – horror of horrors – their products might be confused with journalism. Even when those involved have been trained to write history, the results often suffer from overspecialization, unreadable prose and that characteristic fault: unreality. At the same time, the pressures of American-style 'publish or perish', reinforced in Britain by state-ordered 'Research Assessment' exercises, mean that a huge amount of academic work in progress is thrown into book form. Here, too, the ratio of quantity to quality has surely changed for the worse.

So I maintain that, for all its pitfalls, the literary enterprise of writing 'history of the present' has always been worth attempting. It is even more so now, because of the way history is made and recorded in our time. And it has suffered from developments in the professions of journalism and academic history. Yet you can soon have enough of such methodological self-examination. Altogether, the habit of compulsive labelling, pigeon-holing and compartmentalizing seems to me a disease of modern intellectual life. Let the work speak for itself. In the end, only one thing matters: is the result true, important, interesting or moving? If it is, never mind the label. If it isn't, then it's not worth reading anyway.

T.G.A., Oxford, February 1999

History of the Present

1990

1 January. Introduction of economic 'shock therapy' to make the transition to a free market in Poland. This is called the 'Balcerowicz Plan', after the finance minister Leszek Balcerowicz.

11 January. Soviet president Mikhail Gorbachev visits Lithuania, attempting to stop the movement for independence.

12–13 January. Oxford. At a Franco–German–British conference to discuss what the West should do about the great changes in the former East, senior politicians, officials and diplomats express blank horror at the suggestion that Poland, Hungary and Czechoslovakia should join Nato.

20–22 January. The Fourteenth Special Congress of the League of Communists of Yugoslavia ends with the virtual dissolution of the party that held Yugoslavia together.

27–30 January. The Polish communist party is succeeded by two 'social democratic' parties. Youthful former Central Committee member, Aleksander Kwaśniewski is elected leader of one of them.

January–February. Albanians in Kosovo protest against their province being stripped of its autonomy by Serbian leader Slobodan Milošević.

1 February. East German prime minister Hans Modrow announces a plan for 'Germany, United Fatherland'.

6–7 February. The Central Committee of the Communist Party of the Soviet Union accepts Mikhail Gorbachev's proposal to abandon the 'leading role' of the Communist Party and move towards political pluralism.

10–11 February. West German chancellor Helmut Kohl and foreign minister Hans-Dietrich Genscher visit Moscow. President Gorbachev gives the green light for unification of Germany.

12–14 February. A formula for negotiations on the external aspects of German unification is agreed at an Ottawa 'open skies' meeting between Nato and the Warsaw Pact, with the participation of the two German states and the four post-war occupation powers: the United States, Britain, France and the Soviet Union. The occupying powers call this formula '4+2'; the Germans call it '2+4'.

17–21 February. Berlin. 'You can't come through here,' says the East

German frontier officer at the Brandenburg Gate. Why not? 'Haven't you heard of the four-power status?' And then, rather wittily, 'It's your government which prevents you crossing here!' When an East German frontier officer starts appealing to the four-power status, I think the end of the East German state is in sight. When he finally lets me through – saying, with a shrug of his shoulders, 'Anyway, it's the British sector' – I know the end is near. Further on, an East German guard stands on top of the Wall, while under his very feet people chip away pieces to sell as souvenirs. High up on the Brandenburg Gate itself, I spy a large, white graffito. It says, 'Vive l'Anarchie.'

I visit Egon Krenz, the last communist leader of East Germany, in the pleasant East Berlin villa to which he has moved from the politburo compound at Wandlitz. In real life, his white teeth are every bit as distractingly large as on the photographs. ('Granny, what large teeth you have!' said the posters at last autumn's demonstrations.) He has time on his hands and tells me his life story. The illegitimate son of a Pomeranian peasant woman, he knew poverty in his childhood. What did socialism mean to him as a young man? 'A better life!' Then he hastily adds, 'I mean – also for other people . . .' Krenz is working on his memoirs and has published advance titbits in the *Bild-Zeitung*. So, just weeks after being deposed as communist leader, he has sold himself to a right-wing West German tabloid which stands for everything he has denounced for forty years.

One thing he wants to tell me. He much admires Margaret Thatcher's stalwart and far-sighted opposition to German unification. A great woman, that Mrs Thatcher.

24 February. Lithuanian elections are won by the independence-movement Sajudis.

26 February. Social Democrat Ingvar Carlsson is reappointed prime minister of Sweden.

26–27 February. The Soviet Union agrees to withdraw its troops from Czechoslovakia by July 1991.

23–27 February. Prague. I find Václav Havel installed in the magnificent Castle, traditional home of rulers of the Czech lands. The presidential office still contains some of the old communist furniture: square brown armchairs of superhuman size, set yards apart, silently eloquent of endless fraternal non-conversations between totalitarian rulers. The ghastly pictures have mostly been removed from the walls, to be replaced by large nudes and a prayer rug from the Dalai Lama. Unlike Egon Krenz, Havel now has no spare time at all. But, dashing along the long back corridors to a press conference, he pauses for a moment to show me a room with a huge ancient metal door. This is the starvation chamber traditional in Central European castles. 'We shall use it for talks.'

Walking down Wenceslas Square, I bump into an old friend, the Hungarian writer Árpád Göncz. We go for a coffee in the marvellous Jugendstil café of the Hotel Evropa. 'It seems we have reached a compromise on the matter of the new president of Hungary,' he tells me. Oh yes, and who will it be? 'It seems it will be me.'

4 March. Democratic elections to republican parliaments and local councils in the Soviet Union.

10 March. The Soviet Union agrees to withdraw its troops from Hungary by July 1991.

11 March. The Lithuanian parliament votes to 're-establish' the independence of Lithuania.

15 March. Gorbachev is given powers of an executive president in the Soviet Union.

17 March. Warsaw Pact foreign ministers, meeting in Prague, agree that both the Warsaw Pact and Nato should continue to exist.

18 March. Free elections to the 'People's Chamber' in East Germany.

The Solution

THE SOLUTION
After the rising of the 17th June
The secretary of the Writers' Union
Had leaflets distributed on the Stalinallee
In which one could read that the people
Had forfeited the confidence of the government
And could only recover it through
redoubled work. Would it not then
Be simpler, if the government
Dissolved the people and
Elected another?

Thus Bertolt Brecht – but only privately – after the East German workers' rising in the summer of 1953.

In the summer of 1989, on 31 August to be precise, Erich Mielke, the eighty-one-year-old minister for state security of the German Democratic Republic, held a conference with his regional commanders to discuss growing discontent in the state. Extracts from the transcript of that meeting are among the first documents from the now dissolved Ministry for State Security to have been published, in a remarkable book commissioned by the East German 'Round Table' of government and opposition groups.[1] At one point in this meeting, Mielke interrupts the report of Comrade Colonel Dangriess from Gera to ask, 'Is [the situation] such that tomorrow the 17th June will break out?'

All along one had guessed that the old men at the top were haunted by that memory. But it is still extraordinary to find the fear so plainly expressed, black on white. 'That is [sic] not tomorrow,' replies the

Comrade Colonel, 'that will not happen, that's why we exist.' A little later it is the turn of the Comrade Lieutenant-General from Leipzig. 'The atmosphere is wretched,' he says. But, 'So far as the question of power is concerned, Comrade Minister, we have things firmly in hand . . .'

How wrong they were, how the protests grew, how Leipzig in particular became the centre of enormous but peaceful popular protests – these events I have described elsewhere.[2] The documents reinforce the impression that the GDR came close to bloodshed. Here, for example, is the text of Erich Honecker's telex message to regional party secretaries on 8 October, the day after the GDR's fortieth anniversary, ordering that further disturbances are 'to be prevented from the outset'. And here is the matching order from the minister for state security, including the following: 'Members [of the State Security Service] who are regular weapon-carriers should carry their service weapons with them, appropriately to the given challenges.' In a long conversation, Egon Krenz, Erich Honecker's successor as party leader for just forty-four days, told me that in his view the country did come to the verge of bloodshed, for in such a tense situation one spark – one shot fired in panic – could have set the country alight.

The turning point was probably 9 October, when a large peaceful demonstration in Leipzig was not dispersed by force. While local initiatives, rather than Krenz, were responsible for averting violence at that critical moment, these documents give some credence to Krenz's claim to have maintained the line of non-violence. Thus his otherwise combative message to regional and local party secretaries on 24 October contains the crucial phrase 'We assume that all problems will be solved by political means.'

By 4 November, the day of a huge opposition demonstration in Berlin, Mielke is sending a pathos-laden telex to his deputies and regional leaders. He offers thanks to all his 'dear Comradesses and Comrades' for their 'staunch behaviour and responsible fulfilment of their duty'. 'I know', he writes, 'how difficult it is [not to be provoked or unsettled] especially in this tension-loaded atmosphere, how much self-restraint, staunchness and courage that requires.' The crimes of the Stasi are truly not comparable with those of the SS, yet the language of this message recalls nothing so much as Himmler's infamous Posen speech of 1943.

The last document in the collection is a report from Erich Mielke to Krenz and other party leaders, dated 7 November. It records how Church and opposition groups such as the New Forum have begun to defend State Security buildings against angry demonstrators. A few days later this terrible, pathetic old man stood before the 'People's Chamber', East Germany's previously rubber-stamp parliament, and said, in words that provide the title for this first documentation, and will surely become immortal, '*Ich liebe doch alle . . .*': 'But I love everyone . . .'[3]

That was the revolution, phase one: a peaceful popular uprising that grew slowly through the summer and early autumn, and flowered from 9 October. A new '17 June'. Phase two of the revolution began a month later, on 9 November, with the opening of the Berlin Wall. Within a very few weeks, the tidal wave of popular demands turned decisively in the direction of unification. Instead of '*Wir sind das Volk*' ('We are the people') the crowd chanted, '*Wir sind EIN Volk*' ('We are one nation').

Meanwhile, thousands voted for unification with their feet: moving to West Germany and taking up their automatic rights of citizenship. First the power of the party and the Stasi, then the authority of the government collapsed. Even after taking opposition leaders into his cabinet, in a so-called Government of National Responsibility, Prime Minister Hans Modrow could not slow the internal collapse or the external haemorrhage. So the promised free election was hastily brought forward, from 6 May to 18 March.

By this time, West German politicians from all the major parties were already stumping the country, and it was clear that the main contestants in the election would be the East German partners or protégés of the main West German parties. The East German Social Democrats, who had originally called themselves the SDP (Sozialde-mokratische Partei) precisely to distinguish themselves from the West German SPD (Sozialdemokratische Partei Deutschlands), changed their name to SPD. Although their leading candidate was called Ibrahim Böhme, their chief crowd-puller was the legendary former West German chancellor Willy Brandt. The West German Free

Democrats helped put together a Federation of Free Democrats, whose chief crowd-puller was the West German foreign minister, Hans-Dietrich Genscher. The West German Christian Democrats were instrumental in forging a so-called Alliance for Germany out of the formerly puppet CDU (East), under its new leader, Lothar de Maizière, the newly founded German Social Union (DSU), under the Leipzig pastor Hans-Wilhelm Eberling, and the smaller opposition group, Democratic Awakening (DA), which chose as its leading candidate a lawyer, Wolfgang Schnur, who had been active for several years in Church-based opposition circles. But here, too, there was no doubt that Helmut Kohl was the key man. During the campaign he spoke at six mass meetings across the land.

In the case of these three parties, or party groupings, the West German influence was overwhelming. It was not just that prominent West German politicians of the appropriate party came over to support them. It was not just the financial support, important though that was. Their very posters looked the same: those of the SPD (East) in the distinctive colours and orthography of the SPD (West). So too for the CDU and the Free Democrats, while the DSU, based in Saxony and Thuringia, took its symbolic cue from its Bavarian neighbour, the Christian Social Union (CSU). Their language was increasingly the same: so many little Genschers, Kohls and Brandts springing fully armed out of the television screen. Indeed, most of them had learned the language of democratic politics watching West German television. Moreover, the actual content of their campaigns was inseparable from the impression and promises made by their West German patrons.

The only major contestant with substantial resources of its own was the former ruling communist party (SED), now renamed the Party of Democratic Socialism (PDS), and fiercely insisting that it was a completely different outfit. 'We are the new,' said one of its posters, showing Hans Modrow ogling a baby in a studiedly informal group of mostly young and casually dressed people on a Berlin street. Besides the two former puppet, or 'block', parties, the Democratic Farmers' Party and the National Democratic Party, the other parties or party groupings on the ballot paper – twenty-four in all – included such exotic flowers as the Spartacist Workers' Party, the Carnations, and the German Beer-drinkers Union. Seriously notable was the

Alliance '90, a coalition of three opposition groups – New Forum, Democracy Now and the Initiative for Peace and Human Rights – which, as the Stasi documents amply confirm, had been instrumental in preparing and leading the country's 'October revolution'.

The election campaign, fought at mass meetings, on posters and flysheets, and on both East and West German radio and television, was quite bitter, with two basic themes. The first theme was the past. Charges of collaboration with the former communist dictatorship flew to and fro like custard pies in a bad comedy. Thus, for example, the western CDU, desperately conscious that the eastern CDU was compromised by having been a puppet party, whereas the eastern SPD was a wholly new organization, tried to make up for it by reminding voters of the awful way in which the western SPD had previously chummed up with the ruling communists in the east. One poster showed the western SPD's candidate for chancellor, Oskar Lafontaine, waving brightly next to the former East German leader Erich Honecker, a fellow Saarlander. Underneath it said, 'Now what belongs together is growing together' – the already famous words with which Willy Brandt greeted the opening of the Berlin Wall. (Yet the Social Democrats would have had little difficulty finding photographs of leading Christian Democrats grinning broadly while shaking hands with Honecker, starting with Franz Josef Strauss.) When accusations about the lawyer Wolfgang Schnur's past collaboration with the Stasi began to be made, leading Christian Democrat politicians dismissed them as outrageous electoral mud-slinging – until, just a few days before the election, they turned out to be true.

Yet the results suggest that the issue of the past was not decisive. If it had been, the group with much the strongest claim to be uncompromised, the Alliance '90, would have got more votes than it did. What decided the issue were the contrasting proposals for the immediate future, which boiled down to one essential question: How far, how fast, and by what means should East Germany be united with West Germany? The differences between the SPD and Kohl's Alliance for Germany on this issue were not fundamental. Both said unity should come, and both said they would protect the people of East Germany against the economic and social costs. But there was a significant difference of emphasis. The Alliance for Germany and, above all,

Chancellor Kohl himself made a clear, simple case for the fastest possible integration into the existing structures of the Federal Republic. There should be a rapid currency union. 'We', the Alliance said in effect, 'will give you the Deutschmark.' Then, following intergovernmental negotiations, and the reconstitution of the historic states (*Länder*) in East Germany, they should join the West under Article 23 of the Federal Republic's constitution, which is called the Basic Law. This, after listing the *Länder* of West Germany in which the Basic Law applies, says simply, 'In other parts of Germany it [i.e. the Basic Law] is to come into force after their entry.' *Basta!*

The SPD, by contrast, argued for a somewhat slower and more considered process, in which East Germany would bring more of its own 'identity' into the new Germany. Although it did not absolutely preclude unification by Article 23, the SPD inclined more to the path envisaged in the final article of the Basic Law, Article 146, which says, 'This Basic Law loses its validity on the day on which a constitution comes into force which has been resolved upon by the German people in a free decision.' In other words, there would be some sort of constituent assembly that would write a new constitution, perhaps formally incorporating some of the different property rights or so-called social rights established in the GDR. Altogether, the SPD offered more ifs and buts about the process of unification.

The renewed communist party, the PDS, put the ifs and buts before the 'yes' to unification, although the practical difference between the 'confederation' or 'treaty community' for which it originally argued and de facto unification became increasingly thin. One of its two leading candidates, Hans Modrow, had, after all, as prime minister himself put forward, at the beginning of February, a plan for what he called, echoing a slogan from the streets, which in turn took up a line from East Germany's national anthem, 'Germany, United Fatherland'. The other leading candidate of the PDS, a clever lawyer called Gregor Gysi, said, 'We want a new Germany, better than the GDR but also better than the Federal Republic.'

Curiously enough, the party closest to the post-communists in its reservations about what was described as an *Anschluss* by the Federal Republic was the grouping of those whom the communist party had previously considered its worst enemies, the Alliance '90. When a telephone number is unavailable in Germany you hear a message saying, 'No *Anschluss* [i.e. connection] on this number.' The Alliance '90 had an election poster saying, 'Article 23 – no *Anschluss* on this number!'

Yet the opinion polls soon showed that the Alliance '90 had no chance of winning with this slogan. The SPD initially had an over-whelming lead in the polls, but as the campaign progressed the Alliance for Germany, which people increasingly referred to just as the CDU, gained on it rapidly. The choice was clearly going to be between the medium and the fast track to unification. As this became apparent, so one had the curious spectacle of the communists and the dissidents joining together at the Round Table talks, and in the Government of National Responsibility, to try to save what they thought deserved to be saved from the ruins of the GDR. Sitting in his Spartan government office, one of the most determined and longest serving dissidents, Gerd Poppe, now a minister without portfolio, explained to me how the government had hastily put together a 'social charter' and laws on different ownership, so that there would be at least some formal, codified starting point for the discussion of what 'good' from the GDR could be preserved in a larger Germany. The feelings of the former dissidents during this period were profoundly mixed, for whereas in the rest of East Central Europe the Round Tables and the provisional governments were clearly laying foundations for the (re-) building of democracy, here their work was more like throwing up temporary huts which would be bulldozed away as soon as the real builders moved in.

I

Sunday 18 March was a beautiful spring day. Almost a summer's day, in fact. The sun shone without ceasing. People voted early, then took off into the countryside. There seemed to be universal good humour. An old lady in Pankow asked how many times she should fold the ballot paper. 'You can fold it as many times as you like,' said the volunteer official – 'it's a free election!' By the time I got to the polling station in the small village of Seeberg, at midday, more than 80 per cent of the electors had voted. When I say 'polling station', I mean the back room of the local pub. And when I say '80 per cent', I mean about fifty people, for there were only sixty-five electors in this village – and eight of them were on the supervisory electoral commission.

These electoral commissions, containing, where possible, representatives of the main parties, took their tasks very seriously indeed, scrupulously checking off names and insisting that people use the polling booths. Previously, to use the polling booth was a sign that you were not toeing the line: good conformists openly marked and folded their paper and put it straight into the box. A friend once described the few paces to the polling booth as 'the longest walk of my life'. Another recalled how, at the local-government elections only last May, her hand was shaking so much that she could not get her deliberately spoiled ballot paper into the slot. Today, these sounded like tales from a distant epoch.

In Buckow, where Brecht probably wrote his poem about the 17 June rising in his charming lakeside house, there was the same quiet excitement, especially among younger voters. However, when I asked one old woman how it felt to take part in her first free election she grunted and said, 'Well, it was rather complicated.' The agonies of choice! Actually, compared with the system in Poland or Hungary, the election procedure was simplicity itself. All you had to do was put one cross, or other clear mark, against the party or party grouping of your choice. According to the election law, no party propaganda was allowed within 'some 100 metres' of the polling station. So instead of the canvassers there were the journalists. Interviewers from West Germany's television asked thousands of voters to repeat their vote on simulated ballot papers.

Within a few minutes of the polling station closing at 6 p.m., television was able to announce the shock result: a triumph for the CDU. As the evening wore on, the simulated results were replaced by real ones, slightly reducing the scale of the triumph so that the Alliance for Germany narrowly missed an absolute majority. But the message was plain. In the huge metal and glass Palace of the Republic in the centre of East Berlin, where three competing German television channels (two West, one East) had their studios on the *belle étage*, a desperate scrum of reporters mobbed the winners, and collared anyone who seemed interesting, while yesterday's men like Mieczysław F. Rakowski, former leader of the former Polish communist party, peered longingly at the limelight. In one corner I spotted Daniel Cohn-Bendit, the hero of '68 in Frankfurt and Paris, known as Danny the Red. As I approached, he was saying to an interviewer, 'You know, I was never a communist . . .'

The balladeer Wolf Biermann wandered like a friendly bear through this frantic scene. 'Today,' he said, 'here in this glass palace, is the funeral of the GDR.' In another corner the writer Stefan Heym observed, 'There will be no more GDR. It will be nothing but a footnote in world history.' The Republic had voted to end the Republic.

I say 'the Republic' advisedly, for in East German popular usage 'the Republic' is counterposed to Berlin. And Berlin voted differently: nearly 35 per cent for the SPD, only 18 per cent for the CDU, and nearly 30 per cent for the PDS, the renamed communist party. This last, rather astonishing, figure may partly be explained by the heavy concentration of former party functionaries and state employees of all sorts in the capital. Yet it seems that the PDS also managed to attract both old and young voters by its skilfully propagated warnings against the costs of 'capitalist' unification: unemployment, higher rents, and so forth.

But Berlin was outvoted by the rest of the country – 'the Republic' – and above all by the lands of the south: Thuringia, Saxony and Sachsen-Anhalt. Before the war, these were strongholds of social democracy. (It is sometimes claimed – although this is hotly disputed – that in the 1950s the West German chancellor Konrad Adenauer pressed less hard for reunification than he might otherwise have done, because he feared these constituencies would have swung the electoral balance against him.) But now the electoral regions of Dresden, Erfurt, Gera, Suhl and Karl-Marx-Stadt – that is, as Chancellor Kohl repeatedly insisted, Chemnitz – all turned in votes for the Alliance for Germany of around 60 per cent, with less than 20 per cent for the SPD and less than 15 per cent for the PDS. According to a survey, some 58 per cent of workers throughout the country voted for Kohl's Alliance.

To label this a 'swing to the right' would be, at best, a half-truth. It is true that, as elsewhere in the former Eastern Europe, the more straightforwardly anti-communist the party, the better its chance.

Here, as elsewhere, forty years of communism calling itself socialism has made socialism a dirty word. But it would be wrong to suggest that people went from one extreme to the other. The neo-Nazi far-right groups that made such a terrible impression on international television by their rowdy behaviour, and chants of 'Foreigners out!' at the later Leipzig demonstrations, remained marginal. Even the markedly conservative DSU got no more than 15 per cent of the vote in its original southern heartlands, and just 6.3 per cent overall. What people chose – in spite of its past as a puppet party – was the moderate, liberal conservative CDU, which alone got almost twice the SPD vote (40.9 per cent to 21.8 per cent). This was, first and last, a vote for Chancellor Kohl and the fast track to unity. *Anschluss*? Yes, please!

Bärbel Bohley, the artist who was one of the founders of the New Forum, commented bitterly that 'People really have no more trust in their own strength. They are swapping the tutelage of the old SED for that of the CDU and hope that not the red but the black state will do everything for them.' Again, this seems to me at best a half-truth, seen from the rather special and atypical viewpoint of East Berlin. An old friend in Dresden drew my attention to an article in the West German weekly *Der Spiegel* by an East Berlin intellectual which said, in effect, 'We don't need unification now that the Wall is open.' If I want to get a Western book, observed the author of this article, I just take the train to Bahnhof Zoo (in West Berlin) and pop down to the Heinrich Heine Bookshop there. But, said my friend, that's precisely what you *can't* do from distant Dresden. If you want to have easy access to books – or building materials, or clothes, or cars – from the West, then you need unification. And, anyway, only the privileged intellectual would have the hard currency to slip over so casually to pick up a book. Hard currency earned, for example, by writing an article against unification in the West German weekly *Der Spiegel* . . .

Moreover, for the people of Dresden, this is not a loss but a gain in identity. For what they identify with is not the GDR but the old *Land* and former kingdom of Saxony. (The grand duke, I understand, proposes to move back to Schloss Moritzburg.) Here, on the dusty house fronts and outside the neglected, antiquated factories, you see everywhere two flags: black, red and gold for Germany; green and white for Saxony. And it is as the reconstituted *Land* of Saxony, not as the former GDR, that the Saxons wish to join the Federal Republic.

In the country at large, it seems to me, the real motto of the campaign – though no one, to my knowledge, actually used it – was Adenauer's slogan from the 1950s: 'No Experiments!' They had experienced enough experiments to last several lifetimes: Hitler's experiments, Stalin's experiments, Ulbricht's and Honecker's. They'd had quite enough of being guinea pigs. There were certainly aspects of West German life and attitudes about which they had reservations. But, so far as the economic, political and legal system was concerned, West Germany's was the best one going. Arguably, it was the best system Germany had ever had. Now they wanted to have it as fast as possible: first the Deutschmark of course, but not just the Deutschmark, also the free press, the rule of law, local self-government, and federal democracy. In many ways, their priorities also recalled those of the 1950s in West Germany – starting with the passionate drive to rebuild for private happiness from the ruins. Understandably, the enthusiasm was greatest among the young, while the middle-aged were more worried about their ability to adapt, and the old were concerned about the conversion rate and the value of their pensions. Indeed, the old might wearily remark, like the grandmother in Edgar Reitz's film *Heimat*, 'Yet another new era!'

There are plainly immense problems of learning democracy for people who have lived even longer than Czechs or Poles under successive dictatorships, although the Czechs and Poles, unlike most East Germans, were not able to watch democracy in practice every night on their television screens. But it is deeply condescending to suggest that this vote was simply a sell-out or a cop-out, and little short of revolting for intellectuals in the West to suggest that the East Germans should try – as it were, on our behalf – yet another experiment. (Why the hell should they? If you want to make another experiment, kindly perform it on yourself.)

To be sure, in comparison with Poland, Hungary or Czechoslovakia, there *is* a certain special melancholy about East Germany's transition to democracy. For it is only of the first phase of the revolution – from the great Leipzig demonstration of 9 October 1989 to the opening of the Wall on 9 November – that people can say, with justified pride and unqualified truth, 'We stood up for ourselves! We did it our way!' The first peaceful revolution, the first *self*-liberation in German history, did not remain a self-liberation. East Germany did not first build its own democracy and then join hands with West Germany. From 9 November, the liberation, though still the work of Germans, was led as much by West as by East Germans. But it remains a liberation. And, with all due caveats, the prospects for a swift, successful transition to a flourishing market economy, a stable parliamentary democracy and the rule of law are now brighter in this central patch of old Europe than east of the Oder or south-east of the Erzgebirge.

2

The reunification of Germany began on 9 November 1989. It happened from below. Wherever I went in East Germany, I found evidence of new ties: from person to person, family to family, enterprise to enterprise, town to town, *Land* to *Land*. I talked to a floor tiler in Buckow. His cooperative had established links with a West German firm. They just came knocking on the door. I gave a cheerful agricultural worker a lift home from the pub/polling station in Seeberg. Yes, he said, a baron from West Germany was going to invest in their poultry farm. The Reclam publishing house (East) has come to an arrangement with the Reclam publishing house (West). And so on.

Yet this election was a turning point. It closed the second phase of the revolution, and opened the period of formal negotiation about the terms of unification between the democratically elected governments and parliaments of the two post-war German states.

The process of unification is of such complexity, with so many interacting unknowns, that merely to indicate the main issues would require another essay. Whereas the Bundesbank president initially observed that the currency union should come at the end of the transformation to a market economy, it will now come at the beginning: probably by early July, according to the Bonn government. 'Engagement in spring, marriage in the summer, and then off on holiday,' said the West German economics minister, blithely. But who knows what will come after the honeymoon? Inflation for the West? Mass unemployment for the East?

How will a swift currency union be reconciled with East Germany's Soviet and East European trade? And how will the new government resolve the ghastly tangle of claims on expropriated, nationalized, collectivized or socialized property in the GDR?

The critical argument for a hasty currency union was to stem the haemorrhage of emigration from East Germany, and the Bonn government announced that the special treatment for migrants from East Germany will be ended simultaneously with the introduction of the Deutschmark. But what guarantee is there that this will halt the flood? The *Länder* of East Germany will still be much poorer than those of West Germany, with lower wages for the same work, and in a condition of profound social and economic dislocation. How will the social and economic strains of unification affect popular attitudes in East and West? Could they boost the vote for the far-right Republicans? East German society has scant experience of living peacefully with either political conflicts or foreigners. One of the more worrying side effects already observable in both East and West is a street-level tendency to see an answer to the problem of accommodating more Germans (including those from elsewhere in Eastern Europe) in the accommodation of fewer foreigners (Turks in the West, Vietnamese in the East, and Poles all over). Then there is the terrible problem of so-called *Vergangenheitsbewältigung* – 'overcoming' the past – in East Germany: witness the Schnur case, and the beginning of a verification procedure to check that the people elected on 18 March had not formerly worked for or collaborated with the Stasi. There are no completely reliable figures, but if one takes the estimates made by the commission dissolving the State Security Service then it would appear that at least one in every hundred GDR citizens was an official or unofficial collaborator.

And these are only a few of the internal aspects of unification. I have not begun to list the problems that most exercise the outside world: the so-called external aspects of unification, the stuff of the '2+4' talks, the ending of Allied rights over Berlin and 'Germany as a whole', the Polish frontier treaty, the difficult substantive issues of integration into the European Community and, most intractable of all, the whole complex of political-military security arrangements, the future of Nato and the Warsaw Pact.

For years, German politicians have never tired of repeating that the key to German unity lies in Moscow. Recently Chancellor Kohl's main foreign-policy adviser, Horst Teltschik, was reported as saying that the key to German unity now lies in Bonn. Even if he actually formulated it a little more cautiously, the basic point is right. Moscow has, of course, still a great deal to say, above all on security issues. But even on security issues the first question at the moment is, What do the Germans want? Yet they disagree among themselves about what they want, as the SPD leader Oskar Lafontaine has recently demonstrated once again in advocating what would amount to German withdrawal from Nato.

On the evening of 18 March, Chancellor Kohl was so full of himself that I was afraid he might burst. Exuding sentimental assurance, he obviously felt that the CDU had won not only the East German elections but also the West German elections in December, and that he would therefore go down in history as the chancellor of German unity. The SPD, by contrast, had hoped to sail into the federal elections with the wind from an East German triumph behind it, and was shocked by the defeat. I would not be quite so confident as the chancellor. As the East German elections themselves showed, the firmest predictions can be overthrown. We are in unchartered waters: the chancellor has raised great expectations, and there are any number of things that can go wrong in the process of unification. Nobody knows exactly what has begun. All that is certain is what has ended. This has a name. It is called the German Democratic Republic.

Late that night, I found myself wondering how Brecht would have reacted. Had he offered himself, like Heym and Biermann, to the television interviewers in the frantic mêlée of the Palace of the Republic, he would probably have said something clever and dishonest. But, in the tranquil privacy of Buckow, I think his lyric spirit – honest in spite of the man – might perhaps have written:

> THE SOLUTION
> In the election of 18th March
> The people
> Dissolved the republic and
> Chose another.

1990

24 March. Margaret Thatcher summons a group of historians and specialists on Germany to a private meeting at Chequers to discuss German unification. See below, p. 48.

8 April. The second round of Hungarian parliamentary elections produces a government majority for the nationalist Hungarian Democratic Forum.

9 April. Leaders of Czechoslovakia, Hungary and Poland meet in Bratislava to discuss Central European cooperation. They will subsequently become the 'Visegrád group'.

18 April. French president François Mitterrand and German chancellor Helmut Kohl send a joint message to the current president of the European Council of the EC, proposing an intergovernmental conference on 'political union' of the existing EC, as well as that already planned on economic and monetary union (EMU).

3 May. Árpád Göncz – writer, translator and former political prisoner – becomes acting president of Hungary.

4 May. The Latvian parliament proclaims the country's independence from the Soviet Union.

6 May. The nationalist Croatian Democratic Union wins parliamentary elections. Its leader, Franjo Tudjman, becomes president of Croatia.

8 May. Estonia declares independence.

11 May. Lech Wałęsa declares a 'war at the top' which will divide Solidarity in Poland.

16 May. Nationalist conservative József Antall forms a right-wing coalition government in Hungary.

20 May. The National Salvation Front, led by the former communist Ion Iliescu, wins elections in Romania. Iliescu becomes president.

29 May. Creation of the European Bank for Reconstruction and Development (EBRD) to finance reconstruction of post-communist countries.

30 May. Boris Yeltsin is elected president of the Russian Republic.

May–June. Continental European countries impose ban on imports of British beef, for fear of bovine spongiform encephalopathy or 'mad cow disease'.

7 June. A Moscow summit of the Warsaw Pact seeks to transform it into a 'political-military' rather than a 'military-political' body.

10 June. In the first free elections in Czechoslovakia since 1946, victory for the movements that led the 'velvet revolution': the Civic Forum in the Czech lands, the Public Against Violence in Slovakia.

14–15 June. Romanian miners are bussed in from the provinces to attack protesting students, 'intellectuals' and opposition parties in Bucharest.

10 and 17 June. In Bulgaria, former communists – now called Socialists – win parliamentary elections, closely followed by the Union of Democratic Forces, an opposition coalition.

20 June. In Yugoslavia, the Croatian Republic removes 'Socialist' from its name and adopts the chequerboard flag of the wartime fascist Croat state. Serbs in the Croatian province of Krajina start forming their own de facto authority.

25–26 June. As urged by President François Mitterrand and Chancellor Helmut Kohl, European Community leaders, meeting in Dublin, decide that an intergovernmental conference on political union should be held in parallel with that already planned on economic and monetary union.

26 June. The Hungarian parliament votes for the country to negotiate its withdrawal from the Warsaw Pact.

28 June. Vienna. I hear Lech Wałęsa speak at a conference on 'Central Europe on the Way to Democracy', together with several former Solidarity leaders against whom he has declared his 'war at the top'. Wałęsa is given a tour of the Habsburg capital. His guide points out a statue of the empress Maria Theresa. A little later, Wałęsa muses, 'Hm, interesting that Mother Teresa already has a monument.'

1 July. German 'Monetary, Economic and Social Union'. The Deutschmark comes to East Germany.

2 July. The Slovenian parliament issues a declaration of sovereignty, giving republican laws priority over federal ones. The Kosovo assembly declares the province to be an 'independent republic' in the Yugoslav federation.

5 July. Václav Havel is re-elected president of Czechoslovakia.

5–6 July. A Nato summit in London concludes with a declaration marking the end of the Cold War.

1–13 July. The Twenty-eighth Congress of the Communist Party of the Soviet Union.

14–16 July. Helmut Kohl and Hans-Dietrich Genscher visit Moscow and the Caucasus. Crucial German–Soviet agreements on the external aspects of German unification, with Gorbachev accepting that united Germany will be in Nato.

14 July. British trade and industry minister Nicholas Ridley resigns after telling the Spectator *that the proposed European monetary union is a 'German racket designed to take over the whole of Europe'.*

16 July. Slobodan Milošević is elected leader of the post-communist Socialist Party of Serbia.

Après le Déluge, Nous

I telephoned Jacek Kuroń, the veteran oppositionist, now Poland's minister for labour and social affairs. A woman answered the phone.

'Could I speak to Minister Kuroń, please?'

'But this is the censors' office!' the woman politely replied. (The telephone numbers differ by only one digit.)

'I thought censorship had been abolished?'

'Yes it has, but our contracts run until the end of July, so we're still here.'

'Well, I wish you pleasant inactivity.'

'Thank you, and all the very best to you.'

She sounded charming.

Former censors, former border guards, former apparatchiks, former secret policemen: what is to be done with them? Or, rather, what is to be done with Them – *Oni* – as the communist power-holders, great and small, were universally known. There is the question of justice. Should the men at the top be brought to trial for the evil they did, or that was done under them? If so, on what charges and by what laws? At a lower level, it becomes almost a question of social justice. Is it fair, people ask, that those who had comfortable office jobs under the communists should still have them today, when ordinary people are having to tighten their belts yet more? Is it fair that members of the *nomenklatura* (those nominated to leading positions by the ruling communist party) are exploiting the unclear legal conditions of privatization to take over as capitalists the enterprises they have previously commanded as communists?

Yet the requirements of justice can clash with those of efficiency. If the choice is between a compromised, incompetent person and an uncompromised, competent one, then the decision is easy. But what if the choice is between a compromised but relatively professional person and an uncompromised but wholly amateur one? I dine with the new ambassador of an East Central European country, a charming person, Catholic, brave, honest, unbowed. The number-two man at the embassy, by contrast, is plainly from the old guard, at best an unprincipled careerist, complete with regulation dandruff and greasy smile. He starts telling me how this year he hoped they would lay a wreath at the monument to the American rather than the Soviet liberators. A perfect turncoat. Yet at least he has some rudimentary professionalism in foreign affairs, whereas the ambassador tells me that 'our foreign minister has introduced a new element into international relations – it's called trust.' Oh dear.

There is the problem of Them, but there is also the problem of Us. 'We are not like Them,' chanted the crowds in Prague during the revolution of 1989. Six months later, some of those same people can be heard muttering about how the new power-holders resemble the old. In Poland, the disgruntled now speak of a 'new *nomenklatura*'. The Citizens' Committees, they claim, are beginning to work like the Party Committees of yore. As in the old days, they say, a telephone call from the Committee decides the issue.

Many things contribute to this inchoate discontent. Partly it is that, having known no other power-holders than the communists, people do not distinguish between what is common to all power-holders and what was peculiar to communist ones. Partly it is that, in the first post-revolutionary phase, these countries' new would-be-democratic leaders are almost bound to resort to the method of placing 'one of Us' instead of 'one of Them' on the commanding heights, whether of the secret police or of the media, by nomination rather than election or free competition. This has been true of Czechoslovakia – one writer called it Havel's 'anti-February', referring to the communists' February 1948 coup – and of Poland under its post-Solidarity prime minister Tadeusz Mazowiecki, although the nominations are often the outcome of complex negotiations, and in no case imposed by force or the threat of force.

One may have some sympathy with those at the top, for they are damned if they do and damned if they don't. If they leave old communist appointees in place, people say it's not fair and nothing has really changed. It's like the Polish police cars: same vehicles, same colours, same people inside, but where before it said *Milicja* it now says *Policja*. If, however, they replace the communist appointees with their own, then people cry 'Foul!' and 'New *nomenklatura*!' On the one hand they are required to make changes fast and effectively, on the other hand democratically and constitutionally. As one speaker remarked at a stormy session of Lech Wałęsa's Citizens' Committee, the trouble is that there are no generally accepted 'rules of the game'. This leads into temptation.

Visiting old friends catapulted from jail to cabinet, from stoker to parliamentarian, from being a victim of the secret police to being the head of it, I was interested to see how the acquisition of power had changed them. Could they prove exceptions to Lord Acton's rule that power tends to corrupt?

Everyone, but everyone, is changed. It's not just the externals, although these are important. Offices with secretaries – most of them ladies of a certain age, inherited from the *ancien régime*. Chauffeur-driven cars – avoiding, if at all possible, the old black Tatras, in favour of Volvos, Mercedes or, as in Havel's new presidential motorcade, super-sexed BMWs. Suits and ties instead of the regulation dissident sweaters. (With the exception of the former dissident Adam Michnik – still defiantly wearing jeans – and the Hungarian Young Democrats, who, even in the sumptuous, gilded Budapest parliament, have a quite distinctive line in casual summer wear. 'Yes, they discuss it in their caucuses,' an MP told me.) The unaccustomed press of business exacerbated by deep tiredness, poor institutional back-up, and the endless flow of Western visitors. Changes in bearing, manner and manners. When Havel became president, he adopted a ramrod-straight posture and a rather gruesome imperial stare that I had never noticed before. One sees it often now, on television, far away. Just playing the part?

Many others exhibit the same features to a lesser degree. 'I feel as if I'm two different people,' says one. 'My old, private, writer-self and a new public self.' There is irony here. Against what did they set out to do battle? Why, against the double life, against the split between public and private selves, the daily toll of public conformity and mendacity which, as Havel demonstrated better than anyone in his essays, played a vital role in sustaining the previous system. Yet now they are themselves condemned to live a sort of double life. Not that the new public language is comparable with the old. The Havelspeak now used by Czechoslovak television commentators is quite depressing, but it is still a world away from Newspeak. Nonetheless there is – in Poland and Hungary, as well as Czechoslovakia – a certain incipient divergence between the public and private language of the new leaders.

Corruption by power? The germs of it, in some cases, yes: a little too much enjoyment of the new privileges; perhaps a few too many trips abroad – 'for the good of the country', of course. (Oh, the hard life of luxury!) The arrogance of power, subtly reinforced by the feeling that you have deserved it after so many long years of struggle. 'Where were you in November?' Havel recently retorted to a crowd of Slovak hecklers. 'Where were you in August?' 'Where were you in '68?' 'Where were you in '56?' Explicitly or implicitly, these are also the challenges made in Polish and Hungarian politics. But this line of argument is as dangerous as it is understandable. When the writer Wiktor Woroszylski attacked the Polish parliamentarian Ryszard Bender for having been a member of parliament under the Jaruzelski 'normalization' regime, Bender retorted by recalling Woroszylski's own communist past. Where do you stop with the reckoning? Where do you draw the line?

Everyone finds it difficult to come to terms with the loss of the common enemy. Of course there were endless personal conflicts inside the opposition movements, and deeper differences of tradition and ideology. But, sooner or later, people pulled together against the common oppressor. This was true, at a rather basic level, of all the East Central European societies under communism. In your circle of friends you could always find common ground in grumbling about Them. A young Dresdener described to me his shock at discovering, during the election campaign, that his friends could actually think differently. Unheard of! What was true of the majority of the population in a mild way was true of the politically engaged minority in a much stronger way. For all the tensions and conflicts, the emotional experience of Solidarity in Poland was, indeed, that of solidarity. The heyday of the Civic Forum in the Czech lands was a shorter but no less intense experience of triumphant social unity. Yet, to put it in Hegelian terms, the triumph of unity was also the beginning of its negation.

The one great conflict is succeeded by many small conflicts. However much you may rationally appreciate that there is no pluralism without conflict, the mere fact of these conflicts is somehow felt to be abnormal and disturbing. Often they involve the severing of old friendships, with sadness and bitterness. There is a lack, not only of the forms and procedures in which to regulate these conflicts, but of the language in which to express them. In Poland and Czechoslovakia the civic movements came to power with a rhetoric derived from the anti-political language of the democratic oppositions – a language of philosophic and moral absolutes, of right against wrong, love against hate, truth against falsehood. To communism as a monopoly system of organized lying they counterposed the anti-political programme of 'living in truth'.

Now we expect many things of politicians in a well-functioning parliamentary democracy, but 'living in truth' is not one of them. In fact the essence of democratic politics might rather be described as 'working in half-truth'. Parliamentary democracy is, at its very heart, a system of limited adversarial mendacity, in which each party attempts to present a part of the truth as if it were the whole. When Václav Havel was asked at a public discussion in London whether he thought it would prove possible for the new politicians to continue to 'live in truth', he replied, 'Either yes or no. If it proves not, I certainly won't go on being one.' Now it may just be possible for the president, as moral father-figure, to go on 'living in truth' – although some might think that campaigning for the Civic Forum in the election while protesting that you are not campaigning at all comes pretty close to the line. But it is certainly not possible for any lesser mortals who actually have to compete for power.

Partly for tactical or strategic reasons – 'Unity is strength', as the crowds chanted in Prague – but also for intellectual and emotional ones, there is a reluctance to move from anti-political to explicitly political language. Instead, there is a tendency on all sides to Manichean overstatement. Having lost the communist devil, says Adam Michnik, we find the devil in each other.

I

New political divisions are clearly emerging. But how to describe them? Western observers grasp for simple, comprehensible dichotomies: the functional equivalents of the categories of 'reformists versus hardliners' or 'regime versus opposition' which served understanding (and misunderstanding) in the past. Polish, Hungarian, Czech and Slovak participants and analysts are only too happy to offer new, clear dichotomies – partly in an attempt to understand the situation, partly to mould it. Unfortunately, they offer not just one or two but ten or twenty new dichotomies.

The real issue is pluralism versus the 'new monopoly' of his former advisers, says Lech Wałęsa. No, it is parliamentary constitutionalism versus extra-parliamentary populism, says Solidarity's parliamentary floor leader Bronisław Geremek. It is Europeans against nationalists, says Adam Michnik. No, say others, the real conflict is between under-represented workers and over-represented intelligentsia. Or between country and city. Or simply between those who now have power and those who want it: the Ins and the Outs. Then someone else comes along and says, to the relief of many baffled Westerners, that, after all, the fundamental argument is still between left and right. But no, says another; the crucial difference is rather between liberals of right or left and illiberals of right or left.

In the U-shaped Hungarian parliament you have, starting from the speaker's left, a few independent members, then Socialists (i.e. former communists), Young Democrats, Free Democrats, Smallholders, the Democratic Forum and the Christian Democrats. That looks clear enough: left to right. But, wait a minute: the economic policy of the Free Democrats is far more radically free-market, or 'Thatcherite', than that of the Democratic Forum, while at the far right of the Democratic Forum sit members of what is described as the Protestant, populist *left*: communitarian and anti-capitalist.

Let's try again. The basic divide is between two Hungaries: the cosmopolitan, urbanist, Western-oriented Hungary represented archetypically by the multilingual Jewish intellectuals of the Free Democrats, and a nationalist, populist, sometimes anti-Semitic,

27

Transylvania-oriented Hungary, represented by the monolingual intellectuals of the Democratic Forum. But then the Forum's foreign minister, Géza Jeszenszky, a diplomatic historian, spends twenty minutes explaining to you with eloquence and passion, in fluent English, why this is a caricature. And the populist 'left' (or is it 'right'?) rather prove the point by their furious attacks on their own prime minister, József Antall, and his cosy cabinet of Christian Democrat or Gladstonian-liberal gentlemen. But, then again, it is Antall, a devout Catholic, rather than the Protestant populists, who has pressed one of the policy proposals most offensive to Free Democrats and Young Democrats: that there should be religious instruction – initially it was even implied that this might be compulsory Catholic instruction – in schools. So is that all clear?

In Poland, things are no less complicated. Take, for example, two prominent exponents of opposing points of view: Adam Michnik, chief editor of the Solidarity daily, *Gazeta Wyborcza*, and Jarosław Kaczyński, chief editor of the Solidarity weekly, *Tygodnik Solidarność*, and a leading light of the so-called Centre Agreement, a pro-Wałęsa party. Michnik essentially argues that the basic divide in Polish politics today is still that which can be found, in one form or another, in the histories of all East and Central European countries – between Slavophiles and Westernizers, populists and urbanists, *Kultur* and *Zivilisation*.

One problem with his position is that it does not really allow for the possibility of a modern, liberal, European Christian Democracy in East Central Europe. Early in July, Prime Minister Tadeusz Mazowiecki attended a meeting of, precisely, European Christian Democrats, hosted in Budapest by József Antall, and starring the German chancellor, Helmut Kohl. Some politicians close to Mazowiecki founded a Forum of the Democratic Right, which clearly aimed to be just that. But in Michnik's judgement the dynamics of Polish politics would almost certainly sweep a would-be liberal, tolerant, European Christian Democracy into the flood waters of an intolerant, nationalistic, chauvinist National Democracy.

Kaczyński offers a quite different dichotomy. Michnik and Geremek, he says, represent 'the left'. He, by contrast, claims to represent the 'centre-right'. What, I asked him, distinguished this 'left'? Without hesitation he spelled out four points. First, he said, there was the attitude to property. He and his colleagues were unambiguously in favour of private property, 'the left' much more ambiguously so. Second, there was Michnik and Geremek's attitude to communists. For a year since last June's election they had been far too ready to make compromises with the communists. As late as the autumn, Michnik had argued that the most important thing was to forge an alliance with reformist (ex-) communists. According to Kaczyński, this also reflected ideological preferences: a red–pink continuum. Third, there was the attitude to the Church. To be sure, Michnik often referred to Christian values, and professed admiration for the historic anti-totalitarian role of the Church, but there was still an underlying suspicion, an anticlericalism, which they, the 'centre-right' did not share. Fourth, Michnik and Geremek had a basic, underlying mistrust of ordinary Polish people: they, the 'centre-right', by contrast, believed in the common sense of the common people.

Kaczyński is a clever man, and there is something in at least the last three of these points. Yet the truth of the whole is less than that of any one of its parts. For the whole picture he paints is that of a conspiracy: a conspiracy to dupe the common people, organized in what *Tygodnik Solidarność* writers refer to as the 'Warsaw–Kraków salon', and led by the satanic pair, 'Michnik & Geremek', whose names are repeated over and over again.

To suggest this is covert anti-Semitism (both Michnik and Geremek are of Jewish origin) would be as crude as it would be to suggest that Polish-Jewish history has nothing to do with the argument. The best way to describe it is, I think, in terms of residual images. In what Jarosław Kaczyński says, and even more in what some of the more explicitly right-wing groups say, there is the residual image of a Jewish conspiracy. In what Adam Michnik says there is the residual image of a pogrom. (Of course these residual images are not historically symmetrical, for there never was a Jewish conspiracy, whereas there were pogroms. Indeed, it must not be forgotten that Poland saw a communist-led anti-Semitic campaign as recently as 1968.) Yet the emphasis in both cases should be on the word 'residual'. To suggest that this is somehow the 'real' difference, the bottom line, would be as wrong as it would be to reduce the present arguments to any other single dichotomy: left–right, European–nationalist, monopoly–pluralism, workers–intelligentsia, Ins–Outs.

Perhaps the beginning of wisdom is to recognize that what the communists have left behind is an extraordinary mishmash, a profound fragmentation and cacophony of interests, attitudes, views, ideals, traditions: what in Polish is called a *miazga*. The system of late communism may not have qualified for the label 'totalitarianism', but it was certainly post-totalitarian. Many elements of civil society – elementary property rights, legal structures, intermediate institutions which still existed under the dictatorships in Spain, Greece or Latin America – were destroyed in Eastern Europe and, even more thoroughly, in the Soviet Union. In this sense, the totalitarian–authoritarian distinction may yet be found to have some validity.

A Russian joke about the transition from communism makes the point better than any learned disquisition: 'We know that you can turn an aquarium into fish soup; the question is, Can you turn fish soup back into an aquarium?' In East Central Europe things are not quite so hopeless. Here one has something more like a goulash than a fish soup. (After goulash communism comes the post-communist goulash.) There are large lumps of civil society swimming around like meat in the goulash: private farmers, Churches, universities, small-scale entrepreneurs. But it is still a very long way from the regular meat and two vegetables of developed West European societies, with relatively coherent blocs of interests, aspirations and traditions finding their political expression through a small number of relatively durable political parties.

In East Central Europe today there are a few elements of political differentiation according to socio-economic positions. For example, ever since the formulation of the Mazowiecki government, the private farmers have been the most clearly defined and determined interest group in Polish politics. But it is still very difficult to imagine a class-based politics. Wałęsa and his political allies may still sometimes speak in the name of 'the workers', but in reality the working class is almost as divided as the intelligentsia is between those who stand to gain from this or that measure or marketization and those who stand to lose by it. In Poland there is still no significant property-owning middle class. In Hungary, the sociologist Elemér Hankiss argues that one can already identify a small *grande bourgeoisie* (the 'red barons' of the cities, and the 'green barons' of the agricultural cooperatives), and a larger *petite bourgeoisie*, numbering perhaps as many as 2 million. But he cannot yet offer any significant correlation between these new-old classes and particular parties.

Indeed in both Poland and Hungary the more important divide may be between those who believe that parliamentary politics can change something in their everyday lives and those who do not. In these countries' first free elections in more than forty years, the rate of abstention was staggeringly high: nearly 40 per cent in Poland's parliamentary elections in 1989, nearly 60 per cent in the local elections in May 1990, 35 per cent in the first round of Hungary's parliamentary elections, 55 per cent in the second.

It would be wrong to say that there are no ideological divides. Of course there are. They emerge, for example, in one of the most important debates in all contemporary East Central European politics: how to proceed with privatization. Should the present management of state enterprises be allowed to turn them into joint-stock companies? Or should ownership be given to the workers? Or should shares be distributed to the whole population, perhaps through a system of holding companies or investment funds? And what, if any, should be the limitations on foreign ownership? But, again, these differences are not sufficiently clear and simple to form the basis of different political parties. The arguments are precisely about how to proceed with privatization, not about whether to.

If the basis of post-communist politics is neither class nor ideology, then what is it? At the moment the answer would seem to be: history and the West. Western models play a major role, both in the design of the new political institutions of East Central Europe and in the formation of parties. Everywhere, teams of Western experts have been called in to give their advice. In domestic debates about the new constitution, the 'French model', the 'Italian model' and the 'German model' are basic terms of reference. The last-mentioned is particularly noteworthy.

Germany has offered many things to East Central Europe over the centuries, but democracy has rarely been among them. Now, however, the German model of democracy is arguably the most relevant of all, because it is a model built on the rubble of a totalitarian dictatorship and very deliberately designed to prevent the return of such a dictatorship. It is, one might say, a Western system built on Central European experience. Constitutional elements such as the rule that parties must win more than 5 per cent of the popular vote to gain any seats in parliament or the parliamentary institution of the 'constructive vote of no-confidence' – that is, a vote of no-confidence that simultaneously appoints a new prime minister – have been copied directly in Czechoslovakia and Hungary respectively. The West German parties, together with their wealthy and active party foundations, also play an important role. At the moment, the CDU seems to be most successful, the SPD having the problem that all over East Central Europe ex-communists are now calling themselves Social Democrats.

On the other hand, there is history. I have referred already to some residual images that shape and colour Polish and Hungarian politics. In Czechoslovakia, the only relatively clear divides at this moment are historical-national ones, with separate Czech and Slovak versions of the revolutionary civic movement dominating the Czech and Slovak governments, while both are challenged by Slovak nationalists, by Hungarian nationalists in Slovakia, and by Moravian and Silesian autonomists. But these echoes of the inter-war period are only one part of the story. Both the more recent and the more distant past also play a role.

To understand present conflicts you really need a collective biography of the last forty years. Members of the Hungarian Democratic Forum, for example, often charge the Free Democrats with being former Marxists, while claiming they themselves had no illusions about communism. Similar charges are heard in Poland. Yet many of those who never had any illusions about communism were also never particularly active against it. Gáspár Miklós Tamás, the Transylvanian philosopher and Free Democrat MP, memorably calls them 'the sleepers'. In present-day politics, you have the class of '48, the class of '56, the class of '68, the class of '80 and – largest of all – the class of '89. Both between the classes and within each class there is a complex personal history of friendships and rivalries. You cannot begin to understand the personal alignments of today unless you know *who did what to whom* over the last forty years.

Sometimes, however, one can try to dig too deep. For example, there were, to be sure, obvious differences of tone and style between Tadeusz Mazowiecki and Lech Wałęsa over the last ten years: Mazowiecki always diplomatic, cautious to a fault, a cabinet politician; Wałęsa direct, instinctive, a tribune of the people. Yet the origins of the conflict between them are essentially to be sought in developments over just the last year (1989–90), when Tadeusz Mazowiecki was sitting in the prime minister's office in Warsaw while Lech Wałęsa was sitting in Gdańsk.

'How you see things depends on where you sit,' as Wałęsa himself put it. Last autumn the civic movements in Poland and Czechoslovakia believed that they were embarking on a sort of 'march through the institutions', to recall the German student slogan of '68. But what we have seen was almost the opposite: a march of the institutions through people. It is remarkable how quickly and fully people identify with that particular part of the political system in which, initially almost by chance, they have come to serve: with government as opposed to parliament, with parliament as opposed to the extra-parliamentary movement, with the presidency (in Prague Castle) as opposed to the government, and so on.

At the same time, one cannot ignore the elements of history, tradition and political culture stretching back not months but centuries. Obviously these are more difficult to analyse and assess. But they are certainly there. Watching a meeting of Lech Wałęsa's Citizens' Committee in the main lecture-hall of Warsaw University, with people making theatrical entrances and exits, passionate speeches, furious interjections from the floor and then plotting in the corridors, I wrote at the top of my notes one word: 'sejmik' (literally 'little parliament' – that is, the gentry parliaments of pre-partition Poland). Then the film director Andrzej Wajda slipped into the chair beside me and said, 'You see, all they need is sabres and they'd be fighting each other outside.'

Amid this baffling cacophony of intelligentsia politics – baffling to a large part of the population as well as to the outsider – with its strange admixtures of Piłsudski and Olof Palme, Horthy and Thatcher, Masaryk and von Weizsäcker, Bundestag and sejmik, the only serious path to real understanding is a detailed historical and, in the case of the leading actors, biographical narrative. But, short of that, there are still a few generalizations that might be risked.

2

A friend of mine has a thick file labelled simply 'TD'. It contains invitations to conferences on the subject of the 'Transition to Democracy' in Eastern Europe. 'TC' might be a more accurate label. What one can certainly observe in the whole of Eastern Europe, and in much of the Soviet Union, is the Transition from Communism. But the only case in which one can be almost 100 per cent certain that the transition will indeed be *to democracy* is that of the former German Democratic Republic, which will cease to be called Democratic but actually become so. It is, however, no disrespect to the people of East Germany to say that this will be as much an imported as a home-grown democracy.

Inside the Soviet Union, the aspirations of such European peoples as the Lithuanians, Estonians and Latvians, and of European Russians, are clearly in the same basic direction – towards liberal democracy, the market economy and the rule of law – but the problems they face are both of a different kind (being part of a multinational internal empire) and of a different degree (fish soup rather than merely goulash). In the Balkans, too, there is a rather different pattern, with what seems at the moment to be a transition from a (notionally) communist dictatorship to a non- (or ex-?) communist dictatorship in Romania, and Yugoslavia facing ethnic-national problems more comparable with those of the Soviet Union than with those of East Central Europe.

The heartlands of East Central Europe – Poland, Hungary and Czechoslovakia – are therefore, at the moment, something of a special case. One might also say a test case, for the success or failure of their attempts will influence future developments in the countries of the Balkans and the Soviet Disunion. Poland, Hungary and Czechoslovakia are the three ex-communist countries that are at the moment clearly attempting to built their own democracy on the ruins of dictatorship. Hungary and Czechoslovakia have had wholly free parliamentary elections, which all observers accept to have been fair.

Poland has had partly free but wholly fair parliamentary elections and wholly free local elections. These elections were not contested by a 'normal' party spectrum, as in Western Europe, but nonetheless they produced real parliaments. New constitutions are being written. There is already legally guaranteed freedom of speech, assembly and worship. There are a free press and free media, although the practice of independent journalism still leaves much to be desired – especially in the all-important medium of television. People can travel freely, limited only by shortage of hard currency. The increasing convertibility of their own currencies is itself a vital element of freedom and dignity. Everyday life is less abnormal.

So these countries are travelling hopefully; but will they arrive? It is a commonplace to say that the chances for the political transition from dictatorship to democracy depend to a very large degree on the economic transition from a planned to a market economy. However, it is also true that the chances for the economic transition depend on the politics of transition. It is, I think, slightly misleading to describe the problem as that of a possible 'failure' of the economic transition, for even 'success' will be agonizing in the early stages. This transition is, as Ralf Dahrendorf has written, unavoidably a valley of tears. The valley may be shallow or deep, short or long, but a valley there will certainly be. Even the Germans, with far better starting conditions in 1948, got poorer before they got richer. (There is also a problem of unrealistic popular expectations in East Central Europe, based on a mental elision of the idea of the 1950s *Wirtschaftswunder* with the visible reality of West German prosperity in the 1990s. Perhaps the Goethe Institute should organize a travelling exhibition showing every-day life in Germany in the early 1950s.) In Czechoslovakia, there is talk of achieving a soft landing. But the real question is whether they can achieve a soft take-off. Even East Germany is not going to have that.

The immediate question, therefore, is, What variant of democratic politics can, on the one hand, provide sufficiently strong, stable, consistent government to sustain the necessary rigours of fiscal, monet-ary and economic policy over a period of several years, while, on the other hand, being sufficiently flexible and responsive to absorb the larger part of the inevitable popular discontents through parliamentary or, at least, legal channels, thus preventing the resort to extra-parliamentary, illegal and ultimately anti-democratic means? This challenge has already been posed in a quite direct way in Poland, with peasant farmers physically occupying the agriculture ministry and blocking highways across the country.

For some in Poland and Czechoslovakia, the requirements implicit in this question seem to point to the need for a strong presidency. In an opinion poll conducted in Poland in mid-July 1990, 52 per cent of those asked said the highest power in the state should be the president, against 43 per cent for parliament. In Hungary, by contrast, the argument seems already to have been decided in favour of parliament, with a presidency having little real power, although lots of real influence. The American political scientist Alfred Stepan has forcefully argued that the South European and Latin American experiences of attempted transitions from dictatorship to democracy suggest that an unambiguously parliamentary system has a better chance of striking the necessary balance than a presidential one. Executive presidents are less able to create consensus behind painful (e.g. anti-inflationary) policies than parliamentary coalitions are. The executive president therefore either becomes a weak president, because he bows to the majority, or a strong but anti-democratic one, because he does not. It is, of course, questionable how far such experience is applicable to a regime with a very different history and with the unprecedented task of transforming not just an authoritarian but a post-totalitarian polity, not just a controlled but a central command economy.

Nonetheless, what I have seen on the ground in East Central Europe would support the general argument. Given the fragmentation and confusion of interests, aspirations and traditions that I have sketched above, it is very difficult to see how any president, however popular or charismatic, could sustain a voluntary consensus over a sufficient period for those painful policies of economic transition to have a chance to work, unless it were by mobilizing nationalistic fervour against a real or alleged common enemy: a new devil – Russian? German? Jewish? Romanian? – to take the place of the communist one. But such an undemocratic, nationalist mobilization would itself undermine the proposed economic transition, which crucially depends on the continued goodwill and active engagement of Western democracies.

No, the political key to creating such a consensus must be the creation of strong, freely elected coalition governments. At the time of writing, in July 1990, each of the East Central European countries has fulfilled two of these conditions, but none has fulfilled all three. Hungary has a freely elected coalition government. But thus far it seems to be a weak coalition government, one in which junior coalition partners (e.g. the Smallholders) behave as if they hardly belong to the coalition, while the main partner, the Democratic Forum, is itself a coalition with a coalition. Nor has the Antall government found an architect of economic transformation to compare with Leszek Balcerowicz in Poland or Václav Klaus in Czechoslovakia.

Czechoslovakia has a freely elected government – in fact it has three freely elected governments: Federal, Czech and Slovak. If President Havel were to put his authority firmly behind the policies proposed by the finance minister, Václav Klaus, who knows that there is no such thing as a soft take-off, then the federal government might also be a strong government. But it is not a coalition, in the sense of a government constructed as a negotiated deal between distinct parliamentary parties. For here there is at present really only one party, or rather movement. Since the 5 per cent rule (taken over from West Germany) led to the elimination at the polls of virtually all the minor parties contesting the election, the Civic Forum in the Czech lands and, to a lesser extent, the Public Against Violence in Slovakia are left as an overwhelming bloc, with a parliamentary opposition composed only of communists and nationalists (plus some Christian Democrats in Slovakia).

The competing parties will there have to form out of the body of the Civic Forum. There are already nascent political groupings within the Forum, and one proclaimed proto-party, the neo-liberal (or is it neo-conservative?) Civic Democratic Alliance. These parties will have to separate out in time to compete in the next election, scheduled for 1992. The tendency must therefore be for the Civic Forum to pull apart, rather than to pull together. How this necessary pluralization can be combined with the unity required to sustain the hard policies of economic transition over the two-year period, nobody in Prague could tell me.

As for Poland, from the formation of the Mazowiecki government in September 1989 until the spring of 1990, Poland had something that it has not often had in its history: a strong coalition government. This was a broad coalition, dominated by ministers from the Solidarity side, but containing communists in key positions (defence, interior ministry) as well as representatives from the formerly puppet Democratic and Peasant parties. It was a strong coalition, which managed to sustain, in its first six months, a remarkable degree of national consensus through the most radical and painful economic shock-therapy that had yet been seen anywhere in the ex-communist world: the so-called Balcerowicz Plan.

The trouble is that it was not a freely elected coalition government. And when free parliamentary elections had been held everywhere else in Eastern Europe, when Czechoslovakia and Hungary had their playwright presidents (Václav Havel and Árpád Göncz), then it began to seem anachronistic and shameful that Poland – the pioneer throughout the 1980s – should still have a rigged parliament and, heaven help us, General Jaruzelski as president. A seemingly transformed General Jaruzelski to be sure, as mild and discreet and civil and cooperative as any West European constitutional monarch, but nonetheless – Jaruzelski.

In the event, Polish politics were transformed by Lech Wałęsa's challenge from Gdańsk. But even if Wałęsa had behaved like – well, like Jaruzelski – the problem would still have become acute. It seems to me quite unlikely that, in these external circumstances, the Mazowiecki government and, so to speak, the Geremek parliament could have stuck to the timetable of first holding completely free parliamentary elections in 1991 and only then electing a new president. Even if they had, there would still almost certainly have been a crystallization of competing parties from within the broad Solidarity movement, and its Citizens' Committees.

These Citizens' Committees are strange creatures. The central one started life as a group of intellectual advisers to Lech Wałęsa. In the first half of 1990 it was expanded to include representatives of very different political groupings, at Wałęsa's behest, but against the wishes of many of its founding members. The regional Citizens' Committees were set up on the initiative of the Solidarity leadership (Wałęsa, Geremek and Mazowiecki, then working in close harmony) to win the historic June 1989 election. They had no clear structure or membership. Anyone 'who felt good there' could come, as one member explained. This sort of spontaneous, quasi-revolutionary grass-roots democracy has, of course, led to countless tensions and conflicts ever since that glorious fourth of June.

In fact the dilemma of the Citizens' Committees in Poland is comparable with that of the Civic Forum in the Czech lands. Once the electorate had shown that its confidence still lay with the heirs of the revolution (and the Citizens' Committee lists secured over 41 per cent of the vote in the May 1990 local elections), then it was clear that the process of democratic pluralization must occur inside the movement as well as outside it.

This is one of the things that Lech Wałęsa said most forcefully. But it is not the only thing that he said. In fact, in a series of pyrotechnic interviews and speeches, he said many different and contradictory things – some very acute, some very stupid, some funny, and some less so. There are two ways of viewing the 'war at the top' that Wałęsa launched in spring 1990. One is that Wałęsa, being in touch with ordinary people, saw that all was not going well with the government he had done so much to create. His former intellectual advisers and comrades were growing too comfortable in their undemocratic, rigged Warsaw coalition: their 'new monopoly'. Meanwhile, both political and economic changes were going too slowly. Privatization, insofar as it was happening at all, was benefiting the old *nomenklatura* rather than ordinary people. As prices and unemployment rose, so did popular discontent: witness the railwaymen's and other strikes, which only Wałęsa, with his authority and charisma, managed to pacify.

What was needed, therefore, was an 'acceleration'. Acceleration of privatization and marketization, to be sure, but above all political acceleration: meaning free parliamentary elections, Wałęsa for president, and the faster removal of communists at all levels. Wałęsa sometimes adopted the argument, made by Jarosław Kaczyński and others, that, since people could not be offered economic goods, in the

39

short term they should be offered symbolic political goods instead – that is, communist heads on a silver platter. Not salami tactics but Salome tactics.

The other way of describing Wałęsa's campaign is more simple. Having contributed more than any other single human being, with the exception of the Pope and Mikhail Gorbachev, to the end of communism in Eastern Europe; having won the elections; having formed the Mazowiecki government; he suddenly found himself marginalized, up there in Gdańsk, while all the action was in Warsaw. Then he found that his popularity was slipping in the opinion polls prominently published by *Gazeta Wyborcza* – the paper whose editor, Adam Michnik, he, Wałęsa, had personally chosen. According to one of these polls, he even scored lower than Jaruzelski as a suitable candidate for the presidency. His former advisers made it plain that they, too, did not see him as president. Then news leaked out from the Belweder, the presidential palace, that Jaruzelski, resenting the attacks upon him, and realizing that his time was past, was ready to resign. So, if Wałęsa wanted to be president, it was now or never.

There is truth in both versions. The discontents and problems to which Wałęsa pointed were real, but so was his personal sense of destiny. Like a commander-in-chief, he replaced the chairman of the Citizens' Committe with his own appointee, Zdzisław Najder. Then he sacked – by public letter – the secretary of the Citizens' Committee, Henryk Wujec, for many years one of his closest comrades. When Wujec politely objected that, since he had been elected by the Citizens' Committee, only the committee could dismiss him, Wałęsa wrote back, no longer to 'Henryk', but to 'Representative Henryk Wujec', the now famous line 'feel yourself dismissed'. Then he attempted to sack Adam Michnik from *Gazeta Wyborcza*. Then he peremptorily summoned the prime minister to a meeting in front of the workers in the former Lenin Shipyard, now once again called simply the Gdańsk Shipyard. 'Let us meet at the source,' he wrote, as if 'the source' of the prime minister's power was somehow still the workers' muscle that gave birth to Solidarity in August 1980, rather than the election of June 1989 that gave birth to the Mazowiecki government. (But then, and here's the catch, it wasn't a wholly free election, and people were voting for the 'candidates of Lech Wałęsa'.)

In a newspaper interview in mid-June he said:

For today, when we are changing the system, we need a president with an axe: decisive, tough, straightforward, doesn't mess around, doesn't get in the way of democracy, but immediately fills the holes. If he sees that the people are profiting from the change of system, stealing, he issues a decree, valid until the parliament passes a law. I would save half of Poland if I had such powers.

3

Is this merely a specific, Polish, problem, with one very special history and one very special person, or is it a more general one? Bronisław Geremek has spoken dramatically of the 'totalitarian temptation' in post-communist countries. As an analytical (as opposed to a rhetorical) proposition, this goes too far. One cannot see in any East Central European country today the combination of specific features which the French philosopher Jean-François Revel characterized as the totalitarian temptation. But one can see the seeds of an authoritarian temptation.

This is least apparent in Czechslovakia, the country with the strongest twentieth-century democratic tradition. To be sure, one can hear criticism of Havel's high-handed, arbitrary style, and, as you would expect, much more outspoken criticism of his 'court'. But, in his speech to the newly elected Federal Assembly, Havel himself came out in favour of somewhat reducing the powers of the presidency from those he currently enjoys. If the government(s) can remain coherent and strong, even while the Civic Forum breaks into different proto-parties – a very big if – then there is a chance that Havel could withdraw slightly further from the everyday political arena, in the best case becoming to the Czechoslovak transition what King Juan Carlos was to the Spanish one.

In Hungary, the temptation is perhaps slightly greater. As one Hungarian writer put it to me a little time ago, 'The Czechs are so lucky. When they look under the carpet they find Masaryk, whereas we find Horthy.' Fortunately, Hungary's new president is no Horthy, but instead is that same Hungarian writer – the liberal, genial and charming Árpád Göncz. In the present design of Hungary's new political system, if there were to be a new 'strongman' it would probably be in the position of prime minister rather than president. His rule would be reinforced, it is suggested, by an alliance with an extra-parliamentary 'movement', a *Bewegung*, and buttressed by a complaisant, government-dominated media. But the Democratic Forum really does not yet qualify as a *Bewegung*. Although the press may not be as fiercely independent as it should be – ironically enough, the former party paper *Népszabadság* is now said to be one of the best dailies – it is still very far from being a transmission belt for government policy.

Even in Poland, where the authoritarian temptation actually has a name and a moustache, the immediate danger is certainly not that of a Balkan-style transition from communist to non-communist dictatorship. In fact one might say that the immediate danger here is of too much democracy, not of too little. The immediate effect of Wałęsa's extraordinary campaign was to accelerate – to use his own buzzword – the process of pluralization and political fragmentation.

If Hungary needs the element of strength, and Czechoslovakia the genuine coalition, Poland needs the free election. But will the freely elected government then be a strong coalition, as the half-freely elected Mazowiecki government was for its first six months? Or will it rather be a weak coalition, with members from numerous smaller parties or factions, subject to endless conflicts and frequent reshuffles? This is, after all, what happened last time Poland regained its independence and attempted to build a parliamentary democracy, in the years 1918 to 1926. Then, as the historian Norman Davies jocularly observes, 'the proliferating profusion of possible political permutations ... palpably prevented the propagation of permanent pacts between potential partners'.

At a meeting of Lech Wałęsa's central Citizens' Committee in late March, at the very beginning of the 'war at the top', Tadeusz Mazowiecki expressed his fear that the fledgling Polish democracy could turn into 'a Polish hell. A Polish hell of squabbles, intrigues and conflicts.' At the dramatic thirteenth meeting of that committee, in

June, Wałęsa said, 'Maybe we have to go through the Polish hell.' And that is rather how it looks at this writing. One could, perhaps, afford such fissiparous politics – the Italians seem to manage – if one already had a flourishing free-market economy, with only a small state sector, and a developed civil society. But here, in the immediate post-communist period, too much still depends on the state. It is the state that has to organize the withdrawal of the state from the economy, the state that has to create the conditions for 'building' civil society. One might, therefore, offer an alternative definition of the Polish hell: Italian politics without the Italian economy.

Altogether, if there is a threat to democracy in East Central Europe, it will probably come through a period of, so to speak, excessive democracy. In Czechslovakia and Hungary, as well as in Poland, one can see three major elements that give cause for concern. First, there is popular disgruntlement, not only about the costs of economic transition, such as price rises, reduction of subsidies and unemployment, not only about new injustices and the slowness of visible change, but also about the processes of parliamentary democracy, which are themselves held to be responsible for the slowness of change. It is difficult to adapt psychologically from the dramatic fast forward of last year's revolutions to the slow motion of this year's parliamentary democracy. Seeming indifference to the new politics (reflected in the very high abstention rates in Poland and Hungary) and revolutionary impatience are, in fact, two sides of the same coin.

Second, the processes of the fledgling democracy are, indeed, often slow, ramshackle and flawed. If there is abnormally low popular tolerance or understanding of political conflict ('Why can't we still be united?'), there is also an abnormally high level of political conflict inside the new political elites: because there are no clear dividing lines, no proper parties, and few 'rules of the game'; because the new leaders, too, are unused to living with routinized, multilateral conflict, and have difficulty moving from anti-political to ordinary political language; and, yes, because power is a dangerous drug. Finally, the inevitable dislocation and distress associated with the conversion to a market economy could increase both the fissiparity of the elite and the disillusionment of the population. One could then all too easily imagine these three elements – elite dissension, popular disillusionment, economic distress – combining in a vicious circle, each exacerbating the other.

After 1918 came 1926, and Piłsudski's coup. Yet, although in so many ways the past seems to be returning with a vengeance, there are at least two powerful reasons for believing that history will not simply repeat itself. The first is the popular experience of dictatorships (of right and left) over the last half-century. When the expatriate Nobel Prize-winning Polish poet Czesław Miłosz was asked, on a recent trip to Poland, what he thought people might have learned from the years under communism he replied, 'Resistance to stupidities.' An optimistic interpretation, you may say, but there are some grounds for believing that fifty years of bitter experience have given the people of East Central Europe a resistance to certain kinds of stupidity. The kinds of stupidity associated with dictatorships, for example.

As we have seen, people are unfamiliar with, and therefore some-times distrustful of, the forms and habits of democracy. But the habits of dictatorship? With these they are all too familiar. 'Though I may not be able to define freedom,' wrote another Polish poet, 'I know exactly what unfreedom is.' Suppose a would-be strongman comes along and, using populist demagogy, attempts to overturn the parlia-mentary government. How, then, would he rule? By an extra-parliamentary mass movement? By police terror? By censorship? By martial law? The repertory of dictatorship is relatively small and, in this region, quite comprehensively discredited.

Against this argument you may cite Romania, where an authori-tarian regime has succeeded the Ceauşescu dictatorship. Without insisting too much on differences of tradition and political culture between East Central Europe and the Balkans, I would point to a second, powerful, reason for believing that these countries can after all resist the authoritarian temptation. This is the international context. If more or less authoritarian regimes flourished in East Central Europe between the wars, this was partly because there were examples of authoritarianism elsewhere in Europe which could somehow be associ-ated with the dream of modernity. Today there are no such examples, and modernity is unambiguously associated with democracy.

It would be nice to think that Poland, Hungary and Czechslovakia could coordinate their 'return to Europe', supporting each other's fledgling democracies. But, despite the goodwill of the new leaders, symbolized by the Bratislava summit in April, the present reality is as much one of competition as it is of cooperation. In almost every field, at almost every international gathering, one finds the Polish, the Hungarian and the Czechoslovak representatives quietly pushing their own particular claims for the special attention of the West. This competition is not unhealthy, but it underlines the new-old dependency of these countries – on the West.

Part of the attraction to Czechslovakia and Hungary of the so-called 'Pentagonale' cooperation between them, Yugoslavia (especially Slovenia and Croatia), Austria and Italy may be the sentimental revival of old Habsburg ties. But there is also the more vulgar charm of being closely involved with two highly developed Western countries – one a leading member of the EC, the other trying hard to get in. In their different ways, the Czechoslovak, Polish and Hungarian foreign ministers have all observed that, if these three countries are to achieve a new democratic partnership, it will only be in the context of belonging to a larger European community – and by that they mean, above all, a larger European Community.

The responsibility of the West in general, and Western Europe in particular, is therefore immense. A cartoon on the front page of the leading Czech independent daily *Lidové Noviny* expressed a sentiment about the West that can be encountered in Budapest and Warsaw as well as Prague. It showed a rather gloomy man saying, 'The European Home is shut. If we want to get in we have first to solve all our key problems.' At times the attitude of some Western leaders does still recall Dr Johnson's famous definition of a patron: 'Is not a Patron, my Lord, one who looks with unconcern on a man struggling for life in the water, and, when he has reached ground, encumbers him with help.' Of course, Western investors have no moral obligation at all to invest unless the conditions are right. But Western democracies do have a moral obligation and, what is more, a hard political interest in helping the man while he is struggling in the water. Provided, of course, he is really trying to swim, and not just shouting about swimming.

Perhaps the greatest risk of the kind of super-democratization that I have suggested is possible – with more shouting but less swimming

– is that it will diminish the overall Western interest in the transitions in East Central Europe, an interest which may yet prove to be as shallow as it is currently broad. 'Why should we help them if they cannot help themselves?' will be the cry.

There are two sides to this coin too. The West, if it is to help, has a right to ask for certain rigorous, consistent economic policies – let us call them, in shorthand, a Balcerowicz or Klaus plan – and for the kind of governments that will be able to sustain such policies. The political desiderata may, I have suggested, be summarized as strong, freely elected coalitions. But, if the countries of East Central Europe produce such governments, then they must be confident that the help will really be there. For without it such policies are simply unsustainable.

West Germany is currently reckoning to pay something in the order of DM 300 billion over the next three years for the transition in East Germany. As with all building plans, the final bill will almost certainly be higher. And that is for a ready-made transition – a turnkey democracy, so to speak – for just 16 million people in the most prosperous country of the former Eastern Europe. How much larger then would be the bill for home-made, trial-and-error democracies for 63 million people in three rather poorer countries?

There is, to be sure, a general consensus among Western governments and political elites that 'we should help' the transition to democracy in East Central Europe. But how many politicians are prepared even to contemplate action on a scale comparable with that which West Germany, after a very sober examination, considers to be necessary for East Germany? Above all, how many politicians are prepared seriously to make the case to their own electors for such help? If presented with such a prospective bill, most West European electors would, I fear, say, 'Sorry, no!' Ironically, the kind of West European consumer democracy to which East Central Europeans so passionately aspire may be the kind least likely to help them. If West German taxpayer-electors are so reluctant to pay even for their fellow-Germans, who would seriously expect them to cough up for Poles?

Nonetheless, the challenge of democratic leadership would be precisely to make this unpopular case as eloquently and convincingly as possible, stating plainly that this is a moment when short-term personal and material interests should be sacrificed to long-term national and European ones. What we are witnessing is therefore not just a testing time for the fledgling democracies of East Central Europe, but also a testing time for the established democracies of Western Europe.

Finally, my exclusive emphasis on just three countries of East Central Europe may raise an objection. What about all those other Europeans, to the east and to the south-east, who are also crying out for democracy? My answer is a purely pragmatic one. Poland, Hungary and Czechoslovakia are the countries where the fate of democracy hangs in the balance today, and where the weight of the West can make the difference between success and failure. You cannot do everything at once. With German unification, the eastern frontier of democratic Europe has already moved from the Elbe to the Oder. I sincerely hope (against hope) that in ten or fifteen years the frontier of democratic Europe may be at the Urals and the Black Sea. But the question for today is, Will democratic Europe end on the Oder or on the Bug?

The Chequers Affair

In July 1990, in the midst of far, far more important developments, such as Nato's London Declaration, the Twenty-eighth Congress of the Communist Party of the Soviet Union, and the Stravropol accord giving Soviet approval to the full sovereignty of a united Germany, Anglo-German relations suffered a little shake. The first part of this little shake was an interview given to the *Spectator* by Britain's then secretary of state for trade and industry, Nicholas Ridley, in which, after lunch, but only one glass of wine, Mr Ridley talked about the proposed European monetary union as 'a German racket designed to take over the whole of Europe', and declared that, if you were prepared to give up sovereignty to the Commission of the European Communities, 'you might just as well give it to Adolf Hitler, frankly'. Saltily written up by the new editor of the *Spectator*, Dominic Lawson, son of former chancellor of the Exchequer Nigel Lawson, and adorned with a characteristically vivid cartoon by Nicholas Garland showing a schoolboy-like Mr Ridley daubing a poster of Chancellor Kohl with a Hilter moustache, this 'outbreak of the Euro-hooligan Ridley', as the normally restrained *Frankfurter Allgemeine Zeitung* described it, caused a political storm and the resignation of the trade and industry secretary.

The second part of this little shake was the publication in the *Independent on Sunday* and *Der Spiegel* of a leaked, highly confidential memorandum of a meeting between Mrs Thatcher and a small group of historians held at Chequers, the prime minister's country residence, on 24 March, to discuss Germany. The memorandum, which I had not seen until its publication, although I participated in the Chequers meeting, was written by Mrs Thatcher's private secretary for foreign affairs, Charles Powell. 'Ver-bloody-batim' was how one British minister reportedly described this singular document. But ver-bloody-batim is precisely what it was not. Rather it was a report, with no views attributed specifically to anyone but some by implication to all. And, like all good Whitehall rapporteurs, Mr Powell managed to flavour this rich cream soup with a little of his own particular spice.

One sentence was particularly rich: 'Some even less flattering attributes were also mentioned [at the meeting] as an abiding part of the German character: in alphabetical order, angst, aggressiveness, assertiveness, bullying, egotism, inferiority complex, sentimentality.' Well, perhaps in the course of a long discussion those attributes were mentioned by some participants, along with many more positive ones. But plainly they were never listed like that by anyone; nor, indeed, was there anything like a collective view of 'the German character' – if such a thing exists. Still, as one might expect, this was the sentence that made the headlines, whether in London, Paris or Frankfurt.

What really happened was this. Mrs Thatcher invited six independent experts on Germany to give their views at a private meeting in which the foreign secretary, Douglas Hurd, also participated. Besides two leading American historians of Germany, Fritz Stern of Columbia University and Gordon Craig of Stanford, there were four British historians and commentators: Lord Dacre (Hugh Trevor-Roper), Norman Stone, George Urban and myself. This was no ideological cabal. The guests had different views on Germany, and different views on Europe. Thus, for example, Norman Stone is a member of the Bruges Group, named after Mrs Thatcher's Bruges speech, which opposes further steps of federal integration in the European Community, while I have repeatedly criticized Mrs Thatcher for not going further in that direction. Fritz Stern is not only an outstanding authority on Germany history but also an outspoken defender of the 'L word' (Liberalism). All spoke their own minds. Fritz Stern said nothing that he has not said already in his published work; I said nothing that I have not said in mine.

Yet the most remarkable feature of this quite diverse group was the degree of unanimity that emerged in answering the central question of whether and how Germany has changed, and what we might expect from the new, united, Germany. As the main body of Mr Powell's memorandum fairly indicated, the weight of the argument was over-whelmingly positive. We explained why 1945 was a great caesura in German history. We described how, self-consciously but increasingly self-confidently, the democratic West Germany differed from its prede-cessors; and how the unification of Germany in one democratic state, bordering on East Central European states that were also choosing their own governments, was a development heartily to be welcomed. And we argued that it should be, precisely, welcomed.

Of course concerns were also expressed about this new Germany. Historians will always find continuities as well as discontinuities. But almost every doubt or question that was raised by the guests around the Chequers table could also have been heard in Bonn, from distinguished German historians, commentators and, indeed, leading politicians. For, as several participants pointed out, one of the signal strengths of West Germany has been its capacity for constant, relentless, sometimes almost masochistic self-examination and self-criticism, soundly based on a strong, free press and an exemplary historiography. Neither Japan nor Italy, nor indeed Austria, could match this. Thus I think it is fair to say that, if Chancellor Kohl himself had sat in on that meeting, he would have agreed with, or, at the very least, accepted as fair comment, 90 per cent of what was said around the Chequers table.

For a private, no-holds-barred brain-storming session, that is not a bad percentage. After all, everyone, but everyone, speaks slightly differently *about* his neighbours than he does *to* them. Auden says somewhere that if men knew what women said about them in private, the human race would cease to exist. The same might almost be said about the nations of Europe, and the European Community. (Men as much as women, of course.) If we had a completely frank account of, say, President Mitterrand's discussions with some French intellectuals on this issue, would the score even be as high? Or, for that matter, in a comparably frank discussion between Chancellor Kohl and some German specialists about Britain?

The remaining 10 per cent was as much a matter of style as of content, of tone rather than analysis. This was, of course, the problem a fortiori with Nicholas Ridley's remarks, as presented in the *Spectator*. As it happens, Mr Ridley's analysis was wrong. (If there is a danger, it is not Germany's commitment to further West European integration, but rather a weakening of that commitment as a result of the new possibilities opening to the east.) But, even if he were right, he would have been wrong for the way he said it. I have thought a good deal about this particular British tone and style in discussing Germany and Europe – a tone and style reflected outrageously in Mr Ridley's remarks, somewhat also in the *Spectator*'s representation of them, but also, to a much more limited degree, and in a more defensible way, in the personal spice of Mr Powell's memorandum.

I am told this is a matter of age and personal experience, and no doubt it is easier for someone of my generation, born after the war, to come to like and admire present-day Germany, and to make friendships unburdened by the past. Yet the generation gap does not quite account for this peculiar British tone – a unique mixture of resentment and frivolity. It may, I think, partly be explained by geography and history. America is far enough away, and still big and powerful enough, to be relaxed about the re-emergence of Germany as a great power in Central Europe. France is too close, too small and relatively too weak to be anything but deadly serious about it. But Britain is somewhere in between: close enough to be worried, and weak enough to be resentful ('Who won the war anyway?'), yet also far enough away, and still self-confident enough, to be outspoken and outrageous.

This slightly resentful insouciance is, like so many national weaknesses, the flip side of a strength. With a few notable exceptions, most German political speeches and commentaries are still so earnest, learned, scrupulous and responsible that they are better than any sleeping pill. British political speeches and commentaries, by contrast, are still often amusing, original and uninhibited – to a fault. But the fault in this case was a serious one.

It is not just that it is profoundly offensive to the leaders and people of a democratic Germany to paint Hitler on the wall (or on the remnants of the Wall). It is also consummately counter-productive. Such sauce does not make the meat of substantive criticism more interesting. It means that the whole dish is pushed away. It does not mean that Britain's voice is listened to more attentively in the counsels of Europe. It means that it is listened to even less.

In a sense, the July crisis was just another chapter in a much longer story: the story of how numerous responsible British policy-makers, including successive foreign secretaries, have worked extraordinarily hard to produce a positive yet still distinctive British contribution to the development of Europe, and how this work has again and again been frustrated. There are many reasons for this frustration – in the EC itself, in the legacy of past mistakes, in the Labour Party as well as in the Conservative Party – but some of the responsibility must plainly lie with Mrs Thatcher. The buck stops there. A large part of this most persistent problem lies in that 10 per cent region of tone and style: in the failure to find a distinctive language of British Euro-peanism – a language in which criticisms do not automatically become accusations, and praise does not sound like blame.

The very fact that Mrs Thatcher invited six independent experts for a day's seminar, and listened, shows a genuine wish to come to a serious, informed judgement on these extraordinary developments in the centre of Europe, and hence to find an appropriate response to them. There are those, including some in Bonn, who say that her interventions on these issues were more obviously measured, informed and helpful in the second quarter of 1990 than perhaps they were in the first. Yet the effect of the leaked Powell memo, coming on top of the Ridley affair, was to set things back once again.

Chancellor Kohl took it all very sportingly, saying that Mr Ridley was not the only person to have made tactless remarks, and recalling his own gaffe a few years ago, when he compared Gorbachev to Goebbels. In Britain, an investigation was ordered into the source of the leak. Few thought the culprit would ever be found. Questions were asked in the House of Commons. The prime minister defended Mr Powell. The foreign secretary invited his counterpart, Hans-Dietrich Genscher, to the Glyndebourne Opera. Then the Germans went on uniting and the British went on holiday.

However, the 'Chequers seminar' has entered the mythology of Anglo-German relations. For several years after 1990, I was tackled by people in Germany who started by telling me that of course they hadn't taken the incident at all seriously, and then talked about it very seriously for hours. In 1996, George Urban published a very extensive account of the meeting, drawn from his diaries. He records Mrs Thatcher saying, at the end of the meeting, 'Very well, very well . . . I promise you that I shall be sweet to the Germans . . .' Now I vividly remember her sitting up like a schoolgirl and saying, 'All right, I shall be very nice to the Germans.' I wonder how many of the other participants (including Douglas Hurd, well known as a diarist) have recorded slightly differing versions of the same event.

1990

1 August. Non-communist philosopher Zhelyu Zhelev becomes president of Bulgaria.

2 August. Iraq invades Kuwait.

3 August. Árpád Göncz is elected president of Hungary.

17 August. Beginning of a Serb insurrection in the Croatian province of Krajina.

23 August. The East German 'People's Chamber' votes for East Germany to join the Federal Republic under Article 23 of the West German constitution.

31 August. Signature of the Unification Treaty between the Federal Republic and East Germany.

7 September. Ethnic Albanian delegates of the recently dissolved Kosovo assembly meet secretly in Kaçanik and adopt a constitution for their 'independent republic'.

11–12 September. The concluding '2+4' meeting and signature in Moscow of the 'Final Treaty with respect to Germany' – informally known as the '2+4 treaty'.

17 September. Lech Wałęsa declares that he will stand for the presidency of Poland. The European Community agrees arrangements for the former East Germany to join the EC.

1 October. Britain joins the Exchange Rate Mechanism of the European Monetary System at a central rate against the Deutschmark of DM 2.95 to £1.

3 October. East Germany joins the Federal Republic. The 'Day of German Unity'.

Germany Unbound

He wished to be the chancellor of a liberated not a defeated Germany, said Willy Brandt on the evening of his election victory in 1969. Yet only on 3 October 1990 did Germany liberate itself. Not all alone, of course. Every German politician pays tribute to Gorbachev, to the pioneers of emancipation in Eastern Europe, to the Americans, French and British, without whom, as authors say in their Acknowledgements, this book could never have been written. But it was the Germans who wrote the book.

For all the discontinuities of West Germany policy since 1949, one can but admire the grand continuity in which all chancellors from Adenauer to Kohl, all foreign ministers, all federal governments over forty years, now this way, now that, now in the West, now in the East, pursued the cause of German liberation.

Historians will argue whether Adenauer's integration into the West or Brandt's Ostpolitik contributed more to the success of the past year. There is much to be said for the claim that the East Central European year of wonders, 1989, was a late triumph of Adenauer's 'magnet theory' – the idea that the attraction of a free and prosperous West Germany embedded in a free and prosperous Western Europe would sooner or later draw the unfree and impoverished East Germany irresistibly towards it. But could the magnet have exerted its full attractive force if the blocking Iron Curtain had not first been drawn back by the Ostpolitik which Willy Brandt launched in the late 1960s? And it was not Bonn's Western but rather its Eastern ties – above all, those to Moscow – which directly permitted the transformation of an East German movement for freedom into an all-German state of unity.

Yet this East German rising for freedom was not contemplated in Bonn's policy towards East Germany. Those in the GDR who contributed most to Germany's peaceful October revolution – the tiny minority of human- and civil-rights campaigners – had benefited least from the Federal Republic's governmental policy towards the GDR. Bonn politicians now ritually celebrate the 'peaceful revolution'. Two years ago most of those same politicians would have described it as 'dangerous destabilization'. Yes, it was a 'dangerous destabilization' that made German unification possible. Without the brave minority that faced down armed police on the streets of Leipzig, Dresden and Berlin, the ultimate goal of Bonn's policy would never have been achieved – Gorbachev or no Gorbachev. (The real greatness of this year's Nobel Peace Prize winner consists in the ability to accept often undesired and unintended faits accomplis – or what Mr Gorbachev likes to call 'life itself'.)

The pioneers of social emancipation and democratization in the GDR were then rapidly overtaken by those who wanted to have done with the GDR altogether. By this time the two parallel sets of negotiations for unification – the 'internal' ones, between the two German states ('1+1'), and the 'external' ones, between the two German states and the four post-1945 occupying powers ('2+4') – were already under way.

Chancellor Kohl, after giving initial consideration to alternative models, such as that of a 'treaty community' or confederation, had decided by the end of January to go full steam ahead for one federal republic. The votes of the East German population gave him the domestic political strength to do this. It was his political decision, against the advice of most experts, to introduce monetary union on 1 July, and to do so with a large degree of one-to-one parity (Deutschmark to GDR Mark). This had a traumatic impact on the East German economy – according to West German statistics, industrial output in August 1990 was down 51 per cent from that of August 1989 – which in turn imparted a desperate urgency to the last months of negotiation.

To describe these seven hectic months of intricate negotiation would require not an essay but a compendium. The 31 August treaty on unification between the two German states is a book in itself – 243 pages of small print in the official government bulletin. Formally, they were '1+1' and '2+4' negotiations. In practice they were '1+¼' and '1+1+1' negotiations. The first and last freely elected East Berlin government was not an equal partner in the German–German talks. The Bonn government basically set the terms of the internal unification, its officials drafting treaties that bore a remarkable resemblance to the finished product. Many East German politicians, and intellectuals in both halves of Germany, were understandably miffed by this procedure. '*Anschluss*,' said some. Yet was it not for this that the majority of the people had voted in March? And, despite widespread economic distress, the majority expressed its basic satisfaction with the result, on 14 October, in the first elections for the five reconstituted *Länder* of the former GDR. Chancellor Kohl's CDU was the overall winner everywhere except in Brandenburg (where the Social Democrats' leader is a prominent Protestant churchman), and secured more than 45 per cent of the vote in Saxony and Thuringia.

The external negotiation was basically between the Federal Republic, the Soviet Union and the United States, in that order. The Bonn government makes no secret of the fact that it was the United States, rather than France or Britain, that was its crucial Western supporter in the whole process. Washington was not just self-evidently more important in talks with Moscow, but also more unreservedly supportive than London or Paris – a fact that has done some damage to the Franco-German 'axis'. Yet the central negotiation was that between Bonn and Moscow. In Moscow in February, Chancellor Kohl secured Gorbachev's assent to unification in one state. In Stavropol in July, he secured Gorbachev's assent to the full sovereignty of the united state, including its membership in Nato – although a Nato redefined by the 'London Declaration' a few days before. Soviet troops would leave Germany by 1994.

In return, the united Germany would have no atomic, biological or chemical ('ABC') weapons and no more than 370,000 men and women under arms; it would make a hefty financial contribution to the repatriation costs of Soviet troops; and it would become, even more than it was already, Gorbachev's leading partner in his desperate attempt to modernize the Soviet Union and bring it 'to Europe'. That was the essential German–Soviet deal which opened the door to unification on Adenauer's terms. To celebrate this remarkable deal, Kohl and Gorbachev appeared in V-necked cardigans and open shirts. Surrounded by men in suits, they peered into a Caucasian river and mused upon the meaning of life itself.

In Europe these days 'sovereignty' is a controversial word – and not just for Mrs Thatcher or Jacques Delors. When German conservatives celebrate Germany's recapture of full sovereignty, German liberals (and liberal conservatives) hasten to say, 'But of course this is no longer sovereignty in the classical sense', and 'After all, we share sovereignty in the European Community.' So let us put it more precisely. Until 3 October 1990, the Federal Republic had somewhat less freedom of action than the United Kingdom or the French Republic, both de jure and de facto. After 3 October 1990, it has almost precisely as much de jure, and de facto slightly more. Britain and France have no comparable international treaty restrictions on their armed forces. But their relative economic weakness and their geographical position give them less room for manoeuvre than Germany, which is once again the great power in the centre of Europe.

The liberation from the bonds of the Western Allies' residual rights over Berlin and 'Germany as a whole' is but a marginal advantage by comparison with the liberation from the half-nelson grip of Soviet control over East Germany. At a meeting in Moscow just a few days after unification, I heard a very senior German official say simply, 'Now we are no longer open to blackmail.' 'Are the Russians our brothers or our friends?' asked an old East German joke. Answer: 'Our brothers – you can choose your friends.' By 1994, at the latest, the brothers will be gone – and Germany can choose her friends.

3 October will now officially replace 17 June, the anniversary of the East German rising of 1953, as 'the day of German unity'. A better description might be 'the day of Germany liberty'. Externally, the new German state is free – and can use its freedom of action for good or ill. Internally, more than 16 million men and women are free who until a year ago were not. Of course they have hard times ahead. Of course their new freedom is relative. But one of the messages of the East Central European '1989' is precisely to warn against the confused and exaggerated relativization of values in which all too many German intellectuals so wordily indulged throughout the 1980s.

A few weeks before the great day, we had to stay with us in Oxford a young man, Joachim. As the son of a very remarkable Protestant priest in East Berlin, he had been prevented from completing an ordinary secondary schooling. When I visited him in the early summer of 1989, at the rectory behind the Wall, he described to me how small demonstrations to protest against the falsification of the local-election results in May, and the East German leadership's endorsement of the repression on Tiananmen Square in early June, had been brutally dispersed. Here, in this very garden, the marchers had assembled. There, on that street, they had been 'pulled away', the police dragging them along the cobbles by their long hair. He was pale, nervous, angry.

In the early autumn of 1989 he wrote to me from West Berlin. He had fled across the frontier from Hungary to Austria. (On the first attempt, the Hungarian border guards had caught him and turned him back.) Life in the West seemed to him in some ways poorer than in the East, he wrote – 'inwardly poorer'. But he was still glad to be here – 'and I hope to remain so'. Yet the separation from his family, just a few miles away in East Berlin, was very bitter. His little brother and sister had insisted that their mother take them to a point near the Wall where, clambering on some stones, they could at least see their big brother, a distant figure waving from a platform on the other side.

Now, in the early autumn of 1990, he was a different man: bronzed, confident, relaxed. He had just been to America for the first time. 'That's great!' he kept exclaiming colloquially. He was just off to Dublin to improve his English. But he would probably go back to join his family in Berlin for Christmas. Suddenly he was the citizen of a free, prosperous and – dare one say? – normal country. The word 'liberation' has long been tainted in Central Europe, and most especially since the Soviet 'liberation' of 1945. But there comes a time when even the most polluted words must be reclaimed. This, in a single life, was liberation.

So when, around half past two on the morning of 3 October, as we wandered through the streets of Frankfurt, none of our party being perhaps entirely sober, Adam Michnik turned to me and said, 'Now tell me, Tim, what do you really feel about German unification?' my immediate response was 'You know, I really *am* pleased.' And when, seven hours later, and not perhaps entirely rested, I set out from the Hotel Unter den Linden in the former East Berlin to walk westward through the Brandenburg Gate (look for the new asphalt, it's all that's left of the Wall) and across a corner of the Tiergarten to the official ceremony for German unity in the Berlin Philharmonic concert hall, my step was light.

At first glance I thought the governing mayor had acquired a wig. But when he began to speak I, together with the rest of the gala audience in the Philharmonic, soon realized that this was an uninvited guest. He had walked through all the security controls and right up to the microphone. Before him, in the first row, sat President Richard von Weizsäcker, Chancellor Helmut Kohl, Foreign Minister Hans-Dietrich Genscher and grand old Willy Brandt, and behind them the country's most important political leaders. If the uninvited guest had been a terrorist with a gun, he could have decapitated the German body politic on the day of unification.

Fortunately he was just a nutcase with a cardboard folder, containing a long speech. 'Allow me fifteen minutes,' he said, and began a complicated tale of some outstanding grievance against the justice ministry. After several seconds of silent bewilderment, the audience began loudly to applaud him, hoping to clap him away. He would not stop. The master of ceremonies, in white tie and tails, politely asked him to leave the stage. On he went, describing in detail the excellent wine he had drunk in the course of his extensive litigation. The interior minister, Wolfgang Schäuble, could be seen rising from his seat. After whispered consultations, and a good minute more of barmy speech plus ironic applause, two plain-clothes policemen very gently led this Herr Walter Mitty away. (According to subsequent press reports, they simply took him out to the entrance and released him into the holiday crowds.) Then, at last, we looked down on the familiar bald pate of the governing mayor of Berlin, the next speaker on the official programme.

Far more than any of the official speeches, the proclamation of peace and goodwill to all men, the painfully responsible press commentaries, more even than the grave and beautiful cadences of Richard von Weizsäcker, this little incident exemplified everything that was good about the forty-one-year-old Federal Republic of Germany: civil, civilian, civilized. The small deed matched the big words – and the music, which was splendid.

With hindsight, since Wolfgang Schäuble was actually shot and badly wounded by another disturbed man at a rally less than a fortnight later, the episode looks less amusing. And of course the German police are not always so civil. That same afternoon there was what seemed a quite excessive police turnout in the centre of Berlin to control a demonstration against unification by squatters, anarchists and the far left. Riot-squad vans roared through the former Checkpoint Charlie (now a flea market) into the former East Berlin, and police helicopters chuntered overhead, as if to say, 'We are the masters now.' Yet the way in which Herr Mitty was treated was nonetheless representative of celebrations that were peaceful and merry, without being triumphalist.

In fact, it all seemed almost too good to be true. Like the East Central European revolutions of 1989, the German wonder of 1990 was so swift, peaceful and civil that it is still hard to believe it has really happened. If the first unification of Germany was made with blood and iron, the second took only words and money. Among the countless intellectuals asked by newspapers for their response to unification, the (once East) German writer Reiner Kunze stood out. 'I expect of Germany', he replied, 'that after 3 October 1990 it will prepare itself for this day.'

There is still a vast gulf between the new *pays légal* and the *pays réel*, between the legal fact of unity and the social fact of continued division. On the backstreets, in the factories, and in many, many heads, the GDR still exists. Something like one out of every ten in the former GDR workforce is unemployed. Pensioners have been terribly hard hit by the upward leap in prices. Tenants fear for their security – not to mention their low rents – as old private landlords return, or new ones arrive. And the psychological adaptation after forty years of socialism is perhaps even more difficult than the material ups and downs.

How long will it take before Germany is prepared for 3 October 1990? One reads widely varying estimates of the number of years it will take before the five *Länder* of the former GDR are pulled up to a level comparable with that of even the poorest *Land* of the old Federal Republic. Undeterred by their failure to reveal the full disastrous state of the East German economy in the past, the economists and research institutes are making confident predictions about its future. As diverse are the estimates of the financial cost of reconstructing East German industry. The round figure of a trillion Deutschmarks over ten years is tossed about. Chancellor Kohl has bravely promised an official guess at the costs, even before the federal election on 2 December. The finance minister, Theo Waigel, does not quite say, 'Read my lips', but reckons the government should be able to get by without major tax increases. In the former GDR, as elsewhere in the former Eastern Europe, the costs and problems of economic transformation are far bigger and more fundamental than in Western Europe after 1945. But if anyone in Europe can master the task of post-communist economic reconstruction, it is the Germans.

The real question is less the economic cost than the political implications of the economic cost. These will be seen first on the streets rather than in parliament. The enthusiasm with which ordinary West Germans greeted their liberated compatriots a year ago has largely evaporated, as the newcomers take scarce housing and jobs from poorer West Germans, and jam the checkout lines at the cheaper supermarkets. But the swelling resentment against the so-called *Ossis* is sweetness and light compared with street attitudes to Poles, Romanians and Turks. In a West Berlin supermarket a sign says, 'Polish citizens may only purchase one carton.'

At present the new Germany is home to some 5 million foreigners, out of a total population of 78 million. With the social tensions that will arise from the reconstruction of the East, the tolerance even of those foreigners who have lived in Germany for a long time is likely to diminish. Already one hears of second-generation Turkish-German citizens losing their jobs to East Germans. It is here, on the streets, that the political culture of the Federal Republic will be put to the test.

At the same time, with the combination of political liberation and economic disintegration in the former Eastern Europe and Soviet Disunion, the press of would-be immigrants or *Gastarbeiter* ('guest workers') will increase, adding to the existing pressure from across the Mediterranean. A new spectre is haunting Western Europe: the spectre of a huge post-communist movement of peoples, something like the great *Völkerwanderung* of the early Middle Ages. This is a formidable challenge for the whole European Community, but for Germany above all.

How will it cope? By building a new wall along Germany's new eastern frontier, the Oder–Neisse line? Or by opening to the East while supporting, with more billions of Deutschmarks, the transformation to a market economy from Poznań to Vladivostok, thus encouraging the peoples to stop wandering westward? The answer given by Germany's political leaders is, not surprisingly, a qualified version of the latter possibility rather than the former. 'We lift our voice for a constructive and common Ostpolitik,' said President von Weizsäcker in his 3 October speech. 'All the frontiers of Germany should become bridges to our neighbours.' But, even as he spoke, on the day of unity, a visa requirement was introduced for all Poles, many of whom had previously been able to travel without visas to East Germany and West Berlin. So, if the German–Polish frontier is a bridge, it is a half-closed one. Reality did not quite match up to rhetoric. However, the Bonn government has now declared its readiness in principle to lift the visa requirement for Poles as it has already done for Hungarians, Czechs and Slovaks.

Altogether, the problem with the foreign policy of the new Germany would seem to be not that it has any bad intentions but that it has too many good ones. Hans-Dietrich Genscher says, 'We Germans want nothing else than to live in freedom, democracy and peace with all the peoples of Europe and the world.' A modest aspiration. Germany as Europe's 'honest broker'. But, as Richard von Weizsäcker's unification speech reached its climax with an appeal to Germans to set about 'preserving the creation' (i.e. the natural world), I could not help recalling the description of Germany's possible role that Bismarck rejected in his 'honest broker' speech. Germany, said the chancellor of the first unification, should not aspire to be the schoolmaster of Europe.

The schoolmaster of Europe – that seems to me perhaps the best summary in a phrase of the aspirations of Germany's present political leadership. The schoolmaster has passed his own exams over the last year with flying colours. There is a great deal of sense in what he has to say. But one does wonder how much of the school book can ever be translated into practice, even by the Germans themselves – let alone by more recalcitrant pupils (J. Delors, smirking in the front row; F. Mitterrand, looking grandly out of the window; M. Thatcher, giving her own lesson in the corridor). Are they not perhaps aiming a little too high? As Robert Browning has it in 'A Grammarian's Funeral':

> That low man goes on adding one to one,
>> His hundred's soon hit:
> This high man, aiming at a million,
>> Misses an unit.

In the immediate future, German foreign policy will face some hard choices. American readers may think first of the decision about how far, and in what form, Germany should take greater responsibility outside Europe. Within Europe, I see two major choices, which in a deeper sense are one. The first concerns the former Eastern Europe and the Soviet Union, the second the (West) European Community.

Since 1955, when Adenauer opened diplomatic relations with the Soviet Union (but with no other Soviet-bloc state), then very clearly since the Moscow Treaty of 1970, the relationship with the Soviet Union has taken top priority in Bonn's Ostpolitik. On a sober analysis of national interests, this has been wholly understandable. As many observed, 'The key to German unity lay in Moscow' – from 8 May 1945, one might say, until 3 October 1990. Plainly this priority remained throughout the negotiations on German unity. Chancellor Kohl emphasized that he would have liked to have signed a comprehensive friendship treaty with Poland at the same time as he signed the treaty with the Soviet Union. As it turned out, in 1990 as in 1970, the Moscow treaty preceded the Warsaw one, which is still to be negotiated. And what a treaty this Moscow one is!

Francis Fukuyama has proclaimed the end of history, but the German–Soviet friendship treaty, initiated in Moscow on 13 September, goes one step further. 'The Federal Republic of Germany and the Union of Soviet Socialist Republics,' says its preamble, 'wishing finally to put an end to the past . . .' To put an end to the past! 'Determined to follow on from the good traditions of their [i.e. Germany and the Soviet Union's] centuries-old history', the two sides produce another catalogue of good intentions, mainly gluing together prefabricated phrases from German–Soviet documents of the last twenty years, but also declaring that 'They will never and under no circumstances be the first to use armed forced against each other or against other states. They call upon all other states to join in this commitment to nonaggression.' If we take this literally, it means that Germany is joining the Soviet Union in calling upon, say, the United States not to use armed force against, say, Iraq.

'But', your German colleague will respond privately, 'you mustn't take it literally!' Then why write it if you don't mean it? Well, to get Russian agreement to unification, of course! Fair enough: Machiavelli dressed as Luther. The question then becomes, Is this really the last page of an old chapter – the forty-five-year-long story of German liberation – or the first page of a new one? ('Germany and the Soviet Union at a New Beginning,' a headline in the *Frankfurter Allgemeine Zeitung* memorably announced at the time of the Stavropol agreement in July.) Time will tell – meaning the Germans will decide. Or perhaps will not decide. For my impression is that German policy-makers do not at the moment have a private set of priorities in foreign policy that is much clearer than the public rhetoric.

On present form, the consciousness of promises made, gratitude, habit, the faint hope of a great market to open, above all a deep fear of disorder and chaos – the dreaded 'instability' – all these will incline Bonn to make quite substantial efforts to help the Soviet leadership (and the *Soviet* leadership, rather than, say, the Russian, Ukrainian or Baltic leaderships) to proceed along the path of economic transformation. Yet the Soviet Union is collapsing at such a rate that these efforts are probably doomed to failure, at least in this well-ordered form (Germany–Soviet Union). Moreover, so long as the Soviet–American relationship remains highly cooperative, German–Soviet cooperation need not adversely affect German–American relations. In the short term, then, the 'Big Three' of post-Cold War Europe – America, Germany and Russia – can probably remain more or less in sync.

The immediate problem lies closer to home. At the same time as promising extensive help to the Soviet Union – to be set out in a second comprehensive treaty on economic, scientific and technological cooperation – German policy-makers say they want especially to help their neighbours in 'Central, Eastern and South-Eastern' Europe. But, as the Germans have themselves discovered in the GDR, the problems and costs of the transition from a planned to a market economy are vast. If this is true of the small and relatively prosperous GDR, how much more is it true of Czechoslovakia, Hungary and Poland, let alone of Romania and Bulgaria – not to mention the east European republics of the Soviet Union? If German, European and Western help is spread more or less indiscriminately across this whole vast region, then the three mutually dependent transitions – to market economy, to parliamentary democracy and to the rule of law – will not succeed even in the nearest east of Europe, in East Central Europe. And then that region could indeed become Europe's Near East: not the Central Europe of the intellectual anti-politicians' dreams, but the *Zwischen-europa* of a nightmare – an area of weak, undemocratic states, riven by social and national conflicts. This would obviously be bad for all of Europe, but it would be especially bad for Germany, since the resulting chaos would be just thirty miles east of the capital, Berlin. The pressure of immigrants would grow, not decline, and they would be knocking first at Germany's doors.

'The western frontier of the Soviet Union must not become the eastern frontier of Europe,' says President von Weizsäcker. A noble sentiment, but open to question in two respects. First, the Soviet Union is ceasing to exist, and Lithuanians, Estonians, Latvians and Ukrainians no longer wish to recognize 'the western frontier of the Soviet Union' as 'the eastern frontier of Europe'. (The Ukrainian republic recently signed a separate treaty with Poland, including mutual recognition of frontiers.) Second, if we understand by 'Europe' a community of more or less liberal democratic states with social-market economies, then the real question for the next five to ten years is not 'Will Europe end on the present western frontier of the Soviet Union?' but rather 'Will Europe reach even that far?' Unless a clear and very high priority is given by Germany and the whole European Community to East Central Europe, where the transition still has a sporting chance, Europe – in the constitutional and economic sense – will not end on the river Bug. It will end on the Oder and Neisse.

This relates intimately to the second hard choice that faces German policy: that about the (West) European Community. As national unification reached its climax, so German policy-makers and commentators redoubled their insistence that the E C must move forward, in both domestic and external policy. Where Bismarck said, 'Let us put Germany in the saddle', the Nestor of German liberal journalism, Theo Sommer, says, 'Now we must put Europe in the saddle.' Poor girl: up into the saddle, whether she wants it or not! And, of course, she herself is, as always, in several minds. A significant part of Germany's present political elite still has a genuine commitment to moving forward to closer integration at the E C intergovernmental conferences on political and on economic and monetary union (although there are also substantial reservations, for example on the part of the Bundesbank, which fears a softening of the Deutschmark). This commitment is shared, in different ways and varying degrees, by significant parts of the political elite in most of the other Continental members of the E C. But there is one quite fundamental and immediate problem.

Germany's present political leadership says it wants to deepen the Community, but also in the foreseeable future to widen it, to include East Central Europe and some countries from the European Free Trade Association (EFTA). But many people at the highest levels of the E C consider deepening and widening to be not complementary but contradictory goals. Jacques Delors argues that if you are to deepen, for example by adopting a common currency and a central bank, then you cannot afford to widen. Mrs Thatcher advocates a rapid widening, partly out of genuine concern for the fledgling democracies of East Central Europe, but also to foil Brother Jacques's designs of rapid deepening.

One can quite plausibly argue that the E C is on the horns of a dilemma. If it moves forward soon in the general direction of a United States of Europe, then East Central Europe will join it only late or never. If East Central Europe joins soon, then the E C will move forward in the direction of a USE only late or never. In the former case, the position of the former Eastern Europe will differ from that of the former Soviet Union in degree, but not in kind. 'Europe' will, in some very significant senses, end on the Oder–Neisse line. In the latter case, however, in a looser *Europe des Patries*, Germany would willy-nilly come back somewhat more to the old post-Bismarckian dilemmas of the nation state in the middle. So German policy-makers quite rightly see that they must try to both deepen and widen the Community. But how?

There are a few people in Germany seriously seeking answers. (Perhaps it is always only a few.) Whether they find any, and, if so, what those answers will be, we will probably begin to learn only after the federal election on 2 December. The starting point must surely be, as it was for Adenauer and Brandt, the definition of national interests. For the last forty years (some would say for the last two hundred) the question of German national *identity* has provoked some of the longest, deepest, most contorted answers ever given to any question by any branch of humankind. The question of national *interest*, however, has been much easier to answer. For the last forty years the answer was, in a nutshell, 'recovery of sovereignty and overcoming the division of Germany'.

Now, in one united, western Germany, the question of national identity should be easier to answer – although to judge by the hypo-chondriac effusions in recent weeks of many German writers lamenting unification (like Günter Grass) or discovering a late love for the cosy old Federal Republic (like Patrick Süskind), there is no guarantee that their answers will actually become any simpler. The question of national interest, by contrast, necessarily becomes more complicated. On my analysis, besides the consolidation of the constitution of liberty and an open society inside Germany, the first strategic answer would be: 'to combine in one design the enterprise of sustaining the demo-cratic transition in East Central Europe and that of further, primarily political, integration of the EC'.

If, however, such a design is not clearly spelled out, if the hard choices are ducked, then national (and therefore European) interests will be defined on the hoof – dictated by dramatic external develop-ments, such as the further collapse of the Soviet Union, or by domestic pressures, such as swelling resentment against immigrants, or by a combination of both.

The second part of my answer to Adam Michnik, on the streets of Frankfurt, at 2.30 on the morning of German unification, was: 'If I have a fear for the next few years, it is not that Germany will turn outward in any sort of bid for domination as an economic great power. It's rather that it will turn inward, become obsessed with the problems flowing from unification, a little self-pitying, self-protective. And build a new wall on its eastern frontier which its other West European partners will only help to reinforce.'

In short, the German eagle is unbound. The broken chains lie on the hillside. He has raised his wings a little, and given a few friendly cries. Will he now spread his wings and rise up, this time to help, not to attack? Or will he rather, like the eagle donated to Washington Zoo by Chancellor Helmut Schmidt, sit sulkily on his perch, gobbling his ample food and disconsolately scratching his breast feathers with that great beak?

1990

12 October. Signature of a German–Soviet treaty on the arrangements for remaining Soviet troops in Germany and their planned withdrawal by December 1994.

15 October. Mikhail Gorbachev is awarded the Nobel Peace Prize.

25 October. The Slovak parliament votes to make Slovak the official language of Slovakia.

28 October. At the Rome summit of the EC, eleven leaders agree to proceed to a 'second stage' of monetary union on 1 January 1994, and to achieve full monetary union by 2000. British prime minister Margaret Thatcher refuses to join them, denouncing this as the 'back door to a federal Europe'.

1 November. British deputy prime minister Geoffrey Howe resigns in protest at Mrs Thatcher's attitude to Europe.

6 November. Hungary joins the Council of Europe – the first post-communist country to do so.

7 November. Mary Robinson is elected president of the Republic of Ireland.

9 November. Chancellor Kohl and President Gorbachev sign a German–Soviet friendship treaty on the first anniversary of the opening of the Berlin Wall.

14 November. Signature of a German–Polish frontier treaty.

19–21 November. Paris summit of the Conference on Security and Cooperation in Europe. Launch of the Paris Charter for a New Europe. Member states of Warsaw Pact and Nato sign the Treaty on Conventional Armed Forces in Europe.

28 November. Margaret Thatcher resigns as prime minister of Britain and leader of the Conservative Party. She is succeeded by John Major.

2 December. The first all-German elections to the Bundestag result in a clear victory for the existing centre-right coalition government led by Helmut Kohl.

9 December. Lech Wałęsa is elected president of Poland, promising an 'acceleration' of de-communization. Slobodan Milošević is elected president of Serbia on a nationalist platform.

14–15 December. The European Council in Rome launches twin

intergovernmental conferences, on economic and monetary union and
on political union.
20 December. Soviet foreign minister Eduard Shevardnadze resigns,
warning of the risk of a renewed dictatorship in the Soviet Union.
22 December. In its 'Christmas constitution', the Croatian parliament
proclaims Croatia 'the national state of the Croatian people'.

1991

4 January. Liberal Jan Krzysztof Bielecki becomes prime minister of
Poland.
11–12 January. Paris. At a grand dinner in the Hôtel de Ville, Henry
Kissinger twits Jacques Chirac, the Gaullist mayor of Paris, about his
earlier admiration for the Iraqi leader Saddam Hussein. Chirac replies,
'Oh, he's changed you know.' Politician's wisdom.
13 January. 'Bloody Sunday' in Vilnius. Some fifteen Lithuanians are
killed following action by Soviet forces.
17 January–8 February. Gulf War to liberate Kuwait from Iraq under
Saddam Hussein.
January–February. A wave of emigration by Albanian 'boat people'
attempting to enter Italy.
27 January. Former communist leader Kiro Gligorov becomes presi-
dent of the Yugoslav republic of Macedonia.
6 February. Stockholm. A memorable conversation with Carl Bildt,
leader of the Swedish conservatives. The social-democratic 'Swedish
model' or 'third way' has failed, he says. For too long Sweden has
stood apart, considering itself somehow closer to Africa than to
Germany. And he talks, almost like a Polish or Czech politician, about
the need for his country to 'return to Europe'.
9 February. Overwhelming vote for independence in a Lithuanian
referendum.
15 February. The 'Visegrád Declaration' constitutes the so-called
Visegrád group for Central European cooperation, comprising Hun-
gary, Czechoslovakia and Poland.
23–25 February. A congress of the Solidarity movement in Poland
elects Marian Krzaklewski to succeed Lech Wałęsa as its leader.

25 February. The Warsaw Pact agrees to dissolve its military structures by 1 April. The trial of former Bulgarian communist leader Todor Zhivkov begins.

3 March. Referendums produce clear majorities for independence in Estonia and Latvia.

4 March. The Supreme Soviet ratifies the '2+4 treaty' together with the accompanying German–Soviet treaties.

11 March. John Major declares that Britain is 'at the very heart of Europe'. In Greece, former prime minister Andreas Papandreou goes on trial, charged with bribery and embezzlement.

11 and 14 March. Rallies for Slovak independence in Bratislava.

14–16 March. Dresden. For forty years, the British–German Königswinter Conference has met either in Königswinter on the Rhine or in Cambridge. Now, for the first time, it breaks this tradition to meet in Dresden, the beautiful city – 'Florence on the Elbe' – destroyed by British and American bombs in February 1945. This is a moving event in many ways, but it is striking that, in the first Königswinter meeting after the liberation and unification of Germany, we come to the place in Germany where Britain has most to apologize for. It's almost as if, after forty years of apologizing for Hitler, the Germans are saying, 'Now it's your turn.' The balance of apologies shifts with the balance of power?

Late March. First outbreaks of inter-ethnic fighting between Serbs and Croats, in Serb-populated Krajina and eastern Slavonia regions of Croatia.

March–April. The Civic Forum in the Czech lands splits into three successor parties.

1 April. Formal dissolution of the military structures of the Warsaw Pact.

After Solidarity

Between *Sesame Street* and *Twin Peaks*, Polish television shows President Lech Wałęsa making his first ceremonial appointment of an army general. The new general is – a bishop. Around the corner from Piłsudski Square, formerly Victory Square, a guardsman peers longingly into the new Mercedes showroom. The Palace of Culture, the most famous symbol of Soviet domination, now contains a large shopping mall. In front of it, a huge billboard advertises P O L A M E R, a Polish-American travel agency. The irony is so crude as to be somehow appropriate: kitsch beats kitsch. Down Nowy Świat, Warsaw's Regent Street, a farmer snores in his vegetable truck, just a few yards from the freshly opened Christian Dior boutique. Everywhere, but everywhere, in the country as in the city, you see signs announcing a new *hurtownia* for this or that. *Hurtownia* means a wholesale warehouse, which means you pay less taxes, so every fledgling corner store is a warehouse now.

In this crazy wholesale warehouse which is Poland, with its German cars and American films, its bishop-generals and wheeler-dealers, all the old certainties have gone; no new ones have yet replaced them. The shop windows are full, but for most Poles the familiar, myriad shortages of goods have been replaced by one great shortage: that of money. Here is a country in upheaval, full of extremes and contradictions, with casinos and lines of people on the dole, a triumphant Church and tons of pornography, a few new rich and many old and new poor. A country on the move, but in what direction? West? South? Or perhaps in several directions at once?

All over Warsaw you hear 'Radio Z', a new radio station offering pop music interspersed with advertisements and a little news.

American style again. Between Christian Dior and the snoring farmer, a shabby staircase leads you up to the headquarters of 'Party X', a mysterious political party founded by Stanisław Tymiński, the Polish-Canadian-Peruvian dark horse in last autumn's presidential election. The Warsaw headquarters of Party X is – or appeared to be on Monday 22 April 1991 – one room in the offices of the Grunwald Association, a notorious extreme nationalist group which in the past almost certainly had close ties to unsavoury parts of the communist party–state apparatus. In this room, when I visited it, there sat several poorly dressed, puffy-faced women and a computer. After some debate, one of these women agreed to give me – as a potential member – a 'Letter X' intended for 'members and sympathizers of Party X'.

On its first page this bulletin prints a 'Declaration', the beginning of which seems vaguely familiar. Translated from the Polish, it reads, 'When in the course of human events, it becomes necessary for one people to dissolve the political bonds which have bound them . . .' After three paragraphs of the Declaration of Independence, almost word for word, the Party X Declaration concludes with a paragraph saying, roughly, that this is just about where Poland is now, folks. On the next page a headline in fluent English declares, with reference to Jeffrey Sachs, the Harvard professor who had an important part in helping to design and publicize the Balcerowicz Plan for Poland's economic transformation, 'Sachs, go home and don't come back!'

Without looking any further into the programme, or non-programme, of this ridiculous party, I will merely recall that its leader, Stan Tymiński, beat Tadeusz Mazowiecki, Poland's first non-communist premier, veteran Solidarity adviser, honoured intellectual – the 'force of calm', as his election posters had it – into third place in the presidential elections. And the leaders of all the main contending parties with whom I spoke take very seriously indeed the threat, if not from Party X, then at least from what Jacek Kuroń calls Phenomenon X. They all agree that a substantial part of the electorate is so disgruntled and disoriented that it can fall even for such rubbish.

Between Party X and Radio Z one almost feels like talking of Country Y. So much is new, unpredictable, bewildering, even to those who are supposed to be shaping this new Poland. The variables far outstrip the constants, the unknown the known.

I

Mrs Danuta Wałęsa, Madam President, attends the signing ceremony for a new Franco-Polish macaroni factory, called Danuta in her honour. It will be built, according to the publicity handout, in a 'new, post-Solidarity style'. And what, pray, is that? Of Poland's future architecture, as of the Danuta macaroni factory, one thing alone is certain: it will be post-Solidarity.

On the road out of Warsaw a solitary sign advertises Radio Solidarność. How long, how brave was Solidarity's struggle for access to the mass media! But now everyone listens to Radio Z. The Mazowsze region of the independent self-governing trade union Solidarity has a handsome headquarters on one of Warsaw's main streets. But life is elsewhere. The nationwide union Solidarity has a new, young chairman, Marian Krzaklewski, and a couple of million members. But most of Solidarity's great figures have moved on – to the presidential palace, to parliament, to different political parties – and there is little solidarity among them today.

From 1982 until 1989 the leading underground weekly, *Tygodnik Masowsze*, carried on its masthead the following words: 'Solidarity will not be divided or destroyed – Lech Wałęsa.' And, indeed, General Jaruzelski did not succeed in dividing or destroying Solidarity. Lech Wałęsa did. What he, more than anyone, had kept together through the whole decade of the 1980s, he, not alone of course, but more than any other single person, pulled apart at the beginning of the 1990s. More generally, liberation and democracy succeeded where dictatorship and repression failed. 'There's no liberty without Solidarity,' proclaimed the masthead of Poland's first genuinely independent opposition daily, *Gazeta Wyborcza*, echoing the strikers of 1988 who had set Solidarity back on the path to legality via the Round Table negotiations of early 1989. When Lech Wałęsa subsequently asked the editors of *Gazeta Wyborcza* to remove from their masthead the word 'Solidarity' (printed, of course, in the characteristic red jumbly lettering, and now a registered trademark of the union), someone suggested that they should leave a truncated motto: 'There's no liberty . . .' But a more accurate revised version might have read, 'There's no Solidarity in liberty.' And that could apply not only to Solidarity with a large S, and not only to Poland.

Of course there is a danger of retrospective, sentimental idealization. Even with the intense, uniting pressure of a common enemy, Solidarity was full of internal conflicts and divisions. Tensions were constantly surfacing between different groups, tendencies and regions; between peasants, workers and intellectuals; between conservative Catholics, liberal Catholics, agnostics and atheists; between left liberals, right liberals and anti-liberals; and just between individual personalities. One might say that only the combined efforts of Wałęsa – intentionally – and Jaruzelski – unintentionally – kept it together. Jacek Kuroń once joked that Wałęsa deserved another Nobel Peace Prize for his efforts to reconcile Solidarity's warring factions.

It is, moreover, a dangerous oversimplification to suggest that the society from which Solidarity sprang and in which it operated, and European societies under communism more generally, were characterized by a solidarity (with a small s) not found in the West. To be sure, there were forms of solidarity not found in the West. These ranged from the quotidian mutual dependence of consumers in a shortage economy, to the less quotidian support of the directly oppressed and the exhilarating unity of the crowd at a papal rally. But there were also forms of un-solidarity little known in the contemporary West: collaboration, denunciation, bribery as the sine qua non for medical care.

When all this is said, the fact remains that there existed, in Poland in the 1980s, an extraordinary thing called Solidarity, and that for many individual men and women it offered an extraordinary experience – of solidarity. This was, it seemed, something more than just the comradeship of men and women at war with an alien 'power'. Yet today, it seems, even less remains than usually does of wartime comradeship when the war is over. A few veterans squabble over the remnants of the flag, while the rest of the country slopes off to the *hurtownia*, to Radio Z or even to Party X.

Solidarity is a thing of the past. But, just because it is suddenly past, perhaps we may see it more clearly for what it was. In such a moment of radical, historical discontinuity, in the heat and dust of systemic transformation, the immediate future is uncommonly obscure, but the recent past comes into uncommonly sharp focus – both because we have information that we do not usually have so soon after the event, and simply because we know what we do not usually know: how the story ends.

2

A short stroll through Warsaw's bookshops reveals a plethora of interesting publications about the recent past. These bookshops, incidentally, are themselves a small symptom of the country's present turmoil. Where once you had to wait in line for a little plastic basket in order to view a stale array of books from state publishing houses (and the most interesting of those were sold out in a few days, or kept 'under the counter' for acquaintances), you can now browse at will amid a colourful if haphazard display of books from state publishing houses, former samizdat publishers, ecclesiastical publishers, émigré publishers, new commercial publishers, all together for the first time. Best-selling translations of Robert Ludlum lie next to Adam Michnik's *From the History of Honour in Poland*; Mills & Boon romances rub shoulders with earnest sociological texts: pornography lies on top of martyrology.

If something you want in the bookshops is sold out, you may get it, perhaps in a pirate edition, and certainly at a higher price, from the bookstalls on the street outside. Grzegorz Boguta, former head of one of the most dynamic underground publishers, Nowa, is trying to organize a new publishers' and booksellers' association, to bring some rudimentary order into this chaos. A lively new newspaper supplement, *ex libris*, attempts to review new books promptly and sharply – an essential part of publishing 'normality'. Meanwhile, the market gyrates between the old East of state publishing and the new (Wild) West of commercial publishing.

Among the best-sellers, up there with the Ludlums, are the memoirs or 'revelations' of the former communist leaders: two volumes from the party leader of the 1970s, Edward Gierek, a third from the former premier and last ever leader of the Polish United Workers' Party, Mieczysław F. Rakowski, and, apparently most successful of all, the scurrilous *Alfabet* of the former government spokesman Jerzy Urban. (Jaruzelski's memoirs are on their way.) These volumes – the kiss-and-tell of Polish communism – are interesting not only for what they tell us about the people who ruled Poland for the last twenty years, but also as a phenomenon of the present.

Although there are occasional flurries about the alleged collaboration of this or that politician with the secret police, the contents of the secret-police files are not at present the sort of political issue in Poland that they are in Czechoslovakia, let alone in East Germany. What is a major issue, however, is the way in which former communists have got rich by smartly turning themselves into capitalists. And these books are a prime example of just that. In one of Poland's most successful measures of privatization to date, the country's former communists are not so much, to recall Harold Macmillan's famous jibe at Mrs Thatcher's privatization programme, 'selling off the family silver' as selling off the family secrets. (The word 'family' may here also be understood in its Sicilian sense.) The publisher of most of the books, a firm called simply BGW, is reputedly one of the most commercially successful book publishers in Poland today – and surely a most fitting potential partner for Mr Robert Maxwell. Meanwhile, from the columns of his weekly *Nie* ('No'), a skilful mixture of soft porn and political guttersniping, Jerzy Urban sneers and jeers at the post-Solidarity politicians who have taken power from him.

Morally and aesthetically, this profitable self-privatization by former communists is deeply offensive to many people. It formed one major plank of the attack by the Centre Agreement Party – and by Lech Wałęsa – on the government of Tadeusz Mazowiecki. Yet the responsible Centre politicians now in government and the president's office have little more idea than their predecessors how, in a country that aims to build both a market economy and the rule of law, you can legally punish a former communist for becoming a successful capitalist.

At the other end of the post-Solidarity bookshelf we find a long and richly informative book describing the negotiated end of communism in Poland in 1989; the second volume of Lech Wałęsa's memoirs, ghost-written by one of his aides and covering the period from the end of 1984 (when his last volume broke off) to his election as president in December 1990; and a vivid and perceptive short sketch of Wałęsa in action by his former press spokesman Jarosław Kurski.[1]

The Year 1989 is a book of interviews with Bronisław Geremek, conducted between August and November 1990 by the press spokesman of the Solidarity group in parliament, which Geremek led. The small print at the end reveals what Polish publishing is now capable of, for it records that the last interview was conducted on 20 November and the text typeset between 25 November and 5 December, while the book – well produced, and illustrated with a splendid profusion of photographs – was on the market early in 1991. To anyone who knows Polish publishing of old, these are the coordinates of a minor miracle. I read *The Year 1989* with fascination, for Geremek is a unique witness, being both one of the major actors in the drama and a trained historian – indeed, he defiantly insists, 'above all a historian' – with a remarkable capacity to give a detached analysis of the events in which he participates.

Given that these interviews were conducted at the height of a furiously emotional presidential contest between Lech Wałęsa, Tadeusz Mazowiecki and, as it emerged, Stan Tymiński, the cool sobriety of the analysis is remarkable. Almost unsettling, in fact. Geremek remarks at one point that, as a historian, he has always been fascinated by structure and process, which alone give sense to events and anecdotes. While there are some fine anecdotes here, one sometimes wishes that the relentless analysis of structure and process might now and then give way to description or evocation of the scenes and emotions with which this year was, after all, packed full. But emotions mainly figure here as the 'frustrations' of other people.

Nor are there many ordinary men and women in these pages. Geremek himself says that when he set out on the election trail he had no experience of speaking to crowds, although he did have considerable contact with workers in Solidarity. He was, and is, above all a man of the corridor and the salon, the small circle and the elite group – although an elite defined by talent, not birth or class. Typically, one of the very few chance encounters described here is with an old schoolmate who reminds him of his love of the order and clarity of Latin grammar. What we have here is the Latin grammar of Poland's transition from communism – albeit a grammar laced with anecdotes.

At one point, asked why the authorities were especially hostile to him in the seven lean years when Solidarity was banned, he replies modestly, 'It's hard to say why.' In fact it's easy to say why. The authorities were especially hostile to him because he was the most skilful political tactician and strategist close to Wałęsa, and one who was able to analyse better than most what they were up to, as well as the international background and what Solidarity should do. Yet he was not just a politician. He talks several times of his 'moral discomfort' at sitting down at the same table with General Jaruzelski and, worst of all, with the appalling Mieczysław F. Rakowski. And, in a passage which it is hard to imagine coming from any West European intellectual, he speaks of 'playing my small part in the mission of the Polish intelligentsia, which has always served Poland above all, and not selfish ambition or advantage'. A romantic self-image, no doubt, but hardly an ignoble one.

The story he has to tell is that of Solidarity's historic triumph, and the beginnings of the disintegration which followed so quickly on that triumph. While Geremek suggests that everything went as well as possible in 1989, then fell apart in 1990, his own narrative shows how the seeds of collapse were sown in the very moment of victory, with the formation of the Mazowiecki government following the election of 4 June 1989.

The story begins in late 1988, with 'signals' from the authorities that they might be prepared to negotiate with Solidarity – signals decisively strengthened by two waves of strikes, with young workers chanting, 'There's no freedom without Solidarity!' Geremek then gives a wonderful description of a whole bevy of intellectuals trying to prepare Lech Wałęsa for his television debate with the head of the official trade unions, Alfred Miodowicz. The film director Andrzej Wajda lectures Wałęsa about camera technique. Economists, sociologists, lawyers stuff him with facts and figures about the state of the nation. A nun plies him with herbal potions for his sore throat. Then off he goes, and trounces the party hack with a line that is pure Lech: 'The West goes by car, and we're on a bike.' Here was Solidarity at its best, and that best was superbly sustained over the next half year, through the unprecedented Round Table talks and the election campaign.

Geremek describes these negotiations in exhaustive detail. He shows how the basic precondition for the talks was the removal by the Gorbachev leadership of the barriers of Soviet refusal and their replacement by direct and indirect encouragement for reform. (At one point, a senior party official jokingly asked Lech Wałęsa to prohibit Adam Michnik from reading Soviet newspapers.) In this situation, and faced with the country's deteriorating economic condition, the new political initiative came, as Geremek repeatedly stresses, firstly from the army and the police, from General Jaruzelski and the interior minister, General Kiszczak (who had the best possible information on the level of popular discontent), and only secondly from the reformist wing of the party. Their negotiating adversaries were representatives of what Geremek calls the three streams of Solidarity – workers, peasants and intellectuals – of diverse groups and persuasions, but all at this point carefully coordinating their public speeches at the main Round Table, their semi-public statements at its many sub-tables, and above all their fall-back positions at the famous 'Magdalenkas', the secret summit meetings in a government guest house just outside Warsaw.

Behind this opposition elite, however, was the essential force of popular support and pressure from below. Geremek says he could almost directly correlate the willingness of the authorities to concede this or that point with the rise and fall of 'social pressure'. Last, but by no means least, there were the representatives of the Church, who were the hosts to several crucial meetings, served as mediators, reminded everyone of their shared responsibility, and, as the recently published notes of General Kiszczak's secretary record, ended the last Magdalenka with a blessing 'in the name of the Father, the Son and the Holy Ghost'.[2]

Here, then, was the unique Polish mixture, with ingredients found nowhere else in Eastern Europe – the workers' movement, the intelligentsia counter-government, the private farmers, the influence of the Church, the position of the generals. At the beginning of the Round Table, Wałęsa and his advisers believed they would be negotiating about the political price that they would have to pay for the relegalization of Solidarity. This, they thought, would consist in offering support for painful but indispensable measures of economic reform, and in legitimating a rigged election. At the end of the negotiation, after many twists and turns, and greatly helped by the oxygen of publicity (for the first time since 1981 Solidarity representatives were seen on television, making their self-evidently reasonable demands), it was the authorities who ended up paying a political price for the legalization of Solidarity. To be sure, the authorities had the promise of a strong presidency (for which their candidate was obviously Jaruzelski), and what seemed like a guaranteed 65 per cent of seats in the lower house of parliament (the Sejm) for the communist party (which, however, had only 38 per cent for itself) and its coalition partners. But Solidarity could get 35 per cent of seats, and there would be a wholly free election for the revived upper house of parliament (the Senate) – a proposal originally made by a young party reformist, Aleksander Kwaśniewski.

Yet Solidarity's leaders were not at all sure they could win. It was the authorities who insisted on an early election date, for they had the money, the organization and control of virtually all the mass media. Since in retrospect the election result looks inevitable, it is salutary to be reminded just how difficult and how uncertain this campaign was, and how tense and fraught were the further negotiations leading to the compromise first publicly suggested by Adam Michnik in the famous formula 'Your President, Our Premier'. For no one had been here before. The Soviet reaction was still unpredictable. The Berlin Wall still stood. The old communist reactionary Gustav Husák was still in Prague Castle. Even Hungary had not come so far. Poland was the ice-breaker.

Then, after the nine years of struggle, after the negotiated breakthrough, after doing what Geremek's party counterpart at the Round Table, Professor Janusz Reykowski, insisted had never been done before in the history of the world – that is, changing a political system completely without violence – after all this, the Solidarity camp began to fall apart. By the end of the year, the picture was one of frustrated, feuding factions, with the Solidarity group revolting against its own leadership, poor coordination between this group and 'its' government, and dramatically worsened relations between Gdańsk and Warsaw and, above all, between Lech Wałęsa and Tadeusz Mazowiecki. Between these two men there was, Geremek says, from the very formation of the Mazowiecki government a 'more or less silent war'.

To make a full and fair reconstruction of this silent war we should wait for Tadeusz Mazowiecki's memoirs. But if we combine Geremek's account with those by Wałęsa and his former spokesman, Jarosław Kurski, we get the same basic picture. It is plainly not fair to compare Wałęsa's memoirs directly with Geremek's. Wałęsa is not a historian; his magic is not to be found in the printed page. His memoirs, ghost-written by Arkadiusz Rybicki, a Catholic intellectual trained as a historian and with a long record in Solidarity, are actually a curious mixture of three different books. First, there is a rather stiff, portentous account of Wałęsa's various political initiatives and encounters, notably with foreign dignitaries and the foreign press. Second, there is an account of his family, and his belief in the hearth, the Church and the fatherland. The chapter on his wife, headed 'Danka – Calm at the Foundations', begins, 'The family is the main pillar of life, the source of balance, and woman – wife, mother – is the core of the family.' Somehow one feels this language is not entirely Lech.

Third, there is some genuine Lech, talking about politics. He insists that he should be seen as a practising politician – not, he says, 'an empty symbol' but rather 'a clever fox'. A key word in his self-description – it recurs twice on the last page – is 'skuteczny', meaning 'effective'. This matches precisely the description of him by close associates, quoted by Kurski, as a supremely political animal, mistrustful of everybody, calculating always – a 'political machine', as the Solidarity veteran Krzysztof Wyszkowski puts it.

The second point to note is that, quite remarkably for someone who is now president, this book is simply bristling with raw, naked hurt and resentment at his former Warsaw intellectual advisers who then stood against him. After just a few pages we read:

I wasn't an *inteligent* [that is, a member of the intelligentsia], and one must realize that, in Poland, *inteligenckość* [belonging to or being of the intelligentsia] is a value in itself. It matters less what a professor, doctor or famous actor who speaks in the name of the nation represents; what matters more is that he has a degree, good manners, 'knowledge of what's what', and proper elocution.

And so it goes on. Wałęsa recalls his own blistering attack on the 'eggheads' at the second Solidarity congress in April 1990: 'Must the president really speak fluent French in order to improve the lot of the working class?'

Wałęsa continues:

In this situation – to put in order the most important things – the country should be governed for some time by a decisive, strong hand. For you cannot 'democratically' catch a thief.

But the 'gentlemen from the capital', 'my antagonists (drinking coffee with cream)', did not see it this way:

After the interviews of Messrs Michnik and Geremek – full of venom and unfulfilled political ambitions – it was somehow forgotten that I am a Nobel Peace Prize winner, and this great honour is after all not given just for a pretty face. In the accounts of many [Western] journalists I once again became only an electrician – a limited *robol* [a contemptuous term for a worker] with ambitions to lead a 40 million strong nation in the heart of Europe.

How did such bitter recrimination come about after nine years of working so closely together – years that are still held fast, like the ghost of times past, in photos at the end of the memoirs showing Wałęsa laughing together with Geremek, Michnik and Mazowiecki? Was Solidarity held together only by the common enemy? From the accounts by Geremek and Kurski, it is very clear that the trouble began as soon as Mazowiecki, Wałęsa's choice of premier, did not consult Wałęsa about the composition of his government in August and September 1989. Not the membership of the government, just the fact that Mazowiecki was determined to be his own man seems to have offended Wałęsa.

From this point, relations between them worsened very quickly, despite efforts at mediation by Geremek and the Church. Kurski chronicles the deterioration, and notes the irony that the last, vain, effort at reconciliation took place in Gdańsk on 31 August 1990 – the tenth anniversary of the Gdańsk agreement and the birth of Solidarity. Solidarność, 31 August 1980–31 August 1990, RIP. Seventeen days later Wałęsa formally announced his candidacy for the office of president. Mazowiecki stood against him, and was trounced.

Geremek is inclined to blame Wałęsa's political advisers in Gdańsk, and notably the twin brothers Lech and Jarosław Kaczyński, for much of this poisonous estrangement. Certainly this was no simple division between 'workers' in Gdańsk and 'intellectuals' in Warsaw. It was an argument between politicians in Gdańsk and politicians in Warsaw, with workers – or former workers – on both sides. But this Gdańsk group was important only because Wałęsa made it so. Wałęsa was, and is, nothing if not his own man. In this period of political 'war at the top' he was often a deeply unattractive figure, showing all the weaknesses of his strengths: decisiveness became bullying, the common touch turned to coarse anti-intellectualism, the golden tongue to demagogy. A few isolated quotations serve him even less fairly than they would most politicians, for, as he himself observes, enunciating what should be the first law of Lechology, 'I've said many other things, because I'm a chatterbox and my mouth closes only with difficulty.'

Describing a meeting with the Pope in August 1990, and suggesting, rather misleadingly, that the Pope backed his candidacy, he writes, 'My accumulators were once again loaded up. My doubts and complexes resolved.' And the passages quoted above show that, for all his fame, self-confidence and sense of mission, he was still plagued by certain complexes which the politics of the last year reactivated with a vengeance.

It would, however, be quite wrong to put all the blame on the wild man from Gdańsk, on his complexes and 'frustrations'. Geremek himself observes that the Mazowiecki government proceeded too slowly in many matters (e.g. privatization), that its public relations were poor, that it failed to consult widely enough – and not just with Gdańsk. The mounting popular dissatisfaction in the spring of 1990 was not just a figment of Wałęsa's imagination, although he did conflate it with his own, very personal, dissatisfaction. The way in which some of his former friends and advisers characterized Wałęsa after the rift was exaggerated, reflecting their own personal resentment and even complexes – which were, in some ways, almost a mirror image of his. Wałęsa refers here to the characterization of him as a 'coarse proletarian' trying to 'cut Poland off from Europe with an axe', and indeed Adam Michnik's polemical opposition of a party called 'Europe' to a nationalist, racist, chauvinist darkness did scant justice to a complex reality. Recent history offers few spectacles sadder than this one of friends and comrades who had gone through so much together, with such dignity, honour, wit and, yes, solidarity, now belabouring each other with rusty clubs and blows beneath the belt.

In April 1990, a group of Wałęsa's veteran Solidarity advisers, including Geremek, Michnik and Mazowiecki, told him that they envisaged an orderly political transition in which he would become president in the spring of 1991, together with a freely elected parliament and a new constitution – one promulgated to coincide with the two-hundredth anniversary of the historic Polish constitution of 3 May 1791. It is possible that, if Wałęsa had accepted this offer, Poland would be in a better condition today, politically, socially and economically. But, given that Wałęsa would not accept it, the historian's verdict must be that they made a mistake in not responding more swiftly to his concerns, ambitions and even complexes – starting in the summer of 1989. For there had to be a special place for Wałęsa; Geremek's own book is one long testimonial to that. If they would not give it to him – and fast – then Wałęsa would take it. He would fight dirty if need be. And he would win.

The phenomenon we are discussing here is not 'workers' or 'society'. It is Wałęsa. To be sure, an understanding of structure and process is essential to uncover the deeper roots of what happened in 1989. To be sure, class and class consciousness played a part in the end as they had in the beginning of Solidarity. But the key to this particular passage of Polish history is to be found not in sociology or economics, but in old-fashioned politics, in the clash of personalities and the competition for power. Not Marx, not Hegel, but Machiavelli and Thucydides must be at our side when we write this last, sad chapter in the annals of Solidarity.

3

Where does this leave Polish politics now? In a great muddle. Neither the exaggerated hopes nor the exaggerated fears of Wałęsa's presidency have yet been realized. He has not proved a great dictator. On a number of issues – price rises, a special anti-inflationary tax, the

restoration of expropriated property – he has made decisive interventions, only to withdraw them, or have them blocked, a few days
later. On the other hand, and by the same token, he has not delivered
the 'acceleration' which was his main election promise. When I asked
Jarosław Kaczyński, now head of the president's chancellery, what
'acceleration' had actually taken place, he replied that (1) a number
of high (ex-) *nomenklatura* officials had now been sacked from the
Council of Ministers office (but, he sourly observed, had found good
jobs in banks); (2) the new leadership had got debt reduction from
the West (although he conceded that this was partly the work of finance
minister Leszek Balcerowicz, during the Mazowiecki government); (3)
the new president had been more energetic than Jaruzelski in foreign
policy.

It was late in the day, and Mr Kaczyński was tired, but this list did
not seem overwhelmingly impressive. However – and here one has a
nice illustration of the present muddle – Mr Kaczyński was not
necessarily concerned to make it so, since Wałęsa had chosen a premier
from the so called Gdańsk 'liberals' (meaning, essentially, neo-liberal
in economics), rather than the candidate of Kaczyński's Centre Agreement Party. As a good party politician, Kaczyński therefore performs
the Genscherish trick of being both in government and critical of it.

The government of 'liberal' prime minister Jan Krzysztof Bielecki,
which contains two Centre Agreement ministers, is perhaps slightly
more effective than its predecessor in some areas of economic policy.
However, because of the hiatus created by the presidential election
and the change of government, it has taken several months to get what
should be the centrepiece of its economic programme – privatization of
the still dominant state sector – under way, and this will now be
interrupted again by the parliamentary election campaign. In financial
and monetary policy, there is an overwhelming continuity in the
person and policies of Leszek Balcerowicz, retained partly at the fierce
insistence of the West, and particularly the United States: 'Washington
replacing Moscow,' say some, darkly. These policies are, however,
threatened by, among other things, a large budget deficit, which partly
results from the absence of the planned proceeds from privatization.

As Wałęsa himself ruefully observed in a recent interview, 'It is
difficult to transfer what is said at a rally to the process of governing.'

He has built up a large presidential office, with a wide circle of advisers from the intelligentsia. Jarosław Kaczyński told me that, whereas for Jaruzelski the presidential secretaries of state had been substitute secretaries of the Central Committee, now they were needed 'on account of the educational level of the president' – hardly a complex-soothing observation. In one of the most important areas of presidential responsibility – foreign policy – cooperation between the presidency and the government has thus far been excellent, partly because the foreign minister and the president's foreign-policy adviser are old colleagues from Poznań University. Here, if nowhere else, impressive consistency has been achieved. The Polish presidential palace, the Belweder, is clearly a significant centre of power, although, to keep this in perspective, it probably still has less effective power than Václav Havel's presidential palace, known to all as 'the Castle'. Both Havel and Wałęsa are currently still using the formal presidential powers defined with deliberate vagueness for their communist predecessors, together with informal powers derived from their leading role in the struggle against their communist predecessors.

Despite Bronisław Geremek's best efforts, it has not proved possible for the politicians to agree on a new constitution defining a new separation of powers. The celebrations of the two-hundredth anniversary of the constitution of 3 May 1791, the first democratic constitution in Europe, were therefore not all that they might have been. Debate continues between, say, the 'French model' and the 'German model' of the relations between president, prime minister and parliament. This debate cannot, however, be resolved by the rigged parliament resulting from the Round Table agreement. At best, this parliament will pass on a draft constitution to its democratically elected successor. Meanwhile, the country winds up for an election this autumn whose rules have actually been set, after long wrangling, by this rigged parliament.

Even today, Polish politics run the risk of reinforcing certain cliché images of Poland – images of endless discord and noble anarchy. Although the external environment, to east and west, is currently more favourable than it has been for a very long time, these things can change, and Poland is not an island.

One version of this alarmist analysis would go on to predict, irrespective of possible external threats, the emergence of calls for a 'strongman'. Enter Lech Wałęsa, with an axe. Cut to a photograph of Marshal Piłsudski. But post-communist (and post-Solidarity) Poland is not Poland after the First World War, and Wałęsa is not Piłsudski. (Apart from anything else, as Kurski wryly comments, Piłsudski was loyal to his colonels.) Here, too, one could obviously be proved wrong, but, for all his bragging and bullying, I still cannot see Lech Wałęsa using soldiers or police to put his political opponents into camps. Even if he wanted to, this is not a Poland, or indeed a Europe, which would easily let him. But beyond this I also think that, despite his autocratic style and alarming rhetoric, Lech Wałęsa does actually have some sort of a vision of a normal, democratic Poland.

What is this vision? Wałęsa is very careful not to be pinned down on anything, and certainly not on his own 'politics' in the usual sense of that word (i.e. 'left or right'). As Kurski reports, he has been heard to say, 'Wałęsa is for, and even against.' But this does not mean he has no politics. At one of the 'Magdalenka' meetings, he produced, according to the notes by General Kiszczak's secretary, the following remark: 'I propose my socialism. There are three bakers in town: one private, one cooperative and one state-owned. The one which produces the cheapest rolls does best.' This is socialism with a Thatcherite face. And his politics may be described – for all the obvious differences – as those of a Polish Thatcherite.

On his visit to Britain he made a special point of receiving Mrs Thatcher – something protocol by no means necessarily demanded. In his memoirs he makes very favourable mention of her visit to Gdańsk in 1988, adding, 'I have long been a fan of her vision of an entrepreneurial society, rewarding every initiative.' This is one of his own leitmotifs. Like Mrs Thatcher, he sees the key to change in individual enterprise. Despite the occasional populist sop thrown to workers at the hustings, he is in favour of radical, rapid privatization: 'I have already said a thousand times that I see two Polands. The first – that is the huge, post-communist enterprises. The second – a private Poland, which we are just beginning to build. We need to reconstruct two-thirds of Poland, to catch up with the Europe that is running away from us . . .'

His chosen prime minister, Bielecki, is a 'liberal' in precisely the sense that Mrs Thatcher is. Like her, Wałęsa looks for short, sharp presentations, and work, work, work. Like her, he combines philistinism with a deep respect and liking for clever men of ideas. (Bronisław Geremek was, so to speak, his Keith Joseph.) Coming, like her, not from the old, established 'upper' classes of his country (that is, in Poland, the intelligentsia), he looks for a society in which the less well-off have an equal chance to climb the ladder to wealth and power, by their own initiative and hard work. He combines this, like Mrs Thatcher, with a strong, simple, even simplistic, attachment to the traditional values of family, Church and country. 'Victorian values' à la polonaise. If Mrs Thatcher had a vision of democratic capitalism, with the emphasis slightly more on capitalism than on democracy, then so does he.

Clearly, this comparison can be taken too far. Wałęsa is also capable of saying, as he did in a radio phone-in programme shortly after he became president, 'Let all share Poland's poverty equally.' There is, moreover, the obvious objection that he is perhaps the world's most famous trade-union leader, whereas Mrs Thatcher is one of the world's best-known union-bashers. Yet Solidarity was from the very outset much more than a trade union, and, even as Solidarity chairman, Wałęsa never spent much time on bread-and-butter labour issues. Solidarity's new chairman has announced a protest action against the economic and social policies of the government. Unemployment reached 1.37 million (7.3 per cent of the workforce) at the end of March, and this is before the large state enterprises have been privatized or shut down. It will be fascinating to see how Wałęsa now reacts to growing unemployment and labour militancy. But, whatever he says, my guess is that when it comes to real policy choices he will put the needs of business before the demands of labour.

A Thatcherite Poland, then, as the final outcome of Solidarity? Carefully avoiding the word 'irony', one should say that there are worse possible outcomes for a country emerging from fifty, and, in a deeper sense, from two hundred, years of dependency and unfreedom. These include the outcome in which Poland goes from the abnormal extreme of Solidarity to an abnormal extreme of un-Solidarity: a dissipation of political energies which would hinder the building of both capitalism and democracy.

4

On 13 December 1981, when martial law was declared, Solidarity could be seen as just the latest in a series of failed East Central European risings against Soviet-imposed communism: '53, '56, '68, '80–81. In 1989 that judgment was proved wrong, or, at least, radically incomplete. In 1991 we can see Solidarity a little more clearly for what it was: a pioneering Polish form of social self-organization, with the general objective of achieving, by means of peaceful, popular pressure combined with elite negotiation, the end of communism. In this, it succeeded.

Geremek quotes, with understandable pride, the Soviet dissident Lev Timofeyev's remark (made in Paris, in December 1988) that 'Without Poland's Solidarność there would be no Gorbachev, nor Sakharov in Paris'. Historians of the Soviet Union must tell us how much truth there is in this remark. But certainly, demonstrably, Solidarity was a path-breaking movement in East Central Europe. Nowhere else, to be sure, was there the mass workers' movement. But elements of the new politics developed by Solidarity in Poland – the forms of peaceful protest and civic resistance, the negotiations symbolized by the Round Table – spread directly to its neighbours. Poland was first. If the division of Europe which we call in shorthand 'Yalta' began in Poland in 1945, then there is an important sense in which the end of 'Yalta' also began in Poland. No country did more for the cause of liberty in Europe in the 1980s, and no country paid a higher price.

And how will Solidarity look in another ten years, in 2001? To imagine answers to this question, we must imagine Polish futures. If things go very badly indeed, if what misleadingly present themselves as the 'realities' or 'laws' of geopolitics once again intervene in Poland's internal affairs, then the answer will be simple. Solidarity will be seen as just the latest in a long line of legendary insurrections. As Jacek Kuroń in prison found strength from a book about the 1863–4 January Rising against Russian rule,[3] so now people will draw inspiration and courage from the history of 1980–81. As, in the days of Solidarity's underground struggle, young men read books about the wartime

Home Army and old men came forward with their forgers' stamps from the days of the Nazi occupation,[4] so now the experience of Solidarity will be passed on to a new generation of fighters. Wildly improbable though this seems today, no one who knows even a little Polish history can believe it impossible.

At the other extreme there is the future in which, by 2001, Poland has become a normal country, in the sense that Spain, Portugal and Greece are today normal countries. Still relatively poor, messy, divided, no doubt, but nonetheless having the essential sinews of democracy, the rule of law and a market economy, reinforced by membership of an enlarged European Community and militarily protected by membership of Nato. This Poland may have no Wałęsas, but it will also have no need of Wałęsas. In this normal, perhaps even boring, Poland there will be a new generation of politicians who want to be just that – politicians, neither more nor less.

In this Poland, with its strong middle class, the identities (and complexes) of those three great classes, intelligentsia, workers and peasants – each and all of them 'abnormal' in late-twentieth-century Europe – will have been intermingled and transformed. In this Poland, history, and the historians, will be found in the university, the academy and the schools, where to the younger pupils Solidarity will seem almost as remote as the January Rising.

Into this Poland there will then come a new generation of post-revisionist historians, fresh-faced young men from Oxford and Kraków, eager young women from Maryland and Łódź. They will swiftly dispose of the older generation of witnesses like myself; gut the archives; grill the survivors; put the Geremeks and Wałęsas in their place. And they will tell us how it really was.

1991

16 May. Serbs in the Croatian province of Krajina call for the union of their territory with Serbia.
19 May. Croatians vote for independence in a referendum boycotted by Serbs living in Croatia.
29 May. Basque terrorists (ETA) bomb a Civil Guard barracks, killing nine people.
12 June. Boris Yeltsin is elected president of the Russian Federation.
12–14 June. In Prague, François Mitterrand attempts to launch his European Confederation.

12–14 June. Prague. I am among those invited to found the European Confederation. Even before we arrive, it is clear that this is essentially a French scheme for a grand, velvet-wallpapered waiting room in which the former communist countries can wait a long, long time before joining the EC. The EC, meanwhile, would remain a right, tight little West European affair with – and here's the real point – France at its political centre, as it had been throughout the history of the European Community in the Cold War. At the political centre of an enlarged EC, by contrast, would be Germany.

Fortunately, in the first day of discussions, it soon emerges that many other delegates see and object to this too. Although Václav Havel had agreed to co-host the meeting, the Czechs also understand that it is not really in their interest to make it work. Soon the French participants are fighting a magnificent rearguard action, with all the formidable intellectual brilliance and diplomatic trickiness at their command. The French justice minister, Robert Badinter, who serves as President Mitterrand's field commander, pleads eloquently for a '*structure très légère, très légère . . .*' The Germans, Britons, Dutch and others present are not having even that.

In the concluding session, Mitterrand gives one of the finer rhetorical performances that I have witnessed, disguising what is, in fact, a quadruple backward somersault as a great, balletic leap forward. But the European Confederation will remain a joke.

17 June. Signature of a German–Polish treaty on good neighbourliness and friendly cooperation.

20 June. The Bundestag votes to move the federal capital from Bonn to Berlin.

25 June. Croatia and Slovenia declare their independence.

25 June. A newspaper photograph shows men having their beards shaved off in Prague. They began to grow these beards on 21 August 1968, when Soviet troops invaded, and swore they would shave them off only when the last Soviet soldier had left their land. Now he has.

27 June. Additional units of the Serb-dominated Yugoslav federal army enter Slovenia but subsequently withdraw after Slovene armed resistance and Western diplomatic protests. The 'ten-day war'.

27 June–1 July. EC despatches the current 'troika' of foreign ministers – Jacques Poos of Luxembourg, Gianni de Michaelis of Italy and Hans van den Broek of the Netherlands – to bring peace to Yugoslavia. M. Poos declares, 'The hour of Europe has dawned.'

28 June. Comecon, the economic organization of the former Soviet bloc, formally dissolved.

1 July. The Warsaw Pact is formally dissolved.

26 July. The Central Committee of the Communist Party of the Soviet Union approves Gorbachev's party programme leading to a free market and multi-party democracy.

30 July. Russian president Boris Yeltsin signs a treaty recognizing Lithuania's independence.

July–August. Fighting between the Serb-dominated Yugoslav federal army and Croatian troops in eastern Slavonia.

29 July–1 August. A Bush–Gorbachev summit in Moscow. Signature of the Strategic Arms Reduction Treaty (START).

19–21 August. A coup is attempted against Mikhail Gorbachev, intended to reverse changes in the Soviet Union. Yeltsin leads resistance in Moscow.

23 August. The Communist Party is suspended in Russia.

27 August. EC countries agree to establish diplomatic relations with the Baltic states.

29 August. Soviet legislators vote to suspend all activities of the Communist Party of the Soviet Union. Formation of the 'Weimar Triangle' of foreign-policy cooperation between France, Germany and Poland.

7 September. An EC peace conference on Yugoslavia opens in The Hague under the chairmanship of Lord Carrington.

17 September. Estonia, Latvia and Lithuania are admitted to the UN.

26–28 September. Kraków, Poland. At a conference to mark the end of the Fondation pour une Entraide Intellectuelle Européenne, a foundation dedicated to helping opposition intellectuals in Eastern Europe during the Cold War, Adam Michnik warns in dramatic terms of the danger of a new clerical, nationalist authoritarianism in Poland. I think he overdramatizes the danger, partly in a quest for the kind of clear, Manichaean dichotomy between good and evil in which dissidents like him lived under communism. We argue all the way to passport control at Warsaw Airport.

26–30 September. Kosovar Albanians hold an unofficial referendum on independence.

3 October. Carl Bildt heads a new centre-right coalition government in Sweden.

4 October. The Czechoslovak federal parliament passes a 'lustration' law, providing for the vetting and banning from public service of people who collaborated with the communist secret police or held certain positions in the communist state.

8 October. The Soviet Union agrees to withdraw its troops from Poland by November 1992.

13 October. The opposition Union of Democratic Forces wins Bulgarian parliamentary elections

15 October. Bosniak (or 'Muslim') and Bosnian Croat members of the parliament of Bosnia-Hercegovina vote for independence. Bosnian Serbs leave in protest.

27 October. The first free parliamentary elections in Poland produce a fragmented parliament.

October–November. The Serb-dominated Yugoslav federal army destroys the Croatian city of Vukovar and attacks Dubrovnik.

14 November. The German Bundestag passes a law giving people access to their Stasi files from January 1992.

21 November. Following a referendum, the Macedonian parliament proclaims the sovereign, independent Republic of Macedonia. The head of state is the former communist leader Kiro Gligorov.

1 December. In a referendum in Ukraine, a clear majority votes for independence. Former communist Leonid Kravchuk is elected president.

8 December. Leaders of Russia, Ukraine and Belarus agree to establish the Commonwealth of Independent States (CIS).

9–11 December. The EC's Maastricht summit agrees terms of the Treaty on European Union. Monetary union is to happen by 1 January 1999 at the latest, providing that 'Maastricht criteria' are met. EC and other 'pillars' of institutionalized cooperation between its member states will be combined in a 'European Union'.

14–16 December. Oxford. At the suggestion of the Czech prime minister Petr Pithart, a conference brings together, in Magdalen College, a Czech delegation led by him and a Slovak delegation led by their prime minister Ján Čarnogursky. Pithart, who spent some time in Oxford after the Soviet invasion in 1968, touchingly hopes that they will all see reason in these civilized, dignified and neutral surroundings. Czechoslovakia will be saved in Oxford.

At the meeting, the Czechs talk grandly about the 'civic principle'. The Slovaks talk bitterly about the way they have been exploited in the shared state. A Slovak literary historian reels off fantastical statistics about Czech economic discrimination against Slovakia. Then they all slip away together to do their Christmas shopping at Marks & Spencer.

15 December. The UN Security Council resolves to send peace-keeping forces to former Yugoslavia. These will become known as the United Nations Protection Force: UNPROFOR.

16 December. The signature of so-called 'Europe Agreements' between the EC and Poland, Hungary and Czechoslovakia. Under pressure from Germany, EC foreign ministers agree to diplomatic recognition of former Yugoslav republics on 15 January, if certain conditions are met.

19 December. The Bonn government announces that it is going ahead with the recognition of Slovenia and Croatia before Christmas, as it had previously, unilaterally, promised. Serbs in Croatia proclaim the 'Serb Republic of Krajina', with its capital in Knin.

21 December. At Alma Ata, eleven republics of the former Soviet Union sign agreements creating the Commonwealth of Independent States.

23 December. The conservative anti-communist Jan Olszewski forms a government in Poland.

25 December. Gorbachev resigns as Soviet president, marking the effective end of the Soviet Union.

1992

15 January. The EC's 'Badinter Commission' says only Slovenia and Macedonia, among former Yugoslav republics, qualify for diplomatic recognition. Most EC states nonetheless proceed to recognize Croatia as well as Slovenia – but not Macedonia, because of opposition from Greece.

19 January. Zhelyu Zhelev is confirmed as president of Bulgaria in direct elections.

3–10 February. Moscow. I meet General Sergei Kondrachev, once head of KGB operations in Western Europe, but now rapidly retooling as 'historian' and 'archival specialist'. He argues that the spies in East and West saved us from a Third World War, since through their efforts both sides knew so much about each other's defences that the danger of either risking a nuclear attack was diminished. On the moral chessboard of the post-Cold War world, I call this the Kondrachev Defence.

Kondrachev was stationed in London during the 1950s. In perfectly modulated, slightly old-fashioned English, he tells me, 'I have the fondest memories of my trips to Cambridge . . .'

7 February. Signature of the Maastricht Treaty on European Union.

February. Beginning of arrests in a growing Italian political-corruption scandal. The first focus of investigation is the Italian Socialist Party of Bettino Craxi.

28 February. Slovak prime minister Ján Čarnogursky says he would like Slovakia to enjoy international recognition.

3 March. President Alija Izetbegović declares Bosnian independence, after a referendum boycotted by Bosnian Serbs.

5 March. German foreign minister Hans-Dietrich Genscher presses for international recognition of Bosnia-Hercegovina.

6 March. Formation of a Council of Baltic Sea States, including

Denmark, Estonia, Finland, Germany, Latvia, Lithuania, Norway, Poland, Russia and Sweden.

11 March. After a year of failed attempts to negotiate a new Czecho-Slovak federation, the heads of the Czech and Slovak parliaments suspend talks until after June elections.

27 March. Bosnian Serbs, led by Radovan Karadžić, declare a 'Serb Republic' in Bosnia-Hercegovina.

Late March/early April. Outbreak of war in Bosnia.

2 April. President Mitterrand appoints socialist Pierre Bérégovoy prime minister of France.

5 April. The siege of Sarajevo begins.

6 April. Sali Berisha, a cardiologist from the northern part of the country, is elected president of Albania.

7 April. The USA recognizes Bosnia-Hercegovina, Slovenia and Croatia.

9 April. A general election in Britain returns to office a Conservative government under prime minister John Major.

27 April. Declaration of a new Federal Republic of Yugoslavia (FRY), consisting of Serbia (including Kosovo and Vojvodina) and Monten-egro. Not recognized by the West.

29 April. A list of suspected agents of the communist secret police is published in Prague.

18 May. Hans-Dietrich Genscher resigns after eighteen years as Ger-man foreign minister. He is succeeded by Klaus Kinkel.

22 May. Slovenia, Croatia and Bosnia-Hercegovina are admitted to the UN.

24 May. Kosovar Albanians hold clandestine elections. Ibrahim Rugova is elected 'president of the republic'. In Austria, Thomas Klestil is elected president, replacing disgraced Kurt Waldheim.

25 May. Oscar Luigi Scalfaro becomes president of Italy.

27 May. Massacre of civilians in Sarajevo.

30 May. The UN agrees on sanctions against the Federal Republic of Yugoslavia.

2 June. In a referendum, Danish voters reject ratification of the Maastricht Treaty by a narrow majority.

5 June. The Olszewski government falls in Poland after identifying leading politicians as former collaborators with the communist secret police: the 'night of the files'.

5–6 June. Parliamentary elections in Czechoslovakia. The Civic Democratic Party of Václav Klaus wins in the Czech lands, and the Movement for a Democratic Slovakia of Vladimír Mečiar wins in Slovakia.

15 June. Writer Dobrica Ćosić becomes president of the Federal Republic of Yugoslavia.

17 June. The Slovak parliament votes a declaration of 'sovereignty'.

18 June. Giuliano Amato becomes prime minister of Italy.

June. Serious escalation of the war in Bosnia and the siege of Sarajevo. Student protests against Milošević in Belgrade.

June–August. Czech prime minister Václav Klaus and Slovak prime minister Vladimír Mečiar agree to dissolve the Czecho-Slovak federation by the end of the year.

3 July. Bosnian Croats declare their own statelet in western Bosnia-Hercegovina.

10 July. A summit meeting of the Conference on Security and Cooperation in Europe, which now has fifty-one member states.

12 July. Hanna Suchocka, from a liberal-conservative post-Solidarity party, forms a coalition government of seven parties in Poland.

14 July. Milan Panić, a Serb-American businessman, becomes prime minister of the Federal Republic of Yugoslavia.

17 July. Following Slovakia's 'declaration of sovereignty', Václav Havel announces his resignation as president of Czechoslovakia, with effect from 20 July.

2 August. Croatian nationalists (HDZ) led by Franjo Tudjman win Croatian parliamentary elections. Tudjman is re-elected president of Croatia.

26–28 August. At the London Conference on the former Yugoslavia it is agreed that borders should not be altered by force and that ethnic cleansing should cease. War and ethnic cleansing continue.

30 August. Sarajevans standing in a bread queue are killed and wounded.

3 September. Lord (David) Owen and Cyrus Vance become joint chairmen of a new EC–UN conference on former Yugoslavia.

4 September. Former Bulgarian communist leader Todor Zhivkov is found guilty of embezzlement.

16 September. Massive speculation against the pound forces Britain to 'suspend' its membership of the Exchange Rate Mechanism of the European Monetary System: 'Black Wednesday'.

17 September. The Italian lira is also forced out of the Exchange Rate Mechanism.

20 September. In a referendum called by President Mitterrand following the Danish referendum, 51 per cent of French voters approve ratification of the Maastricht Treaty. In Estonia, parliamentary elections are won by parties of the centre-right. Only Estonian citizens are enfranchised, so most of the nearly 40 per cent non-Estonian population are not able to vote.

27 September. Ion Iliescu is confirmed in office as president of Romania. His authoritarian National Salvation Front wins most seats in parliament.

5 October. Nationalist intellectual Lennart Meri becomes president of Estonia.

11 October. Former Soviet foreign minister Eduard Shevardnadze becomes head of state in Georgia. He faces a Russian-supported revolt in Abkhazia.

13 October. The veteran socialist Andreas Papandreou again becomes prime minister of Greece, replacing the right-wing government of Constantine Mitsotakis.

25 October. Lithuanian parliamentary elections produce a landslide victory for former communists under Algirdas Brazauskas.

26 October. Czech prime minister Václav Klaus and Slovak prime minister Vladimír Mečiar agree on a customs union after Czecho-Slovakia is divided on 1 January 1993. Erich Mielke, former head of the East German State Security Service (Stasi), is convicted for his part in the murder of a policeman in 1931.

3 November. Bill Clinton wins the US presidential elections.

The Visit

'Are you bringing any laundry?' asks the porter at the fortified entrance to Moabit prison.

When I laugh, he says defensively, 'I was only asking', and grimly stamps my permit to visit remand prisoner Honecker, Erich.

Into a waiting room full of chain-smoking wives and spivs in black leather jackets. Wait for your number to be called from a loudspeaker. Through an automatic barrier. Empty your pockets and put everything in a locker. Body search. Another automatic barrier. Unsmiling guards, barked orders. '*Moment! Kommen Sie mit!*' Then you've come to the wrong place. Collect all your belongings again. Pack up. Walk around the red-brick fortress to another gate. Unpack. Sign this, take that. Another huge metal door. The clash of bolts. A courtyard, then the corridor to the prison hospital, bare but clean.

Somehow this all seems increasingly familiar. I have been here before. But where and when? Then I remember. It's like crossing through the Friedrichstrasse underground frontier station into East Berlin, in the bad old days. West Germany has given Honecker back his Berlin Wall.

Inside it is warm and safe. There is food to eat – plain fare, to be sure, but regular and ample. There is basic, free medical care for all. Good books are to be had from the library, and there is guaranteed employment for men and women alike. And life is, of course, very secure. Just like East Germany.

The first time I saw, at close quarters, the Chairman of the Council of State of the German Democratic Republic and General Secretary of the Socialist Unity Party of Germany was at the Leipzig trade fair in 1980. A horde of plain-clothes Stasi men heralded the arrival of the leader. Eastern functionaries, West German businessmen, British diplomats – all flapped and fluttered, bowed and scraped, as if at the Sublime Porte of Suleiman the Great. His every move, every tiny gesture, was studied and minutely interpreted, with all the arcane science of Sovietology. Significantly, graciously, the Chairman and General Secretary stopped at the Afghan stand, which displayed rugs and nuts. 'And these are peanuts and those are salted peanuts...' came the breathless commentary of the rattled Afghan salesman. Graciously, significantly, the Chairman and General Secretary clapped him on the shoulder and said, 'We regard your revolution as a decisive contribution to détente. All the best for your struggle!' Ah, happy days, the old style.

Now the door opens and there he stands in a tiny corner room, sandwiched between the doctor's washbasin and a table. He is very small, his face pallid and sweaty, but he still stands bolt upright. 'Bodily contact is not permitted,' says my permit. But he extends his hand – graciously, significantly – and I shake it. He is clad in khaki prison pyjamas, which remind me of a Mao suit. But on his feet he still wears, incongruously, those fine, black leather slip-on shoes in which he used to tread all the red carpets, not just in Moscow and Prague but in Madrid, in Paris and in Bonn. 'Fraternal greetings, Comrade Leonid Ilyich,' and a smacking kiss on each cheek. 'How do you do, Mr President.' '*Guten Tag, Herr Bundeskanzler.*'

We sit down, our knees almost touching in the cramped room, and the accompanying warder wedges himself into a corner. All my notes and papers have been impounded at the gate, but fortunately the doctor has left some spare sheets of lined paper and a pencil. Fixing me with his tiny, intense eyes – always his most striking feature – Honecker concentrates on answering my questions. He talks at length about his relations with Moscow, his friendship with Brezhnev, his arguments with Chernenko and then Gorbachev. Even under Gorbachev, he says, the Soviet Union never ceased to intervene in East Germany. The Soviet embassy's consular officials behaved, he says, like provincial governors. So much for the sovereignty of the GDR that he himself had so long trumpeted! At one point he shows staggering (and I think genuine) economic naivety, arguing that East Germany's hard-currency debt, in Deutschmarks, has to be set against its surplus in transferable roubles.

His language is a little stiff, polit-bureaucratic, but very far from being just ideological gobbledygook. Through it come glimpses of a real political intelligence, a man who knows about power. Was it his conscious decision to allow many more ordinary East Germans to travel to the West in the second half of the 1980s? Yes, definitely – a conscious decision. He thought it would make people more satisfied. But did it? 'Nee,' he says, 'offensichtlich nicht.' 'Nope, obviously not.'

With the tiny pupils of his eyes boring into mine, he speaks with what seems like real, almost fanatical, conviction – or at least with a real will to convince. This is somehow more, not less, impressive because of the humiliating prison surroundings, and because of the obvious physical effort it costs him. (He has cancer of the liver. The doctors give him only months to live.) Once he has to excuse himself to go to the lavatory, accompanied by the warder. 'You noticed I was getting a little restless,' he says apologetically on his return.

Then he resumes his defiant refrain. East Germany, he insists, was 'to the end the only socialist country in which you could always go into a shop and buy bread, butter, sausage etc.' Yet people wanted more? Yes, but now they regret it. Look at the unemployment in the former GDR! Look how few apartments are being built! He gets hundreds of letters from people in the east. They say they lived more *quietly* in the old days: '*Sie haben ruhiger gelebt.*'

And look what's happening on the streets now – the racist attacks, the fascists. It reminds him of 1933. Really? 1933? Well, he concedes, perhaps 1923. Hitler's first attempt was also a flop. But look what happened then. He's warning us. We've been here before. At least, he's been here before. Which, indeed, he has: held as a remand prisoner in this very prison in the years 1935–7, after being caught working for the communist resistance.

And now he is here again. West Germany's leaders denounce him as a criminal. Yet only yesterday the same politicians were competing for the privilege of being received in audience by him. Oh, the tales he could tell! His talks with West German Social Democrats were, he says, 'comradely'. Some other West German politicians were more reserved. He had great respect for Franz Josef Strauss. Helmut Schmidt was the most reliable and punctilious partner. But he also got on well with Helmut Kohl. He had often talked on the telephone to Chancellor Schmidt and to Chancellor Kohl. Why, he had even dialled the number himself.

Then the former Chairman of the Council of State of the former German Democratic Republic and former General Secretary of the former Socialist Unity Party of Germany pulls out of the pocket of his prison pyjamas a slightly dog-eared card on which his former secretary had typed the direct telephone number to the chancellor in Bonn. He places it before me, urges me to copy the number down. 0649 (West Germany) 228 (Bonn) 562001. (I try it later. It takes you straight through to the chancellor's office in Bonn.)

A quarter-century of divided Germany's tragic, complex history is, it seems to me, concentrated in this one pathetic moment: the defiant, mortally sick old man in his prison pyjamas, the dog-eared card with the direct number to Chancellor Kohl.

The warder clears his throat and looks at his watch. Our time is up. Honecker rises, again standing almost to attention. A formal farewell. Then the bare corridors, the clashing gates, the unsmiling guards, the belongings from the locker, the fortified entrance. But now I *am* carrying laundry. Scribbled in pencil on a doctor's notepad: the dirty linen of history.

1992

6 *December. In a referendum, Swiss voters reject membership of a European Economic Area, seen as a stepping-stone to membership of the EU. Milan Kučan is elected president of Slovenia.*
9 *December. John Major announces that the Prince and Princess of Wales are to separate.*
11 *December. EC summit in Edinburgh.*
20 *December. Slobodan Milošević is re-elected president of the republic of Serbia.*

1993

1 *January. The Single European Market comes into effect in the EC, now renamed the EU. Czechoslovakia splits into the Czech Republic and Slovakia: the 'velvet divorce'.*
2 *January. Presentation in Geneva of the 'Vance–Owen plan' for Bosnia as a federal republic with ten ethnically based cantons enjoying substantial autonomy.*
3 *January. US president George Bush and Russian president Boris Yeltsin sign the START II treaty, eliminating all multiple-warhead intercontinental ballistic missiles and reducing their stocks of strategic nuclear weapons by two-thirds.*
20 *January. Bill Clinton takes office as US president.*
26 *January. Václav Havel is elected the first president of the Czech Republic.*
January–December. Italy is engulfed in a massive political-corruption scandal which effectively destroys the political system that had survived throughout the Cold War. In the so called 'Mani Pulite' ('Clean Hands') investigation, numerous senior politicians, including four former prime ministers, and many business leaders are arrested or interrogated on charges of corruption.
14 *February. Former communist Algirdas Brazauskas is elected president of Lithuania.*

22 February. UN agrees that there should be criminal prosecution of those responsible for war crimes in former Yugoslavia.

1 February. Sweden, Norway, Finland and Austria – all members of the European Free Trade Association (EFTA) – begin negotiations to join the EU.

5 March. Michal Kováč, an independent-minded former associate of prime minister Vladimír Mečiar, becomes president of Slovakia.

March. UN convoys reach the besieged Bosnian town of Srebrenica.

March–April. The centre-right Swedish government of Carl Bildt pushes through major cuts in public expenditure, especially on welfare programmes.

12 April. Nato begins enforcement of a no-fly zone over Bosnia.

20 March. Russian president Boris Yeltsin attempts to impose 'special rule', effectively suspending parliament until fresh elections.

29 March. A new government of the centre-right in France, under prime minister Édouard Balladur. 'Cohabitation' with socialist president François Mitterrand.

April. A referendum on political reforms in Italy. President Scalfaro asks non-party Carlo Azeglio Ciampi, governor of the Bank of Italy, to form a government, following the resignation of Giulio Amato. Veteran Christian Democrat politician Giulio Andreotti, seven times prime minister, is accused of complicity with the Mafia.

7 April. Macedonia is admitted to the UN as 'The Former Yugoslav Republic of Macedonia' (FYROM), despite Greek opposition.

24 April. The Dutch government under Christian Democrat Ruud Lubbers agrees a programme of radical reductions of the Netherlands' generous welfare spending.

1–2 May. Representatives of the main combatants in Bosnia sign the 'Vance–Owen plan'. Thorvald Stoltenberg replaces Cyrus Vance as UN co-chairman of the London Conference on the former Yugoslavia.

5–6 May. The Bosnian Serb assembly in Pale rejects the 'Vance–Owen plan'.

6 May. UN Security Council Resolution 824 declares Sarajevo, Tuzla, Žepa, Bihać, Goražde and Srebrenica to be 'safe zones'. These are often called 'safe areas' or 'safe havens'.

18 May. In a second referendum, Danish voters approve ratification of the Maastricht Treaty, after their government has negotiated a number of 'opt-outs'.

31 May. Serbian writer Dobrica Ćosić is compelled to resign as president of the Federal Republic of Yugoslavia.

6 June. Spanish elections return the Socialists under prime minister Felipe González to power, though dependent on Catalan and Basque votes for a majority.

21 June. The Copenhagen summit of the EU sets out basic criteria for post-communist countries to become members of the European Union.

14 July. The Belgian parliament votes to complete federalization of the country, with far-reaching devolution to largely Flemish-speaking Flanders, French-speaking Wallonia and the mixed city of Brussels.

1 August. After intensive speculation against the French franc, remaining currencies in the Exchange Rate Mechanism are allowed to fluctuate within margins of 15 per cent above or below the central rate. Only the Deutschmark and the Dutch guilder remain within a narrower band.

2 August. Britain ratifies the Maastricht Treaty.

Late September–early October. President Yeltsin suspends the intransigent parliament and calls for fresh elections. Following resistance by parliament and some armed forces, forces loyal to President Yeltsin bombard and storm the parliament building, Russia's 'White House'.

3–15 October. Germany. I spend the evening of the third anniversary of German unification in the beer tents of the Oktoberfest in Munich. The editor of a women's magazine tells me how they live from images of Princess Diana. Every time they put her on the front cover, sales go up by at least 20 per cent. On television, I see Chancellor Kohl toasting German unity in Saarbrücken. 'Here's to Gorbi,' says someone from the crowd. 'Yes, here's to Gorbi,' says Kohl. Forgotten or abhorred in Russia, Gorbachev is still a hero here. But Kohl has a new friend: Boris Yeltsin.

In Bonn, the Social Democrat leader Rudolf Scharping hastens to tell me about his early contacts with dissidents in Poland. I ask him what he replies to German voters who ask, 'Why do we need Europe now?' 'I have only fragments of an answer,' he says. An associate of Helmut Kohl tells me that the chancellor is adamant that other EU states must agree to the European Monetary Institute, and hence the European Central Bank, being located in Frankfurt – 'Otherwise,' Kohl apparently said, 'I'll enter the election campaign in short trousers.'

In an East German city, I share a platform with a new dean at the local university, a west German. He's an example of the kind of second-rater who would never have got such a senior position in the west, but now lords it over the east Germans like a British district commissioner in nineteenth-century India. He hardly lets the east Germans in our audience get a word in edgeways. Germany has another political first: colonialism in one country.

12 October. The German Constitutional Court rules that Germany can ratify the Maastricht Treaty.

26 October. Following a decisive victory in Polish elections held in September, under a new electoral law, a coalition government of post-communists and the Polish Peasant Party is formed, under prime minister Waldemar Pawlak.

29 October. EU leaders agree that the European Central Bank will be in Frankfurt, and that monetary union should happen at the latest by 1999.

1 November. The Maastricht Treaty comes into force in all member states of the EU.

1–4 November. Amsterdam and Antwerp. A tour for the Dutch edition of my book about German Ostpolitik. For these purposes, Flanders is treated as a part of Holland. It's as if Belgium does not exist.

The Dutch, in both Holland and Belgium, are better informed about Germany than the Germans themselves are. But they are also astonishingly suspicious and fearful of Germany and the Germans. Several times I am told the story of the banner, held up to greet German visitors at some large public event, saying, 'Give us back our bicycles!' (During the wartime occupation, bicycles were confiscated.) And when young German tourists ask the good people of Rotterdam, 'Excuse me, where's the old town?' they receive the acid reply, 'Ask your grandfather.' (The old town of Rotterdam was destroyed by the Germans during the war.)

This suspicion and fear is mitigated but also strengthened by the present relationship with their mighty neighbour. For the Dutch accept, almost fatalistically, that their economy, and therefore their fate, is inextricably bound up with that of Germany; that their interest rates automatically follow the Bundesbank's; that the Dutch guilder will merge with the Deutschmark in monetary union. One Dutch journalist confides, 'You know, in the end, we're left saying, "We hope they'll be nice to us!"' The national purpose is to preserve nothing so grand as sovereignty – just their language and a distinctive way of life. From 'Give us back our bicycles!' to 'Please let us keep our bicycles.'

9 November. The old bridge in Mostar is destroyed in fighting between Bosniaks and Bosnian Croats.

11 November. The UN Tribunal on War Crimes in former Yugoslavia is inaugurated in The Hague.

12 December. The first free multi-party parliamentary elections in Russia since 1917. Strong vote for communists under Gennady Zhuganov and for the far-right nationalist 'Liberal Democratic Party' of Vladimir Zhirinovsky. A new constitution is approved, giving more powers to the president.

15 December. British prime minister John Major and Irish prime minister Albert Reynolds issue the 'Downing Street Declaration' on the way forward in Northern Ireland.

19– December. Milošević's Socialist Party wins parliamentary elections in Serbia.

21 December. Former interior minister and moderate nationalist Peter Boross becomes Hungarian prime minister following the death of József Antall.

1994

1 January. The 'second stage' of economic and monetary union comes into effect with the establishment of a European Monetary Institute, as a precursor to a European Central Bank.

10–11 January. At a Brussels summit, Nato leaders launch the Partnership for Peace with former members of the Warsaw Pact.

14 January. The US, Soviet and Ukrainian presidents sign an accord detailing arrangements for the transfer of Ukrainian nuclear warheads to Russia.

5 February. A mortar attack on the market place in Sarajevo, with heavy loss of life. UN secretary-general Boutros Boutros Ghali asks Nato to prepare for possible air strikes against Serb artillery positions around Sarajevo.

16 February. Greece imposes a trade embargo on Macedonia. The EU declares this to be in violation of European law.

23 February. The Russian parliament votes an amnesty for those involved in the October 1993 revolt by the Russian parliament.

9–10 March. The EU's Committee of the Regions, established under the Maastricht Treaty, holds its first session.

14 March. Vladimír Mečiar resigns as prime minister of Slovakia after losing a confidence vote.

18 March. The Washington Agreement creates the Federation of Bosniaks and Bosnian Croats.

26–27 March. The new 'Forza Italia' party of business magnate Silvio Berlusconi wins Italian parliamentary elections as part of a 'Freedom Alliance'.

27 March. A referendum called by the pro-Russian president of the Ukrainian republic of Crimea results in a vote for greater autonomy of the Crimea.

Seven Cities

VIENNA

Driving into town from the airport, I pass a café called the Espresso Ilidza. On the radio, a reporter discusses the arrangements in Austrian schools for teaching in Croatian. Then comes the weather forecast: for Austria, Hungary, Slovenia, Croatia and Northern Italy. I read the diminutive *Neue Kronen Zeitung*, clipped to its *Zeitungshalter* (newspaper stick) like a little flag. In a fighting interview, Frau Klestil, the jilted wife of Kurt Waldheim's successor as president, tells us she is determined to remain Austria's first lady. The operetta continues. I am back in Central Europe.

Later, at the editorial meeting of a more elevated journal, a German feminist exclaims, 'Eastern men are such pashas.' Yes, a colleague agrees, they could do with some 're-education'. I glimpse a new Central Europe, where Polish men are to be 're-educated' by German feminists.

Then to the fellows' meeting of the Institute for Human Sciences, a meeting place to rival even the Café Landtmann. Bronisław Geremek lectures on 'The Collapse of Communism and European Security'. He makes a politician's speech, mustering every argument for Poland to be admitted to Nato. Eloquent, as always, but some in the audience are disconcerted. Somehow they had expected him to speak as an intellectual to intellectuals. But times and roles have changed, and Geremek, unlike many from the anti-communist oppositions of the 1970s and 1980s, has made a clear choice: while he is a politician he will be a politician. I'm sure he's right. All we've seen in Central

European politics since 1989 confirms an old truth. You may, in the course of your life, be both intellectual and politician. Try to be both at once and you'll be neither.

BRATISLAVA

Before the wars – Second and Cold – you went by tram from Vienna for an evening at the theatre in the Slovakian capital of Bratislava, or vice versa. Now you could do so again, if the authorities would only relay a few miles of track. Meanwhile, it is just over an hour by train, and you slide across the border as if the Iron Curtain had never been. Amid the seemingly endless, dusty allotments – small plots of land on which people grow vegetables – I spy garages flying the flags of Volkswagen and Audi, like crusader castles. Giggly Slovak schoolgirls scream pop songs out of the train windows, startling the people digging in their gardens below. But the nice girl sitting next to me demurely studies a German textbook on management economics. She hopes to work in the hotel trade.

As I arrive, the government falls. The populist prime minister, Vladimír Mečiar, has been ousted by a parliamentary vote, following outspoken criticism of him by the president, Michal Kováč.

On the evening television news, the chubby, avuncular president is shown sitting beside a carefully polished tile oven, with a large bunch of flowers in a vase on the table before him. At one side of the screen you see a large microphone, held motionless by a female hand with brightly painted fingernails. The president talks about democracy, constitutionalism, civic engagement, on and on, but the more he talks the less he convinces me – because of that painted hand. After about five minutes we briefly catch sight of the woman interviewer. Her feeble 'question' gives the cue for another five-minute sermon, delivered to the long-suffering painted hand. President Clinton, President Mitterrand or, for that matter, President Klestil can only dream of such a complaisant medium; but then they work in a fully fledged democracy.

My acquaintances are divided over whether Mečiar's fall is a good thing. All sigh with relief that the vulgar, nationalist rabble-rouser has got the boot. But some fear this ouster gives him the perfect chance to bounce back – as self-styled victim – in the elections that are due to be held in September. After all, he did it once before, in 1992, after being ousted by the parliament in 1991. Well, we shall see.

Meanwhile, I am in search of old Bratislava – that is, the German-Hungarian-Jewish-Slovak city of Pressburg, and before that the Hungarian royal capital of Pozsony. As I walk the dilapidated streets of the old town in the company of a local journalist, we meet an elderly gentleman in a black felt hat and formal grey coat, with a semi-precious stone on a ribbon round the collar of his slightly grubby white shirt. 'Ah, here is the oldest Pressburger!' says my acquaintance, and makes the introduction. This is Jan, Hans or 'Hansi' Albrecht, a retired musicologist and son of a celebrated local composer.

Later, over coffee and cognac in the inspissated gloom of his cluttered apartment, Albrecht tells tales of old Pressburg, while kids smash out the window glass from a derelict house across the road. ('Yes, that house belonged to the Esterházys,' he says; crash goes another window.) He shows me a programme for one of his father's concerts: printed in German, Hungarian and Slovak. The Pressburg of his youth really was trilingual, he says. Someone would address you in Hungarian, you might reply in German, another would interrupt in Slovak.

Even after the first wave of Slovakization, which began with the establishment of Czechoslovakia in 1918, the statistics still show a population of some 15,000 Jewish, 20,000 Hungarian and 30,000 German citizens of Pressburg, as well as 60,000 Slovaks. It was only the next two waves of Slovakization that effectually purged the city of all but a very few survivors of the other nationalities. First came the proclamation of Slovak independence under Hitler's protection, in March 1939. (Outside the Slovak Philharmonic's concert hall, a pathetic gaggle of old men in shabby suits and cheap ties can be seen gathering to celebrate the anniversary.) The fascist puppet state of Father Jozef Tiso got rid of the Jews, and made the Hungarians unwelcome too.

After 1945, the new Czechoslovak government got rid of the Germans. Finally, to celebrate the enhanced status which Slovak Bratislava received after the Soviet invasion of Czechoslovakia in 1968, the communist authorities drove a huge suspension bridge, the 'Bridge of the Slovak National Uprising', across the Danube and through the heart of the old town, destroying the synagogue and much of the old Jewish quarter. On a high wall they inscribed in large letters, 'Bratislava, City of Peace'.

Alas, poor Pressburg! Hansi Albrecht, the musicologist, argues that there has also been some cultural gain – the effete, decadent bourgeois culture of the late Habsburg empire has been reinvigorated by an injection of raw Slavonic folk spirit – but one feels an overwhelming sense of loss. Alma Münzová, another charming survivor of old Pressburg, well-read, multilingual, soignée, gives me the text of a talk she recently delivered (in German) on the history of the city. In it, she quotes a wry old joke: 'When will things finally get better?' 'What do you mean? They already were!' In many ways, to propose multi-culturalism in Central Europe really is to suggest going forward to the past.

However, one must beware the siren song of nostalgia. The balance was never even. Before the Austro-Hungarian *Ausgleich*, or comprom-ise, of 1867, the Austro-German element dominated Pressburg life. After the *Ausgleich*, the Hungarians there launched a programme of systematic Magyarization. At the end of the century, this would arouse the sympathy of visitors such as the historian R. W. Seton-Watson, who described it, under the pseudonym 'Scotus Viator', in the *Spectator*. So at the end of the First World War he was among those who advocated that Slovakia – 'Northern Hungary', as it then was – should be taken away from Hungary and joined with the Czech lands, in the newly independent state of Czechoslovakia.

All this is not just history. It has immediate political relevance. For, as a result of the post-1918 territorial settlement, reaffirmed after 1945, and again in the Helsinki Final Act of 1975, some half a million Hungarians now live just inside the Slovak frontier, on the north bank of the Danube. In Czechoslovakia, they were a small minority: about one in thirty of the population. In Slovakia they are a much larger minority: about one in ten.

The Slovak government, under Mečiar, has been a model of nation-alist stubbornness in resisting even the most reasonable demands for bilingual road signs, the restoration of the Hungarian forms of personal names, and so on, despite pressure from, among others, the Council of Europe. On the other hand, it was the now deceased Hungarian prime minister József Antall who famously declared that he wished to be the prime minister of 15 million Hungarians – that is, roughly 10 million inside Hungary's frontiers and 5 million beyond them. When Czecho- and Slovakia were splitting up, radical Hungarian nationalists even argued that what was laid down by the Allies in 1920, in the Treaty of Trianon, was the new frontier of Czechoslovakia, not of Slovakia – which would therefore have to be negotiated anew. Incredibly, though Slovakia and Hungary are both members of the Visegrád group, together with the Czech Republic and Poland, Slovakia currently has no ambassador in Budapest.

Slovakia's Hungarians are represented in the Slovak parliament, by their own Hungarian parties. Except on a few tactical votes (and to some extent, interestingly, in the ex-communist party) they do not mix with the Slovak parties. Regrettably, the Hungarian and Slovak sides seem to be getting not closer together but further apart. I am told that, in a recent poll, 35 per cent of those asked thought the Hungarian parties should not be in the Slovak parliament.

It is a worrying state of affairs.

BUDAPEST

I cross the Slovak–Hungarian border on the so-called Balkan–Orient Express. Its Romanian carriages provide a very credible setting for a murder. The old peasant woman sitting opposite me puts the Hungarian–Slovak conflict in its proper place. To the Slovak passport officer she says, in Slovak, 'I'm Slovak.' To the Hungarian passport officer she says, in Hungarian, 'I'm Hungarian.' To neither does she show a passport. Maybe there's hope for Central Europe yet.

I tell a Hungarian friend that I'm staying at the Hotel Gellért, that splendid art-nouveau blancmange on the right bank of the Danube, with its majolica-walled thermal baths and granite-faced masseurs. 'Oh,' she says, looking disapproving, 'it's a Forum hotel.' Thinking of the rather good Forum Hotel on the Pest side of the river, I'm about to exclaim, 'So has the Forum taken over the Gellért?' Then I realize that she means the Hungarian Democratic Forum, the conservative nationalist party which has been in power since 1990 and now faces an election in which the former communists are favoured to win. How out of touch can you get?

She's right, too. I had forgotten how the tone, the decor, the very smell of the Gellért exude that particular aesthetic of populist Hungarianness. Even the 'Do Not Disturb' signs to hang out on your doorknob are done in the national colours of red, white and green. Meanwhile, the modern Forum Hotel is bursting with Western consultants, most of them wasting large sums of our (that is, Western taxpayers') money which is meant to be going to the struggling new democracies of post-communist Europe. In German, one talks of *Spesenritter*: expense-account knights. O brave new world, that has such people in't.

This evening, however, something of the old world – almost a flashback – can be witnessed just along the embankment. A large crowd gathers at the invitation of the Democratic Charter, a liberal civic initiative, or anti-Forum forum, to protest against the recent sacking of 129 state radio employees. This was the latest act in the so-called 'media war', and a quite blatant attempt by the government to skew the radio still further to its side during the election. As dusk falls, the crowd, in which I meet several old friends, moves picturesquely down the left bank of the Danube, flaming torches held aloft, to reassemble at the statue of the poet Sándor Petőfi.

It was 146 years ago tomorrow, on 15 March 1848, that Petőfi led a Budapest crowd in what is generally taken to be the beginning of the country's 'lawful revolution' – Hungary's 14 July. And tomorrow it will be celebrated as a national holiday, with all the fetid pathos of which the Forum is capable. But this evening the liberals have stolen a march on them. At the feet of the poet, fine speeches are delivered by flaming torchlight: for democracy! for civil rights! for freedom! O brave old world, that had such demos in't.

As we watch the march, a publisher friend explains to me his worry that Hungary is once again being polarized into two nations, locked in a *Kulturkampf*. If someone talks of 'structural problems', of 'this country' or 'this agricultural country', you know at once that they come from the camp known before the war as 'urbanist'. If someone talks of 'fate issues', of 'my land' or 'our homeland', they belong to the camp known before the war as 'populist'. He fears history is repeating itself.

Another friend puts his personal dissatisfaction, frustration, melancholy, in a different way. 'I grew up', he says, 'in what I knew was an "abnormal" state. I thought that, if the communists and the Soviet Union went, Hungary would be a "normal", that is, a Western, country. Now they've gone and it isn't. We're governed by the Forum, and I have to accept that Hungary is in some ways an Eastern country.'

He gropes for an image, and finds it. 'There was a statue, covered by a heavy sheet. We believed it was beautiful. One day, miraculously, after forty long years, it was uncovered. Our hearts rose, great were our hopes. But then we found that the statue was chipped and dirty, and not so handsome after all.'

PRAGUE

The sleeping beauty of Central Europe has not merely been awakened by a prince's velvet kiss. She has put on black tights and gone off to the disco. (That is, after all, what contemporary princesses do, whether in Monaco or Mayfair.) While Budapest gradually developed into a modern consumer city, starting in the 1970s, Prague has emerged from its time warp suddenly and explosively. Instead of the magical museum, lovely but decaying, there is colour, noise, action: street performers, traffic jams, building works, thousands of young Americans – would-be Hemingways or Scott Fitzgeralds – millions of German tourists, betting shops, reserved parking places for France Telecom and Mitsubishi Corporation, beggars, junkies, *Spesenritter* of all countries, car alarms, trendy bars, gangsters, whores galore, *Bierstüben*, litter, graffiti, video shops and Franz Kafka T-shirts.

I have mixed feelings about this transformation scene. But I am quite won over by walking the streets with my friend Jáchym Topol, a young poet, novelist and editor of the formerly samizdat journal *Revolver Revue*. Jáchym – long-haired, chain-smoking, deeply Bohemian in both senses of the word – stalks along simply fizzing with enthusiasm for the way Prague has come alive. 'Look at it – it's great!' he exclaims, as we are nearly run down by a speeding car. The rock groups now write their lyrics in English, he says. Street kids use the Albanian word for prison, because there is now a strong Albanian 'mafia', besides the Russian and local ones. And there's a new kind of savoury bread roll. It's called a *crazy chleba*, a grammatically eccentric name translatable roughly as a 'bread crazy'.

Jáchym's new novel, out of Döblin and Joyce by way of Hrabal, is to be published next month, and he's dashing around trying to arrange publicity for it. But he has to do almost everything himself. The publicity department, so important a part of most Western publishers, is still almost unknown here.

The cliché is that the Czechs are the Prussians of the Slavs. Certainly the orderly, Western qualities of Bohemia, its pre-war industrial record, the economic credibility of premier Václav Klaus and, above all, its cheap skilled labour have combined to attract foreign, and especially German, investment. (An hour's skilled labour costs the employer about DM 35 in Germany compared to just DM 4 in Bohemia.) Yet even here there is the characteristic post-communist mixture of enterprise and corruption: large kickbacks paid in the course of privatization, mysterious enhancement of party funds, the dubious involvement of ex-*nomenklatura*, criminal, semi-criminal and corrupt official elements, all combining to give many ordinary people a slightly jaundiced view of both capitalism and the politicians who preach it.

The frequently encountered and loosely used term 'mafia' points to the ubiquitous element of organized crime. The Russian word '*prikhvatizatsiya*' – that is, roughly, pritheftization (*khvatat'* = 'seize', 'grab') – catches another aspect of the post-communist scene; as does the phrase 'the privatization of the *nomenklatura*'. Alfred Stepan, the American political scientist and new rector of George Soros's Central European University, reminds me of the term 'kleptocracy', already used in Latin America and Africa. The former foreign minister Jirí Dienstbier talks of an 'Italian-type political system'. And, finally, there is the special part played by the consultants and the *Spesenritter*. German businessmen, I am told, are particularly free with the bribes. What we need, however, is a term that encompasses the whole distinctive post-communist combination of all of these.

A friend who works for the Helsinki Committee for Refugees adds another colourful tessera to the post-communist mosaic. She tells me the story of a former Afghan police chief who had fled with his family to Moscow. There he was told that he could get to Germany, at a cost of $12,000 per head. He paid up for himself, his wife and their two youngest children, leaving two older children behind. (How an Afghan police chief had collected $48,000 one can perhaps imagine.) They were given false passports, travelled for many hours by train, by bus, by train again, until they finally arrived. 'Well,' said the Russian who escorted them, 'here you are, in Germany.' Setting them down in the station buffet, he asked for their false papers back and then went, as he said, to get some cash. Of course he never returned. So there they were, without papers, money or a single acquaintance, in what they thought was Germany. That is, in Prague.

Walking along Národní Street, I suddenly notice a black metal plaque inscribed simply with the date 17 November 1989. It marks the student demonstration which began the 'velvet revolution'. But you feel that event is already almost as remote as the resistance to Nazi occupation commemorated by other plaques around the city. Here more than anywhere else the last forty years seem just to have evaporated, almost as if they had never been. Certainly no one, except a very few historians, is interested in the communist past. Inasmuch as anyone is interested in the past at all, it is that of Tomáš Garrigue Masaryk's first republic, before 1939.

Next day I am driven out to Masaryk's country house at Lány, to see President Havel. Recovering from flu, he sits with a small group of friends and counsellors in a rather formal salon, while the rain buckets down on the park outside. Watched by the ghost of Masaryk, we talk about the idea and the reality of Central Europe. Masaryk's definition of Central Europe, or *Střední Evropa*, elaborated in London during the First World War in R. W. Seton-Watson's journal *The New Europe*, included 'Laplanders, Swedes, Norwegians and Danes, Finns, Estonians, Letts, Lithuanians, Poles, Lusatians, Czechs and Slovaks, Magyars, Serbo-Croats and Slovenes, Romanians, Bulgars, Albanians, Turks and Greeks' – but no Germans or Austrians. The German liberal politician Friedrich Naumann articulated a very different vision of Central Europe at the same time. His *Mitteleuropa* was all about the Germans and Austrians, with the others included only insofar as they were subjects of the German and Austro-Hungarian empires.

One of the great questions of the new 'New Europe' is whether this old tension between *Mitteleuropa* and *Střední Evropa* can finally be laid to rest. Very much with this in mind, Havel has invited seven presidents to an 'informal' meeting in Litomyšl, the birthplace of the composer Smetana. Besides the presidents of the 'Visegrád four' (Poland, Hungary, the Czech Republic and Slovakia), and the president of Slovenia, a country with which the Czech Republic has developed its own miniature special relationship (some make jokes about 'Czecho-Slovenia'), the 'L7' – as Havel's foreign-affairs adviser Pavel Seifter wryly christens it – will include Austria's President Klestil and Havel's good friend, the outgoing German president, Richard von Weizsäcker, whose birthday will also be marked by the occasion.

The inclusion of Germany in the group may raise a few eyebrows, not least in France or Italy, but I think it is vital. Even if Germany only stands in Central Europe 'with one leg', as Havel himself observes, it is the biggest leg in town. There is a lively debate about Germany inside East Central Europe, and there is a lively debate inside Germany about East Central Europe: it is vital that the two debates should intertwine.

At one point I ask Havel when he is going to write his fundamental essay about the intellectual and the politician. 'Only when I stop being president,' comes the instant reply.

Back in Prague, I visit another old friend, Petr Pithart, a highly respected opposition intellectual who in 1990 became prime minister of the Czech Republic, but is now – with relief – an intellectual again. After working hard to keep Czechoslovakia together, he now finds himself being invited to Belgium and Quebec, to tell them how you make a velvet divorce.

On Sunday, I drive myself out, along bad roads, through poor, dusty villages – no Prague transformation scenes here – to the castle of Častolovice, in north-eastern Bohemia. Diana Phipps – née Sternberg – has had the castle returned to her, under the so-called 'restitution' law. Not so many great families of the Bohemian aristocracy have in fact been eligible for this restitution, because the condition sine qua non is that they were still there at the time of the February 1948 communist coup. Many, seeing the writing on the wall, had already left. Of those eligible, by no means all have reclaimed their property, which often requires a large investment for a very doubtful return. Diana has, with enormous difficulty, got back more than 7,000 acres of the estate which originally sustained the castle, mainly forest, with herds of white deer and gruntles of wild boar. But, as for all but a very few country houses or castles in the world today, Častolovice's future will depend on people coming to see it.

Častolovice will be well worth seeing. There is the breathtaking Renaissance Knight's Hall, the dining room adorned with portraits of all the kings of Bohemia, the library left virtually untouched for forty years, like Miss Havisham's boudoir in *Great Expectations*, the rusty old weapons, the furniture (much of it 'restituted' from other locations), the ancestral portraits – Diana's great-grandfather in the full splendour of a general in the service of Emperor Franz Joseph, her father as a dashing dragoon galloping through some Ruthenian hamlet in the First World War; then the 'English' park and the boar-filled woods; and all this restored with Diana Phipps's rare taste and imagination. If you stand with eyes half-closed you can almost see Count Leopold Sternberg's hunting party lined up in the great courtyard, waiting impatiently for the American ambassador to join them, as described in Cecilia Sternberg's memorable autobiography, *The Journey*.

Here as elsewhere in the Czech lands, the local people do not seem to be overwhelmingly enthusiastic about the return of the aristocrats. (There is perhaps a contrast to the traditional gentry nations of Poland and Hungary.) I personally find it not just fabulous, in the original sense of the word, but also moving. Like, at the other social extreme, Jáchym Topol's street kids tossing off Albanian slang between bites of *crazy chleba* this is all part of the larger return to diversity, to history and to freedom – with all the tensions and conflicts that necessarily brings.

In the ante-room to the 'museum' part of the castle, we contemplate a display, left over from the communist period, listing the successive owners with their coats of arms. The Sternberg arms show a star with the motto '*Nescit occasum*' – 'It will not set.' Underneath, the communist curators have written, 'Sternberk family (1694–1948)' – as if the star had set. We discuss how this entry should be amended. Perhaps the simplest and most eloquent thing would be just to add, '(1992–)'.

WARSAW

In the evening I fly, with a plane-load of screaming French teenagers and wearily networking American, German and British consultants, to Poland, where it is the ex-communists' star that has risen again. For me, this is really just a stopover on the way to Lithuania, but there is time to see a few old friends.

Konstanty Gerbert, who still sometimes uses his underground pen-name of Dawid Warszawski, takes me out to lunch in an unexpectedly good Chinese restaurant (culinary worlds apart from the old, state-owned Shanghai). He talks, vividly as ever, about Bosnia, where he now spends much of his time. 'But,' I ask, 'what about Poland?'

'*Słuchaj, nudnie!*' he says. Boring! 'Poland has become an ordinary, provincial country with ordinary, provincial problems.' We both agree that this is a very great achievement indeed. After all, until 1989, boring, provincial normality was beyond all but the most far-fetched dreams. And the fact that this can more or less continue to be the case under a government dominated by the ex-communists (or ex-ex-communists) levered out only five years ago is a twist that nobody imagined.

Everywhere jackets and ties, suits and ties – scarcely a trace of the old underground sweaters and jeans. I feel almost underdressed.

Grzegorz Boguta, once the tyro of the underground publisher Nowa and now the smartly suited head of Polish Scientific Publishers (P W N), gives me the 1992 supplement to their dictionary of the Polish language. It contains words that have entered the language since the dictionary was first published in 1978 and those that had been excluded for political reasons (including reasons of communist prudery). This is a fascinating semantic register of fifteen years in which so much has changed: from *aborcja* (abortion, one of the most controversial issues in Polish politics over the last few years) to *żydokomuna* (a hateful new-old term for communists of – or allegedly of – Jewish origin). The entries under 'B' include *beton* ('concrete', referring to communist-party hard-liners), *bingo, bioenergoterapia, bogoojczyźniany* (one of my favourites, meaning literally 'god–fatherlandized', and used to refer to excessively pious patriotic persons), *bolszewik, briefing* and *broker*. 'V', a letter not generally used in Polish, has just three entries: *video* (explained as 'wideo'), *video-* (as prefix) and *votum separatum*.

VILNIUS

Puttering along in yet another twin-propeller plane, across snow-covered fields, enchanting lakes and enchanted woods, I arrive in Vilnius. Like Bratislava, this is a capital city which lies in one corner of its country and is in many ways quite untypical of it. Where Bratislava (Pressburg, Pozsony) was once German, Hungarian and Jewish as well as Slovak, Vilnius (Wilno, Vilna) was once Polish and Jewish as well as Lithuanian. Memorably evoked in recent times by two of its native sons, the Polish poet Czesław Miłosz and the Lithuanian poet Tomas Venclova, Vilnius is a wonderful irregular composition of baroque churches, small palaces, and town houses, courtyard leading into courtyard – 'a city of clouds resembling baroque architecture and of baroque architecture like coagulated clouds', as Miłosz puts it in his *Native Realm*.

However, Vilnius is Central Europe only from the knees up: the pavements and roads are full of Soviet-style potholes and slush. Near the university, I see a car with its rear wheel completely jammed in a three-foot-deep pothole. An acquaintance tells me you can actually get some modest compensation for the damage from the local authorities, but only if you land in a registered pothole.

A Lithuanian poet shows me around the Jewish museum, which goes by the curious name of the Jewish State Museum of Lithuania. The exhibition is striking because, even when you have found it, which is not altogether easy, there is almost nothing there. A few

Torah scrolls and Hanukkah lamps, some prints ('Portrait of Sir Moses Montefiore, Lithograph, Warsaw'); that's about it. Fragments of fragments from a lost world. 'We rely on the visitors to tell us what we have,' says the poet. In the visitors' book, a young German thanks the museum for this reminder of 'our very, very bad history'.

Not far away, on Gedimino Boulevard, there is another exhibition. In the basement of what until just three years ago was still the KGB headquarters, you can visit the cells. I am shown around by a former inmate, Stasys Katauskas. Speaking Polish with the rolled Lithuanian 'l', he tells me how he was caught in 1946 after passing a radio set to the anti-Soviet partisans. Then he takes me through the cells as if I myself were being admitted – first the strip search; then locked up in a tiny, windowless cupboard; then the registration, photographing and fingerprinting (the original equipment is still there); finally, into the cells. These were repainted by the KGB before they left, but the association of former inmates has paid a picture restorer to strip off the paint, layer by layer. On a small, two-foot square patch you have twenty carefully numbered layers: so many despairing messages, so much filth, so much blood have these walls seen. Down the corridor there is the freezing solitary-confinement cell, and, most horrible of all, a cell heavily padded with stuffed canvas, still bloodstained. The torture room.

To sophisticated Western ears, Lithuanian nationalism often sounds strident and crude. But if you walk through these cellars, contemplate the catalogue of occupation which this one building has seen over the last century – tsarist Russian courts, Polish courts, NKVD, Nazi *Sicherheitsdienst*, KGB – and look at the grainy photographs of the partisans on the walls, then you may have a little more understanding of the traumatic experience from which that raw, naive nationalism comes.

However, I am told that, after the first great wave of recollection and mourning and celebration in the independence struggle, most young Lithuanians, perhaps most Lithuanians altogether, no longer want to look back, whether in sorrow, pride or anger. They have elected former communists to the government after the anti-communist patriots led by Vytautas Landsbergis turned out to be inept. They are more concerned with today's chances, and today's problems, such as the omnipresent mafia, with their car-theft and protection rackets; the *biznes*-men who buy politicians and a favourable press; the politicians enriching themselves from the public purse and the proceeds of privatization. (Once again, I feel the lack of a term to embrace this entire complex phenomenon.)

I visit some of the politicians in the parliament building which the people of Vilnius defended against Soviet forces in 1991. A section of the concrete and barbed-wire barricade has been left as a memorial, looking strangely like a remnant of the Berlin Wall. Inside, an adviser to the government of ex-communists outlines Lithuania's foreign-policy options: to take the 'northern' route to Europe, via Sweden and Denmark, or the 'western' route, by way of Poland and Germany. Interestingly, many Lithuanians favour the northern route mainly because it does not involve going by way of Poland, which is still seen here as a historic oppressor.

Romualdas Ozolas, a small, wiry, bristling opposition MP, has a sticker on his office wall in the blue and yellow colours of the European Union. It proclaims, 'My Country Europe'. Is that his sentiment? '*Ja*,' he says, in his somewhat broken German, '*genau!*' And what is Europe? Strutting up and down, he barks a short and definite answer: '*Europa ist . . . nicht-Russland!*' 'Europe is not-Russia.' Well, that is one definition – and far from just a Lithuanian one. (It's just that the Lithuanians are naive enough to say so.)

Our wide-ranging geopolitical discussion is interrupted by a sharp knock at the door. A young journalist from the sensationalist newspaper *Respublika* comes in and, without so much as an 'Excuse me', thrusts a tape recorder under Mr Ozolas's nose. Mr Ozolas delivers a few well-chosen words, and the journalist exits as abruptly as he entered.

Playing on the popular theme of political corruption, *Respublika* has offered a large reward to any politician who can prove – against the best efforts of their investigative journalists – that he (or she) is not corrupt. Since politicians have not exactly been rushing to apply, the newspaper has started nominating candidates, allegedly on the basis of a poll of its readers. Mr Ozolas has been thus nominated. He has just told that probing young Lithuanian Woodward 'n' Bernstein that he would not be accepting the kind offer. '*Ich sage,*' he explains, '*ich nicht nehme, weil ich habe Auto gekauft!*' After further enquiries, I finally establish that, along with other MPs, he had voted himself a car at what was, in effect, a subsidized price.

ST PETERSBURG

After a long, cold wait, the Lithuanian Airlines twin-prop just starts up and goes – no safety drill; no 'This is your steward speaking.' The emergency exit next to me rattles like a loose mudguard.

At St Petersburg Airport, however, I am met by a Volvo stretch limo, and swept into the Grand Hotel Europe – a Swedish–Russian joint venture and luxurious even by western standards. 'No detail has been overlooked', says the room card, 'in creating an authentic Russian environment with all the comforts and services of today.' Authentic Russian environment, my foot!

The contrast with the city just beyond the hotel doors is extreme. There, poorly dressed crowds trudge grimly along the muddy pavements – although some stop to indulge in that curious Russian pastime of eating ice cream in the snow. The façades look more grubby than when I was last in (then still) Leningrad, but perhaps it is just the season. What is certainly new is the proliferation of street traders, hawkers, spivs and beggars.

I am here for what turns out to be a fascinating conference, organized by the Hamburg-based Bergedorfer Gesprächskreis with the participation of the German defence minister and the Russian deputy defence minister. Two things strike me particularly. One is that, whereas in Central Europe the central historical reference point is the period before 1939, here it is clearly the period before 1917. This extends even to details of dress and manner. The smart aide-de-camp to the Russian minister looks like an oil painting of a First World War officer. The German military men, by contrast, look like managers in uniform.

The other, more serious, thing is just how difficult even those whom I know to be very liberal Russians find it, emotionally as much as intellectually, to accept the loss of empire. Although the West in general, and the Clinton administration in particular, has done everything to avoid a Versailles-type humiliation, they still feel humiliated. In this, as in other respects, it really is 'Weimar Russia'.

The crucial psychological test case is not the Baltic states – although Russia's relationship with them is difficult enough, especially because of the position of the Russian minorities there and the Russian military exclave of Kaliningrad. The test is Ukraine. With the best will in the world, most Russians I talk to find it difficult to accept the idea that Ukraine can really be an independent state.

One evening we are treated by Mayor Sobchak to a splendid reception in the extraordinary Yusupov Palace, with its rooms of onyx, marble and tooled leather, its white and gold ballroom, and its own small theatre complete with plush stalls, circle and the family box. After the usual banquet of *zakuski*, vodka and speeches, we are shown down to the room in which Prince Feliks Yusupov and his fellow conspirators attempted to poison Rasputin. A wax model of the lubricious monk sits at a table laid with his favourite sweet wine and cakes, while the clean-shaven young prince looks on. A smartly dressed lady guide, exuding perfume and national pride, tells us every last detail of that gruesome night: how the poison was not sufficient to fell the immensely strong Rasputin, how he staggered out into the courtyard, how the conspirators finished him off, how they disposed (or failed to dispose) of the body. His ghost, you feel, has still not quite been laid to rest.

1994

1 April. Hungary becomes the first post-communist state to apply for membership of the EU.

April. Bosnian Serbs attack the UN 'safe haven' of Goražde. The first Nato air strikes on Bosnian Serb forces are abandoned after Bosnian Serbs threaten UN troops.

26 April. The USA, Britain, France, Germany and Russia form the Contact Group for coordinating policy towards former Yugoslavia. Polish president Lech Wałęsa visits Lithuania and signs a treaty of friendship and cooperation.

6 May. Queen Elizabeth II and President François Mitterrand open the Channel Tunnel between Britain and France.

11 May. Silvio Berlusconi becomes prime minister of Italy.

17–19 May. Milan: so rich; so beautiful its women; so stylish its men; so glorious its food. I am here at the invitation of my publisher, Mondadori, which is owned by Berlusconi, although the politics of the editors I meet are very different from his. They give me a few glimpses of the crisis that has engulfed the whole Italian political system. One tells me, 'You know, we in Milan knew there were politicians in Rome, just as we knew that there are wild boar in the forests of Tuscany.' They were strange, remote creatures, southern lawyers and Roman wheeler-dealers. 'But now, suddenly, they are real people – even people we actually know.'

Berlusconi, I am told, started his eruption into Italian politics by conducting extensive and sophisticated opinion polls. Having found out what people wanted, he then offered it to them, wrapped in glittering paper and sold with the latest advertising techniques on the television channels that he owns. It's almost a parable – or is it a parody? – of contemporary television democracy.

I am taken to a television chat show which addresses the question whether there is any connection between the success of the Milan football club, owned by Berlusconi, and his recent triumph in politics. Is politics like football? The presenter, himself of the left, suggests one parallel. Berlusconi's success in football, he observes, comes from buying players . . .

20 May. The Crimean assembly approves an effective declaration of sovereignty.

20–23 May. Sintra, Portugal. Byron's 'Eden'. A moorish castle, fantastic villas and exotic trees, their tops disappearing into the hillside mists. What does this small country, at the westernmost end of Europe, helped on its journey from dictatorship to democracy by the prospect and then the reality of joining the European Community, think of doing the same for the small, fragile new democracies in the eastern mists? The answer, roughly, is 'We'd really like to support them, as we ourselves were supported, just so long as it doesn't take any of the money that we get from the EU.' The money that has, for example, paid for the motorway we drove down on our way from Lisbon.

Talking of money, the Portuguese are determined to be a founding member of the European monetary union. But won't the participation of currencies like theirs mean that the new single currency will be softer than the Deutschmark? 'Yes, exactly,' says a former finance minister. 'That's just what we want.'

23 May. Roman Herzog is elected president of Germany, succeeding Richard von Weizsäcker.

26–27 May. The inaugural conference for a Pact on Stability in Europe is held in Paris.

27 May. Alexander Solzhenitsyn returns to Russia.

29 May. The former East German leader Erich Honecker dies in Chile. Former communists, now called Socialists, win parliamentary elections in Hungary.

30 May. A new currency, the kuna, is introduced in Croatia and in Croatian-controlled parts of Bosnia.

1 June. Partial legalization of euthanasia in the Netherlands.

6 June. Politicians and veterans commemorate the fiftieth anniversary of the D-Day landings in Normandy. Germans are not invited to participate.

Fathers and Sons

Like many British children of my generation, I grew up amid tales of D-Day and the memories of war. When I was six or seven, my mother showed me the citation for my father's Military Cross: 'He landed on 6th June 1944 with the first assault wave of 6th Battalion The Green Howards and in the bitter and continuous fighting in the Normandy bridgehead his coolness and disregard of danger were quickly apparent . . . His conduct, bravery and devotion to duty throughout the whole campaign are deserving of the highest praise . . .' With all their formulaic stiffness, the words move me as deeply now as they did then.

When my children were about the same age, I sat them on a tank outside the D-Day museum in Bayeux and told them how their grandfather had fought to liberate Europe from Nazism. There are few satisfactions to compare with that of passing on history with pride. 'This story shall the good man teach his son . . .' It is a satisfaction which many Polish friends of my generation can share, but only a very few German ones. For, while their fathers often fought with extraordinary courage, resourcefulness and, yes, devotion to duty, they did so in an abominable cause. The brave men and women of the resistance whom Germany will commemorate on 20 July, the fiftieth anniversary of Count Stauffenberg's attempt to assassinate Hitler, are the exceptions.

Yet the subsequent fifty years offer Germany some other causes for quiet pride. Last weekend I took my eldest son, Thomas, now ten, to visit his godfather in Berlin. Thomas's godfather, Werner Krätschell, is an East German priest with a remarkable story. When East Germany was cut off from the West by the building of the Berlin Wall, in August 1961, Werner was on holiday in the West. He made an extraordinary decision. While thousands of East Germans were still desperately trying to get out, he decided to go back. 'People will need me there,' he said. And they certainly did. For twenty-eight long years, Werner did what a churchman could do to alleviate the suffering caused by the communist dictatorship, with quiet courage and devotion to duty. And this story, too, shall the good man teach his son . . .

Thomas can be proud both of his grandfather and of his godfather. That is a fine beginning. But if one takes the argument from the individual to the collective, from single people to the nations to which they belong, things are not so easy. So much of our national pride still derives from our part in the defeat of Nazism: and this is remembered not just as a defeat of Hitler but also as a defeat of Germany. Now Thomas's history teacher at the Dragon School in Oxford will remind him of the complicating truth that the *Wehrmacht*'s back was broken by the Red Army, fighting in the service of another tyrant. But in the British memory it is 'the longest day'. And before that 'the finest hour'.

Yet, read again today, Churchill's famous remark about the Battle of Britain – 'if the British Empire and its Commonwealth last for a thousand years, men will still say, "This was their finest hour"' – seems to contain the hint of a dark premonition: there might not be many more fine hours to follow. It is, I think, really a little worrying that a British schoolboy in the 1990s is still expected to derive so much of his national pride from the achievements of fifty years ago, as if nothing really important had been done since. But of course he asks questions. What *has* happened since? Is Britain or Germany now the richer and more powerful country? Which has the stronger currency? And it is not easy to avoid, in the substance if not in the phrasing, the hoary old cliché that 'Britain won the war but Germany won the peace'.

Germany has a different problem – or, rather, the other side of the same one. It was well illustrated by the little rumpus last year about Chancellor Kohl's possible participation in this year's ceremonies to mark the fiftieth anniversary of D-Day. Denying that Chancellor Kohl had ever sought to be included, his spokesman remarked at a press conference, 'Do you seriously think that the chancellor would wish to take part in a ceremony [marking an event] in which German soldiers suffered a defeat?' While the spokesman subsequently elaborated his off-the-cuff remark – the chancellor, he added, would not want to celebrate the German victories of 1870 either – it in fact perfectly encapsulates a deep ambivalence about a liberation that was also a defeat.

My father, who as I write these lines is once again embarked for Normandy, felt the Germans should not be invited to the veterans' commemoration. It seems to me that the veterans have an absolute right to say this. They risked their lives so that others – including the Germans – could be free. They must decide. But, insofar as the commemoration is also an act of contemporary states, this was, I think, a missed opportunity.

A missed opportunity, above all, for Germany. Had the German president, Richard von Weizsäcker, been invited to participate in some form – and, as head of the state, he would have been the appropriate person to invite – he would have had the opportunity to deliver one more great speech, comparable to that which he delivered on the fortieth anniversary of VE Day, in May 1985.

This speech would have explained how the defeat of the German armies meant liberation even for the soldiers who were defeated. How everything that has been achieved in Germany over the past fifty years – security, prosperity, democracy and, finally, unity – began with and was founded upon that total defeat and unconditional surrender which precluded any but the civilian path to recovery. How, in short, the defeat of Germany was a victory for Germany. (He might have added, but would have been too diplomatic to do so, that Russia today faces a rather similar question – was the end of the Cold War a defeat for Russia or just for Soviet communism? – but in a situation more like that of Germany in 1918 than that of Germany in 1945. For Russia, even more than for Weimar Germany, the military option still remains very much available.)

The German president's great speech would have concluded by explaining why this memory is still important for a united, fully sovereign Germany, the richest and most powerful country in Europe. For if the danger for Britain is that we dwell too much on the past, often in romanticized, Merchant Ivory colours, the danger for Germany is now rather the opposite.

The public memory of the old, pre-unification Federal Republic dwelled almost obsessively on the Nazi past. Everything the Bonn republic did was interpreted in the light of 'the past' – meaning the twelve years of Hitler. But, even then, the private memory was rather different. James Fenton captured this wonderfully in a poem called 'A German Requiem', which he wrote when living in Berlin in the late 1970s: 'How comforting it is, once or twice a year, / To get together and forget the old times.' And again: 'But come. Grief must have its term? Guilt too, then.'

With unification has come a strong inclination to say, 'Enough is enough.' Germany has done its penance through forty years of division, with the East Germans, such as Werner Krätschell, bearing a disproportionate part of the burden. You cannot walk for ever in sackcloth and ashes. What matters now is for the new republic, the Berlin republic, to concentrate on building Europe's future. Anyway, the German past is more than just those twelve years. There are other aspects of German history, before 1933, after 1945, even a very few between those dates, about which Germans can be proud – patriotic, even.

This reaction is not only understandable but right and proper – up to a point. The task, the extraordinarily delicate task, for Germany's political, intellectual and spiritual leaders is to determine: up to what point?

Now, one of the passages of history which I think is already slipping down the memory hole is the specifically British contribution not just to the liberation of Germany from Nazism, but also to the reconstruction of what would become West Germany after 1945, the defence of West Berlin, and the secure position in the West from which the Federal Republic could develop its own relations with the East. I am struck by the extent to which, in the German public debate, the three Western Allies have really become two: France and the United States. (German politicians and officials will of course deny this – unconvincingly.)

This has happened partly because France and the United States have known how to combine the proper memory of war with effective signs of reconciliation – like the 'Eurocorps', in whose ranks German troops will march through Paris on 14 July. But it is even more because France and the United States both seem to have some vision of a new partnership with Germany in Europe, while Britain does not. At which it will be the turn of British politicians and officials to protest – unconvincingly.

In 1944 Britain had a policy for Europe: to liberate as much of it as possible, and then to help reconstruct it. Fifty years on, Britain has neither a policy for Europe nor any coherent vision of our own place in Europe. If we carry on like this, I fear to think what my sons will have left to teach their children.

1994

9 and 12 June. Direct elections to the European Parliament.

12 June. In a referendum, 66.4 per cent of Austrian voters support their county joining the EU.

22 June. Russia signs a Partnership for Peace agreement with Nato.

24 June. The UN endorses deployment of Russian 'peacekeeping' forces in Abkhazia, which has effectively seceded from Georgia.

24–25 June. An EU summit in Corfu. Signature of accession treaties for Austria, Finland, Sweden and Norway. A partnership and cooperation agreement is signed with Russia.

2 July. Former Albanian president Ramiz Alia is condemned to nine years in prison for abuse of power.

6 July. The Contact Group unveils its proposal for division of Bosnia, giving 51 per cent of the territory to the Bosniak–Croat federation and 49 per cent to the Bosnian Serbs.

10 July. Leonid Kuchma, a former director of a missile factory, is elected president of Ukraine. Alexander Lukashenka is elected president of Belarus on a pro-Russian and anti-corruption platform.

12 July. The German Constitutional Court decides that it is constitutional for German forces to participate in operations outside the Nato area.

15 July. Jacques Santer is appointed president of the European Commission from 1 January 1995. A new Hungarian government is formed, with post-dissident Free Democrats serving under post-communist prime minister Gyula Horn. Horn promises a 'historic reconciliation' with Romania.

23 July. Tony Blair becomes leader of the British Labour Party.

29 July. Former Italian prime minister Bettino Craxi is sentenced to eight and a half years' imprisonment for fraudulent bankruptcy but remains in Tunisia, enjoying 'ill health'.

5 August. The Federal Republic of Yugoslavia imposes an economic blockade on Bosnian Serbs.

29 August. The Basque terrorist organisation ETA calls on 600 imprisoned members to go on hunger strike.

29–30 August. The last Russian forces leave Estonia and Latvia.

31 August. The IRA declares a ceasefire in Northern Ireland.

1 September. The last Russian troops leave Berlin, completing their withdrawal from Germany.

6 September. Irish prime minister Albert Reynolds meets Sinn Fein leader Gerry Adams and SDLP leader John Hume to talk about peaceful solutions in Northern Ireland.

8 September. The USA, Britain and France withdraw their remaining troops from Berlin. The last Soviet forces leave Poland.

September–November. Nato member Turkey threatens war against Nato member Greece if the latter extends its territorial waters in the Aegean.

1 October. Vladimír Mečiar's Movement for a Democratic Slovakia wins the Slovak parliamentary elections.

7 October. Swedish social democrats return to power, with Ingvar Carlsson as prime minister. Ex-king Michael of Romania is refused entry at Bucharest airport.

16 October. In a referendum, Finns vote to join the EU. Bundestag elections in Germany.

The Banality of the Good

Taking a break from Germany's rather boring election campaign, I dropped in to the fine new museums that have recently been opened in Bonn. Right at the beginning of the permanent exhibition in the splendid new Museum of the History of the Federal Republic I found a strange black pavilion with, inside, pictures from the Nazi extermination camps. A young German guide was just explaining to a group of visitors that there had been a vigorous debate about whether to show these horrifying pictures. The conclusion, he said, was that 'a German museum could not afford not to show these pictures'.

At the towering new exhibition hall just down the road there was an impressive show of the central and east European avant-garde in the twentieth century. One section was entitled 'The Presence of Jewry'. Here another young German guide stood before Chagall's 1914 picture *The Feast Day*, showing a rabbi with a miniature rabbi on his head, pointing in the opposite direction. Trying to explain the figure of the miniature rabbi, the guide, a woman in her early twenties, said, 'I myself have no direct experience with Jewish people, so I can't really judge, but, from what I've read, this spirit of contradiction, this capacity to make fun of yourself, is characteristic of Jewry.'

Yes, the past – that past – is still here. Whenever you come to Germany you are sure to stumble across it, one way or another. It won't pass away. Yet, as the naive comments of the young German guides suggest, it is astronomically remote from the life experience of younger Germans today. Painful innocence, not guilt or even repressed guilt, speaks from those comments.

For me, these flashbacks to a hell made in Germany serve above all as a reminder of the fantastic distance that Germany has travelled over the last half-century: the distance to civility, legality, modernity, democracy. The very fact that, after four years of traumatic change in an only painfully uniting Germany, the election campaign can be boring is itself a measure of that progress. The village pub where I go for lunch with friends turns out also to be a polling station. As we chew our schnitzels, we can watch the civil, genial, utterly matter-of-fact business of voting. In the evening, the 'election parties' in the headquarters of the main political parties are even more hot and crowded than at previous elections, with everyone trying to judge everyone else's mood as the beer (Social Democrats) and wine (Christian Democrats) flow.

An element of drama is given by the closeness of the result, with estimates of the current coalition's new parliamentary majority sinking to as low as a single seat during the evening, before rising again in the small hours to the eventual ten. But the whole nation is hardly biting its nails in suspense. On another television channel there is a comedy show, with a comedian from Paderborn giving a wonderful imitation of the petit-bourgeois concierge type, obsessed with cleanliness and order. The audience loves it. Who says the Germans can't laugh at themselves? On a third channel, there is a light-entertainment programme, with viewers invited to contribute by telephone to a charity for cancer victims. Viewers' names are flashed across the screen, with their contributions: D M 20, D M 30, D M 4,000, D M 40,000. Just before I flick back to the election coverage, the computer announces the latest total. It is D M 5 million.

Germany – from the banality of evil to the banality of good.

I

Of course there are still serious matters to be worried about in Germany – even in the results of this election. But the first thing is to keep those matters in proportion. I have been travelling to Germany for more than twenty years now. For as long as I can remember, I have heard apocalyptic warnings – and none more apocalyptic than those issued by the Germans themselves. The oil-price shock! The terrorists! *Berufs-verbot*! Franz Josef Strauss! Eurosclerosis! The Greens! The peace movement! Nationalist-neutralism! *Anschluss* (of East Germany)! German-dominated *Mitteleuropa*! Neo-Nazis! For as long as I can remember, the Federal Republic has gone on its quiet, successful, bourgeois way, proving one warning after the other wrong, as it has grown steadily richer, stronger and now bigger.

This election, the thirteenth to a German Bundestag but only the second to an all-German Bundestag, is taken so seriously both because of the pre-1945 past – the ghosts in the museum – and because of the post-1995 future, with Germany as the key power in the centre of Europe. And how very seriously it is taken! It is not just the little sermon on television from the president of the Bundestag, Frau Professor Dr Rita Sussmuth, telling people how important it is to turn out to vote, in the dulcet yet pious tones of our Queen's address on Christmas Day. It is not just the three or four highly professional polling organizations, producing unbelievably detailed information on every aspect of the voting. It is also the teams of political scientists and observers from all over the world, flown in to diagnose in minute detail the condition of German Democracy. They remind me of nothing so much as the huge medical teams assigned to check the health of the American president or the Pope. Is there a *slight* irregularity in his pulse?

In the last few years there has been much speculation about a fragmentation of the country's political representation. As a result both of unification and of widespread dissatisfaction with the political elites of the established parties – seen as remote, bureaucratic and unduly interested in lining their own pockets – local and state elections have seen votes flowing away not just to the Greens in the west and the post-communist Party of Democratic Socialism (PDS) in the east, but also to new groupings such as the Hamburg-based *Stattpartei*. The name means roughly 'The Instead Party'. Instead, that is, of the worn-out old established parties.

'Bonn is not Weimar,' went the old saying, meaning that the Bonn republic was not going to fall victim to the political fragmentation which helped to doom the Weimar republic. But perhaps, we all sombrely wisecracked, 'Berlin could be Weimar.' Well, the republic hasn't quite got to Berlin, yet – indeed, the government will probably still be in Bonn in the next federal election, due in 1998. So there is still time for the sombre fears to be realized. There are still real concerns about the reputation and future of the political parties.

Yet this election showed a clear swing in the other direction: back to the established parties. With a 79 per cent turnout, about 85 per cent of the votes cast went to the parties of the old Federal Republic: the wedded Christian Democratic Union and Bavarian Christian Social Union (CDU/CSU), the Social Democrats (SPD) and the Free Democrats (FDP). A further 7.3 per cent of the vote went to the combined list of the Greens, who by now must almost count as an 'established' party of the Federal Republic, and the Alliance '90, the heirs to the alliance of civil-rights and opposition groups formed to fight the elections of 1990.

According to the opinion pollsters, voters were more or less evenly divided about which combination of these parties they wanted to see in power: the present coalition of CDU/CSU and FDP, a 'Grand Coalition' of CDU/CSU and SPD, or 'red–green' (SPD–Alliance '90/Greens). Each of these combinations can already be found in local or state governments. But that they wanted some combination of these four or, inasmuch as the Bavarian CSU still has a separate identity, five established parties was very clear.

2

The two main extremist outsiders, the east German post-communist PDS (Party of Democratic Socialism) and the largely west German, indeed mainly Bavarian, far-right Republicans, fared differently. Most reassuringly, the Republicans got only 1.9 per cent of the vote. In Bavaria they have been completely outplayed by the CSU, which has mopped up their votes by a tough line on the issues of law and order and immigration, together with firmly expressed scepticism about further steps of European integration, while, at the same time, avoiding the Republicans' extreme nationalist or racist tones. ('Jobs for Germans!' said one of their election posters.)

At the same time, the Republicans have been crippled by internal feuding. A few weeks before the election the leadership voted to sack their chairman and founding father, Franz Schönhuber, a former SS man and gifted rabble-rouser, because he had met with the leader of an older-established far-right party, Gerhard Frey of the so-called Deutsche Volkunion. But just three days before the election a Berlin court issued an order suspending Schönhuber's dismissal, on the grounds that the proper procedures had not been followed.

Thinking that I would try to attend all the election parties in Bonn, I inadvertently chose the day of the court hearing to telephone the Republicans' office in Bonn to ask if they were having a party. 'Well,' said a slightly confused woman at the end of the line, 'we have the food and drink here, but we're waiting for instructions as to whether we have a party.' On the election day, I rang again. Yes, I was told, the party was on. At about 8.15 p.m., abandoning the packed, excited scrum in the CDU's Konrad-Adenauer-Haus, I took a taxi down to the Republicans' headquarters in Bad Godesberg.

We had a little difficulty finding it. No flags or posters hung outside the villa at Plittersdorferstrasse 91. The shutters were down on the windows – but a chink of light shone through them. As I advanced to the front door, automatic security spotlights flashed on. A muscular character opened the door. Was the party still on? I asked. Yes, he said, but 'most of them have gone'. Inside, there was a large room with a buffet and drinks. It contained eight people. Two of them were journalists.

The journalists then interviewed the party's spokesman and deputy chairman, a Herr Hausmann. He spent most of the interview denouncing his temporarily reinstated chairman. However, he said, they would not disappoint the confidence which had been placed in them by their voters, by the *Angestellte* (white-collar workers) and *Beamte* (officials); yes, by the *Polizeibeamte* – the police officers.

His reference to the police was a reminder that the Republicans cannot simply be dismissed out of hand. There has been worrying evidence of far-right sympathies among the police. And the Republicans still received a total of some 875,000 votes – the population of a medium-size city. The xenophobic, authoritarian and anti-Maastricht views of these voters will be reflected, not directly but indirectly, especially in the rhetoric of the CSU. Nonetheless, for the time being at least, the result puts the Republicans themselves right back on the outer margins of German politics.

Not so the post-communist PDS, which will have thirty members of the new parliament. Indeed, in a curious twist, the proceedings of the thirteenth Bundestag will actually be opened by a speech from a PDS member. The foxy old East German writer Stefan Heym, elected on the PDS ticket, is automatically granted this right as the oldest member of the house.

To understand why the PDS is in parliament, one must dwell for a moment on the peculiarity of Germany's electoral law. According to this law, each citizen has two votes. The 'first vote' goes to an individual candidate, the 'second vote' goes to a party. It is the *second* vote that mainly determines the total number of seats each party has in the house. Incidentally, it is not only to foreign readers that this peculiarity needs explaining. Surveys and interviews regularly show that many German voters don't understand it either. They think their first vote is as important as or even, as its name suggests, more important than the second vote.

The so-called '5 per cent hurdle' provides that only those parties getting more than 5 per cent of the second votes will enter the Bundestag. This provision was introduced to prevent a recurrence of the fragmented party politics of the Weimar republic – the nightmare of 'Bonn becoming Weimar'.

So how come the PDS has got into parliament with less than 5 per cent of the second votes? Because the law also provides that if a party has three or more direct candidates elected – by the first votes, that is – then it should have the full number of seats to which it would be entitled by its percentage of the second votes. And the PDS got not just three but four direct candidates elected, all of them in what used to be East Berlin.

Through this super-scrupulous loophole in the election law, their Noah's ark sails into parliament, disgorging, besides Stefan Heym, such diverse creatures as the lawyer, wit and gifted demagogue Gregor Gysi; the former East German economics minister Christa Luft; a great-grandson of Bismarck, Count Heinrich von Einsiedel; a former East German Olympic champion, Ruth Fuchs; and, most repulsively, two people who were almost certainly regular Stasi informers, one Rolf Kutzmutz and the curiously named Kerstin Kaiser-Nicht. What a bunch!

The PDS is, without doubt, the most interesting phenomenon in these elections. It is overwhelmingly an east German party, picking up a little over 300,000 votes in the west, but more than 1.7 million in the east. In what used to be East Berlin, it received a good third of the vote and won four of the five constituencies. Since most of the old West Berlin went to the CDU, the capital is now dramatically divided – almost, one is tempted to say, like the division between white and black parts of Washington, DC.

The vote for the PDS is, in part, a familiar post-communist phenomenon, as seen in Poland and Hungary: a diverse vote comprising old comrades and functionaries, the losers from the traumatic process of economic transformation, those who yearn for the good old days of social security when 'we pretended to work and they pretended to pay us', and some younger protest voters. In the east German case the familiar mix of post-communist grievances has been ameliorated by the economic transfers from the west, in the order of DM 150 billion a year; but then it has been exacerbated by two elements.

First, nowhere in post-communist Europe has the change in every single aspect of life been so sudden and total as in east Germany. Not just the political, economic and legal system but the street signs, the banks, the post offices, the health insurance, the cars, the products in the shops, even the bread has changed. Small wonder there is much dislocation and some nostalgia. Second, nowhere else has one had the strange experience of colonialism in one country. Many west Germans have displayed monstrous condescension towards, and sheer incomprehension of, their poorer compatriots in the east. At the same time, the east Germans continue to be paid less, and are bureaucratically discriminated against in countless aspects of everyday life. This is felt most acutely in Berlin, where an easterner working on the next block from his western colleague is paid only 70–80 per cent of his colleague's salary. And the PDS, rather than the heirs of the opposition in the Alliance '90, has become the vehicle of this resentment: the party of eastern protest.

Moreover, the PDS is revelling in the luxury of dissidence, without the risk of persecution (whereas the true dissidents in the GDR were fiercely prosecuted by the ruling communist party from which the PDS was born). It is the gamekeeper turned poacher. Its leaders gather all the available arguments against all the established parties, without worrying unduly about internal coherence or a serious programme for government. The past master of this kind of left-wing populism is Gregor Gysi. The diminutive, fast-talking Jewish lawyer, son of a high-ranking official in the old communist hierarchy, is a Mephisto-phelean figure. Evidence continues to emerge of how, as a lawyer in communist East Germany, he cooperated closely with the Stasi. But, as a speaker, this miniature Mephisto is terrific – and, I would guess, almost single-handedly responsible for attracting the party's younger voters. (Almost a quarter of PDS voters are under thirty.)

I saw Gysi in action at the PDS's last election rally in Berlin. As I arrived, a warm-up band was singing 'Komm schlaf mit mir' ('Come, sleep with me'), which seemed appropriate. 'Once a whore, always a whore,' as Orwell remarked in a similar context. A bookstall displayed, among other wares, some of Stalin's works, at DM 10 a volume. I asked the bookseller whether he had many takers. 'Oh yes, people buy them out of historical interest. You see, they weren't available in East Germany for a long time.'

After speeches by Stefan Heym and two others, it was Gysi's turn. Speaking like a rapid-fire machine-gun, he presented the PDS as the only real party of opposition in Germany. He protested against a 'one-sided view' of the history of the GDR. Of course 'real socialism' had failed because of its own deficiencies, he said, but the alternative was not Herr Kohl but a truly democratic socialism. The east, he said, was being used as a laboratory for the dismantling of the welfare state.

Then there was foreign policy. Of course the Federal Republic had greater responsibilities, but what hypocrisy to call for German participation in peace-making missions when Germany is the third largest arms exporter in the world!

Then there was the growth of right-wing extremism, racism and anti-Semitism. How about changing the country's citizenship law? How absurd that a Turkish citizen living here for years (he was talking in Kreuzberg, where many Turks live) cannot vote, whereas a German from Argentina can come here for three months, vote for Helmut Kohl, and then go back to Argentina, leaving us with Kohl . . .

Then there was the dismantling of higher education. This must be stopped. Not that he was arguing for endless study. Helmut Kohl had taken sixteen semesters to get his doctorate. In the GDR, he, Gysi, was allowed only eight. 'The difference is clearly visible, but I try to make up for it by life experience.' At this remark even the policemen standing next to me were laughing.

Then there was the environment. Why didn't they keep up the East German system of recycling basic raw materials? Of course the GDR had done it for economic rather than ecological reasons. But it was still sensible. (No mention of the huge environmental damage in East Germany.)

Then there was the bureaucracy. 'I thought the GDR was the most bureaucratic country in the world. What a mistake!' The west German bureaucracy is much worse. (This is a complaint you hear from east Germans in every walk of life.)

And so on. A catalogue of well-made individual points, appealing to the particular experience of particular groups, above all in the east. And the whole spiced with acid wit. It doesn't add up to a policy. But in expressing radical populist opposition it is very effective.

Later I talk with one of the most distinguished of the former East German opposition leaders, the biochemist Jens Reich, about the PDS phenomenon. Like me, he finds it utterly repulsive that these former functionaries, hacks and Stasi narks are rearing their heads again, even behaving with some of their old arrogance. On the other hand, looking at it coolly, he concludes that it is better to have these people integrated into the democratic system than to have them working outside and against it. Better to have them inside the tent pissing out rather than outside pissing in, as President Lyndon Baines Johnson once elegantly observed.

After all, so the argument continues, that's what the Federal Republic did with the old Nazis after 1949: integrate them. Ah yes, comes the answer, but at least the old Nazis were working in newly constituted democratic parties, not in a direct successor to the Nazi Party, the NSDAP. Imagine, says a conservative politician, if the NSDAP had just renamed itself the PDSAN – and been voted back into parliament.

In practice, the PDS has so far only affected one major decision in national politics. It was the votes of the PDS members of the Bundestag that, in 1991, gave the narrow majority for the decision to move the capital to Berlin. Whether the PDS can establish itself as a more permanent feature of the political landscape will clearly depend on the progress of reconstruction and 'internal unification' in the east in general, and in the former East Berlin in particular. But for the period of the thirteenth Bundestag it will be a colourful, raucous, disturbing presence in Bonn, a presence indeed recalling – in a figure like Gysi – the radical left-wing politics of the Weimar republic, but also seen by many as 'the voice of the east'.

3

So much for the small but interesting margins. What of the large but boring centre? 'He's done it again' is, of course, the first thing to be said of Helmut Kohl, written off by many commentators at the beginning of the year, just as he was being written off by many, even in his own party, in early 1989. Five years ago, it was the way in which he seized the opportunity of unification that brought him back. This year it was three things.

First, it was his personal authority, conviction and energy. The Christian Democrats fought a presidential election campaign around Helmut Kohl: the colossus of Oggersheim, the 'chancellor of unity', the 'Bismarck in a cardigan'. His face alone stared down from the posters. For the first time ever, polls showed that he was more popular than his party. Indeed, some well-informed sources wonder what exactly will be left of his party when he is gone. By contrast, the Social Democrats had, rather late in the campaign, to bring in two other politicians – their last candidate for chancellor, Oskar Lafontaine, and the man who many think should be their next one, Gerhard Schröder – to stand beside the lacklustre Rudolf Scharping in a so-called leadership 'troika'.

Second, the economic upturn in west Germany and the signs of lasting economic recovery in east Germany came just in time to save Kohl's bacon. Napoleon famously asked about one of his generals the single, all-important question 'Is he lucky?' Helmut Kohl is lucky. In the west, he benefited from the familiar 'feel-good factor' at this point in the economic cycle. In the east, it was something more dramatic. Here he had been first adored and then reviled for his famous promise of 1990 to create 'blooming landscapes' within a few years. In fact, the transformation has been much slower and more painful than he predicted. Some 14 per cent of the east German labour force are still unemployed, and another 4 per cent hold artificial, government-subsidized jobs.

Nonetheless, if you travel through east Germany today it is one big building site. In a bold move, Helmut Kohl went back to every place where he had campaigned in the elections of 1990 and said, in effect, 'I told you so.' And enough people felt their own lives had in fact improved. So, in the east, the CDU got the most votes – more than 38 per cent to the SPD's 32 per cent. Altogether, any claim or perception that the PDS is the 'voice of the east' must be qualified by the plain fact that 80 per cent of the east German vote went to the established parties and the Alliance '90/Greens.

The third reason why Helmut Kohl won is that he managed ever so slightly to tar the Social Democrats with the communist brush. They foolishly gave him the opportunity to do so, by forming a minority government in one of the east German states, Sachsen-Anhalt, in coalition with the Alliance '90/Greens but depending on the votes (or abstention) of the PDS for its continuance in office. Aha, said Kohl, here is a fundamental break with the continuity of the democratic politics of the Federal Republic: a Social Democratic government that is there only on sufferance from the PDS. And, adapting a phrase of the early post-war Social Democratic leader Kurt Schumacher, he described the PDS as 'red-painted fascists'. This, Kohl said to the voters, is what you might get if you vote for the SPD. It was a tactical, some might even say a cynical, argument, and it is difficult to judge its precise effect. Perhaps in east Germany it even won the PDS a few more protest votes. But I think Kohl knew exactly what he was doing.

With this single argument he artfully polarized a contest in which, up to that point, the differences between the Christian Democrats and Social Democrats had been very blurred – so much so, in fact, that wits had combined the two leading candidates for chancellor into an imaginary 'Chancellor Kohlping'. At the same time, by summoning up the ghost of 'red-painted fascists' in a popular front with the SPD, he activated some deep-seated Cold War reactions and fears, reinforcing the feeling that it was safer to stick with the devil you know.

Yet it was still a close-run thing. In fact, the coalition got its working majority of ten only thanks to another peculiarity of the German electoral system. I said earlier – choosing my words carefully – that the percentage of second votes won by a party 'mainly determines' the number of seats it has in parliament. However, if a party gets more direct candidates elected in a particular state (*Land*) than it would be entitled to from its proportion of the second votes in that state, then those extra members enter the Bundestag as so-called 'overhang mandates'. The CDU/CSU got twelve 'overhang mandates' against the SPD's four, thus significantly increasing its majority.

Kohl himself immediately pointed out that Helmut Schmidt had governed for four years after 1976 with a majority of ten, and that Willy Brandt had come to power in 1969 with a majority of twelve. Yet Kohl knows as well as anyone that Brandt's majority was then pared down to almost nothing by defections in protest at his Ostpolitik. Narrow majorities sit uneasily with bold policies. And Kohl's position now is significantly weaker than Brandt's or Schmidt's was then.

4

To describe Kohl as already a 'lame duck' would, however, be once again to underestimate a man who has made a habit of being underestimated throughout his extraordinarily successful political career. Helmut Kohl is still the most formidable politician – and statesman – in Europe. He will not lightly be deflected from pursuing the last great task that he has set himself: to bind united Germany into a united Europe. In his view, the Maastricht Treaty was a crucial step in that direction.

However, the goal most important to Chancellor Kohl personally is not the top priority of most of his compatriots. A poll result published on election night showed 'foreign policy' at the very bottom of the list of issues that concerned the respondents. At the very top was job creation, then issues such as the restructuring of the welfare state, health care and the environment. Despite its strong economic recovery, Germany has daunting domestic problems. It clearly has to cut budgets in order to reduce the public debt, which has soared to

DM 2 trillion as a result of the costs of unification. It has to try to restore Germany's competitive edge in world export markets, which probably involves doing some of the things that Britain and America did in the 1980s – privatization, deregulation, and reducing employment costs and tax disincentives to enterprise. It has to work out what to do about long-term, structural unemployment: a problem common to all of Western Europe, but particularly sensitive because of the disproportionately larger number of long-term unemployed to be found in east Germany. Yet it is not only in east Germany that Gysi's polemic against a 'dismantling of the welfare state' will fall on fertile ground. And it is not only in west Germany that the Greens' ecological and feminist concerns will further complicate the process.

With the results of the elections, it is clear that, within the present political system, these issues can be addressed only by negotiation between all the established parties. In other words, this is the greatest test so far of what has long been the Federal Republic's greatest strength: its ability to achieve change through consensus. If the attempt fails, then next time round we may yet see a more significant flight of disillusioned voters from the boring centre to the interesting margins. Then, indeed, the Berlin republic might after all begin to look like Weimar.

But there we go again: worrying and warning, because of ghosts in the museum. The Federal Republic has proved the Cassandras wrong so many times before. Let's hope it can do so again. In any case, it's worth remembering that, when looking at Germany, most people from most of the world, even from quite prosperous countries in the West, will exclaim, 'If only we had your problems!'

Intellectuals and Politicians

Imagine a theatre critic who is suddenly hauled up from the stalls to act in the play he meant to review. What should he do then? Write the review without mentioning his own part? Appraise his own performance? This is the strange dilemma in which I find myself as I sit down to write this essay. Yet it is a dilemma curiously appropriate to the subject – as will, I trust, emerge. Let me explain.

Earlier this year I received a letter informing me that I had been elected an honorary member of Czech PEN. I was touched by the gesture. The letter also invited me to attend the Sixty-first World Congress of International PEN, which would be held in Prague in November.

Now there is a great deal to be said against attending any international congress of writers, anywhere, any time. But Prague is a city where writers and intellectuals, especially the numerous banned writers and intellectuals, published only in samizdat or in the West, had a singular importance up to 1989. This occasion would take place five years to the month after the 'revolution of the Magic Lantern'[1] that had catapulted many of them quite unexpectedly into positions of power, which some retain but others have in the meantime left or lost. Those characteristic post-communist mutations, dilemmas and ironies are concentrated – almost as in an archetype – in the person of the writer-president Václav Havel. All this, I thought, might make this particular writers' congress more than usually interesting.

It did.

I

On the plane out, I looked back through my notebooks from the heady days of November 1989 in the Magic Lantern theatre, and recalled the leading actors in the play then directed by, and starring, Václav Havel. Among my visiting cards I found one given me in the Magic Lantern by someone who, at the time, had only a minor part – as an economist prized for his professional expertise by the writers, philosophers, journalists and historians then leading the Civic Forum. I have the card before me as I write. Actually nothing more than a typewritten slip of paper, it reads, 'Dr Václav Klaus, Head of Department for Macroeconomic Analysis, Institute for Forecasting, Czechoslovak Academy of Sciences'.

In Prague, I soon found that the position of intellectuals was very much a live subject and one that, like so many others in the Czech lands today, had come to be politicized around the, so to speak, magnetic polarity between the two Václavs, now better known as President Havel and Prime Minister Klaus. Havel was understood to be calling for the voice of independent intellectuals to be heard more clearly, enriching the country's political debate. Klaus, the intellectual anti-intellectual, was heard to be sceptical of this notion, both on general grounds and because Havel was for it.

I talked briefly to the prime minister in the days before the PEN congress opened. Dr Klaus received me in his tastefully appointed office, its walls decorated with framed honorary doctorates, prizes and photographs of himself with very important persons. In the course of an interesting conversation, mainly about Europe, he thrust into my hands a selection of his lectures and speeches from the last three years, which he had got his office to type up, photocopy and bind. This collector's item of, as it were, prime-ministerial samizdat – entitled *Dismantling Socialism: An Interim Report* – well documents his characteristic mixture of sharp economic analysis and bold political salesmanship. Helpfully, he pointed out the best pieces.

The PEN congress itself was opened by President Havel. Welcoming his fellow writers from around the world 'first and foremost as a colleague and only secondarily as a representative of the Czech Republic', he went on to express the hope that our presence would 'introduce important spiritual and intellectual stimuli into this sometimes too materialistic and somewhat provincial setting'. Intellectuals, he argued, have a responsibility to engage in 'politics in the broadest sense of the word'. And not just in the broadest sense:

I once asked a friend of mine, a wonderful man and a wonderful writer, to fill a certain political post. He refused, arguing that someone had to remain independent. I replied that if you all said that, it could happen that in the end no one will be independent, because there won't be anyone around to make that independence possible and stand behind it.

However, 'I am not suggesting, dear colleagues, that you all become presidents in your own countries, or that each of you go out and start a political party.' But we should, he suggested,

gradually begin to create something like a worldwide lobby, a special brother-hood or, if I may use the word, a somewhat conspiratorial mafia, whose aim is not just to write marvellous books or occasional manifestos but to have an impact on politics and its human perceptions in a spirit of solidarity, and in a coordinated, deliberate way . . .

He continued:

Politicians – at least the wiser ones – will not reject such activity but, on the contrary, will welcome it. I, for instance, would welcome hearing, in this country, a really strong and eloquent voice coming from my colleagues, one that could not be ignored no matter how critical it might be, a voice that did more than merely grumble, or engage in esoteric reflection, but became a clear public and political fact.

He then concluded with an eloquent appeal for us all to stand up for Salman Rushdie, for Wole Soyinka, and for Bosnian intellectuals.

Emboldened by this speech, the assembled PEN delegates could begin their usual round of reports, resolutions and the all-important business of supporting persecuted and imprisoned writers – work in which Czech writers who had themselves long been persecuted or imprisoned could now join. But you could see at once (though I'm not sure how many of the international PEN delegates did see at once) that Havel's speech was addressed to the domestic audience as much as to us. And it was a blow – a pen-thrust – at Klaus, whom Czech readers, radio listeners or television viewers would immediately understand not to be among those 'wiser' politicians who would welcome independent intellectual criticism.

Indeed, that very day Czech readers could find in the newspaper *Lidové Noviny* a column by Václav Klaus rejecting, in the name of liberalism, the demand recently made by a group of intellectuals that the showing of violence on television be regulated by the state. President Havel had come out in support of the intellectuals' petition.

In the evening, the prime minister, who as a regular newspaper columnist and essayist is himself a member of Czech PEN, gave a reception for the PEN delegates. His speech of welcome was also in part an answer to Havel's welcome speech in the morning, thus producing further symptoms of slight bafflement among those delegates who thought they were just attending a writers' congress. As we left the reception, officials distributed free copies of two books (in Czech) by Klaus, almost as if to say, 'Look, *he* writes books too!' One of the books is called *Why am I a conservative?*[2] and begins with a glowing tribute to Margaret Thatcher, entitled 'Inspiration'.

The next day there was a panel discussion on the very general theme of 'Intellectuals, Government Policy and Tolerance' in a large hall at the foreign ministry. The most prominent panellist was none other than the writer-premier Václav Klaus. He was joined on the platform by the Hungarian essayist György Konrád (himself a former president of International PEN, and someone who has written extensively on the role of intellectuals), the Czech novelist Ivan Klíma, writers from Germany, Sweden and Turkey, and myself. Extracts from the discussion were to be broadcast on Czech television. Good press coverage for the prime minister among these intellectuals would no doubt enhance his public image, which might be useful in the imminent local-government elections. In fact, the prime minister was going straight from this discussion to campaign for his party in the provinces.

Before the discussion we were handed copies of an essay on tolerance, nicely printed in five languages. And who was the essay by? Comenius? John Locke? Voltaire? No, by Václav Klaus. That philosopher of tolerance then opened the discussion with a remarkable short statement in which he announced that in a free country, such as the

Czech Republic had now become, the distinction between 'dependent' and 'independent' intellectuals no longer had any real importance. Some intellectuals were in politics, others not. Expert advice was always welcome. But it made no sense to speak any more about a special role for 'independent' intellectuals.

Now the critic was hauled on stage. For this sally could not go unanswered. I began my reply by saying that it was both appropriate and moving to discuss the subject of 'Intellectuals, Government Policy and Tolerance' in Prague, where, for twenty-one long years, from the Soviet invasion of 1968 until the 'velvet revolution', some individual Czechs – and Slovaks – had given us a shining example of what intellectuals can do in opposition to a repressive state. The names of Jan Patočka and Václav Havel must stand for many, many more whom I would have liked to name.

Five years on, however, we happily found ourselves in very different times in Central Europe. What was the role of intellectuals now? I argued, against Klaus, that independence is a crucial attribute of what it should mean to be an intellectual. Not just in a dictatorship but precisely in a liberal, democratic state, independent intellectuals have a crucial role to play.

There should be, I suggested, a necessarily adversarial (but not necessarily hostile) relationship between the independent intellectual and the professional politician. The intellectual's job is to seek the truth, and then to present it as fully and clearly and interestingly as possible. The politician's job is to work in half-truth. The very word 'party' implies partial, one-sided. The Czech word for party, '*strana*', meaning literally 'side', says it even more clearly. Of course, the opposition parties then present the other side, the other half of the truth. But this is one of those strange cases where two halves don't make a whole.

The position of a non-executive president or constitutional monarch may, I noted, be a partial exception to this rule. Such a person, standing above party politics, may contribute to setting certain higher intellectual or moral standards in public life. But as a rule there is a necessary and healthy division of labour in a liberal state between independent intellectuals and professional politicians. Arguably this is as important as the formal separation of powers between executive, legislature and judiciary. It is part of the larger and all-important creative tension between the state and civil society.

Having made my main point about 'intellectuals', I commented briefly on the other words in the theme that PEN had asked us to discuss: 'government policy and tolerance'. The liberal state – but mainly the legislature and the judiciary rather than the executive branch of government – may sometimes have to limit the freedom of the enemies of freedom. If, say, a private television channel were to mix popular light entertainment with consistent advocacy of the extermination of gypsies, a liberal state should stop it being used for that purpose. If a writer is threatened from abroad with assassination, like Salman Rushdie, the government has a duty to protect him.

Beyond this, however, the contribution of politicians in power to 'tolerance' lies less in specific acts or policies than in a certain attitude and style of political conduct. No politician likes being criticized. Mrs Thatcher would often complain about 'the media'. Her successors blame 'the chattering classes', which, I noted, is the current English phrase for intellectuals. Yet the closer the politicians can stick to the attitude summed up in the famous phrase 'I do not agree with what you say, but I will defend to the death your right to say it', the more secure freedom will be. This, I suggested, is where the business of PEN and the business of prime ministers meet.

Now if these thoughts were expressed around a seminar table at Harvard or Oxford they might be questioned for their simplicity or banality, but they would hardly be thought provocative.[3] Here, with the Czech television cameras rolling and the famously arrogant prime minister locked in this strange intellectual-political wrestling match with his own president, they were accounted so.

Dr Klaus was not amused by my comments. He wanted to reply immediately. He sat fuming while our strong-minded American chair-woman let all the other panellists have their turn. Then he let rip. In his essay on tolerance he had written, 'The responsibility of a tolerant person is to listen attentively to others and to attempt to understand what they are saying.' This was not my experience of Dr Klaus. Instead, I found him a sharp political debater, happy to twist an argument in order to score a point. But then, what else would you expect of a politician sitting in front of TV cameras at the beginning of an election campaign?

Yet, by behaving in this way, he actually made my point far more effectively than I could myself. If he had listened attentively and then calmly made a reasoned argument in response to mine, he would have brilliantly illustrated his own proposition that there is no fundamental difference or clear dividing line between the roles of independent intellectual and professional politician. There he would have been: a professional politician, yet arguing as an intellectual among intellectuals . . .

But, instead, he began by exclaiming, in his peculiarly effective tone of aggressive exasperation, that he found what I had said 'incredible'. He knew me as an intellectual, an essayist, he said, but I had just delivered a 'political speech'. But there again he was, in a backhanded way, making my point. For the criticism has meaning only if there is, indeed, a fundamental difference between an intellectual speech and a political speech, between the way intellectuals use words and the way politicians do.

He went on to say that there is nothing worse than an intellectual delivering a political speech. Politicians may not like to be criticized, he observed, but do intellectuals? And he also found 'incredible' my observation that politicians 'live in half-truth'. This was a rather revealing misquotation, since one of the most famous leitmotifs in the whole Central European debate about intellectuals and politics is Václav Havel's pre-1989 formula 'living in truth'. But what I said was that politicians *work* in half-truth.[4] The phrase characterizes the professional party politician's job, not his life.

No politician worthy of the name will seriously maintain in private that what he has said in a public, party-political speech is the whole truth on a particular issue. It may possibly have been the truth; it might even have been nothing but the truth; but it is most unlikely to have been the whole truth – or he will not be a very effective party politician. Every time a politician says to a journalist 'Off the record . . .' he is recognizing this elementary fact about his profession. Off the record, Václav Klaus would doubtless acknowledge this.

Here I need to explicate two issues which were not clarified in the subsequent discussion – partly, I would have to add as a critic, through my own fault. Both were raised by Ivan Klíma, in interventions which effectively supported his prime minister. First, Klíma objected to what he saw as the implication that intellectuals are morally superior to politicians, or somehow possessed of 'Truth' with a capital T. We have heard too much of these claims, especially in Central Europe, suggested Klíma, in a discussion which we had begun earlier and subsequently continued in private.

Look what a mess intellectuals in power have made of things! Look at the damage done by their utopias! And look what monsters they have been in their private lives! In which connection he quoted Paul Johnson's book *Intellectuals*. The charge about private lives is probably the least pertinent, but there is much in the rest of the indictment. Intellectuals obviously do bear a heavy load of responsibility as architects or accomplices of some of the greatest political crimes of the twentieth century. As George Orwell caustically observed of fellow-travelling intellectuals, 'No ordinary man could be such a fool.'

Yet I am not making any such high moral, let alone ideological or metaphysical, claim for intellectuals. Many politicians are no doubt better people than many intellectuals. They may also be more intelligent, better read, more cultured. My argument is only that they have, and should have, a different role, which is reflected, crucially, in a different use of language. If a politician gives a partial, one-sided, indeed self-censored account of a particular issue, he is simply doing his job. And if he manages to 'sell' the part as the whole then he is doing his job effectively.

If an intellectual does that, he is not doing his job: he has failed in it. The intellectual is not the guardian or high priest of some metaphysical, ideological or pseudo-scientific Truth with a capital T. Nor is he simply the voice of the 'ethics of conviction' (*Gesinnungsethik*) against the politician's 'ethics of responsibility' (*Verantwortungsethik*), to use Max Weber's famous distinction. But he does have a qualitatively different responsibility for the validity, intellectual coherence and truth of what he says and writes.

I therefore have an answer to the question which Ivan Klíma injected into the discussion: 'What do you mean by an intellectual?' What I mean is a person playing a particular role. It is the role of the thinker or writer who engages in public discussion of issues of public policy, in politics in the broadest sense, while deliberately not engaging in the pursuit of political power.

I certainly don't mean all members of the 'intelligentsia', in the broad sociological definition of 'intelligentsia' officially adopted in communist Eastern Europe; that is, everyone with higher education. Nor do I mean the 'intellectuals on the road to class power' of György Konrád and Ivan Szelényi's book of 1974.[5] Or the pre-1989 Václav Klaus, an employee of the Czechoslovak Academy of Sciences under President Husák. These were all intellectuals, but in a different sense.

My description of the intellectual's role, which is both a Weberian ideal type and simply an ideal, certainly has more in common with the self-understanding of the opposition intellectuals in Central and Eastern Europe before 1989; of the pre-1989 Václav Havel (who barely qualified as an 'intellectual' in communist sociology, since he had scant formal higher education and for a time did manual labour); of the patriotic Polish, Czech or Hungarian 'intelligentsia', in their idealistic, pre- and anti-communist interpretation of their own role. Yet it differs also fundamentally from this. In the 'abnormal' conditions which have actually been normality for much of Central Europe over much of the last two centuries, intellectuals have been called upon, or have felt themselves called upon, to take roles that they did not take in the West. The conscience of the nation. The voice of the oppressed. The writer as priest, prophet, resistance fighter and substitute politician.

Since the liberation of 1989, all these extra roles have fallen away, with stunning rapidity. This is healthy, and long overdue. As Brecht's Galileo exclaims, 'Unhappy the land that has need of heroes.' The role of the intellectual as critic of a democratically elected government cannot be equated with that of the intellectual as leader of the opposition against an alien, totalitarian power. But I am deeply convinced that Hans Morgenthau expressed a universal and not a particular truth when he observed: Truth threatens power and power threatens truth. That applies not just to totalitarian or authoritarian power, as described in Václav Havel's great essay 'The Power of the Powerless', but also, albeit to a lesser degree, to democratically elected and constitutionally limited power.

Now, obviously, this ideal of the intellectual has never fully been achieved. Indeed, as the twentieth century closes, the catalogue of the *trahison des clercs* is a thick volume; the list of those who preserved real independence is a thin one. In our own free societies, we see examples of journalists who have been corrupted by their proximity to power. American academics will perhaps know, in their own universities, scholars who have politically trimmed their analyses, or at least their conclusions, in the hope of following Kissinger or Brzezinski to a job in Washington. But to say that an ideal has never been fully achieved is merely to say that it is an ideal.

We have Orwell. We have Raymond Aron. We have other writers, academics and journalists who have maintained a high standard of intellectual independence while engaging in political debate. Even in a free society, there is still an important part to be played by the *spectateur engagé*. By the critic on stage.

2

And by the playwright on stage? Václav Havel was, of course, the invisible panelist in our discussion. Klaus certainly interpreted much of what I said in the light of his running argument with Havel. Doubtless many Czech listeners did. And from what I have written so far you might also think that I was, so to speak, taking Havel's part – breaking a lance for Václav I against Václav II. That would be a misunderstanding.

It is wholly true that I feel strong ties of admiration for and friendship with Václav Havel. It will also be clear that I think he is right to argue that independent intellectuals should take an active part in the public life of a democracy. Yet I also have a serious disagreement with him about the role that intellectuals can play in politics, in the narrow sense of competing for power and holding office. The sharp distinction I drew on that panel between the roles of the intellectual and of the politician is one that ever since Havel became president of Czechoslovakia at the end of 1989 he has consistently refused to accept. As it happened, I went straight from the panel discussion in the foreign ministry to a lively private discussion with the president on precisely this issue, in the more congenial surroundings of a riverside pub. (György Konrád also came from the panel to the pub, and joined cannily in the debate.)

Now on this particular issue a discussion with Havel is obviously far more important than any argument with Klaus. Klaus will be judged on his record as a politician, and on his very considerable achievements in the rapid transformation of the Czech economy. Despite his at times almost comical desire to be taken seriously as a writer, his views on intellectuals are, so to speak, an optional extra. By contrast, the subject is central to Havel's whole life and work. His essays, lectures and prison letters from the last quarter-century are, taken altogether, among the most vivid, sustained and searching explorations of the moral and political responsibility of the intellectual produced anywhere in Europe. Indeed, it is difficult to think of any figure in the contemporary world who has more cumulative authority to speak on this issue than Václav Havel.

If you said 'the intellectual and politics' in the 1960s, the immediate free association might be 'Sartre' or perhaps 'Bertrand Russell'. Say it now, whether in Paris, New York, Berlin or Rome, and one of the first associations will be 'Havel'. If he is right, what he says will be important not just for the Czech lands; if he is wrong, it matters for the rest of us too.

Fortunately, I don't just have to rely on a pub conversation for this judgement. Three volumes of Havel's speeches have now appeared in Czech, and a Prague publisher has just issued a selection in English, entitled *Toward a Civil Society*.[6] Although the English selection is heavily biased towards his major foreign appearances, and to that extent gives a slightly misleading impression of what he has been doing for the last five years, it does contain the most important and systematic statements of his views since he became president. Havel told me that he regards his presidential speeches as the intellectual continuation of the essays, lectures and prison letters of the dissident years. 'Then I wrote essays, now I write speeches,' he said, suggesting that only the form of what he does with words has changed, not the essential content of the intellectual activity.

Certainly as presidential speeches go these are extraordinary. Extraordinary in the range of subjects they address, from Maastricht to the

Anthropic Cosmological Principle, from European security to the legacy of the Czechoslovak security police, from Kafka to the need for a higher something which Havel cannot quite bring himself to call God. Extraordinary in their literary quality. Extraordinary in their frank and vivid insights based, like his earlier work, on a kind of wry agonizing about his own existential dilemmas. Since his present dilemma – or, at least, one of them – is that of the intellectual in politics, there is much on that in his speeches. And sometimes in unlikely places.

Nearly two years ago, a mutual friend brought me, with the president's greetings, the typescript of a speech delivered in the Asahi Hall in Tokyo in April 1992, and now reproduced in this volume. The speech is devoted to the place of the intellectual in politics. Having described the peculiar post-communist situation in which 'poets, philosophers, singers became members of Parliament, government ministers or even presidents', he proceeds to take issue with 'a British friend of mine' who 'has said that one of the biggest problems of the post-communist states lies in the inability of their leaders to make up their minds about who they are. Are they independent intellectuals or practising politicians?'

Having explained that he understands only too well what I have in mind, he goes on to ask if this may actually be 'not a dilemma, but a historic challenge? What if in fact it challenged them to introduce a new tone, a new element, a new dimension into politics?' Based on their specific experience under totalitarianism, might they not inject 'a new wind, [a] new spirit, a new spirituality . . . into the established stereotypes of present-day politics?' Faced with the huge challenges of overpopulation, poverty, pollution, ethnic and social unrest, what is needed is a change 'in the sphere of the spirit, of human consciousness and self-knowledge . . .'

Politics is increasingly becoming the domain of specialists, but it should be the domain of people,

with a heightened sense of responsibility and heightened understanding for the mysterious complexity of Being. If intellectuals claim to be such people, they would virtually be denying the truth of that claim if they refused to take upon themselves the burden of public offices on the grounds that it would mean dirtying their hands. Those who say that politics is disreputable in fact help make it so.

He does not know, he says in conclusion, who will be proved right, but he regards it as 'a challenge to take a great risk and launch a great adventure. It is up to those of us whom fate has put in this position to demonstrate whether my British friend has shown foresight, or has simply been too influenced by the banal idea that everyone should stick to his own trade.'

Heaven only knows what the Japanese audience made of the president from Prague conducting a long-range discussion with someone in Oxford from a platform in Tokyo. But the result is certainly one of the clearest and fullest statements of his position. Elsewhere he restates and elaborates on various parts of it. Right at the outset, in his 1990 new year's address, he expresses the hope that the new Czechoslovakia can 'permanently radiate love, understanding, the power of the spirit and of ideas', with a new version of the founding president Tomáš Garrigue Masaryk's concept of politics based on morality. ('Jesus, not Caesar,' as Masaryk famously wrote.)

'If the hope of the world lies in human consciousness,' Havel tells a joint session of the US Congress in February 1990, 'then it is obvious that intellectuals cannot go on forever avoiding their share of responsibility for the world and hiding their distaste for politics under an alleged need to be independent.' And he says there what he repeated in opening the PEN congress nearly five years later: that if everyone remained independent then in the end nobody would be independent.

Perhaps his most remarkable treatment of the subject, however, is a speech he delivered in Copenhagen in May 1991. Here he confronts head-on what he calls the 'diabolical' temptations of power. He now finds himself, he writes,

in the world of privileges, exceptions, perks, in the world of VIPs who gradually lose track of how much a streetcar ticket or butter costs, how to make a cup of coffee, how to drive a car and how to place a telephone call. In other words, I find myself on the threshold of the very world of the communist fat cats whom I have criticized all my life. And worst of all, everything has its own unassailable logic.

'Someone who forgets how to drive a car, do the shopping, make himself coffee and place a telephone call is not the same person who had known how to do those things all his life.' The politician becomes 'a captive of his position, his perks, his office. That which apparently confirms his identity and thus his existence in fact subtly takes that identity and existence away from him.' This is vintage Havel, probing through a combination of ironical observation and agonized introspection to a larger truth, as he did in 'The Power of the Powerless'. It hints at a great essay to come: on the powerlessness of the powerful.

Yet the conclusion of this speech is surprising. It does not follow, he says, 'that it is not proper to devote oneself to politics because politics is in principle immoral'. What follows is that politics requires people of higher responsibility, taste, tact and moral sensitivity. 'Those who claim that politics is a dirty business are lying to us. Politics is work of a kind that requires especially pure people, because it is especially easy to become morally tainted.'[7]

He returns to the theme in a speech at New York University in October 1991, comparing himself to a literary critic well known for his sharp judgements who is suddenly called upon to write a novel. First he quotes his own refutation of the charge that politics is 'an essentially disreputable business':

Of course, in politics, as anywhere else in life, it is impossible and pointless to say everything, all at once, to just anyone. But that does not mean having to lie. All you need is tact, the proper instincts, and good taste. One surprising experience from 'high politics' is this: I have discovered that good taste is more useful here than a degree in political science.

(This may be less surprising to anyone who has studied political science.)

Then he notes that in the few weeks since he wrote those words 'fate played a joke on me. It punished me for my self-assurance by exposing me to an immensely difficult dilemma. A democratically elected parliament passed a bill I considered to be morally flawed, yet which our constitution required me to sign.' This was the so-called 'lustration' bill, which, as Havel explains, banned from public service whole categories of people who had been implicated in the communist regime, with inadequate rights of individual appeal. He describes his

163

decision: to sign the bill and then propose an amendment to parliament.

He does not know, he concludes, whether his decision was the right one, whether this part of the 'novel' he is writing would meet the standards he set earlier as a critic. 'History can probably be the only judge of that.' He still does not think that politics requires one to behave immorally. 'My latest experience, however, makes me want to underline five times a sentence that, until a few weeks ago, I thought unnecessary to underline even once: that the way of a truly moral politics is neither simple nor easy.'

Six months later comes the Tokyo long-range argument with me, which is, so far as I can judge, his last major stab at this issue before his resignation as the president of a now clearly dissolving Czechoslovakia in July 1992. (The English edition rather glosses over this discontinuity, but what is described as his 'abdication speech' can be found in the relevant Czech volume.[8]) Since he came back to the Castle as president of the Czech Republic in January 1993, courtesy of the votes of Václav Klaus's party, and with much reduced powers, he has returned to the theme on various occasions, most recently in his welcome speech to the PEN congress, but without, so far as I can see, adding significant new elements to his argument.

I have quoted what Havel has to say on this subject at some length, because his reflections are always interesting, but also because only through extensive quotation does a problem become apparent. The problem is that what he has to say is often vague and confused, and this analytical confusion reflects a deeper confusion about his own role.

In his PEN speech, for example, he confuses the intellectual's engagement in politics in the broader sense (that is, without being directly involved in the pursuit of power or office) and in the narrower sense (the anecdote about urging his writer friend to take office). But, as I argued against Klaus, the distinction is very important.

The argument in the Copenhagen speech is also confused. Is he saying that politics is or is not a dirty business? If it isn't a dirty business, then why should it require exceptionally 'pure' people to get involved without being corrupted? Anyway, why should we imagine that intellectuals are any better equipped to resist the temptations of power, to remain decent, upright and uncorrupted, than ordinary mortals? One might well argue, with Ivan Klíma, quite the contrary: the record of intellectuals in power in the twentieth century suggests that they are among the least likely to resist the insidious poison, precisely because they are most able to rationalize, intellectualize or philosophically justify their own submission or corruption by referring to higher goals or values. Orwell's faith in 'ordinary men' may also be misplaced, but the history of Europe in the twentieth century gives us no grounds for believing that intellectuals will do any better.

The argument about the irresponsibility of not taking political responsibility is also a highly questionable projection from the very particular situation of post-communist Central Europe, and specifically of V. Havel, to the general one. Of course, in the unique situation of 1989, in countries where the only alternative to the *nomenklatura* was a new political elite drawn largely from the ranks of more or less independent intellectuals, it would have been shirking responsibility not to take office. 'Someone had to' is, for the year 1990, an entirely valid observation. But even then it could be the polite and, as it were, PC (or, rather, MC – morally correct) guise for personal ambition. Lech Wałęsa's '*Nie chcę, ale muszę*' ('I don't want to, but I must') has become proverbial in Poland. In any case, this is the particular problem of a particular historical moment. As a new class of professional politicians emerges, there is no reason at all why those intellectuals who do not feel comfortable in professional politics – with its different rules of play, its different way with words – should not return to their desks, laboratories or studios.

Then there is Havel's powerful argument about the need to change consciousness. But why need intellectuals be in politics in order to change the consciousness of their own societies or a wider world? To be sure, it is good to have politicians with a larger vision. In conversation, Havel mentions the examples of de Gaulle, Adenauer and Churchill. But, if the point is to change consciousness, then the classics of the samizdat reading list – Orwell, Hayek, Popper and, of course, Havel – have done as much or more. You don't have to be a president or a prime minister to change consciousness. In fact, you may stand a rather better chance if you're not.

There remains the general claim about introducing a new moral, intellectual and spiritual dimension into our routinized, specialized, unimaginative party politics – a 'new wind', to recall Havel's own metaphor. At this point, at the latest, one has to turn from the writing to the man. For Havel now differs fundamentally from most writers or philosophers, in that the test case of the truth of the propositions he is advancing is himself. As he constantly points out, the test of what Václav Havel argues in these speeches is what Václav Havel does as president – which is, of course, now mainly to give speeches.

3

So how far has Havel achieved the very high goal that he set himself five years ago? Particularly in his first two years as president of Czechoslovakia, the achievement was immense. Through his words and deeds, he both preached and practised a resolute and morally sensitive moderation, civility, tolerance and decency which contributed a huge amount to the peaceful, civilized nature of the transition from communism in Czechoslovakia. There was nothing inevitable about this. Were it not for him, it could have been much messier, dirtier, even bloody. Beyond that, he has been an extraordinary and much needed voice in Europe, and beyond. While the response of West European leaders to what happened five years ago was woefully inadequate, while they fiddled as Yugoslavia began to burn, he has constantly and eloquently reminded us of the larger historical dimensions of what has happened in Europe, and – if one can say this without too much pathos – of our duty.

Of course he did not become Plato's philosopher-king, or even, to take the obvious comparison, a second Masaryk. At times he does seem to hold the peculiar Masarykian belief which Ernest Gellner ironically sums up as 'No State Formation without Philosophic Justification'. But he is not a systematic philosopher, and 1989 was not 1918. Yet, measured by any but the vertiginous standards he has set himself, the first two years of the playwright-king would be accounted a remarkable success.

Since then, however, and especially since his abdication in 1992 and his return as Czech president in 1993, it has been, to say the least, a more mixed picture. There are many reasons for this, but the one most relevant here is his refusal to choose between the roles of intellectual and politician.

If, when the Civic Forum broke up on the initiative of Václav Klaus in 1991, Havel had allowed himself to be clearly identified with the remaining movement, or some new political movement, or even – perish the thought – a political party, he would certainly have stretched the terms of his office, but he might also have had a real political power base as well as his own charisma and popularity. As it was, he refused to engage in those normal, partisan (and often dirty) politics. His power slipped away. Up came Václav II, on whose reluctant sufferance he was, in a quite humiliating way, elected Czech president in 1993, with very limited powers. Havel himself recalls with anger how members of the Czech parliament openly ignored him, reading newspapers or chatting, while he addressed them. Wryly, but with more than a touch of bitterness, he mutters, in English, the word 'clown'.

Yet, at the same time, his image and voice as an intellectual have become blurred. It's not just the suits and ties (in which he says he still feels uncomfortable), the ceremonial duties and the compromises, such as that on the 'lustration' law. It's not just the privileged isolation from ordinary life – the life in a velvet cage which he describes so vividly in his Copenhagen speech but which has nonetheless alienated many former close associates and friends. All that apart, there is simply the plain fact that a president's speeches are not a writer's essays. Text and context interact in a different and much less favourable way. Life contradicts art.

Even the outward form of *Toward a Civil Society* somehow speaks to us of the blurring of the voice that comes from the confusion of roles. The copyright page tells us this book is published with financial assistance from the Czech foreign ministry. Does a book by Havel really need a subsidy to be published? It comes with jacket endorsements from Zbigniew Brzezinski, Eduard Shevardnadze and one Thomas Klestil, who, readers may like to know, is the president of Austria. Does Havel really need to be puffed by a Klestil? The cover photograph shows a man in a pinstriped suit and tie speaking in front of the yellow-stars-on-blue-background of the Council of Europe and the EU. In other words, this book looks just like a professional politician's piece of government-subsidized vanity publishing – which, of course, it definitely is not. But it looks like it.

'The strongest poison ever known/ Came from Caesar's laurel crown,' wrote William Blake. I do not believe that Václav Havel has been poisoned by power in any normal sense. If mildly infected at all, it is in the rather unusual form of being, so to speak, aesthetically enamoured of the theatre of high politics – which, as he is the first to point out, is even more the theatre of the absurd than the most absurdist of his own plays.

Earlier this year I heard him give a brilliantly funny description of the stage management of President Clinton's visit to Prague, and, in particular, of his visit with Clinton to a typical Prague pub with a typical gathering of typical locals – all carefully identified by the American embassy beforehand. (The typical locals included the writer Bohumil Hrabal.) It was a wonderful foretaste of the book he might write when he ceases to be president. But I must admit that for a moment I did find myself uneasily wondering what the dissident writer Václav Havel would have made of such a stage-managed scene, what subtle lessons he would have drawn about the alienation of the powerful.

Probably the shortest and best retort ever made to Plato's vision of the philosopher-king is Kant's remark that for philosophers to become kings is neither desirable nor possible, because 'the possession of power unavoidably spoils the free use of reason'. Havel's case is an interesting variation on this eternal truth, because it seems to me that the greater threat to his free use of reason may actually be the relative *loss* of power he has experienced since 1992 – a loss which Václav Klaus misses no occasion to rub in. Havel is now fighting to regain some of the lost power, staking out his own political agenda in a series of speeches stressing the importance of education, local government, civic engagement, and so on. He now even seems prepared, at least on some issues, to be a focus for opposition to Klaus – an opposition which is to be found not least within the prime minister's own governing coalition. But to use his 'spoken essays' in this instrumental way would seem to be a departure from the standards he has set himself – and simply a sad come-down from his position five years ago.

Anyway, this is not a French-style *cohabitation*, where an executive president with great powers can, as it were, win the political battle. Havel's present constitutional position as non-executive president is more comparable with that of the president of the Federal Republic of Germany, an office held, until recently, by a man whom he much admires, Richard von Weizsäcker. In his *Summer Meditations*, Havel wrote that, in his dream vision of (as he then still hoped) Czechoslovakia, 'At the head of the state will be a grey-haired Professor with the charm of a Richard von Weizsäcker.' And as I read Havel's speeches, especially the more recent ones, I notice some similarities – not least in a small but revealing feature of the prose. The most characteristic feature of President von Weizsäcker's style was the rhetorical question. 'Of course my office only permits me to ask questions,' he would say, before launching a series of rhetorical questions which added up to an extremely clear statement of his own views. Am I imagining things, or is Havel increasingly using the same device?

One can take this particular comparison a stage further. It is an open secret that there was considerable tension between the patrician, Protestant, intellectual President von Weizsäcker and the provincial, Catholic and less ostensibly intellectual Chancellor Kohl. In private, they could be quite rude about each other. In public, some of President von Weizsäcker's elegant rhetorical questions could be understood as digs at the chancellor; some of the chancellor's remarks could be interpreted as barbs in the other direction. But they certainly never descended to anything like the public Punch and Judy show which the Klaus–Havel duel has at times become, with everyone knowing who is the unnamed object of each elliptical speech; every occasion being interpreted in that light; and ordinary Czechs sometimes having the impression that if Havel came out in favour of eating spinach then Klaus would be sure to come out the next day against eating spinach – on impeccable neo-liberal grounds, of course.

Instead, both Kohl and von Weizsäcker scrupulously observed the constitutional proprieties and, at best, tried to turn their differences into complementarity rather than discord. The result was one of the most effective double acts to lead any European state in recent history. It contributed very substantially to the peaceful achievement of

German unity. If the Czech president and prime minister were to achieve such a division of labour, it would doubtless be a great service to the Czech Republic – at home, in Europe and in the wider world.

To be sure, this, so to speak, Weizsäcker role would be some miles down from that new spiritual dimension which Havel dreamed, and perhaps still dreams, of introducing. Indeed, as the German example illustrates, in the wider European context it would not even be new. There is also a real question whether the ex-president of Czechoslovakia might not actually have a greater influence in Europe and the world today were he again able to speak with his own unique voice as an independent intellectual. But the die is cast. For another few years, at least, he will go on in the Castle, suffering up there for us; a living exemplar of the dilemmas of the intellectual in politics; condemned, like the central character in one of his own plays, to play out a role which he feels is not truly his own; and haunted and taunted by a slightly threatening character who even bears the same name. Such absurdist tricks the divine playwright plays.

4

With that somewhat Havelesque reflection, my Prague tale of intellectuals and politics is told, five years, almost to the day, after I told the story of the revolution of the Magic Lantern. Now, as then, I have tried to tell the story as honestly as I can, at the risk of indiscretion and of causing offence. Are there any conclusions to be drawn, any lessons, even? There are, I think, possible implications for the Czech Republic, for the position of intellectuals in post-communist Europe, and, most tentatively, for the place of intellectuals in Europe altogether.

For the Czech Republic the immediate question is, Can the premier and the president possibly achieve the kind of moderately harmonious public relationship which Kohl and Von Weizsäcker achieved? Almost certainly not. Since this is a new democracy, the constitutional roles are not as clearly defined by law or by precedent. The two have very different political views of the way the new Czech state should be built. Klaus, the Thatcherite, gives absolute priority to economic transformation, even at the cost of corruption and illegality on the way. 'Speed', he says, 'is more important than accuracy.' At times he seems inclined to Mrs Thatcher's view that 'society' does not exist. Havel, whose politics, inasmuch as they can be defined in ordinary terms, are those of an ecologically minded social democrat, stresses the importance of culture, local government, civic participation and civil society.

Above all, though, it is a clash of personalities, and biographies. The Tale of Two Václavs is not simply that of the intellectual Havel versus the politician Klaus. To be sure, Havel is a more important intellectual and Klaus a more effective politician. But what makes it so difficult is precisely that both are intellectuals in politics, as the PEN episode nicely illustrated.

This is what makes the story at once unique and representative, for all over post-communist Central Europe intellectuals are wrestling with similar dilemmas. Many who have gone into and remain in politics will find the dichotomy I present too sharp. The former dissident and former foreign minister Jiří Dienstbier, now the leader of a small opposition party, commented in a newspaper interview after our PEN discussion that, while he agreed with my basic argument, he did not feel that as a minister he had been working in half-truth. Those, now quite numerous, who after 1989 went into but are now again out of politics will find it easier to accept such a clear dichotomy. Those who never ventured into politics will find it easier still. But they have their own problems.

The intelligentsia – one of the characteristic phenomena of modern Central and East European history – is now everywhere engulfed in sweeping change. This world of 'circles of friends', of *milieux*, where artists, philosophers, writers, economists, journalists all felt themselves to belong to the same group, and to be committed to a certain common ethos (albeit often honoured in the breach), was something anachronistic in late-twentieth-century Europe – but also something rich and fine. Its extraordinary character was summed up for me in a phrase than Ivan Klíma used in describing how he and his fellow writers had set out to revive the dormant Czech PEN club in 1989. 'I was', he said, 'authorized by my circle of friends . . .' The peculiar world of the intelligentsia under communism was one in which you sought authorization from your circle of friends.[9]

Freedom has changed all that. With remarkable speed, the intelligentsia has fragmented into separate professions, as in the West: journalists, publishers, academics, actors, not to mention those who have become officials, lawyers, diplomats. The *milieux* have faded, the 'circles of friends' have dispersed or lost their special significance. Those who have remained in purely 'intellectual' professions – above all, academics – have found themselves impoverished. Moreover, it is the businessmen and entrepreneurs who are the tone-setting heroes of this time. Thus, from having an abnormal importance before 1989, independent intellectuals have plummeted to abnormal unimportance.

Yet to say that is to assume that we know what their 'normal' importance would be. But do we? Is there any wider European normality in this respect, towards which post-communist Central Europe might be either moving or contributing? In Britain the term 'intellectual' is rarely used, being regarded as something Continental and slightly pretentious. Yet, as Byron said of the word *'longeurs'*, though we have not the word, we have the thing in some profusion. And the things exist on both left and right – although here, as elsewhere, the right tends to identify the very idea of 'intellectuals' with the left.

In Germany, the days of the great public role of writers like Heinrich Böll and Günter Grass seem to be over. However, some of the country's most interesting political debates are actually conducted by intellectuals, on the *Feuilleton* pages of the *Frankfurter Allgemeine Zeitung* and in smaller journals. Yet here too you have the phenomenon of right-wing intellectuals denouncing 'the intellectuals', meaning left-wing intellectuals: in this case, for their failure to welcome the unification of Germany.

In France there have been writers and thinkers identified and identifying themselves as 'intellectuals' at least since the time of the Dreyfus affair and the *Manifeste des Intellectuels*. Yet I doubt that anyone would today venture to write a *Plaidoyer pour les intellectuels*, as Sartre did in 1972. Partly, no doubt, out of an awareness of the awful misjudgements and moral failures of intellectuals in the twentieth century – and not least French intellectuals, including, notably, Sartre. Partly because there are no obvious new utopias to be embraced – except utopian liberalism, which is a contradiction in terms. Partly, perhaps, because they are too busy appearing on television and generally competing in a crowded entertainment market.

Yet, at the same time, there is, in all the major West European countries, a real crisis of popular confidence in the professional politicians, seen to be out-of-touch, self-interested careerists, tainted by corruption. The Italian debacle haunts us all.

In this sense, Havel's call for a new spiritual and moral dimension to be introduced into politics might seem to be relevant, after all, for Western Europe. That was what many in Western Europe felt and hoped at the moment of the Magic Lantern five years ago. But the lesson is surely not that this is a time for intellectuals to enter politics, in the narrow sense of trying to become prime ministers or presidents. No, this is a time for intellectuals to be both resolutely independent and politically engaged – which means, among other things, criticizing prime ministers and presidents. Politely, of course. Constructively, wherever possible. But above all, clearly.

Four years later, in November 1998, Havel returned to this subject when receiving an honorary doctorate at Oxford. Referring in his acceptance speech to our earlier exchanges, he acknowledged that intellectuals have borne a heavy responsibility for some of the worst regimes in history. But he argued that, at a time when politicians tend to follow opinion polls and the media rather than to lead their citizens, there is a crying need for men and women of larger vision to enter politics. Intellectuals, he said, can participate in politics either by holding office or by holding up a mirror to those in power. You can be an office-holder or a mirror-holder. But I would continue to insist that a healthy democracy requires a very clear separation of roles between the two, and that the primary, even the defining, role of the intellectual in politics should be as mirror-holder.

Marta and Helena

It's November 1994, and we're at the Lucerna Palace in Prague, built by a millionaire developer in the early years of this century, expropriated by the communists, but now returned to his sons, Ivan and Václav Havel. Tonight's guest stars are the Golden Kids, a Sixties pop group who haven't performed together for nearly twenty-five years, since they were banned by the communist authorities after the Soviet invasion. They are Marta Kubišová, now aged fifty-three; Václav Neckář, fifty-two; and Helena Vondráčková, forty-seven. They wear black. They jive. They sing 'Hey Jude' and 'Massachusetts' and 'The Times They Are a-Changin'' and 'The Mighty Quinn' and even, God save us, 'Congratulations'.

The audience, like the Golden Kids, is middle-aged: men in sheeny suits, white shirts and ties, women in blouses, as if for the opera. They sweat amid the faded Jugendstil gilding and candelabra. Sometimes they clap along. But when the Golden Kids sing 'Suzanne' there's just total silence:

> Suzanne takes you down
> To her place near the river.
> You can hear the boats go by;
> You can spent the night beside her.

Tense and heavy with regret: the silence of the middle-aged remembering sex.

There's another story being played out on stage this evening: the story of Marta and Helena. Marta Kubišová was a Czech heroine of the Prague Spring in 1968. A song called 'Hymn for Marta' became a rallying song of the time. After the Soviet invasion, she was banned.

For twenty long years, until 1989, she did odd jobs, worked as a clerk, had close friends among the dissidents. In the middle of the 'velvet revolution' she made her first comeback – a moment I will never forget, at once rapturous and terribly sad. Barely able to sing, due to the engulfing emotion, she whispered into the microphone, '*Časy se mění*.' 'The Times They Are a-Changin'.'

Helena Vondráčková took a quite different path after 1969. She continued performing and was seen often on state television. She collaborated.

Now their paths have met again. Will virtue have its reward? Or does none of that matter any more? Helena – tall, blonde and still very much in practice – seems to dominate at first. She's younger, more professional, and the audience knows her from television. Perhaps they even feel a little easier with her, for most of them collaborated, too, or at least made little compromises to keep their jobs. Marta – older, shorter, black-haired – is a shade slower, and you feel the nervousness in her voice.

But, somewhere in the middle of the evening, the emotion begins flowing towards her. People bring bouquets of flowers up onstage after every number (opera habits), and the flower count is going Marta's way. Then the whole concert stops, and the stage is full of embarrassed men in suits. They represent Supraphon, Fiat, Interbanka, Seagram – the commercial sponsors of the evening. Awkwardly, they hand out platinum discs and bottles of champagne. And there's a raffle: first prize, a Fiat Punto. The prize-winners come up onstage, say a few words into the mike, and kiss the stars.

One, a comfortable-looking man in jeans, shambles up and says he'd like to thank all the performers, every one, 'but above all, above all, Mrs Kubišová'. And we all applaud loud and long, and we know what he's thanking her for, and it's not for her singing this evening – it's for her twenty years of silence.

But now everyone is sweating, and everything is mixed up together, the Marta of then and the 'Mrs Kubišová' of now, the pop heroes of the 1960s and the business heroes of the 1990s, the memories of sex and the memories of national protest, and today's hope of a Fiat Punto.

Yet there's an ever bigger circle closing here: a European circle. For these are also our songs: this is our past. Sixty-eight was one of those very rare moments when the experiences of people in Western and Eastern Europe really did meet. For all the differences between Prague and Paris, Liverpool and Leipzig, people under thirty here and there moved to the same rhythm, sang the same lyrics, shared something of the same protest, the same emancipation. Then the Russian tanks rolled in, and the paths of experience diverged, as did those of Marta and Helena, and the years slipped away.

Now, a quarter-century on, East and West have come together again, like Marta and Helena, here in the Havels' Lucerna Palace, in this postmodern stew of middle-aged longing and regret, under the sign of Seagram, and the shared meaning of history is:

Yeh yeh yeh yeh yeh yeh yeh da da da da
Hey Jude.

1994

25 October. British prime minister John Major announces an inquiry into standards in public life, headed by a senior judge, Lord Nolan. The 'Nolan committee'.

11 November. The USA announces that its troops will no longer enforce the arms embargo against Bosnia.

13 November. In a referendum, 52.2 per cent of Swedish voters approve their country joining the EU on the terms already negotiated.

15 November. The EU's Court of Auditors highlights the problem of fraud in the Common Agricultural Policy and the so-called 'structural funds'.

27–28 November. In a referendum, 52.4 per cent of Norwegian voters oppose their country joining the EU on the terms already negotiated.

9–10 December. An EU summit in Essen outlines the 'pre-accession strategy' for enlargement of the EU to include some former communist countries. It also discusses terms of the EU's relationship with states across the Mediterranean. Other major summit themes are improving competitiveness and creating jobs.

11 December. Russian forces invade the breakaway republic of Chechnya.

13 December. Italian prime minister Silvio Berlusconi is questioned by magistrates investigating corruption in three subsidiaries of his Fininvest business empire. Vladimír Mečiar becomes Slovak prime minister for the third time, leading a 'red–brown' coalition of right- and left-wing parties.

22 December. Berlusconi resigns as Italian prime minister after the Northern League withdraws its support from his coalition.

1995

1 January. Austria, Finland and Sweden join the EU. Establishment of the World Trade Organization. A four-month ceasefire in Bosnia, negotiated by former US president Jimmy Carter, comes into effect, but is ignored in Bihać, one of the UN's 'safe areas'.

9 January. Seven former members of the East German politburo, including former party leader Egon Krenz (see above, p. 3), are charged in connection with shootings at the Berlin Wall.

13 January. In Italy, former treasury minister Lamberto Dini forms a government, after the collapse of the Berlusconi government.

27–30 January. Davos, Switzerland. The World Economic Forum, an extraordinary annual gathering of business and political leaders, with a scattering of intellectuals thrown in for stimulation and entertainment. A giant ego-feast on Thomas Mann's 'magic mountain'. (His great novel *Der Zauberberg*, 'The Magic Mountain', was set here.) I have a memorable dinner with the financier and philanthropist George Soros, whom I know from his pioneering charitable work for open societies in central and eastern Europe. He is one of a very small group of people who have been good both at making money and at spending it.

We meet at a restaurant that is called, promisingly, *Der Zauberberg*, but turns out to be Chinese. Soros says he has always thought of himself as first and foremost a philosopher, not a money man. When he was still a poor exile, he took several years of his life to write a philosophical work called *The Burden of Consciousness*. But nobody really wanted to know. Then he went off and made his billions. Now everyone is eager to hear his lectures on philosophy; great universities and institutions vie to offer him a platform. Yet he can never quite be sure whether it is his philosophy that they are interested in or his money. In a way, his personal experience is an illustration of his own central philosophical principle, which he calls 'reflexivity'.

With its human and philosophical ironies, this seems to me a tale worthy of Mann's magic mountain.

Late January. Russia claims victory in Chechnya.

7 February. Polish prime minister Waldemar Pawlak resigns. He is succeeded by the post-communist Józef Oleksy, heading the same coalition of the post-communist Democratic Left Alliance and the Polish Peasant Party.

21 February. Belarus president Alexander Lukashenka signs comprehensive cooperation treaties with President Yeltsin. Substantial reintegration of Belarus with Russia.

22 February. Irish prime minister John Bruton and British prime minister John Major present a framework document for all-party constitutional talks on Northern Ireland, including proposals for a cross-border body.

12 March. The Hungarian government proposes drastic new austerity measures.

20–21 March. A pan-European 'Stability Pact' is signed in Paris.

26 March. The Schengen agreement comes into effect, abolishing border controls between France, Germany, Belgium, Luxembourg, the Netherlands, Spain and Portugal. 'Schengenland' is born.

7 April. In Poland, General Wojciech Jaruzelski is charged with involvement in the shooting of protesting workers in 1970.

29 April. The British Labour Party votes to replace Clause Four of the party's constitution, which had advocated 'common ownership of the means of production, distribution and exchange'.

1 May. Heavy fighting erupts in Grozny, capital of Chechnya, after Chechen forces return to the city.

1–2 May. Croat forces recapture the Serb-controlled enclave in eastern Slavonia.

7 May. Jacques Chirac wins the run-off election for the presidency of France. Alain Juppé is named as prime minister, heading a centre-right coalition government. In Bosnia, another attack on a market place in Sarajevo.

Catching the Wrong Bus?

Five years ago, in the euphoria at the end of the Cold War, it looked as if we could discern the shape of the twentieth century in Europe. That shape seemed to be a V. The line descended from the first and second Balkan wars before 1914, through what Churchill called Europe's second Thirty Years War, to the depths of Auschwitz and the Gulag, but then gradually rose again from mid-century, through the reconstruction of Western Europe to the liberation of Eastern Europe in 1989. For Poland, VE Day came only in the summer of 1989 – just forty-four years late. And for Germany, that autumn. 'Only today is the war really over,' said an improvised poster in East Berlin as the Berlin Wall came down. So in 1989 the shape of the century looked like a V for Victory. But since then the upward line has faltered, perhaps even turned downward, as we once again witness a Balkan war.

Fifty years on, we remember Britain's unique contribution to the Victory in Europe with wholly justified pride. But we had to fight that war partly because of an earlier British policy based on the mistaken belief that Britain could, by a diplomacy of detachment, insulate itself from those European quarrels in faraway countries of which Chamberlain knew nothing. Wrong then; even more wrong now.

So, fifty years after the end of what we still call *the* war in Europe, and five years after the end of the Cold War, what has Europe come to, and where, if anywhere, is it going? And is there, could there be, a British way of 'thinking Europe'?

Most contemporary British discussion of 'Europe' is not about Europe at all. At best, it is about EU-rope – that is, some aspects of the collective political and economic life of the western, northern and southern European states now organized in something rather misleadingly called the European Union. But mainly it is about Britain. Our so-called 'European debate' is part of a tortured national self-examination, an English, Scottish, Welsh and Irish agonizing about self. In this debate, 'Europe' appears as a threat to the very existence of Britain for (mainly English) 'Euro-sceptics' of the right; as a chance to transform the very nature of Britain for (often Scottish or Welsh) 'Euro-enthusiasts' of the left; as both opportunity and problem for the large centre; but for all sides as something basically external. There is 'Europe' over there and 'Britain' here, and the argument is about the relationship between them and us.

Penser l'Europe is a French book-title, inconceivable as a British one. Thinking Europe is an un-British activity. Those who do it, even as consenting adults in private, risk being stigmatized as 'Euro-intellectuals' – a neologism that neatly combines two things the British deeply distrust.

In the circumstances, it is not surprising that most of our Continental partners regard the very notion of 'a British idea of Europe' as a contradiction in terms. This is a pity. It is a pity for Britain: we lose influence because we are seen on the Continent to be opposed or at best marginal to the mainstream of European development. But it may also be a pity for Europe, since Europe, and especially EU-rope, could perhaps use a little more British thinking at the moment – with 'British' here meant in the deeper sense of our particular intellectual tradition: sceptical, empirical and pragmatic.

For 'Continental' ways of thinking about Europe also have their problems. To use a simple dichotomy of 'British versus Continental' would, of course, be to make precisely the British mistake. There is a huge variety of different ways of thinking about Europe across the Continent. Yet certainly there are some common characteristics of the main French and German approaches which have had a formative influence on the development of EU-rope over the past half-century.

Where British politicians make an artificial separation of the national and the European, ignoring the degree to which the two are already intertwined, French and German politicians utterly conflate the national and the European, so it is almost impossible to distinguish when they are talking about Europe and when about their own nations.

Now the instrumentalization of 'Europe' for the pursuit of national ends is an old European habit. Bismarck famously observed that he had always found the word 'Europe' in the mouths of those politicians who wanted from other powers something they did not dare demand in their own name. His conclusion was '*Qui parle Europe a tort. Notion géographique.*' British Euro-sceptics applaud Bismarck.

Yet in truth things are now a little more complicated. For in the half-century since 1945 there has also been a great deal of genuinely idealistic commitment to Europe among French and German politicians and opinion-formers – a commitment born from personal experience of revolution, war, genocide, defeat and occupation. The trouble is that the conflation of national and European – part instrumental, part idealistic – has become so habitual that they themselves sometimes don't quite know when they are talking about Europe and when about France or Germany.

Idealism in a different though related sense – the tendency to represent things in an ideal form rather than as they are: idealism as opposed to empiricism – is the other salient common characteristic of this French and German Euro-thinking. The 'Europe' of which they have spoken for the past half-century is an idea and an ideal, a dream, a vision or a grand design; this is *faire l'Europe, Europa bauen,* Europe as project, process, progress towards some *finalité européenne*; Europe as *telos*. At its most vertiginous, this comes as dialectical idealism. '*Europa der Gegensätze auf dem Wege zu sich selbst,*' proclaims a German publication: 'The Europe of contradictions on the way to itself.' Which, in English, makes about as much sense as 'The London of traffic jams on the way to itself.'

The difference between the teleological-idealistic and the empirical-sceptical approaches leads to profound misunderstandings. For the former, the great end justifies the often unsatisfactory means. Eurocratic nonsense from Brussels is a price worth paying for the larger political sense. But the teleologists are in trouble. In the Continental elites' building plans for EU-rope, from Messina to Maastricht, the *telos* was a substitute for the absent *demos* – with the hope of eventually contributing to the creation of a new European *demos*, from above, by education and example. But it has not happened. There is still no European people, or *demos*. And, after the signature of the Maastricht

Treaty, the peoples of the very heartlands of EU-rope turned to question what was being dished up in their name. 'For we are the peoples of Europe, that never have spoken yet,' as Chesterton might have written.

In this sense, EU-rope is perhaps now ready for a more (intellectually) 'British' approach. But is any constructive 'British' approach on offer? An approach, that is, which cares about Europe as Europe and not just as a threat or opportunity for a greater or lesser Britain. What follows is an attempt to 'think Europe' in English: to see Europe plain and to see it whole.

For a start, does Europe exist? This most ill-defined of continents has, after all, been open for long stretches of its history not just on one but on three sides: to the south across the Mediterranean, throughout most of what we call 'ancient history' and in some ways again today; to the east, where Europe does not end but merely fades away, into Asia; and to the west, across the Atlantic, especially in our post-1945 'West'. The 'globalization' caused by the technological developments of the past half-century further calls into question the coherence or validity of the unit 'Europe' as compared with smaller entities (state, region, firm) or larger ones (Eur-atlantic, OECD, world).

And what of its internal make-up? What are Europe's essential constituent parts? Its hundreds of millions of individual people who more or less – mainly less – identify themselves as 'Europeans'? Its regions? Classes? Societies? Nations and states? But to say 'nation states', as most British politicians do, obscures the huge diversity of European combinations of nation and state, from the national state, with citizenship rights conditional on membership of one dominant ethnic *Volk*, or the classic east European variant of ethnic nations distributed between several states, through the French civic *état-nation*, to Britain itself: a nation state containing several nations.

Nonetheless, in most of western, southern and now also northern Europe, these individuals, regions, societies, nations, but above all states are now organized in something new – EU-rope – which differs qualitatively both from any previous arrangement of states and from any current arrangement of states on any other continent. The nature of this arrangement is, however, very hard to define. The German

Constitutional Court has described it as a *Staatenverbund*. In English, we might call it a thing. This thing is less than a federal superstate but more than an alliance: an unprecedented, unique and horribly complex combination of the supranational and the intergovernmental, of economic integration and political cooperation.

This thing evolved in the Cold War, like Nato and with Nato, as the western half of a European order which we called in shorthand 'Yalta'. Its development was directly and indirectly influenced, to a degree many devoted advocates of European integration find hard to acknowledge, by that of the Cold War – and of détente, the Siamese twin of Cold War. But, five years ago, this 'Yalta' order ended in a way quite different from that in which previous European orders, whether of 'Versailles', 'Vienna' or 'Westphalia', had ended. Essentially, its eastern half just fell away, with the largely peaceful death of communism in Eastern Europe and the rather less peaceful dissolution of the Soviet Union. The western half remained intact – or at least apparently so.

So today this now slightly expanded western part, this EU-rope, with its fifteen states and some 370 million people, faces the other Europe from which it was so long insulated by the Iron Curtain. (For we lived, as the Hungarian writer György Konrád put it, with our backs to the Berlin Wall.) This other Europe may itself be very crudely subdivided into a second and a third Europe. The second Europe has in all some twenty states, of which fifteen have only recently been liberated from communism, and some 140 million people. The states of this second Europe, among which I do not include Turkey, are mainly small. Except for Poland and Romania, none has more inhabitants than Greater London, and most have far fewer. Most of them, or at least most of their political elites, more or less clearly want to join the Europe of the EU and Nato: to 'return to Europe', in the slogan of 1989. More important, their theoretical claim to belong, sooner or later, is more or less accepted by the political leaders of the EU – although with the emphasis in practice often on the less and later.

Clearly, this is to paint with a very broad brush. Having spent much of the past fifteen years trying to explain to Western readers that Prague, Budapest and Warsaw belong to Central and not to Eastern

Europe, I am the last person to need reminding of the immense differences between Poland and Albania. But to suggest that there is some absolutely clear historical dividing line between the Central European democracies in the so-called Visegrád group and, say, the Baltic states or Slovenia would be to service a new myth.

The third Europe comprises two much larger states, Russia and Ukraine, together with Belarus and perhaps also Serbia. They have a very large combined population of more than 210 million – or 220 million if one includes Serbia. These states are themselves, especially in the case of Russia, somewhat more ambivalent than the second Europe about their own historical belonging to Europe and their current desire to join the first Europe of EU and Nato. But, more important, the political leaders of the EU and Nato do not agree even on the long-term principle of these states' claim to membership.

Again, the division between the second and third Europes is crude, probably unfair to Ukraine, and may understate the long-term possibility of a democratic Serbia reorientated towards Europe. But, wherever the exact lines fall at any given moment, for the foreseeable future this other Europe will certainly be subdivided between states which are recognizably set on a course towards EU-rope and those which are not – with, no doubt, a number straggling in between.

The central political question about the composition of Europe today is therefore whether and how EU-rope can gradually include an ever larger part of the second Europe, while itself continuing to 'work' in the unique, complex, unsatisfactory but nonetheless real way it does; and how this process will both affect and be affected by relations with the third Europe, above all with Russia.

At issue right across the other Europe is the choice not just between democracy and dictatorship but also between war and peace. Banishing the spectre of war between European states and peoples was, of course, the first great purpose of EU-rope's founding fathers. Economic integration was the indirect means chosen to achieve that end, especially after a more direct approach – the European Defence Community – was voted down in the French National Assembly. Now it is a fair question how far it really was the (then still) EEC/EC which kept the peace in Europe, inasmuch as it was kept, up to 1990, and how far Nato and the East–West nuclear stand-off in the Cold War. But certainly the habits and institutions of peaceful conflict-resolution and permanent cooperation in the E C made a contribution.

Yet, while our leaders still mouth the platitude that 'war has become unthinkable' in Europe, war not only has again become thinkable across much of post-communist Europe but is, even as they speak, actually being waged, bloodily and brutally and – with almost too crude an irony – in a place called Sarajevo.

One lesson of the short twentieth century is that political ends are not separable from the means used to attain them. Today, E U-rope's means are threatening its ends. The process of 'making Europe' proceeds *par pro toto*. The elites negotiate for the people and ask them only afterwards, if at all, whether they agree. In this sense, as process, what is happening now is already 'a second Maastricht'. E U-rope also decides for Europe, and future members have to accept the given shape. The Poles send up their old cry, '*Nic o nas bez nas*' – 'Nothing about us without us!' – but, as usual, the West hardly listens.

Within the E U, a number of states – and crucially France and Germany – are contemplating 'going ahead': *pars pro toto* again. Following German unification, France's political leaders feel it to be more urgent than ever to bind Germany into Europe and – curious but true! – Germany's political leaders want their own country to be bound in, so they are not left alone to face the temptations of the past in the centre of Europe. True to the functionalist tradition of proceeding through economic means to political ends, the chosen path is monetary union. This, with its desired political consequences, is to make the process of integration 'irreversible'. The Franco-German avant-garde will form a 'magnetic core' of a uniting Europe, with monetary union as the hard core of the hard core. But where they lead, other states, including Britain, are to follow, as they have done throughout the previous history of the E E C/E C/E U. E U-rope after Maastricht (1 and 2) will be 'multi-speed', but still moving in one direction.

Here, stripped to essentials, is the bold – even breathtaking – Franco-German project for E U-rope in the closing years of the century, and the immediate European challenge for Britain. The trouble is that this project is very likely to fail. Monetary union itself might fail, obviously, at the first or second fences, because even the core economies are not close enough to stand the strains, or because either French or German political opinion turns against it. Monetary union might also fail after the event. Nothing except death is irreversible, and European history offers several examples of failed monetary unions.

Yet it may also fail by succeeding. That is, succeed in the narrow, technical, sense but fail in the broader purpose. A single market is perhaps difficult to sustain without a single currency, but it may be even more difficult to sustain with a clear, formalized division between monetary core and periphery. And how would this work in the councils of EU-rope? Would representatives of the core states have separate meetings on those fundamental issues of fiscal and macroeconomic policy on which they would now need a common stance? (The idea of EMU as gold standard, with each state bound to keep its own budgetary house in order or go broke, is theoretically attractive but not practical European politics.) Or would the core group be a permanent caucus, coming to each Council with an agreed position? One of the great strengths of the EU is its flexibility: you have changing national alliances on different issues. Set one alliance in concrete, and you risk breaking the whole structure.

The great gamble of this Continental project is that the Franco-German core will indeed be magnetic, that, where Bonn and Paris lead, others will sooner or later follow. And the reason why people in Bonn and Paris (and quite a few older 'pro-Europeans' in London) think this will happen is that that is roughly what did happen for about thirty-five years, from 1955 to 1990. But a process that worked, almost with the regularity of a physics demonstration, in the air-cooled laboratory of 'Western Europe' in the Cold War will not necessarily work in the same way in the much larger, messier, post-Wall Europe of today.

Anyone who has played with magnets as a child knows that they can have two effects: one way round they attract, the other way they repel. There is now a serious danger of the would-be magnetic core exerting magnetic repulsion. The best can be the enemy of the good. The rationalist, functionalist, perfectionist attempt to 'make Europe' or 'complete Europe' through a hard core built around a rapid monetary union could well end up achieving the opposite of the desired effect. A procedure aimed at finally overcoming the bad old European ways of competing nation states and alliances risks hastening a return to precisely those bad old ways. Press the fast-forward button, and you go backwards.

Yet even if it succeeds, both economically and politically, even if Britain and others in the EU once again follow where France and Germany have led, this in itself offers nothing to the rest of Europe knocking at our door. Indeed, the current Inter-Governmental Conference threatens to be 'Maastricht 2' in another sense – with the leaders of EU-rope so totally preoccupied with the EU's own internal reforms that they simply don't have enough time, energy and attention left for the parts of Europe where our actions might actually make the difference between democracy and dictatorship, war and peace.

Yet it is not enough to point out – empirically, sceptically and pragmatically – the flaws and dangers in a Franco-German project which is, characteristically, at once teleological, idealistic and instrumental. For the French and Germans will quite rightly retort, Do you have a better one? For anyone who cares about Europe, the task is therefore to come up with a better one. Or, at the very least, to ensure that there is something else under way so that the whole 'European enterprise' at the end of the twentieth century is not seen to stand or fall with this hair-raising adventure, this *Europe as Will and Idea*, of unification through money.

That 'something' should, I believe, be a detailed project both for the enlargement of the present EU to include, over the next twenty years, the recently liberated second Europe, and, simultaneously, for a more closely coordinated and in some respects 'common' foreign, security and defence policy, to meet the challenges and dangers both within Europe itself and from the dangerous world around. This project would therefore approach the political goal directly, by political means, not by the functionalist diversion through economics. Unlike EMU, it would not be one simple big thing but a whole jigsaw of complex, piecemeal things, since it would necessarily involve many other, overlapping, European institutions, and, above all, EU-rope's second true pillar: Nato. But, however precisely it were done, it would require more sharing of power and sovereignty – both in the form of Qualified Majority Voting, without which an EU of twenty and more member states would simply not work, and in the rather different procedures for what one might call Qualified Minority Acting (by varying groups of states, but usually involving France, Germany and Britain) which are what is needed in foreign, security and defence policy.

But if you don't care about Europe as Europe, just about Britain as Britain, why bother and why pay the price? For two reasons: because if we don't we'll be left out, and because if we don't we'll be dragged in. Left out, in the short term, from the next stage of Franco-German EU-ro-building, with (at the very least) high risks for Britain; but then dragged in by the probable failure of that design and by the disorder of the rest of Europe which that design does so little to address.

There is a surreal, even a grotesque, discrepancy between the contorted, rapidly-sleep-inducing, acronym-ridden, polit-bureaucratic detail of the current debate about reforming EU-rope and the huge, fateful, almost melodramatic challenges facing us across the rest of Europe after the end of the Cold War. And yet our answer to the latter must start from the former – for where else should we start except where we are?

And going where? All divisions of time are artificial, and perhaps the last five years of the twentieth century and the second millennium AD should be considered no differently from any other five years. But the millennial deadline does concentrate the mind. In these next five years, we probably have a larger chance but also a greater danger than at any time in the past fifty. The chance is that in the year 2000 more of Europe will be more peaceful, prosperous, democratic and free than ever before in its history. The danger can also be simply described. If we get things wrong now, some time in the early part of the next century we will stop talking about 8 May 1945 as the end of the war in Europe – because there'll be another.

I develop this argument further in 'The Case for Liberal Order', p. 316.

1995

16 May. Milan prosecutors propose that 160 politicians and business people should be tried for bribery and corruption. They also request the indictment of Silvio Berlusconi, Italian prime minister until December 1994.

25–26 May. Nato bombs Bosnian Serb targets. In revenge, Bosnian Serbs take UN peacekeepers hostage and shell 'safe areas'.

31 May. Prince Charles becomes the first member of the British royal family to visit Ireland since it gained independence in 1922.

3 June. Creation of a Nato 'rapid-reaction force' to support UNPRO-FOR in Bosnia.

9 June. Russian president Yeltsin and Ukrainian president Kuchma sign an agreement on the future of the Black Sea fleet.

11 and 18 June. In French local elections, the far-right National Front makes major gains.

19 June. Árpád Göncz is re-elected president of Hungary.

26–27 June. An EU summit in Cannes. Agreement on an 'irreversible' move to economic and monetary union by 1999.

3 July. Serious rioting in Northern Ireland follows the early release of Private Lee Clegg, a British soldier serving a life sentence for shooting dead a Catholic driving a stolen car.

4 July. British prime minister John Major wins the election for leadership of the Conservative Party, defeating John Redwood, who receives votes from Major's 'Euro-sceptic' critics.

11 July. Bosnian Serb forces take the UN 'safe area' of Srebrenica. Dutch UN peacekeepers offer no resistance. Local Bosniak men of military age are subsequently massacred by Bosnian Serbs; older men, women and children are forced to flee. In Russia, President Yeltsin suffers a heart attack, starting a long period of impaired health.

25 July. Bosnian Serb forces take the UN 'safe area' of Zepa. The UN War Crimes Tribunal in The Hague indicts Bosnian Serb president Radovan Karadžić and military commander Radko Mladić on charges of genocide and crimes against humanity.

30 July. A Chechnya peace agreement provides for withdrawal of Russian troops. The issue of formal independence is left unresolved.

4 August. The Italian parliament approves a pension reform plan, cutting public expenditure.

5–9 August. Croatian forces retake Serb-held Krajina in 'Operation Storm'. More than 150,000 local Serbs flee.

August. Holidays in a part of western Poland that was Germany until 1945. The architecture is still overwhelmingly, unmistakably German. The red-brick Gothic church is a German Protestant church with a Virgin Mary and twelve stations of the cross slapped round the walls to make it a Polish Catholic one. Many of the place names are just Polish translations of the original German names. On the murderously busy main road from Poznań to Berlin, a hoarding advertises 'New Cars – after accidents in Germany'. The Germans are not yet coming back in any great numbers, whether as landowners, factory-owners or pleasure-seekers. But as Poland comes closer to the West, and the German capital moves to nearby Berlin, they surely will.

28 August. Another mortar bombing of a market place in Sarajevo.

August–September. Nato responds by a series of air attacks on Bosnian Serb positions, including their artillery emplacements around Sarajevo.

31 August. The son of Slovak president Michal Kováč is kidnapped and taken to Austria. Operatives of the Slovak intelligence service, answerable to prime minister Vladimír Mečiar, are almost certainly involved.

14 September. Bosnian Serbs remove their heavy weaponry from around Sarajevo.

27 September. The European Court of Human Rights condemns the 1988 Gibraltar killing of three unarmed IRA terrorists by British security forces.

7 October. Representatives of Greek and Turkish political parties in Cyprus express commitment to a negotiated solution for the island.

12 October. A sixty-day ceasefire in Bosnia, negotiated by US mediator Richard Holbrooke, comes into effect.

Cleansed Croatia

ZAGREB

I need no visa to enter Croatia. Planinka from Belgrade does. She had to wait for weeks, and got one only because Slavko Goldstein, her editor here, intervened with the Croat authorities. But others have been refused, in both directions. It's as if I, as an Englishman, were suddenly forbidden to visit Cardiff. 'Yugoslavia was a small country,' says Slavko, 'and now we've made five even smaller ones.'

At dinner in one of Zagreb's plush restaurants, we talk about the siege of Sarajevo. 'The Serbs' did this, a Croat friend tells us; 'the Serbs' do that. Planinka, a lady of a certain age, smartly dressed and immaculately made-up, has an almost permanently fixed smile. But I wonder how she feels. Serb?

'Before the war,' says Slavko, and for a moment I think he means, 'Before the war . . .' This is Europe's new semantic dividing line. In Britain, France or Germany, 'the war' still means 1939–1945. Here it means 1991–1995. So far, that is, for no one knows whether the war has really ended or merely paused for a year.

TO GLINA

With Slavko, his son Ivo, and Planinka packed into a puttering Renault 4, we drive south from Zagreb to the Krajina, under Serb rule for nearly four years but now 'liberated' by the Croatian army, in

'Operation Storm'. At Karlovac, where Slavko lived as a boy, we visit the market place bombed by the besieging Serb forces. Look, here's the mark of the mortar bomb on the pavement; that's where the shoppers died.

On the way out of town, we pick up Mate, an elderly Croat farmer who hid Slavko in his village during the war (the last war, that is), when the Ustasha – the Croat fascists – were rounding up the Jews of Karlovac. Slavko then went off to fight with Tito's communist partisans, but Mate hid in the woods, refusing to fight for any side. The old man has a broad, nut-brown face, a ready smile beneath the cloth cap, and quiet dignity.

Leaving Karlovac, we cross what for the last four years was the Serb front line. Suddenly all the houses are roofless, scorched, plundered or simply reduced to rubble. It's like the photographs of German cities in 1945, except in colour and 3D. We come upon a man demolishing, brick by red brick, a wall that is still standing. The bricks are then passed down a line, composed mainly of women and children, to a woman who crouches in the ruins. She carefully brushes off each intact brick and places it on a pile, ready for the rebuilding. In Germany in 1945 they called such women the *Trümmerfrauen*, the women of the ruins.

We drive eastward along the valley of the river Kupa, which for much of its length was the front line, just twenty miles south of Zagreb as the missile flies. In the Croat villages almost every house has been plundered and had the roof burned or blown out by the occupying Serbs. Here and there, we see Croats returning to their houses, starting over, with the chequerboard flag of Croatia flying from the balcony. But for the most part the villages are still deserted.

We stop off at the house of Mate's son-in-law, well-built, with a still intact solid concrete roof and a good view down the valley. It has survived because the Serbs used it as a command and observation post. Inside, red-painted graffiti in the Serbs' Cyrillic script say, 'Welcome to the heroes', 'Keep this place clean!' and 'If you want to eat, wash up the dishes!' Orderly folk.

On down the valley, and then – bang! bang! – two tyres on the little Renault have blown as we hit a giant pothole. A passing farmer takes Mate and Slavko off in his trailer to find someone who has the right kind of spare tyre. Planinka, still smiling, wanders off into the bushes to have a pee, but Ivo shouts at her: 'Stop! The verges are mined!' Half an hour later, Mate and Slavko come back in a lorry with a spare tyre and a thickset farmer, grinning from ear to ear. He is a Serb, married to a Croat, and during the Serb occupation he protected the houses of his Croat neighbours. We can see their roofs along the skyline of a nearby hill, miracles of intactness. Now, we are told, he is a hero to the local Croats. But he does seem desperately eager to please. Fear lines his grin.

Mate's village, Kovačevac, has hardly a house intact. He leads us through some long grass to an area of rubble and twisted metal: all that is left of an eighteenth-century wooden church, a fine and rare example of its kind. Planinka picks up a small piece of twisted bronze and turns it around. It is beautiful. I feel that she would love to place it on her studio table. But then she puts it back. After all, she, too, is a Serb.

When Mate came back from hiding in the woods in 1945, he was elected mayor of Kovačevac. He helped rebuild not just his own village, but also the neighbouring Serb village of Prško, which had been the victim of an Ustasha atrocity. In 1941, some 400 women and children had been rounded up by crack troops of the Ustasha leader Ante Pavelić and slaughtered in the forest. So in 1991, when most of the Croats fled before the advancing Serbs, Mate stayed. He'd seen out four regimes, he said, and he'd see out this regime too. But one night Serb friends came to his house and told him to escape at once. You've seen too much, they said. You know who did the plundering and killing. They're coming to get you. So once again – fifty years on – Mate took to the woods. He stole down to the river Kupa, found a boat, and rowed across to the Croat-controlled side. Next night, Serbs – 'Chetniks' says Mate, using the old term for Serb nationalist partisans – came and killed several of the elderly Croats who had stayed in Kovačevac.

Now Mate and his friends are putting their farms together again. They find the barn roof stacked up as spare timber in a farmyard two villages away. They find the tractor abandoned in a field. And, if they don't find their own possessions, they take someone else's. Mate's immediate neighbour came back with a trailer which Mate recognized as his own. 'Give it me back,' said Mate. 'No,' said his neighbour. 'I found it. You take another one!'

We leave Mate to attend the first normal funeral in this village for four years. A normal death – a cause for celebration. In Prško, the bust of the local Serb hero – a close comrade of Gavrilo Princip, the man who shot Archduke Franz Ferdinand in Sarajevo in 1914 – has been hacked off and thrown into a hedge. Serb houses are still flying white flags. But virtually all the inhabitants have fled, in the exodus of the Serb population of the Krajina, the biggest single exodus of the war. More than 150,000 people filled the roads to Serbia and Serb-controlled Bosnia. A village became a hundred yards of traffic – vans, tractors and trailers piled high with baggage and pets and wailing children. Again, I think of 1945, and the endless columns of Germans fleeing westward before the Red Army, from East Prussia and Silesia. Here, as there, the war has come full circle. Innocent women and children are punished for the crimes of their compatriots. Nemesis.

In one low wooden house we find an old peasant woman, with a deeply lined face, black woollen headscarf, gnarled hands. She, too, had fled with the village, seven days on the road to Belgrade. 'Ay, ay,' she sighs, and lifts her hands. But her son went via Hungary to Belgrade, and brought her back again. They were lucky to get through. Although paying lip-service to the refugees' 'right to return', the Croat authorities are making it very difficult for anyone to do so.

We drive through more eerily empty villages, with just the occasional pig wandering along the verge, to the town of Glina, scene of another Ustasha massacre during the Second World War. Here, Serbs from the local area were told they would be spared if they converted to Roman Catholicism. They marched, singing, along the road into Glina. Then they were herded into the Orthodox church and massacred.

Today, this is a ghost town. The Croats fled in 1991; now the Serbs have fled too, while most of the Croats have yet to return. However, the Croat administration has started the work of reconstruction by converting a memorial pavilion to the victims of the Ustasha massacre into a 'Croat House'. They have removed the marble tablets bearing the names of the Serb victims, raised the chequerboard flag, and held a liberation concert to inaugurate this Croat cultural institute. Western civilization has triumphed.

THE WASTE LAND

Two more days in the 'ethnically cleansed' Krajina, this time heading south with my friend Konstanty Gebert, a Polish writer, and Ana Uzelac, his Serbo-Polish colleague from Belgrade. On the roads, there is no traffic except the Croat military police at the roadblocks, a few white-painted UN vehicles, and, incongruously, the occasional smart BMW or Mercedes with German number plates racing past. Presumably Croat *Gastarbeiter* revisiting family homes, or just on safari.

For hour after hour, we drive through the most spectacularly beautiful countryside, along the wooded valleys of the Plitvicka National Park, across the karst uplands, and down to the fortress of Knin. For hour after hour we see nothing but devastated, burned, plundered houses. Roofs burned out; windows smashed; clothes, bedclothes, furniture, papers strewn across the floor. Everything of value removed. Orchards, vineyards, fields, all with their crops gone to waste. No cars left, no tractors, no farm equipment, no cattle, no dogs. Only a few cats survive.

And, for mile upon mile upon mile, we see no single human being. Nobody. Ana has brought from Belgrade the addresses of Serb families that fled, but their houses are very difficult to find, because the villages no longer have the landmarks the inhabitants remember. Could this have been a grocer's shop? Was that once a white wall? But there is no one to ask for directions.

'Cleansing' is in an awful way the right word for what has been done here. The Krajina, an area the size of several English counties, has literally been picked clean. This was not random looting. The plundering and burning has been done quite systematically – for the most part, it seems, by Croats in one uniform or another. The object, apart from booty, is simple: to ensure that the Serbs don't come back. Croatia is to be, so far as possible, Serb-free. *Serbenrein*.

According to the local UN office, some 100 elderly Serbs who stayed in their homes have been murdered since Croat forces retook the area. At Gračac, we find fresh graves in the cemetery, neatly numbered on the identical wooden crosses. However here, as elsewhere, the

Orthodox church has been left standing, to show that the Croats are western, civilized people, unlike those barbaric Orthodox Serbs, who raze Catholic churches to the ground. But the vicarage has been torn apart. A children's Bible and a Church calendar for 1996 lie among the litter on the floor.

At Kistanje, once a pretty small town, we find three family photo albums laid out on stone tables in the market place. The wedding. A son's christening. The ceremony to celebrate his joining the Yugoslav army. As we turn the pages, a white armoured personnel carrier of UNPROFOR, the so-called United Nations Protection Force, roars through the deserted town. Ludicrous protectors of nothing. The UN self-protection force.

In places like this, journalists say, 'the story writes itself'. Wherever we look, journalistic 'colour' and clichés offer themselves wantonly, like the whores in Amsterdam. Outside a plundered home, a doll is sprawled across the road, one foot torn off. In the ruins of the family home of Milorad Pupovac, leader of a small would-be liberal Serb party in Croatia, I find a book of children's verse, *Robber Katja and Princess Nadja*, published in Sarajevo in 1989. Ana can recite some of the verses from memory. The last poem is entitled 'How Our Yugoslavia Grows'. In the rubble of another house I see what looks like a white scroll. Unrolling it, I discover a black-and-white photograph of Tito – the kind that once hung in every public place and in many private houses too. It has a bootmark pointing towards the face.

Knin was the capital of the self-styled Serb Republic of Krajina. Now 'liberated', its imposing hilltop fortress, with the chequerboard flag flying from the top, forms the background to the main election poster for President Tudjman's nationalist HDZ movement. In the foreground you see Tudjman himself, waving both fists above his head like a victorious football manager. Before the war, some 37,000 people lived in Knin; now even the local government claims only 2,000. Croat soldiers and military police, baseball caps reversed, speed along the deserted streets in their stolen – sorry, 'liberated' – cars: a smart Mercedes, a Renault, a Mitsubishi jeep with the name of the German dealer still advertised on the back. We climb to the top of the fortress and discover the largest flag I have ever seen in my life. It must be at least thirty feet long. Young girls in black jeans and

T-shirts are photographing each other literally wrapped in the flag. The cliché made flesh.

As the sun sets over the mountains like a holiday advertisement, we drive down to the Adriatic, across the invisible line to the part of Croatia the Serbs never occupied, and suddenly there is ordinary life: houses with roofs, electric light, curtains, cars, a young couple snogging on a scooter. In Šibenik, one of the beautiful resort towns on the Dalmatian coast, we gape at the cheerful well-dressed crowds, the nice hotels and the Café Europa.

Ah, Europe – but we've been there all the time.

Three years later, British television commentators celebrated the World Cup football match in which plucky little Croatia defeated Germany. The cameras showed, draped across one side of the stadium, a huge Croatian flag. The Croatian team played well and sportingly, but I could only think of the cleansed Krajina, and of the huge flag flying over Knin, and of how the same people cheering their footballers now must have been cheering their soldiers then. Perhaps it was the same flag.

Bosnian Glimpses

TUZLA

We arrive in the late evening, after an exhausting sixteen-hour bus journey across Bosnia, and enter the dim and cavernous Hotel Tuzla, instantly recognizable as the kind of grimly modernist tower-block hotel built all over communist Europe in the 1970s and 1980s. I step into the lift, press the button for the second floor, and at once subside, powerless, into the cellar. The reception committee in the bar consists of Christopher Hitchens, Susan Sontag and David Rieff. When I join them, Susan is just saying to Michael Ignatieff, 'I can't *believe* that this is your first time here.'

Next morning, we are bussed to a large congress hall, with usherettes in red jackets and black miniskirts. Mary Kaldor, chair of the Helsinki Citizens Assembly, welcomes us 'after this long journey, so difficult for all of us'. But she came by helicopter. Julie Christie reads a poem which goes, according to my notebook, 'Sarajevo, glowing white . . . as a translucent china cup . . .'

Then four local politicians, middle-aged men in suits, make their appeals for international support. Sturdy Selim Beslagić, the mayor of Tuzla, tells us that our planet is based on natural laws and harmonies, and asks us to help defend Europe from fascism. The provincial governor, who comes from President Izetbegović's muslim-led Party of Democratic Action (SDA), says Europe must do something to prevent genocide happening one hour's flying-time from its capitals. The president of the Bosnian parliament says, according to the

199

simultaneous interpretation, 'We are defending the basic principles of the world system', while the head of the Tuzla Citizens' Forum, which co-hosts this meeting, talks of 'the spirit of progressive mankind' represented by the Helsinki Citizens Assembly, and asks, 'Is Europe dying in Bosnia?' He insists that two things are vital: the right of refugees to return to their homes and the punishment of war criminals.

We have been told that Tuzla is an island of liberal, multi-ethnic, multicultural coexistence. The reality I discover over the next three days is more complicated. The style of these men, like that of the congress hall and of the hotel, is unmistakably communist. And one reason – perhaps the main reason – why Tuzla is still relatively tolerant of ethnic diversity is precisely that it was such a strongly communist, Yugoslav industrial city. Yet even Tuzla isn't that multi-ethnic any more. According to the 1991 census, only 55 per cent of the Tuzla region's population identified themselves as 'Muslim'; now the UN estimate is 96 per cent. The Serb Orthodox church is beautifully kept, but the old caretaker says they haven't had a priest here since 1992. For three years, the remnants of the congregation have been improvising, intoning half-remembered chants and hymns, but with no christenings, marriages or funerals. And then, when you talk to people from Mayor Beslagić's city council, you find that for them the main enemy seems to be not the Serbs but rather their Bosnian political rivals from President Izetbegović's SDA.

Like the complex landscape of physical destruction on the way out here, these political complexities spoil the simple picture with which many people started the journey of solidarity: immaculate Bosnian victims ('Sarajevo, glowing white . . .') against child-eating Serb villains. But this is one very good reason for coming. It's what I call the *Homage to Catalonia* test. Can you, like Orwell in Spain, maintain solidarity with the victims without compromising the truth about the faults on the victims' side? When the assembly's concluding statement describes Tuzla as a 'multi-ethnic, multi-religious paradise' it has, in my book, failed the *Homage to Catalonia* test. But that's the trouble with assemblies, committees, platforms: they always do.

SURVIVORS OF SREBRENICA

When Serb forces seized the UN 'safe area' of Srebrenica, marching Bosnian men off to killing fields while Dutch soldiers stood by, most of the surviving refugees came to the Tuzla area. In a bar in Tuzla, Michael Ignatieff and I meet one of the few soldiers from Srebrenica to have escaped with his life. He limps in on crutches, one foot still heavily bandaged, and tells his story through our interpreter. After being operated on by Dutch surgeons in a UN camp at Potočari, he was told by the Dutch that he would be evacuated to Tuzla. Instead, Serb officers strode in and ordered that an old man should be transported in his place.

Now he was told he would be taken to another hospital, shown on Bosnian Serb TV as proof of how well the captives were being treated, and then evacuated. Instead, he was taken to a Serb prison camp. The camp commander deliberately kicked his wounded leg. The wound, undressed, was crawling with worms. An old man hanged himself after learning of his son's death. Another prisoner died in the freezing cold. After more than three months in detention, he was brought out in an exchange of prisoners organized by the International Committee of the Red Cross. His father and two brothers have still not made it to Tuzla.

The story is harrowing enough. But he's a bad witness. His tale is poorly told, confusing, and he seems to be mixing what happened to others with what happened to him. Notebooks open on the table, Michael and I find ourselves pummelling him with questions to get the bloody story straight. Anyone here been crippled and speak English?

In the nearby town of Živinice, a refugee camp was hit by a Serb mortar bomb just a fortnight ago. Six children were killed, four wounded. The camp turns out to be an incongruous toytown of Scandinavian-built terraced houses, each designed as an idyllic suburban home for a nuclear family of four, but now sleeping forty. Old peasant women in headscarves, grubby children with large brown eyes. No work, no money, nothing to do. Empty, numbing hopelessness. Suddenly there is another visiting party, with Julie Christie in black

trousers and grey sweater, camera at the ready. The children immediately form into a group to have their photograph taken. They raise
their hands and make the V sign. V for victory.

DIJANA

In a coffee-break I talk to a girl called Dijana, from Sarajevo. She is
in her early twenties and beautiful, with high cheekbones and large,
liquid, oval eyes; stylishly dressed in black, carefully made-up in white.
At first, she is unforthcoming, almost hostile, until I mention the name
of a good friend who has been coming regularly to Sarajevo in the
worst times of the siege. I add, 'You must be totally fed up with all
these well-intentioned foreigners always asking the same questions.'
'Yes,' she says, and smiles for the first time. 'A lot of people come
just for themselves, to say they've been here, to show off.'

Now she'd like to ask me something. Why did the West do nothing
to help Sarajevo? Sarajevo was a very special place before the war.
They lived well, better than many in the West. Now their life is utterly
destroyed and degraded. Her brother was just starting to study. But
he's been four years a soldier, and she doesn't think he can ever return
to normal life. And the West has done nothing – nothing – just watched
them being killed. She wants to say to UNPROFOR, 'Just clear out
and give me a weapon to fight with, and I'll see if I can avoid being
raped or whatever.' Anger polishes her English.

What is she to do? Perhaps she could emigrate, but she doesn't
want to be a dishwasher somewhere. 'My children might become
Canadian or whatever, but I wouldn't be – I'd always be Sarajevan.'
At the independent Radio Zid, she and her friends try to pretend they
live in a normal country. They do reports on films, play pop music,
and give their listeners beauty tips. For example, water after rice has
been boiled in it is very good for the skin. She smiles, an angry smile.

Like it or not (and she doesn't), Dijana is a Western television
producer's dream victim. Beautiful in black and white, eloquent,
bitter. *Victim*, the new fragrance from Calvin Klein.

SARAJEVO

Dijana's anger was just a small foretaste of what I find here. I have never met such deep bitterness. Despite all the introductions with which I'm armed – several from good friends of mine to people they regard as close friends here – I think some people would hardly have talked to me were it not for the intercession of my interpreter, Senada Kreso. Knowing some of my work, she decides that it may, after all, be worth the effort of helping me. But it's a very bad moment. The American-brokered ceasefire has just come into force – something I didn't anticipate when I planned my trip. Senada and her Sarajevan friends are just emerging from a particularly terrible period of the now three-and-a-half-year-long siege, the worse because it followed a reprieve in 1994.

For days on end they sat at home, freezing, in the dark, without electricity, gas or running water, waiting for a mortar bomb to hit them from the hills. Or they forced themselves to walk to work, although often there was no work to do, risking death by sniper fire at every crossroads. However many descriptions you have read and television reports you've watched, until you see the place for yourself you don't really grasp how its peculiar, unique and beautiful location lays the whole city out as a kind of superbowl target for the snipers in the surrounding hills.

They saw friends wounded or killed. They were degraded in a hundred small, everyday ways. They had to wash themselves and their clothes in a couple of buckets of water. They had to scavenge for firewood. They were impoverished by the black-market prices and the lack of normal incomes. They were humiliated by having to receive charity from visiting foreigners: the discreet envelope, the embarrassed smile. And then there was the noise, early at morning, late at night, as death rained gigantically down.

Now they are like deep-sea divers dragged too quickly up to the surface. They have psychological divers' bends. If you, the West, could stop it now – they say – why couldn't you stop it three years ago? And, because they're sure we could have stopped it, they feel that what they've been through has been senseless. Worse still, British and

French soldiers have been here all the time, patrolling the ghetto walls while they were frozen, degraded, bombarded and picked off like insects.

Quite a few of those to whom I have introductions – academics, journalists, artists, film-makers – have their flats in one large modern housing estate in an area called Ciglane. The estate is built up a steep hillside, with staggered balconies and large windows, like a ziggurat, thus offering perfect target practice for Serb artillery. When I join Senada in the tiny Café Herc, in the middle of the estate (only yesterday they took the sandbags down from the front window), an unshaven, weary, mildly tipsy man says, 'How I hate foreigners!' They are bitter about the indifference of the West, about those who didn't come. But now they are also bitter about those who kept coming back – on safari – and then flew out to safety with their Sarajevo tales. 'It seemed to us a sort of necrophilia,' says Senada.

'Who really helped?' I ask Zdravko Grebo, a law professor and director of Radio Zid, whom every visiting foreigner goes to see. 'Everyone and no one,' he says. Everyone – even Bianca Jagger, who just stayed for a few hours at the airport – helped a little to draw the world's attention to what was happening in Sarajevo. But nobody, because the siege went on, and on, and on.

But they are bitter, too, about their own friends and colleagues who have left. Sitting in the cramped editorial office of the weekly *Dani*, an open metal oven burning firewood in the corner, Ozren Kebo talks of 'cowardice' and 'betrayal'. He describes a pop concert in Zagreb where thousands of Sarajevans wept as a well-known Sarajevan pop group sang the refrain of their hit song, 'Sarajevo, I'm staying here.' But they didn't stay here, says Ozren. He did. With the recent easing of the siege, there's been another wave of emigration.

At times it seems the only people they can still respect, even relate to at all, are those who have stayed, like them, and gone through the same experience. They are proud of how they've continued to produce newspapers, literary quarterlies, weeklies, concerts, radio programmes. The cultural resistance. The black humour of the siege. The wonderful posters by the 'Trio' artists: 'Enjoy Sara-Jevo', a perfect parody of the famous red-and-white 'Enjoy Coca-Cola' poster, or 'Enjoy the Winter Olympics, Sarajevo 1994/95', with the Olympic rings done in barbed wire. (The 1984 Winter Olympics were held here.)

Suada Kapić, editor of the *Survival Guide to Sarajevo*, gives me her latest production, a large glossy magazine called *LIFE* – its title printed with the E reversed – with profiles of people who stayed. (She tells me *Time-Life*'s lawyers have protested at the infringement of its copyright.) Sometimes the pathos of the intellectuals seems a little heavy. And the black humour, too. For example, 'What is the difference between Auschwitz and Sarajevo?' 'In Sarajevo there's no gas.' But I hardly feel in a position to say, 'Come on, it wasn't *that* bad.'

Yet the worst thing is their bitterness about themselves. Four years ago they led a life as normal and civilized as their contemporaries in Budapest or Athens. They enjoyed the easygoing café lifestyle of their own city, went skiing in the hills around Pale, perhaps holidayed in Italy. Now they are reduced to this humiliating role of victim and international zoo exhibit. Zdravko Grebo, unofficial spokesman number one for Sarajevo, says, 'You know, since you're here with Senada, as a friend, I'll tell you what I really want. What I really want is to be left alone, to get back to my books and my music, not to have to travel to conferences, and endlessly answer these questions.'

In the first two years of the siege – the 'romantic period' – they still felt they might save their Sarajevo. Fluid. Tolerant. Multi-ethnic not as the result of a western ideology of multiculturalism – what they ironically call 'multi-multi-multi' – but as a historical reality where people of Serb, Croat, muslim and increasingly mixed backgrounds and relationships shared the same lifestyle. Or divided, if they divided, not on ethnic lines. (To be sure, all this happened under the authoritarian roof of Titoism. In many places I find black-and-white photographs of the old man still displayed on the wall: in Radio Zid, in the PEN Club, even above two stern rows of Sarajevo rabbis in the headquarters of the Jewish community.) But now they feel this Sarajevo – their Sarajevo – has gone for good.

Even if the peace holds, they will find themselves in the provincial capital of a rump Bosnian state, with a gently corrupt and mildly authoritarian government. And what there is of cosmopolitan culture will be living off foreign money, as artificial and ultimately as inauthentic and corrupt as the subsidized culture of West Berlin during the Cold War.

The defence of the café has failed.

But for what some of the same people were saying three years later, see pp. 373–4.

KARADŽIĆ

At first glance, the poet and critic Marko Vešović, with a forehead like a small cliff and wild, swept-back hair, bears an alarming resemblance to the Bosnian Serb leader Radovan Karadžić. In fact, they are both Montenegrins, and before the war were friends. With only the slightest prompting, Marko unfolds his tale of Karadžić.

Radovan – 'Radko' to his friends – came to Sarajevo on his own, at the age of fourteen, to study at secondary and then medical school. His family had suffered terribly in Montenegro from wartime reprisals by Tito's communist partisans, and he always hated the communists. He was good-looking, bright, one of the lads. But then, as still a very young man, he made the terrible mistake of impregnating the dreadful Delilija, whom Marko describes as hideous and weighing a hundred kilos. Her father, the manager of the Europa Hotel, forced Radko to marry her and to come and live in their house. But secretly he went on womanizing. That was when his chronic lying began.

Sonja, now propaganda minister of the Bosnian Serbs, was the child of this ghastly coupling. Marko was put down as her godfather at the christening, but Radko told him about it only afterwards – otherwise, in the Montenegrin tradition, the godfather would have had the right to choose her name.

Like Marko and Zdravko Grebo, Karadžić took part in the '68 demos in Sarajevo. But then he got a scholarship to study in America, and they were sure he had agreed to work for the secret police. For years they shunned him. But eventually they made it up, and again attended the hard-drinking 'salons' which he loved to give. He was a charming host.

He wanted to be a great psychiatrist, but he was too lazy to do any real work. He owed his job at the clinic to his Bosnian muslim boss, Ismet Cerić, to whom he was devoted. Never – not even in the most intimate, drunken conversation – had Marko heard Karadžić say a word against muslims. Once he went away to work in Belgrade. But he came back after a few months and told Cerić he couldn't understand the mentality of the people there. (Those Serbs, you know.)

Then he wanted to be a great poet. But had no voice of his own. His poetry was all bad imitations of Georg Trakl, the Austrian poet of decadence. When he published a book of poems in 1992, Marko and Nikola Koljević (now also a leader of the Bosnian Serbs in the hills) had to rewrite half the verses for him.

Just a few months later, Marko turned on the television and there was Karadžić, up in the hills, looking down at Sarajevo through his binoculars and saying, 'I could take it in two days.' This from someone who never even served in the army. In this, as in all else, a bragging charlatan. A liar, a trickster, a failure at everything he did.

But, as Marko rumbles to the close of his picaresque tale, I think that, after all, Radovan Karadžić has succeeded. He may have to live out the rest of his days in hiding, as a war criminal. He may even be caught and tried, or simply shot. But he's famous at last. His name will live on, in the history books and the stories of future generations.

Bosnia in Our Future

One day, soon, I want to hijack Helmut Kohl, Jacques Chirac, Jacques Santer and all the other leaders of the European Union, on the way to their latest summit, and I want to fly them to a neighbourhood of Sarajevo called Ciglane. There I will drive them, past the graveyards, to the Café Herc, or perhaps, because it has more room, to the Café London. Just for an hour – since I know how busy they all are – I will have them listen to a small group of articulate, English-speaking Sarajevans. Have them listen, not, as they might expect, to yet one more plangent appeal for help, but to the sheer bottomless contempt and bitterness of people who don't expect anything from them any more. Nothing except empty words.

After three and a half years, this acid bitterness, so deep and tired that even the black humour of the earlier siege time hardly surfaces any more, extends to almost everyone. To anything in a blue helmet, of course. To all the endless foreign visitors on their Sarajevo safaris. But now even to some of those journalists, intellectuals and aid workers who came early and really tried to help; even to their own Sarajevan friends who have left; even, worst of all, to themselves, for being forced into this humiliating role of victim. Yet somewhere very near the bottom of the pile is this thing which still calls itself 'Europe'.

Then, when I have got our European leaders safely back to their comfortable hotels in Brussels or Paris or Barcelona, I should like to see if they can still go on smoothly delivering their soft, prefabricated speeches about our Europe of peace and progress and ever closer union.

I

There are so many defeats and failures involved in Bosnia, so many dimensions and intricacies to the whole larger history of former Yugoslavia, that one hardly knows where to begin. But, at a moment when America is making all the diplomatic running over Bosnia, I will, perversely perhaps, but not illogically, begin with Europe.

Most people brought up in Western Europe during the Cold War have imbibed, consciously or half wittingly, a Whig interpretation of European history. European history since 1945 has been told them essentially as a story of progress towards more prosperity, more freedom, more democracy, more unity in something now teleologically called the European Union. What is more, in the 1970s and 1980s people in Eastern Europe increasingly came to believe this story. This is one of the reasons why, in 1989, they voted communism away and set out to 'return to Europe'. Nineteen eighty-nine was thus the greatest triumph of this idea – but also, it now seems, its apogee.

For since then we have, in the south-eastern part of Europe, gone almost all the way back. Here there was violent conflict in the province of Kosovo already in 1989, even as the Berlin Wall fell. Within two years, there was outright war between Serbia and Slovenia, Serbia and Croatia, then between Serbians, Croatians and Bosniaks in Bosnia. With it came a rapid descent to atrocities not seen in Europe for fifty years. These atrocities do not merely reproduce but also, so to speak, elaborate upon the already formidable repertoire of European barbarism from 1939 to 1945.

It is not just war without quarter, massacres of civilians, camps, systematic rapes, mutilation of corpses, but has also added new refinements of the old European art of ethnic cleansing and the refined psychological torture of the siege of Sarajevo – to name but two innovations. Only the worst horror of them all – the systematic attempt to exterminate a whole people, as in the Holocaust of European Jewry – has so far been lacking, although there have been attempts at systematic extermination of Bosnian elites and men of military age. Now, in the Croatian Krajina, we see a familiar last act: Serbian men, women and children fleeing on their tractors from villages where their people have lived for hundreds of years, as punishment for the sins of their compatriots – just like the Germans from the Sudetenland and Silesia in 1945. But Bosnia has still not reached its 1945.

Early in the siege of Sarajevo there appeared on the wall of the half-ruined post office the familiar Serb graffito 'This is Serbia!' Someone scrawled underneath, 'No, you idiot, it's a post office!' My friend Konstanty Gebert has written a whole book about that line, about the defence of the post office. But I want to add a line of my own: 'This is Europe!' For all these things have been done by Europeans to other Europeans in Europe. That in itself should be enough to remind us that the story of recent European history that we have been telling ourselves and our children is little better than a fairy tale. And yet our politicians go on telling it.

The double-think is truly surreal. 'War in Europe has become unthinkable,' say our leaders. Crash go the shells into Sarajevo, and Srebrenica, and a thousand other towns and villages.

2

Of course the war in former Yugoslavia, though entirely comparable in brutality with all but the ultimate horror of the Second World War, is not comparable in scale. But, in two respects, our own relationship to it is worse. In the Second World War, most people in the countries fighting Nazism did not, at the time, know the full extent of the horrors; and, anyway, we were at war with Nazism. But here, sitting in peace and comfort, we have watched it all on our television screens. The Warsaw ghetto in instalments, every night at nine. Death brought to us live.

If there was then the question 'Why did the heavens not open?', there is even more of a question now. Why did all this coverage, these harrowing accounts by brave reporters, fail to mobilize West European public opinion? Is it because of the Rambo loop? The young male fighters we see charging across our screens, with black headbands and cross-slung ammunition belts, partly model themselves on Rambo, but they also look to the viewer like Rambo – that is, fiction. Reality, partly modelling itself on virtual reality, is taken for unreal. Or is it the sheer complexity of the story? 'Bosnia is our Spain,' says the French philosopher Bernard-Henri Levy. But this is so much more complicated, and even Spain, as Orwell reminded us in *Homage to Catalonia*, was complicated enough. Another French intellectual, Alain Finkielkraut, has told us how to be Croats; but Croats, too, have now been ethnic cleansers. And so on.

Worse still, we have not just watched from our ringside seats while people are murdered and Bosnia torn apart. Representing the European Community on a diplomatic mission to Yugoslavia as the war began in the summer of 1991, M. Jacques Poos proclaimed that 'The hour of Europe has dawned.' America should kindly leave this one to us. As foreign minister of Luxembourg, M. Poos informed the peoples of disintegrating Yugoslavia that small states have no future. Ever since that aptly ridiculous moment, the states supposedly united in the European Union, and especially Britain, France and Germany, have been directly involved in what has happened. At the very latest since the imposition of the arms embargo on Bosnia, we have directly affected the military balance of this war and become, willy-nilly, a party to the destruction. Not just we Europeans, of course. Plainly the UN bears its own specific responsibility; and the USA and other non-European states too.

The point here is not to pick over, once again, the whole tortuous diplomatic and military history of the four years from, as it were, Jacques Poos to Richard Holbrooke, deploying the documentary CD-ROM now available with David Owen's memoirs to demonstrate that the Germans were most to blame here, or the British there. Nor is it to distinguish, as one clearly should, between individual politicians, officials and UN commanders on the ground. The point is simply to restate a few bald facts about Europe's failure. In the last four years we have failed to prevent the destruction and partition of a once peaceful and still beautiful part of Europe, with perhaps a quarter of a million people killed and more than 2 million made homeless. To many a professional soldier's profound frustration and anger, British and French soldiers have had to sit there on the ghetto walls while the people inside were humiliated and shot. Worst of all, there is the supposed UN 'safe area' of Srebrenica, where Dutch UN soldiers this summer stood by (if not worse) while Bosnian men were taken off to be killed.

Apart from the valiant but largely vain efforts of Hans Koschnick, the EU administrator of Mostar, the EU as such is represented in Bosnia only by its monitors, known locally as 'the ice-cream men' because of their ludicrous uniform of white shirts, white pullovers, white trousers and white plimsolls. Cricket umpires whom no one obeys. Yet, when all is said and done, the ice-cream men seem less a caricature than a pretty fair representation of the external policy of that thing called Europe, which looked so bright and hopeful just four years ago.

3

Now for the excuses. First, there is the diplomat's eternal refrain: 'What would *you* have done?' 'What was the alternative?' Well, of course we never can know 'What would have happened if . . .' For example, if we had done nothing – including, that is, not stopping anyone get arms – then it is possible that Bosnia would have been simply obliterated, partitioned between a Greater Serbia and a Greater Croatia, as the post-communist opportunist Slobodan Milošević (who started it) and the post-communist nationalist Franjo Tudjman (who has come out on top) discussed at their secret meeting at Tito's villa in Karadjordjevo in March 1991. But it is also possible that the Bosnians would somehow have defended more of their territory, as they somehow defended most of Sarajevo in 1992. We can only make an informed guess.

Many of the 'What was the alternative?' arguments, however, actually come back to the question of political will in the West, and specifically in Western Europe. Few soldiers will disagree with the proposition that what we have done militarily to stop the worst of the siege of Sarajevo could have been done militarily three years ago. All along, the professional soldiers were saying that we needed a large force – of the order of 60,000 men – to stop the fighting in Bosnia. If that is what we are proposing to put in now, why did we not do it then? Ah, because there has been 'a process of ripening', one is told; because it needed three years of our masterly diplomacy to detach Milošević from Karadžić. But Karadžić himself says that 10,000 men could have stopped him.[1]

And then we get to the point: that we were simply not ready to do it then. But who is 'we' in this sentence? The talk turns to the reluctance of parliaments, to how public opinion would have reacted to our soldiers coming back in body bags. Actually, the British and French publics are probably less sensitive to the famous 'body bags' than is American public opinion, so long as they can be persuaded that the end is good and the means patriotic. But nobody even tried to persuade them. Whatever you think of Margaret Thatcher, you can't help wondering what might have happened if she had still been in charge.

In the second line of excuses, there is a whole regiment of arguments from cultural prejudice. Here are the old saws about ancient hatreds and atavistic tribes. 'We can't stop people who *want* to kill each other,' I recently heard a senior EU official say. Here is the view that, after all, what else can you expect of the Balkans? This view is particularly associated in the United States with Robert Kaplan's book *Balkan Ghosts*, but implicit in a great many other analyses and commentaries. Unfortunately, too, the idea of 'Central Europe', revived in the 1980s as a political-cultural distinction against the Soviet 'East', has now been turned southward against 'the Balkans', in effect trying to make it easier for Poles and Czechs to get into the EU by suggesting that Croats, Bosnians or Bulgarians belong to a different world. Cultural determinism as an instrument of foreign policy. And then there is the view, quite widespread among the Western diplomats and soldiers involved, that all sides are as bad as each other – meaning, in particular, that the Bosnian government side is no better than the Serbs or Croats. So a plague on all their houses.

Now plainly it is important not to fall into the opposite mistake: selective idealization rather than collective demonization. To suggest that Bosnia was, as it were, a Switzerland invaded by a Nazi Serbia; that Sarajevo in 1990 was a hotbed of European genius, like Vienna in 1900; that the victims must always be guiltless, because that makes things morally and aesthetically easy for their foreign supporters; and that the current Bosnian state is a model multi-ethnic, multicultural, multi-religious, multi-everything liberal democracy. This is the story that some Bosnian politicians will still try to tell you, but it is not the story that Messrs Kohl, Chirac and Santer will be told when I have sat them down in that café in Ciglane.

With a self-restraint and honesty which is, in the circumstances, quite remarkable, the surviving liberal intellectuals of Sarajevo (who are obviously, by definition, not typical, here as everywhere else) tell a much more subtle and therefore more convincing story. They are the first to be ironical about the ideological flag of what they call 'multi-multi-multi' which has been hoisted over their city and the remains of their country.

In crude summary, the story goes something like this. For centuries Bosnia was, as everyone knows, a unique meeting place of east, west and south, Orthodox, Catholic, Bogomil, muslim, Jew, the Ottoman and Austro-Hungarian empires, and, from the late nineteenth century, self-consciously national Serb and Croat. Coexistence was often fragile, consisting in a peaceful living side by side rather than mixing, a respecting rather than accepting the other's customs. It was punctuated in the first half of the twentieth century by two horrible periods of war and internecine conflict along both ethnic and political lines. After 1945, however, under Tito's iron roof of 'brotherhood and unity', not only was coexistence restored but the mixing advanced. To this mixing, many factors contributed – not least urbanization, secularization and some assimilation to a Yugoslav identity.

Naturally, this process went furthest in the city of Sarajevo, and furthest of all among the younger generation, who had their own zany version of post-'68 youth culture. An editor of the monthly *Dani* tells me he and his friends are fighting 'freedom, human rights and urban culture', and when I query the term 'urban culture' he shoots back, in English, 'Sex, drugs and rock 'n' roll.' It may not have been the world's most creative or exciting place. Many of the best and brightest left, especially for Belgrade. But it had real beauty and charm, a civilized lifestyle, the café raised to an art form.

However – and here's the rub – all of this was still under the political roof of an undemocratic, Titoist Yugoslavia. If you talk to the Croat Catholic Cardinal Puljić of Sarajevo, or to one of the spiritual leaders of the muslim religious community, they both start by explaining how their communities were oppressed under communism. The contortions of Tito's own nationality policy only made things worse, by identifying the heirs of the Bosniak part of the population as a national group called Muslims with a capital M (as opposed to the faith, with a small m).[2] So here, as elsewhere in communist Europe, there was simultaneously the assimilation and the exacerbation of ethnic, cultural and religious differences by communist rule and repression.

The end of communism was therefore bound to be a critical moment, and there was always only a small chance that the repressed grievances and tensions between the different traditions and communities could, even in the most favourable circumstances, have been negotiated peacefully into a stable democratic state. After all, even in the peaceful, prosperous, democratic West, Switzerland is still a great exception. Look at Belgium. Look at Canada. This was true of Yugoslavia as a whole, but above all of Bosnia, which had a Bosniak plurality, but no majority.

Even the slim chance that still existed was, however, then denied them. Tito's heirs, and specifically the post-communist politicians of first Serbia and then Croatia, either adopted a manipulative nationalist programme in order to gain and retain power (Milošević) or used manipulative post-communist methods of gaining and retaining power in order to realize a nationalist programme (Tudjman). As they pulled Yugoslavia apart, they of course found Bosnian Serb and Bosnian Croat leaders ready to join them in the enterprise. Bosnian politics, especially in the country outside Sarajevo, rapidly divided on these lines. The West, and specifically the EC, then hastened to recognize the independence of the former Yugoslav republics of Slovenia, Croatia and, yes, Bosnia-Hercegovina, without beginning to think through what it would need to turn this unique and delicately balanced historic entity into a viable independent state.

Of course Alija Izetbegović and his Bosniak-led SDA were not blameless in this whole process. Of course there are many nasty, corrupt, manipulative and authoritarian aspects of the present SDA regime. Perhaps if you are an UNPROFOR commander or a negotiator on the ground it is the Bosnian government and army representatives who are the most slippery and difficult to deal with, as British and French soldiers in Sarajevo will hasten to tell you. But to jump from that current experience to an assertion of moral equivalence between the three sides is to lose sight of the wood for the trees and to forget how we got to where we are now. In terms of historical responsibility the position is clear.

There is an important difference in the degree of responsibility between the Serbian and Croatian regimes, but there is a difference in kind between the responsibility of the Serbian and Croatian regimes, on the one hand, and that of the Bosnian regime on the other. Bosnia was the victim of aggression from first one side, then the other. Bosnia and the Bosnians have suffered most, lost most, and are still most likely to lose more.

4

It is important to grasp that the reality on the ground today is a Bosnia split *three* ways: between areas of Bosnian Serb, Bosnian Croat and Bosnian-government control. This reality is best represented on paper by an internal UNPROFOR map entitled, pithily, *Warring Faction Update*. It shows that the Bosnian Serbs – with their 'Serb Republic' para-state – control some 48 per cent of the territory of Bosnia-Hercegovina, in an unwieldy shape like two lungs almost cut off in the middle at the so-called Posevina corridor. The Bosnian Croats control some 21 per cent, with the Hercegovinan part relatively coherent and conveniently contiguous to the Croatian fatherland, and then some awkward enclaves in the central Bosnian-government region. Bosnian-government forces themselves actually control less than one-third of the territory, and theirs is much the most fragmented part.

Their capital, Sarajevo, is still surrounded by Serbs, with the gunmen still in the surrounding hills and just a stone's throw across the river Miljacka, in the suburb of Grbavica. Their main portion of central Bosnia is, at this writing, still separated by Croat-held territory from the Bihać pocket in the north-west. And then there is the remaining enclave of Goražde – Bosnia's Leningrad – separated from Sarajevo by some twenty-five miles of Serb-held land. Following the terms of the ceasefire, I was able to visit Goražde, courtesy of a US-embassy armoured Land Rover, but there is still nothing like safe access for ordinary Bosnian civilians. Some call this territory 'rump Bosnia', but at least a rump is one piece. Their territory is also landlocked. Some supplies come in by air (including arms purchased with Arab money), but for the most part they have to come by land via Croatia – and the Croatians have been taking a large cut of the incoming money, goods and, of course, arms.

In theory, the Bosnian-government and Bosnian Croat parts are united in a 'Federation of Bosnia and Hercegovina', created in last year's Washington agreements. But the evidence on the ground is all of a continued, almost total, division, with the Croat parts wholly run by the para-state of Herceg-Bosna, having its own insignia, police, armed forces closely linked to the Croatian army, and children taught from Croatian schoolbooks, and even, since Croatia's parliamentary elections in October, with their own 'diaspora' representatives in the Zagreb parliament. In a wood outside the Bosnian Croat exclave of Kiseljak you suddenly come upon two dirty caravans and two dishevelled frontier policemen: a Bosnian Croat/Bosnian-government frontier post. Hans Koschnick will tell you how all the peaceful pressure that the EU has so far been able (or willing) to exert has not brought the Bosnian Croat authorities in the western half of the divided city of Mostar even to let people pass freely across the river Neretva from the pulverized and miserable Bosnian eastern half. Even though Croat forces supported Bosnian ones in the recent campaign, they reportedly twice went back to fighting each other. And President Tudjman's generous offer in an interview with *Le Figaro* to help 'Europeanize the muslims' hardly makes things any better.

Moreover, if you look at the population figures you find that, through war, murder, flight and expulsion, the ethnic separation, like the territorial, is already far advanced. The Bosnian government maintains a commitment to a multi-ethnic state. There are Serb and Croat members of its presidency. There is a Serb general on the Bosnian general staff, always wheeled out to talk to foreign visitors. The Croat cardinal insists he will stay in Sarajevo, and serve all the Catholics in all of Bosnia-Hercegovina. But the fact is that the Bosnian-government parts are becoming increasingly Bosniak or, to use the misleading term, Muslim. As for 'muslim' in the religious sense, I did find some anecdotal evidence of the growth of religious belief – 'In times of trouble, man remembers his God' – but nothing remotely resembling 'fundamentalism'. ('I consider myself a muslim,' one historian told me, and, as if on cue, someone came in to refill his large glass of local grape brandy.)

What one does find, however, is elements of something which might be described as nascent Bosnian nationalism. For example, the insistence on calling the language 'Bosnian'. This is entirely under-standable, since one could hardly now expect them to call it 'Serbo-Croat' or 'Serb' or 'Croat', but also rather absurd – for if ever there was an area where the Serb and Croat variants of the common language really were intertwined, together with some regional peculiarities and enrichments, it was Bosnia. In a way, this is a *reductio ad absurdum* of nineteenth-century nation-building through language. But then what on earth are they to do if everyone else around them is separating out into national states, with nationality defined in a neo-Herderian way by that combination of blood, language, religion and culture which supposedly makes a *Volk*?

Moreover, though still chronically short of heavy weapons, they are defending themselves. (Who was it who said that a language is a dialect with an army?[3]) They try to make up in numbers of soldiers for what they lack in weaponry. In Goražde, we were told that, of some 57,000 people crammed into the enclave, as many as 10,000 were now bearing arms. Before the war, the Bosniaks were not famed as fighters. But nor, before the Second World War, were the European Jews. Some Bosnians say despairingly that they are fated to become Europe's Palestinians. Others are determined, however wildly unlikely it may sound, that they should become Europe's Israelis.

Contemptuously dismissing my suggestion that Europe might still have anything to offer them, a Bosnian editor ennumerated the three things that they now need: a strong army, help for economic recon-struction, and American support.

5

And so to Dayton, Ohio, where, once again, for the – what? third? fourth? – time this century, America is trying to resolve a European conflict which Europe has failed to resolve for itself . . .

I believe Europe should prepare to take over the leading role in providing the international roof under which the different communities in Bosnia might live side by side and then perhaps, gradually, over many years, grow together again. As a European, I shall do what I can to try to ensure that this becomes a priority for European leaders. But, alas, here, too, I simply don't believe that it will happen. On the flight out to Zagreb I read Helmut Kohl telling the *Süddeutsche Zeitung*, 'We will make the process of unifying Europe irreversible in the next two years or so.' On the flight back, nearly three weeks later, I find the West European papers full of passionate debate about European monetary union.

There are quite other priorities here: no sense of urgency about what is happening just an hour's flying-time away; no sense that there is any contradiction between the claim that Europe is peacefully, irreversibly uniting and the fact that at the very same time a part of Europe is being brutally, and, one fears, really irreversibly, torn apart. The long tortuous process of polit-bureaucratic negotiation at the EU's next intergovernmental conference, scheduled to open in 1996, is supposed to produce improvements to the Union's so-called Common Foreign and Security Policy. But I'm afraid we can already guess what that will mean for Bosnia. More ice-cream men.

6

If a Swiss diplomatic observer had gone to sleep after the Congress of Berlin, which assigned Bosnia-Hercegovina to Austria-Hungary in 1878, and awoke now, he would of course find much to surprise him in the institutionalized cooperation of West European states. Here, he might exclaim, is a permanent Congress of Berlin! So far as the diplomacy goes, he might wonder a little about the blue helmets and white vehicles of the UN, and about Mr Carl Bildt representing the EU. But a great deal would seem very familiar.

In the so-called Contact Group he would see representatives of the same powers – France, Britain, Germany and Russia – pursuing their national interests through their national diplomats and national armies, in what he would probably still call 'the Eastern Question'. Turning to *The Times*, he would read, in a leading article, of a new Franco-British entente 'forged in the Bosnian War'. The only difference is that he would have to substitute the United States for Austria-Hungary.

To him, what has been happening on the ground would probably also make sense, although as a Swiss he would not like it. 'Ah yes,' he would say, 'this crazy modern passion for separating out into national states has obviously proceeded apace. I remember when the Serbs started it . . .'

In other words, it begins to look almost as if the whole twentieth-century European story of post-imperial federations and communist multinational states was merely an interruption of a longer, underlying process of separating and moulding peoples into nation states. In Western Europe, we did it earlier, by and large, through conquest and forced assimilation. In Central Europe, the first half of the twentieth century saw the job largely done, by war, the redrawing of frontiers, and ethnic 'cleansing' on a massive scale (although the two-nation federation of Czechoslovakia still remained, to be finished off in the 1990s). Now this part of south-eastern Europe is following suit – catching up, one might almost say, with modern Europe.

Obviously, this thought can be pushed too far. There are quite specific reasons why former Yugoslavia and Bosnia were pulled apart as they were. Even in former Yugoslavia, Macedonia still fragilely holds as a multi-ethnic state. There are parts of the former Soviet Union where ethnic groups still coexist. Nor does it follow that 'Bosnia is our future.' What we have witnessed on our television screens over the last four years is precisely the simultaneous theatre of continued peace, normality and further (though halting) steps of integration in one part of Europe, and bloody disintegration in another.

Before 1989, Europe was like Berlin: divided between East and West by a single Wall. Now Europe is like a great American city, with

prosperous and relatively peaceful neighbourhoods, such as George-
town or the Upper East Side of Manhattan, existing just a few blocks
away from violent and miserable ghettos. There are no concrete walls
across the streets. In theory, you can drive anywhere. But in practice
the two are still worlds apart. This should shame us in Europe, just
as that should shame America. But somehow we live with it.

Yet this simile, too, is misleading. For the cruellest twist is that the
formation of post-communist nation states with clear ethnic majorities, through policies that combine the philosophy of Fichte with the
methods of Stalin, probably does *not* condemn them to the fate of
being Europe's permanent slums. They are not doomed for ever
to be chronically backward states, with corrupt one-party regimes
maintaining their hold by television brainwashing, xenophobia and
force. For example, I would say that Croatia has a reasonable chance of
gradually evolving into a reasonably liberal, pluralistic and democratic
nation state over the next ten to twenty years. It might even, in the
still longer term, develop a genuine acceptance of minorities and, who
knows, eventually, a civic rather than an ethnic definition of nationality.

With the Polish experience in mind, Konstanty Gebert sarcastically
puts the lesson thus: 'If you want to "return to Europe", first do your
ethnic cleansing, then wait a generation.' One can turn it round
another way, and put it more mildly. Trying to describe the ethnic
and cultural mélange of Sarajevo before the war, the painter Edo
Numankadić said to me, 'We were Europe before Europe.' Hyperbole
perhaps. But with an element of truth. The democratization of Yugoslavia, and of Bosnia in particular, would, had it worked, have been
an unique example of a part of Europe moving peacefully from a truly
multi-ethnic society under an undemocratic (imperial, then communist) political roof to such a society within a democratic framework.
That it failed there does not mean it has to fail everywhere, or that
we should give up trying – let alone that we should accept ethnic
cleansing as a necessary evil. But – alas, alas for Europe! – it does
seem to be the case that almost nobody has yet been able to avoid the
painful path which has led through the formation of nation states, to
– if one is lucky – the securing of human and civil rights by a democratic
nation state, and thence – if one is very lucky – to the peaceful
cooperation and integration of those nation states.

So this not just a matter of confronting Europe's failure and Europe's continued responsibility in this part of Europe. Properly understood, Bosnia does, I believe, compel us to re-examine some of our most basic assumptions about the shape and direction of European history.

Of course the view of Europe you get from Sarajevo is partial as well as bitter. But I trust that my hijacked European leaders will by now have seen the point of their involuntary stopover.

We are now coming in to land at Brussels Airport. Please fasten your safety belts and extinguish all easy speeches.

I return to and develop further this argument in 'Cry, the Dismembered Country', see below, p. 354.

1995

18 October. The Czech parliament approves the new 'lustration' law, overriding the veto of President Havel.

29 October. Franjo Tudjman's Croatian Democratic Union (HDZ) wins parliamentary elections in Croatia.

1 November. Bosnia peace negotiations begin at a US Air Force base in Dayton, Ohio.

November–December. In France, the Juppé government announces cuts in welfare spending, designed to meet the Maastricht criteria for participation in monetary union. Widespread popular protests follow.

5 November. Eduard Shevardnadze is re-elected president of Georgia.

16 November. Populist left-winger Oskar Lafontaine is elected leader of the German Social Democrats.

19 November. Presidential elections in Poland.

Abnormal Normality

The Polish philosopher Leszek Kołakowski has a Law of the Infinite Cornucopia. This states that there is never a shortage of arguments to support whatever doctrine you want to believe in for whatever reasons. The historian's version of this law is that causes can invariably be found for any event or phenomenon, however extraordinary or unexpected. Whatever happens will be explained.

The election of the post-communist Aleksander Kwaśniewski as president of Poland, on 19 November 1995, perfectly illustrates this law. Numerous articles have immediately explained, with clarity, vivid supporting detail and persuasive arguments, why 'Poland chose' a former communist apparatchik in preference to the former Solidarity leader, Nobel Prize-winner and incumbent president, Lech Wałęsa. Never mind that if just 2 per cent of the votes had gone the other way we would have read numerous articles explaining, with equal clarity and persuasiveness, why Poland had re-elected Wałęsa. Thus is history written.

Yet this was an astonishing result. Six years after the end of communism, the country which had the strongest anti-communist opposition and the weakest communist party in the Soviet bloc has both a post-communist government and a post-communist president. If anyone had predicted this in the autumn of 1989 they would have been laughed out of the room. But then so would anyone who had predicted in the autumn of 1983 that within six years Poland would have a Catholic prime minister. Or, for that matter, anyone who had suggested in 1977, when the twenty-five-year-old Aleksander Kwaśniewski joined the ruling communist party, that the party state would soon be engulfed by a 10-million-strong national movement called Solidarity. The kaleidoscope keeps turning. Each turn is a surprise. And each turn changes our view of the past as well as of the present.

I

Now for those explanations. First, there is a regional pattern. Most of post-communist Europe today has post-communist rulers. In Central Europe, the Czech Republic is the only clear exception. There are major differences between, for example, countries like Poland and Hungary, which had intervening periods of transformation under liberal or conservative governments, and those like Romania, which went straight from the communist frying pan into the post-communist fire. Polish and Hungarian communists in the 1980s were, in important ways, already less communist than their Czech comrades – let alone their Russian ones.

Nonetheless, there is a pattern. Post-communist parties inherit nationwide organizations, offices, personnel and funds, which are usually enhanced, at the end of communism, by appropriating the property of the party state. The 'privatization of the *nomenklatura*' – itself one of the reasons why communists gave up political power so relatively quietly – produces a new class of communists-turned-capitalists. Actually, the Yugoslav dissident Milovan Djilas famously described the *nomenklatura* itself as 'the new class', so this must be the new new class. They back their old-new party by funding or fixing, and through the media they own. Former communists also have the habits and discipline of patient, boring political groundwork, which former dissidents and intellectuals generally do not.

To be sure, the business of democratic politics differs from that of communist politics. But there are people slightly lower down the communist hierarchy who very rapidly adapt to the rather different techniques of acquiring and exercising power in a modern television democracy. You may not be able to teach an old dog new tricks, but the young dogs learn them in no time. After all, they joined the party in the 1970s not because they believed in communism but because they were interested in making a career. And in the real politics of power rather than the intellectual and moral 'anti-politics' of dissidence.

In the electorate, they have a hard core of the old faithful. Then they pick up votes from those who have suffered from the transition to a market economy: the unemployed, workers in large state-owned factories, the middle-aged and small-town dwellers who have difficulty adapting to new ways, and impoverished pensioners. When people had the basic, minimal security afforded by a police welfare state, they longed for freedom; now that they have freedom they yearn for the old security as well. Post-communists promise that the state will provide more housing, employment and social security, while preserving the gains of freedom and the market.

Kwaśniewski's victory partly fits this broad pattern, but also has unique Polish features. His Alliance of the Democratic Left incorporates the so-called Social Democracy of the Republic of Poland – the direct successor to Poland's ruling communist party – whose leader he became in 1990. Although it suffers from internal tensions, the Alliance is much the largest, best-organized and best-funded party in Poland. Its backers are classic exemplars of the new 'new class' – corrupt apparatchiks turned corrupt businessmen. During the campaign, it emerged that Kwaśniewski's own wife had a large shareholding – which he had not declared – in one of these *nomenklatura* capitalist companies. Kwaśniewski gave several implausible explanations of why he had not declared this holding in his parliamentary statement of members' interests, including the suggestion that he and his wife had separated their finances and he didn't know about it.

By contrast with the standard practice in many other post-communist countries, his candidacy was not outrageously promoted by the news and current-affairs programmes of state television, which rather favoured the incumbent President Wałęsa. However, he did enjoy the support of papers such as the best-selling satirical weekly *Nie* ('No'), the organ of Jerzy Urban, formerly General Jaruzelski's spokesman during martial law.

Kwaśniewski's campaign was a masterpiece of 1990s designer electioneering, from his immaculate suits and ties to the perfect delivery of his television sound bites. A friend who commutes between Paris and Warsaw told me it was quite as professional as the presidential campaigns in France. Perhaps this is not surprising, since a leading French public-relations consultant, Jacques Séguéla, was advising him. Séguéla who has previously worked for François Mitterrand (he claims to have been behind the slogan '*La France Tranquille*') and was recommended to Kwaśniewski by the Austrian chancellor Franz Vranitsky, says he helped to invent Kwaśniewski's two main slogans – 'Choose the Future' and 'A Common Poland' – and to prepare him for his crucial television debates with Lech Wałęsa. In a telephone conversation, M. Séguéla tells me that he likes to do an election campaign every year or two. It is, he says, his 'hobby'. Besides Mitterrand and Vranitsky, his advisees have included the Bulgarian president Zhelyu Zhelev and the former Hungarian prime minister József Antall. He finds 'Alexander' to be young, clever, courageous and *médiatique*. He is, says M. Séguéla, something between a Kennedy and a Bill Clinton, whom he describes as 'a great president' – although adding cautiously 'at least from the point of view of communications'.

Kwaśniewski also used more old-fashioned methods. He toured the country assiduously, promising good things like more housing (a major worry for the young), social security and pensions – things on which, incidentally, the Polish president has little power to decide, even taking the broadest interpretation of his rather ill-defined constitutional powers.

However, the composition of his vote does not entirely bear out the standard interpretation of post-communist return. It is true that Wałęsa got slightly more votes in cities and large towns – where the effects of economic growth have been more visible – and Kwaśniewski got slightly more in small towns and the countryside. But his was not simply the vote of losers in an economic game in which his close associates are, after all, among the greatest winners. Voting for him, people also chose a personification of success. And he benefited from a 'feel-good factor' in a country which has the fastest economic growth in Europe: 6.5 per cent in the first half of 1995. The liberal architects of Poland's 'economic miracle', such as Leszek Balcerowicz, now leader of the opposition Freedom Union party, wryly observe that Kwaśniewski reaps the harvest of the changes they introduced.

Moreover, Kwaśniewski got significantly more votes from the young and Wałęsa more from the old. Here was the great role-reversal. The former communist became the man of the future, making Wałęsa look like a man of the past. Just forty-three years old (to Wałęsa's fifty-two), suntanned, trim (he dieted specially for the elections), snappily dressed, better educated (although it now emerges that he lied about having received a master's degree from Gdańsk University), smooth-talking, yuppie-like, 'Olek' Kwaśniewski sold himself as modern, forward-looking, Western. Perhaps inspired by M. Séguéla, his supporters even called him 'the Polish Kennedy'. And the whole message was 'Choose the Future.'

2

Yet how could people so rapidly forget the past? In Hungary one might understand it more easily: 1956 was a very long time ago, and by the 1980s the party's iron fist was hidden deep inside a thick velvet glove. But not in Poland, where just a few years ago this same Aleksander Kwaśniewski was, as editor of the communist youth newspaper and then as minister for youth, justifying the imposition of martial law, the internment of political opponents and the banning of Solidarity.

Well, first of all, a lot of people have not forgotten. Many voted for Lech Wałęsa simply in order to stop an ex-communist from becoming their president. Conversely, some of Kwaśniewski's party electorate voted for him precisely because he is an ex-communist. Indeed, for all the slimming and suntanning and smart suits, Kwaśniewski, with his hatchet jaw and slab cheekbones, still has something of the face and posture of the Stalinist worker-hero in Andrzej Wajda's film *Man of Iron*. (People are now speculating about a sequel. *Man of Silicon?*)

For the young, however, communism and Solidarity are already ancient history – something they are forced to learn about from boring textbooks. Here the post-Solidarity leaders are a victim of their own success. So rapid have been the changes, so self-evident has freedom become in just six years, that the young can hardly remember anything else. On election day, I had lunch with a friend who was a samizdat publisher in the 1980s. 'Yes', he reminisced, 'of course in those days you never used to phone beforehand, just appeared at the door.' 'But *why* didn't he phone?' asked his fourteen-year-old daughter. Long pause. 'Oh, you mean because the phone was bugged?' With some young voters, there was an element of conscious revolt. Just because the parents identify so strongly with the post-Solidarity tradition, the children vote against it.

There remains, nonetheless, a question. In 1989, Solidarity leaders negotiated with Polish communists at the Round Table, and made a power-sharing deal summed up in a famous headline in the Solidarity paper *Gazeta Wyborcza*: 'Your President, Our Premier'. The Warsaw Pact still existed, and this seemed the most the Soviet Union would accept. In a spirit of liberal Catholic forgiveness, and having in mind the model of post-Franco Spain, the Solidarity premier Tadeusz Mazowiecki drew what he called a 'thick line' under the past. But did that line have to be quite so thick? And was it still right a year or two later, when the Soviet constraint had largely disappeared, to continue without any systematic purges of former communists or secret-police collaborators from public life (such as happened in Czechoslovakia and East Germany), without Latin American-style truth commissions, tribunals (except one specifically on the responsibility for martial law) or other symbolic steps to remind the public, and particularly the young, of what communists had done to Poland?

This question has divided the post-Solidarity opposition. The right say the revolution should have been completed: not with the guillotine, to be sure, but with purges. Then Kwaśniewski would never have got back. One of their representatives put it graphically on election night. In eighteen post-communist countries, he said, there has been no de-communization and post-communists are back in power; in two, the Czech Republic and East Germany, there has been de-communization and they are not. (The figures don't quite hold up, but one gets the general point.)

At the other extreme is the former dissident and now editor of *Gazeta Wyborcza* Adam Michnik, who has counted Kwaśniewski among his friends since 1989, written a preface to General Jaruzelski's memoirs, and in September published a highly controversial article arguing that the time had come for the post-communist and the post-Solidarity sides to sit down together and try to agree a common version of the history of Poland under communist rule. The significance of the article was less what it said than the fact that it was signed jointly by Michnik and Włodzimierz Cimoszewicz, a post-communist member of parliament who soon thereafter became Kwaśniewski's campaign manager.

Michnik argues that somebody had to break through the social ostracism of the post-communists, which he dramatically describes as 'apartheid'. (But are the former communists now the blacks or the whites in that metaphor?) He also points out that, in spite of de-communization, the post-communists got nearly a fifth of the vote in East Germany at the last parliamentary elections (not far short of what they got in Poland), and suggests that we should wait a little longer to see what happens in the Czech Republic.

On balance, it seems to me that this very conciliatory 'Spanish' approach to the past probably has facilitated the return of the post-communists to power in Poland, although of course one can never prove that a tougher, more 'Czech' or 'East German', approach would have prevented it.

3

Absolutely peculiar to Poland was the role of the Catholic Church. The Church threw its immense authority and influence not so much, initially, behind Wałęsa – for in the first round there were other conservative Catholic candidates, such as the exceedingly devout president of the National Bank, Hanna Gronkiewicz-Waltz – but emphatically against the atheist post-communists. In the late summer, a message from the Episcopate warned against 'choosing for the highest positions in the fatherland people who during the period of the totalitarian state were involved in exercising power at the highest party-government level'. Now who could they mean? The post-communists' support for a liberal abortion law and resistance to ratifying the concordat with the Vatican further sharpened the Church's opposition.

Primate Glemp denounced the representatives of what he delightfully called 'neo-paganism'. (In a subsequent interview, he averred that 'neo-pagan' is a purely descriptive term for non-believers. Such people could not, he carefully explained, be described as 'pagans', since 'a pagan has a specific faith'.) Before the second-round run-off, the Church came very close to telling the faithful to vote for Wałęsa, who famously wears a badge of the Black Madonna of Częstochowa on his lapel. The bishop responsible for the pastoral care of farmers sent a special letter to country and small-town dwellers, headed 'Don't abandon the fatherland in need!' At the entrance to St Stanisław Kostki, the famous Warsaw church of a Solidarity priest murdered by secret police in 1984, I found a Wałęsa election poster displayed beneath the timetable of services. On the very eve of the election, Primate Glemp called on the faithful to pray for 'the elections, President Wałęsa and the fatherland'.

And still Wałęsa lost – especially in the countryside and the small towns. In spite of the Church's appeals; or perhaps even because of them. Three-quarters of those asked in one pre-election opinion poll said that the Church should not try to influence the election result. After the event, the secretary-general of the Episcopate, Bishop Tadeusz Pieronek, told me that he thinks people may well have resented what he called the Church's 'paternalistic' approach, and that he is sure many good Catholics voted for Kwaśniewski. As for young Poles, I suspect many of them will have said, 'Neo-paganism? Mmm, yes please!' It would be a fine irony if it was the Catholic Church which won the election for the neo-pagan.

Yet part of the responsibility must also lie with the whole post-Solidarity side of Polish politics, divided into many, mainly small, parties, with several different presidential candidates, and as much occupied with fighting among themselves as with serious nationwide politics. They have, in fact, done much worse in this respect than their counterparts in Hungary or the Czech Republic, where the liberal and conservative parts of the political spectrum are consolidated into fewer, larger, better-organized parties. Why? Partly because such falling-out is what tends to happen after a revolution, and what Solidarity did in Poland over the whole period from 1980 to 1989 was a revolution, albeit of a new kind. Just because before 1989 people had been more united than in Hungary and the Czech lands, they are more disunited now.

Yet, watching and listening to these theatrical (and sometimes highly enjoyable) quarrels, I am sure that the disunity also has something to do with older Polish traditions. There is the early modern tradition of the so-called noble democracy, with its endlessly disputatious 'little parliaments' and with the gentry, great and small, quarrelling on the election fields of the Polish kings, perhaps even coming to blows, then as theatrically making it up over innumerable beakers of hooch. There is also the tradition of the intelligentsia which the urbanized heirs of the gentry became. This heritage was vividly represented in Warsaw at election time by a fine exhibition of intelligentsia family photographs, spanning five or six generations, from the great-great-grandfather who lost his estates after fighting against the Russians in the January Rising of 1863 to the latest scion graduating from Warsaw University in 1987. Such traditions do not translate easily into the workaday, opportunistic politics of a television mass democracy. Former communist hacks, unburdened by pride or principle, take to it much quicker.

Last, but by no means least, there is Lech Wałęsa himself, who has spent much of the last five years destroying his own monument. Already in 1990, he alienated many former associates and supporters with his 'war at the top' of Solidarity and his demagogic campaign for the presidency. As president, he has been erratic and often authoritarian in his style. He once suggested that he would change prime ministers 'like car bumpers', and he has, in fact, several times destabilized the parliamentary government. He has surrounded himself with a court of mediocre and even shady advisers, some with dubious ties to the security services and the army. Most notoriously, there was his former chauffeur Mieczysław Wachowski, until recently his senior minister of state. Above all, though, the former electrician and workers' leader has failed to become statesmanlike. Not just the Warsaw intelligentsia, whose condescension he so fiercely resents, but many ordinary Poles I have talked to feel that his often undignified manner and broken, ungrammatical Polish do not fit him to represent a proud nation in the world.

Earlier this year, his standing in the opinion polls fell to as low as 6 per cent. Then, having changed his staff – Wachowski and others departing – he tried to adopt a more restrained and presidential style, while, at the same time, successfully polarizing the campaign in historical terms: Lech against the Reds. This brought him a remarkable recovery, back up to a third of the vote in the first round, with the alternative candidate of post-Solidarity liberals and social democrats, the veteran dissident Jacek Kuroń, getting less than 10 per cent. Then most of the post-Solidarity side rallied round Wałęsa. For someone who remembered Solidarity, it was touching to see him together again with former advisers such as Bronisław Geremek and Tadeusz Mazowiecki.

But Jerzy Urban could quote in *Nie*, his satirical weekly, all the devastatingly critical things Wałęsa's former colleagues had said about him over the last five years, giving this mini-anthology the characteristically sarcastic headline 'Wałęsa's a monster, so vote for him.' And many voted for him only as the 'lesser evil', with a heavy heart. 'I don't want to, but I must,' said one voter interviewed on television, ironically using Wałęsa's own words when he announced that he would stand for president in 1990. 'For Wałęsa?' asked the interviewer. 'Unfortunately!' A friend of mine told me, 'All right, I'll drink half a litre and then go and vote for him.' Half a litre of vodka, that is. In the event, we got him there on slightly less.

It was very close. When voting ended at 8 p.m., Polish television's exit polls put Wałęsa ahead at 51.1 per cent to Kwaśniewski's 48.9 per cent. Jubilation and the old street chant of 'Lech Wałęsa! Lech Wałęsa!' from the president's campaign headquarters; defiant chants of 'Olek! Olek!' from Kwaśniewski's. Every half-hour, television gave a later exit-poll result. At 10.30 p.m. the final, cumulative, exit poll, up to the close of voting, still put Wałęsa ahead, but now by just 50.2 per cent to 49.8. Then, at nine minutes past eleven, came the first unofficial result from slightly more than a thousand polling stations: 51.3 per cent for Kwaśniewski, 48.7 for Wałęsa. The final official result was 51.7 per cent to 48.3, with an impressive turnout of 68 per cent.

Opinion polls between the two rounds of voting had shown that Wałęsa lost quite heavily from a rude, unstatesmanlike and incoherent performance in the first of two television debates between the candidates. It is therefore quite possible that, if he had done better and Kwaśniewski worse in that one television debate, the result might have been the other way round. And then, of course, we would all have knowingly explained Wałęsa's triumph, sagely identifying the deeper forces, structures and patterns.

4

So there they are, back on top, the men and women who lied to us for so many years, the cynics, opportunists and careerists, still with their apparatchik's jowls and their lavatory-brush haircuts. Yes, often the very same people. That professor of sociology who went around the world selling martial law while his colleagues were thrown into camps. That 'expert' on international relations who travelled abroad to talk about peace and the environment while Professor Geremek had to sleep in the crypt of a church to avoid arrest by the secret police. And lower down, in the provinces and local government, hundreds of much cruder specimens. What's more, many of them have become privately rich as well as again being publicly powerful. Look at the millionaire Jerzy Urban, for heaven's sake!

A memoir written a few years ago by the now outgoing foreign minister, Władysław Bartoszewski – one of three so-called 'presidential' ministers to resign following Wałęsa's defeat – was entitled *It's Worth Being Decent*. This from a man who was a political prisoner both in Auschwitz and in Stalinist gaols. But, fifty years on, the message for a young Pole would appear to be, *It's Worth Being an Opportunist*.

Aesthetically and morally, the triumph of the post-communists in Poland is profoundly distasteful. But is it dangerous? Not, I believe, so far as their aims and policies are concerned. The leader of Russia's communist party, Gennady Zhuganov, congratulated 'the Polish working masses' on their victory. But you won't catch Mr Kwaśniewski talking about 'working masses'. On the contrary, Poland's post-communists will do everything in their power to live up to the congratulations Kwaśniewski received from Poland's other big neighbour, Germany, and especially those from the new leader of Germany's Social Democrats, Oskar Lafontaine. Kwaśniewski and his friends want desperately to be seen not as eastern post-communists but as regular western social democrats. The president-elect immediately reaffirmed his commitment to Poland seeking membership of the European Union and Nato. Within days, the government was going ahead with the distribution of coupons for the long-delayed mass privatization.

5

It is now commonplace to observe that Poland has become a 'normal country'. But what does this mean? Certainly, to arrive in Warsaw these days is more like arriving in Lisbon or Naples than it is like arriving in Warsaw before 1989. A smart modern airport. No need for a visa. When the passport officers call Polish passport-holders to a separate gate, you simply can't tell the difference, in dress, accoutrements, hairstyles and so on, between the two lines, Polish and Western. A relatively clean taxi, and you are actually charged the local-currency price on the taxi meter. Familiar shops, goods, cars. The same TV commercials. Smart offices. Mobile phones. Professional friends who are now overworked and defend themselves with answering-machines. More and real money, but also more money worries: 'Half our income goes in tax, the other half on school fees!' Great contrasts between rich and poor.

Of course if you dig just a little deeper you find extraordinary things. The man in the Mercedes is a former politburo member. Your mobile-phone salesman is a former secret policeman. In the countryside, you still see peasant houses out of Brueghel. Priests chunter on about 'neo-paganism'. But Europe – our 'normal', 'western', Europe – is also full of extraordinary things. Between observing the Polish elections and writing this essay I had to drop in to Naples for the Premio Napoli awards. The Grand Hotel Vesuvio was even better than the Hotel Bristol in Warsaw, but driving through the city I could see the dreadful slums – far worse than anything in Warsaw – where people still go in fear of the Camorra. Among the Premio Napoli prize-winners was a Jesuit priest, who was being honoured for his fight against usury. ('Why don't you in Britain have a law against usury?' he quizzed me.) The popular post-communist mayor was asked at the televised prize-giving ceremony what he thought of his rival, the post-fascist Signora Alessandra Mussolini (daughter of you-know-who). And, incidentally, was it true that they have been romantically involved? While denying romance, the mayor said that Signora Mussolini had made a very positive contribution to solving some problems in the city. All normal?

So the spectrum of contemporary European 'normality' is very wide, and Poland is now definitely within it. But there is another measure of 'normality': diachronic rather than synchronic. What has been normal for a country historically, over, say, the last two hundred years? By this criterion, Poland today is quite spectacularly abnormal. This country is free, sovereign, prospering? Germany is its best ally in the West? It is not immediately threatened even by Russia? Surely we've got our countries mixed up. I asked the Polish historian Jerzy Jedlicki when before in its history Poland had been so well placed. Scarcely hesitating, he replied, 'Probably the second half of the sixteenth century.'

Poland's transition from normal abnormality to abnormal normality is already a fantastic achievement. The challenge for the next five years is to secure it, internally and externally – which means in the EU and in Nato. Only then will we, and the Poles themselves, begin to see what the Polish version of European 'normality' really looks like. This Polish normality may well not be as interesting as the old abnormality. Indeed, it may at first look like a cheap copy of the West. But, if that is freedom's price, it is surely worth paying. And, anyway, who knows? As the British historian Hugh Trevor-Roper once wryly observed: history is full of surprises, and no one is more surprised by them than historians.

1995

14 November. The European Monetary Institute publishes a timetable for monetary union.

21 November. Bosnian president Alija Izetbegović, Serbian president Slobodan Milošević and Croatian president Franjo Tudjman initial the Dayton peace agreement. This provides for the formal maintenance of a unitary state, but far-reaching de facto division into the Bosniak–Croat Federation, having 51 per cent of the territory, and the Serb Republic, having 49 per cent. The Bosniaks get suburbs of Sarajevo and a corridor to Goražde; the Serbs retain Srebrenica and Žepa. A Nato Implementation Force (IFOR) is to police the agreement.

30 November. President Clinton visits Northern Ireland, encouraging the 'peace process' there.

6 December. The German Bundestag votes for German forces to participate in IFOR in Bosnia.

14 December. The Bosnian, Serb and Croat presidents formally sign the Dayton agreement.

15–16 December. An EU summit in Madrid agrees that the single European currency should be called the 'euro'. Another intergovernmental conference, to review the implementation of Maastricht, will open at the end of March.

17 December. Communists win Russian parliamentary elections, with right-wing nationalists in second place.

20 December. In Bosnia, UNPROFOR hands over to IFOR, which divides the country into American, British and French sectors.

31 December. A customs union between the EU and Turkey comes into force.

1996

8 January. Death of François Mitterrand.

11–13 January. Hanbury Manor, England. At a high-level Franco-British meeting, a senior French businessman gives me his view of the eastward enlargement of the European Union to include former communist countries. '*Il faut toujours en parler,*' he says, '*et jamais y penser.*' 'One should always talk about it and never think about it.' I had always suspected that this was the attitude of much of the French elite to enlargement. But to have it expressed so clearly and elegantly is a kind of bitter delight. A wonderful thing, French *clarté.*

24 January. Józef Oleksy resigns as Polish prime minister following allegations about his collaboration with the KGB and its successors. He will be succeeded by Włodzimierz Cimoszewicz, former campaign manager for President Kwaśniewski.

9 February. An IRA bomb explodes in London's docklands.

3 March. Spanish parliamentary elections end thirteen years of Socialist rule and bring the centre-right Popular Party to power. The prime minister will be José Maria Aznar.

29 March. An EU intergovernmental conference opens in Turin.

5 April. Berkeley, California. We tell our Californian host that we are going to visit Czesław Miłosz, the great contemporary Polish poet, who lives near Berkeley. Later, our kind host collects us and asks, 'Well, how is Milošević?' O happy California, where no one needs to know the difference between a Miłosz and a Milošević!

21 April. Italian parliamentary elections result in victory for the centre-left 'Olive Tree' alliance.

25 April. The German government announces cuts in public expenditure, to meet 'Maastricht criteria' for monetary union.

May. Financial crisis in Bulgaria.

1 June. In Czech parliamentary elections, the Civic Democratic Party of prime minister Václav Klaus loses its overall majority.

June. Controversy in Poland over the post-communist government's decision not to save the Gdańsk shipyard, birthplace of Solidarity, from bankruptcy.

10 June. All-party talks on the future of Northern Ireland open at Stormont Castle in Belfast.

23 June. Death of the veteran Greek socialist leader Andreas Papandreou.

3 July. Boris Yeltsin is re-elected president of Russia, defeating the communist leader Gennady Zhuganov.

14 September. Elections in Bosnia.

15 September. In Italy, Umberto Bossi, leader of the Northern League, declares the independence of the state of 'Padania'.

24 September. The USA, Russia, China, France and Britain sign the Comprehensive Test Ban Treaty.

September. Growing controversy about 'Nazi gold' held by Swiss banks.

15 October. The Council of Europe admits Croatia.

17 October. President Yeltsin dismisses his national security adviser, General Aleksandr Lebed.

29 October. London. I chair a meeting of more than 2,400 people with Mikhail Gorbachev in Westminster Central Hall, jointly arranged by *The Times* and Dillons bookshops to present his memoirs. Only in the central European revolutions of 1989 have I experienced such an explosion of spontaneous emotion as greets him the moment he steps on to the platform. At first, he is brief and sharp. What does he consider his three greatest achievements? I ask him. 'Freedom, openness among nations and an end to the arms race.' He earns wave after wave of applause. But, as the evening progresses, his answers get longer and longer. After a twenty-minute tirade against Boris Yeltsin, he has almost lost the audience; but then he wins them back again.

At dinner afterwards, Gorbachev proposes round after round of toasts, tapping his glass and crying, incongruously, '*Achtung! Achtung!*' (He has told a story about a Lufthansa pilot who kept saying that over the loudspeakers, so this is a kind of joke.) Close impressions: immense strength and warmth of personality. Above all, warmth – human, all-embracing warmth. A man settled in himself: happy to be Russian, happy to have been Soviet. A slightly surprising and very engaging simplicity, for all his experience of the world. His touching, obvious affection towards his wife, Raisa. And the sheer surreality of sitting here, in a London club, as this man who changed the course

239

of the twentieth century proposes toasts with a jovial *'Achtung! Achtung!'*

Raisa seems to feel this surreality too. At one point she feels it necessary to remind us, in her slightly schoolmarmish way, that no previous Soviet leader would have sat with us so informally. 'No, Lenin would not have,' she says. 'Stalin would not have.' Something between a giggle and a shiver goes round the table. 'Not Khrushchev. Or Andropov. Or Chernenko.' 'Well, Andropov might have, you know,' says Gorbachev, indulgently.

31 October. The European Commission accepts the legitimacy of a one-off payment by France Telecom to the French government, to help France meet the Maastricht criteria for monetary union.

Forty Years On

What happened in Hungary in 1956? Here is a fairly typical brief Western summary, from the *Columbia Encyclopedia*:

On Oct. 23, 1956, a popular anti-Communist revolution, centered in Budapest, broke out in Hungary. A new coalition government under Imre Nagy declared Hungary neutral, withdrew it from the Warsaw Treaty, and appealed to the UN for aid. However, János Kádár, one of Nagy's ministers, formed a counter-government and asked the USSR for military support. In severe and brutal fighting, Soviet forces suppressed the revolution. Nagy and some of his ministers were abducted and were later executed. Some 190,000 refugees fled the country. Kádár became premier and sought to win popular support for Communist rule . . .

In Hungary itself, the history of the 1956 revolution was obliterated or traduced for more than thirty years, while János Kádár progressed from Soviet quisling to domestic father-figure and the West's favourite 'liberal' communist. Yet, through all those years, Kádár himself seems to have been haunted and driven by the memory of the comrades he had betrayed and, finally, condemned to death. Imre Nagy was his Banquo – and he was always Macbeth.

A part of the true history was written abroad. Another part was gradually rediscovered by independent historians and oppositional writers inside Hungary in the 1980s, interviewing survivors, publishing suppressed writings, and drawing their own conclusions. Then, in June 1989, Imre Nagy and his closest associates were ceremonially reburied. Beside the coffins of the leaders lying in state on Heroes' Square, there lay a symbolic sixth coffin of the Unknown Insurgent. This was the great symbolic turning point in Hungary's transition from communism to democracy. Banquo's ghost was enthroned.

In a free Hungary, the true history of 1956 could surely at last be revealed. A whole institute was established for this single purpose: the Institute for the History of the 1956 Hungarian Revolution. Archives were opened. Survivors could now talk freely. Young historians set to work. The 1956 Institute produced a new short history of the revolution, which became the Hungarian school textbook.[1]

With the end of communism elsewhere, more evidence also emerged from the Soviet Union, from Yugoslavia, even from China. Not all the evidence, of course, but more. Meanwhile, American, British, French and other Western official documents became available under the 'thirty-year rule'. Some, perhaps the most interesting, remained classified, but scholars pressed for further access and, in the United States, used the Freedom of Information Act to demand it.

I

Now, forty years on, scholars and survivors assemble in the handsome rooms of the Hungarian Academy of Sciences, its high windows looking across the Danube from naughty Pest to haughty Buda. Inside, it looks like just another academic conference.[2] We might be in London, at a conference about the Suez crisis that so fatefully coincided with the Hungarian revolution. This forty-year moment is an interesting one even in more normal countries: the first and generally the last occasion when reasonably digested findings from the archives can be confronted with the reasonably coherent memories of surviving participants. Thirty years after the event, most of the archives are still closed; fifty years on, most of the participants are no longer with us. Yet in Budapest the witnesses have survived not just, say, too many good dinners at the Carlton Club in London, but a death sentence commuted at the last minute to fourteen years in prison. So the occasion is not ordinary at all.

Being tested here is the central proposition of modern historical writing since Ranke: that with the passage of time we know more about the past. This is supposed to be the case because we have greater distance from the past; because we are (supposedly) more impartial;

because we can see the longer-term consequences and therefore the larger historical 'meaning' of the events in question; and, above all, because the documents are now available. The subtitle of this conference is 'The New Archival Evidence'. Following Ranke, we should now learn 'how it really was'. But do we, can we?

In important ways, we certainly learn more. For example, here, from the Soviet archives, are the notes made by V. N. Malin, head of the General Department of the Central Committee of the Communist Party of the Soviet Union, on the Soviet leaders' hectic debates in the Party Presidium.[3] We see them dithering and agonizing in the days after the outbreak of the revolution on 23 October: 'C[omra]de Khrushchev [says] . . . the matter is becoming more complicated . . . the workers are supporting the uprising.' And, later, 'The English and French are in a real mess in Egypt. We shouldn't get caught in the same company.' And their meetings with Chairman Mao's emissaries on 30 October. 'Cde Khrushchev . . . there are two paths. A military path . . . one of occupation. A peaceful path . . . the withdrawal of troops, negotiations.'

So might it really have happened differently? What Gorbachev did in 1989, done by Khrushchev in 1956? These documents warn us against what the French philosopher Henri Bergson called 'the illusions of retrospective determinism' – against the conviction, so hard to resist, that what actually happened had to happen. For years, most of us have lived with the assumption that the Soviet Union could never have tolerated what was happening in Hungary – otherwise it would not have been the Soviet Union. But Soviet leaders plainly did not know that at the time. What would have happened if . . . ?

The openness did not last long. On 31 October, Malin records Khrushchev saying, 'We should re-examine our assessment and should not withdraw our troops from Hungary and Budapest. We should take the initiative in restoring order in Hungary.' What factors were decisive? How important, for example, were concerns about the unity of the international communist movement, with the Italian communist leader Palmiro Togliatti and, finally, also Chairman Mao urging the 'restoration of order'? What difference was made by the assurance given by John Foster Dulles that 'We do not look upon these nations as potential military allies'? What was the impact of Suez? 'If we depart from Hungary,' Khrushchev goes on, 'it will give a great boost to the Americans, English, and French – the imperialists. They will perceive it as weakness on our part and will go on to the offensive ... To Egypt they will then add Hungary.'

'Agreed: Cdes Zhukov, Bulganin, Molotov, Kaganovich, Voroshilov, Saburov' – and behind this sentence the Russian historian Vyacheslav Sereda hears a sigh of relief. The notes continue, 'We should create a Provisional Revol. Gov't (headed by Kádár).' But then, incredibly, 'If Nagy agrees, bring him in as dep. premier.'

Another area of old controversy and new discoveries is the role of Radio Free Europe (RFE), the American-run radio station which broadcast in all the languages of Eastern Europe. Here we have a hitherto unpublished memorandum from William Griffith, then political adviser to RFE.[4] Dated 5 December 1956, it reviews the Hungarian output of RFE and concludes that there were important 'policy violations' by the Hungarian radio journalists involved. One programme on 28 October gave detailed instructions to Hungarian soldiers on the conduct of partisan warfare. 'In the Western capitals,' a commentary on 4 November declared, 'a practical manifestation of Western sympathy is expected at any hour.' Griffith's own conclusion in December 1956 is that the Hungarian service did not *incite* the revolution and '(with one exception) made no *direct* promise or commitment of Western or UN military support or intervention. Its broadcasts may well, however, have encouraged Hungarians to have false hopes in this respect; they certainly did little or nothing to contradict them.'

Now William Griffith, today a distinguished professor emeritus of political science at MIT, is on the platform, together with other surviving participants. He makes essentially the same argument that he did forty years ago. But a journalist who then worked for RFE's Hungarian service angrily suggests that the Hungarian journalists are being scapegoated. They were only following American policy guidance, which, in particular, urged criticism of the communist Imre Nagy, and support for the militantly anti-communist Cardinal József Mindszenty. An American working in RFE at the time jumps up to support him. He remembers the discussions in the newsroom, quotes from the policy guidance given at the time by Griffith, who was, however, himself subject to policy guidance from New York. An old Hungarian, identifying himself as a listener to Radio Free Europe, emotionally declares that it was to blame for the deaths of thousands of Hungarian youngsters.

Pale-faced, her voice trembling, Mária Wittner, one of the street fighters who paid for her part in the revolution with more than fourteen years in prison, reads out extracts from RFE broadcasts in Hungarian. The interpreter gives us some idea of the fiery language: 'The tanks come in . . . invited by the bloody-handed Imre Nagy.' (Basing their judgements too much on official Hungarian radio broadcasts, RFE initially thought Nagy was co-responsible for the first intervention by Soviet troops.) Or, again, 'Where are the traitors . . . who are the murderers? Imre Nagy and his government . . . only Cardinal Mindszenty has spoken out fearlessly . . . Imre Nagy is a base Muscovite.' But afterwards there is some confusion. Are these quotations from RFE's own broadcasts, or from Hungarian radio stations taken over by the insurgents – the 'freedom stations' – some of whose programmes RFE rebroadcast? Jan Nowak, then head of RFE's Polish service, draws the important contrast with Poland, where both the freshly released Cardinal Stefan Wyszyński from inside and RFE from outside immediately and firmly backed Władysław Gomułka, the Polish Nagy.

After this dramatic confrontation of documents and memories, of written and oral history, we can see the historical picture more clearly. With the best of intentions on all sides, and quite understandably, in a confused and drastic situation which changed literally minute by minute, both Hungarians and Americans at RFE got it wrong. Not all of them and not all the time, of course. But in the crucial days of late October their broadcasts attacked Imre Nagy (while the Polish service was supporting Gomułka) and some encouraged armed resistance, with broads hints of imminent Western aid that, in fact, the United States (let alone the Suez-embroiled British and French) had no intention of giving. We can never know what difference this made to the course of events; it probably made little or none to the final result. That does not diminish the moral responsibility.

Here, then, are two cases which seem to justify the implicit, neo-Rankean assumption: that with the passing of time and careful study of the documents we know more about what really happened. Yet this is, on a moment's reflection, a very odd assumption. It was not shared by historians for more than two thousand years before Ranke. And it is not one we usually make in everyday life. Our rather reasonable everyday assumption is that the closer you are to an event, in both time and place, the more you are likely to know about it. 'Well,' we say, 'of course you'd know better, because you were there.'

The fact is that so much of history with a small h – most of it, in fact – is simply lost. To be sure, in some respects we do know more after forty years; but in others we know less. This is particularly true of times of crisis and rapid change, and above all of wars and revolutions. Tolstoy reminds us in *War and Peace* of the mystery at the heart of battles. So also with revolutions. Even now – especially now – do we really know how and why it came to the storming of the Bastille?

The Hungarian revolution of 1956 is an event of that kind – perhaps the last in Europe with the popular, violent and genuinely spontaneous character that we still associate with the word 'revolution'. All subsequent European revolutions – Czechoslovakia 1968, Portugal 1974, Poland 1980–81, the many-in-one of 1989 – have to be qualified with an additional adjective: 'interrupted', 'self-limiting', 'peaceful', 'velvet', 'negotiated'. For that reason, and because of the subsequent decades of political repression and historical falsification, there is a part of its history that is virtually impossible to recover. It may also be the most important part. It concerns, for example, the experience of the mainly young men and women who took up arms on 23 or 24 October 1956: the workers, students, street-fighting kids who, after all, actually made this a revolution. Without them, it might have remained a high level political crisis, an attempt at radical reform, an affair largely of the party and the intelligentsia, with the people playing only a supporting role. Why did they act as they did? What was it like for them? What did they hope to achieve? What kept them fighting? What did they think of in the moment before they died?

I read the contemporary reports, watch the newsreels, look at the black-and-white photographs of those smiling boys and girls amid the broken glass, so like the photos of the Warsaw Rising in 1944. I think of Yeats: 'a terrible beauty is born'. Then I look at some of the meticulous reconstructions of the street fighting by Hungarian historians, using long interviews with survivors. I talk with Mária Wittner, described to me by another survivor as the revolution's Joan of Arc. It is a deeply moving conversation. But even she cannot really explain to me how, as a nineteen-year-old girl from a convent school, she came to pick up that ammunition belt and start reloading the guns for the boys on the roof, shooting back at the guards of the Budapest radio station on 23 October. She talks of 'something in the air', of the 'vibrations'. But the filters of retrospection are too strong.

She wants to speak for those who can no longer speak: her dead comrades, the unknown insurgents. Much of her life since 1989 has been devoted to that purpose. Yet their experience is lost, irrevocably. We don't know, we will never know, what it was really like at the eye of the storm. Beside history regained there is history lost. In history, too, there is always a sixth coffin.

2

The other thing that we are supposed to know more about is the consequences, and hence the larger 'meaning', of the event. For this, we plainly have to consider the alternatives. Purely hypothetical counter-factuals can be fun, and illuminating too, but more important are the alternatives that were seriously considered at the time. As we have found from the documents, major alternatives were considered – for example, by Khrushchev. What if the advice from Togliatti, Tito and Mao had been different? What if American policy had been clearer, one way or the other? What if the British and French had not launched the Suez adventure at exactly the same time? Might the Soviet leadership then at least have tried the second path – withdrawal, negotiations – a little longer and more seriously?

But what would have been the impact of that on Poland? For if the Hungarian revolution started with a demonstration beneath the statue of the Polish General Bem, who himself had been a hero of the Hungarian revolution of 1848–9, the Polish October was hugely influenced by what happened in Hungary. Khrushchev's 'peaceful path' in Hungary would surely have encouraged the Poles to ask for the same, or more. If the Soviet Union might just have been prepared to countenance an Austrian status for Hungary – in which, after all, even Stalin had proposed only a fifty-fifty split with the West, in his famous 'percentages agreement' with Churchill – it was another thing to countenance that for Poland.[5] This, in turn, would have meant countenancing it for Germany – the larger, Western, part of which was already in Nato.

Or take another if: What if Hungary had stopped at radical reform, rather than revolution, as the reform communists around Imre Nagy would have wished, and as Poland did? What might have happened then? Well, look what happened in Poland, where the hopes invested in Gomułka in 1956 were progressively and comprehensively disappointed. Is there any reason to believe that the same would not have happened in Hungary?

Orwell once remarked that 'All revolutions are failures, but they are not all the same failure.' The consequences appear different at different times, and some only emerge decades later. To describe 1956 as 'the victory of a defeat', as the exiled Hungarian historian Miklós Molnár did in his book of 1968,[6] was not merely romantic hyperbole and wishful thinking. Perhaps the simplest and most direct consequence is one that could be seen immediately, but has endured. This is quite simply the sympathy and positive feeling towards Hungary on the part of people around the world who either had hardly noticed its existence before or had had a rather negative image of the country, seeing it as an oppressor of minorities before 1914 and Germany's ally in two world wars. This basic positive association from 1956, supplanting a negative or non-existent one, has persisted, and remains a national treasure – or asset, to use language more appropriate to the 1990s – as the country strives to join the EU and Nato.

Another consequence that emerged immediately, but also endured, was the impact on the left throughout the world. This was a moment of bitter disillusionment with Soviet communism, of growing doubts in communist hearts, and the parting of ways between democratic and undemocratic socialists. The Chinese historian Jian Chen argues that it also hastened the great split between communist China and the Soviet Union.

Beyond this, however, someone reflecting on the tenth anniversary of the revolution, in 1966, would have been pushed to find many more elements of positive legacy, of clear gain to set against the obvious loss. On the twentieth anniversary, in 1976, one could already add something more. By this time it was clear that the Kádár regime was, if not more 'liberal' than other communist regimes in Eastern Europe – that label was always misplaced – then certainly more cautious, circumspect, indirect, subtle, velvet-gloved in the way it treated its own people.[7] This could be, and was, traced back to the trauma of 1956, when the communist party and state had collapsed in a matter of a few days, and perhaps also, more even than we guessed at the time, to Kádár's personal sense of guilt. On the thirtieth anniversary, in 1986, one might have added the growing importance in Hungarian independent and oppositional thinking of the rediscovery of intellectual and political tendencies of 1956 – for example, the work of the distinguished political thinker István Bibó, author of a famous last declaration on behalf of the Nagy government.[8]

The great temptation, of course, is to draw a straight line from 1956 to 1989. There is a thin line between the historian's privilege of hindsight and Bergson's 'illusions of retrospective determinism'. Nonetheless, there are connections to be made. For example, I do not think that it is fanciful to make a connection between Soviet policy towards Eastern Europe in 1956 and that in 1989. Top Soviet policy-makers, starting with Gorbachev, clearly remembered the political cost to the Soviet Union of the interventions in 1956 as well as 1968. In 1956, the Soviet leaders did not know what to do, and therefore used force. In 1989 the Soviet leaders also did not know what to do – but they did know what not to do: use force.

Nor is it fanciful to see Hungary 1956 as an important milepost in what may be described as the cumulative learning process of Central European oppositions and governments, from the sheer outburst of popular fury in East Berlin in 1953, through 1956 in Poland and Hungary, 1968 in Czechoslovakia, 1980–81 in Poland, to the sophisticated peaceful change of system in 1989–90, which I christened 'refolution'.[9] Moreover, it is undeniable that the largest symbolic event in the Hungarian refolution of 1989 was the ceremonial reburial of Imre Nagy on 16 June, the anniversary of his execution in 1958. The six coffins laid out on Heroes' Square, the revolutionary flags once again hanging from the lamp-posts: an occasion unforgettable to anyone who was there. And the past was a catalyst of the future.

However, the emergence of new evidence already slightly changes our view even of that very recent event. Documents found in the interior-ministry archives by the long-time oppositionist János Kenedi now show how both the party leadership and the still active secret police used all possible means at their disposal – including, for example, 'agents of influence' who had access to the American ambassador – to ensure that the reburial and attendant ceremonies passed off peacefully.[10] Kádár's successors, the new reform communists of 1989, appealed, directly and indirectly, to Nagy's surviving comrades, the reform communists of 1956.

The kaleidoscope does not stop turning. Now, in 1996, it is a free Hungary. The president of the republic, Árpád Göncz, was himself imprisoned for his attempts to mediate after the 1956 revolution, having been tried together with István Bibó. Wise, warm, avuncular, he is supremely fitted to mark the anniversary. The famous Plot 301 in a remote corner of the municipal cemetery, where Nagy and his comrades were given indecent burial after their execution in 1958, was a site of weeds and rubbish dumps when I first visited it in 1988 and still a place of freshly turned earth and recent clearing at the reburial in 1989. Now it has neat turf, marble tablets, paving stones, a monument – everything that belongs to an official place of public memory.

So far, so good. But the current government of the country is dominated by the Hungarian Socialist Party, the main successor to the ruling communist party. The Socialists were elected, with a landslide majority, in 1994, and govern in coalition with the Alliance of Free Democrats, the main heirs to the liberal-democratic opposition of the 1980s, who now find themselves a junior and uncomfortable partner of the post-communists. And the prime minister, Gyula Horn? Well, he was a reform communist in the 1980s and, as foreign minister, he was partly responsible for opening the Iron Curtain to Austria in 1989 and letting the East Germans out later that year – thus beginning the end of the Berlin Wall. But in 1956? No, in 1956 young Gyula, aged twenty-four, was a member of the feared and hated volunteer militias, known on account of their distinctive heavy quilted jackets as the *pufajkások* (roughly, 'quilted-jacket guys'), who fought, detained and beat up those who continued to resist.

He has explained his actions. He was young, and he blamed the revolutionaries for the death of a much loved elder brother. He has, up to a point, apologized. He has, in a way, tried to make amends – for example, by increasing special pensions for the survivors. But his way of dealing with the problem is deeply ambiguous. For it also involves trying to draw a line under the past – and to claim Nagy's inheritance. Soon after becoming prime minister, he joined Imre Nagy's daughter in a ceremony at Plot 301 to mark the anniversary of the revolution. Then, earlier this year, it was Horn who proposed in parliament a special commemorative law to mark the hundredth anniversary of the birth of Imre Nagy. The Free Democrats did not know which way to turn. Of course Nagy should be honoured, but at the initiative of a man like Horn? In the end, they abstained. This strange custom of the commemorative law, incidentally, has a history in Hungary reaching back into the nineteenth century. The hero of the 1848–9 revolution, Lajos Kossuth, for example, was thus commemorated after his death. However, the last person to have been so honoured by the Hungarian parliament was Joseph Stalin. And the man who proposed that tribute? The then president of the parliament, Imre Nagy. In Hungary, the ironies and ambiguities just never seem to stop.

How many more turns of the kaleidoscope will we see? As it looks now, Hungary has a very good chance of celebrating the fiftieth anniversary of the revolution as a full member of what we unreflectingly call 'Europe' and 'the West'. Of the EU, that is. And of Nato. It will thus become, to recall John Foster Dulles's words in 1956, a military ally of the United States. But what will those two things mean in 2006? What will the internal condition of Hungary be then, and how will it affect Hungarians' views of 1956? How much more, and how much less, will we then know about the revolution? It is precisely the mark of great events that their meaning constantly changes, is forever disputed, with some questions never finally answered. Questions like, What happened in France in 1789?

1996

1 November. Slobodan Milošević's Socialist Party of Serbia wins Serbian parliamentary elections. In Bulgaria, opposition leader Petar Stoyanov is elected president.

5 November. Bill Clinton is elected for a second term as president of the United States.

17 November. In Serbia, the Zajedno ('Together') coalition win municipal elections in several major cities, including Belgrade, but the Milošević regime fraudulently denies them their victory.

22 November. Beginning of student demonstrations in Belgrade, protesting at the fraudulent denial of opposition victories in municipal elections. In Romania, anti-communist Emil Constantinescu is elected president.

24 November. A referendum in Belarus gives President Lukashenka far-reaching powers, but these are contested by parliament.

13–14 December. An EU summit in Dublin agrees a 'stability pact' which would penalize future EMU members who exceed budget deficit targets.

19 December. Denmark, Finland and Sweden become full members of the Schengen group.

20 December. A Nato 'Stabilization Force' (SFOR) replaces IFOR in Bosnia.

25 December. Italy rejoins the Exchange Rate Mechanism of the European Monetary System.

1997

16–18 January. Versailles. An Anglo-French meeting in the wonderful Petit Trianon hotel. A tablet in the dining room announces that in this very room M. Clemenceau dictated the terms of peace to the defeated Germans after the First World War. The French delegation to our meeting – a glittering collection of stars from the country's business, political and intellectual elite, almost all of them graduates of the *grandes écoles* – argue with brilliance, lucidity and near-unanimity the French case for the Cartesian imperative of binding Germany into a European monetary union. I cannot help wondering if one day some Germans won't come to regard monetary union as the new 'Versailles'.

20 January. Bill Clinton starts his second term as president of the United States.

January–February. In faxes apparently sent from a supermarket in Switzerland, a Kosovo Liberation Army claims responsibility for terrorist attacks on Serb police in Kosovo.

5 February. The Swiss government agrees a fund to compensate relatives of victims of the Holocaust whose assets were held in Swiss banks.

11 February. The Serbian parliament recognizes opposition victories in municipal elections.

19 February. The European Commission allows Italy to impose a one-off tax to help it try to meet the Maastricht criteria in preparation for monetary union.

21 February. After student and opposition demonstrations force the Serbian regime to recognize the true results of municipal elections, opposition politician Zoran Djindjić starts work as mayor of Belgrade.

March. Albania collapses into anarchy. Arsenals are plundered.

The Serbian Tragedy

'People compare this to the "velvet revolution" in Prague,' I say to Momčilo. 'Yes,' he retorts, 'but the Czechs only lasted thirty-seven days!'

On the one-hundred-and-fourth day of the Belgrade student protest, Momčilo Radulović – thickset, with a two-day stubble, short dark hair and black leather jacket – has just burst into the room exclaiming, 'We've occupied the rector's office!' He is twenty-three, and studies political science. As he leads me to the new centre of action, he stops in the middle of the street to explain, 'I just want to live in a normal country. I want to get up in the morning, go to a normal shop, read my books, have the rule of law and democracy. And to travel.' 'I'm not a child of the Internet,' he adds, referring to a frequent characterization of the students, 'but I'd like to be.'

Around the heavy conference tables in the rectorate are packed some eighty students belonging to what they call the Main Board. 'Silence!' people shout at the top of their voices. 'Silence!' A tall, bespectacled history student called Čeda Antić tries to keep order: 'Kolega Gavrilović to speak next.' A girl with long brown hair and a little pink-and-white plastic handbag takes longhand notes in a ring-file binder, as if at a lecture. She is the official minute-taker. From the window I can see the student masses gathering below, with their flags, posters and badges, while pop music blares out: 'She loves you, yeah, yeah, yeah.' How touching to hear the Beatles still.

The Main Board is discussing the route for today's Walk. Walking, with a capital W, is the students' characteristic form of protest. Today they'll parade around the rectorate courtyard, then walk to the education ministry to support their deans. Instructions are given by mobile phone – a major technological advance on Prague in 1989. The mobile phones are a present from Bogoljub Karić, one of the country's best known multimillionaires and until recently – or perhaps still – a close associate of the hated president Slobodan 'Slobo' Milošević. 'After ninety days, Karić decided that he supports us,' Momčilo says, with nice irony. The student next to me has a multicoloured badge saying 'Propaganda'. Their other departments included Information, Security, Culture and Protocol. Information is for foreign visitors like me, Propaganda for their own rank and file. Protocol is now on the mobile phone to his colleague at the loudspeaker jeep outside.

The sound of singing comes from the square below. Everyone in the room rises to their feet, some standing to attention. This is the 'Hymn of St Sava', a patriotic hymn of nineteenth-century Serbia, celebrating the patron saint of education, and only recently revived as the university anthem. Some sing along quietly, with expressions of mildly ironical affection on their faces; most are respectfully silent; one or two look embarrassed or resentful. At the end, a few – mostly the singers – cross themselves after the Orthodox fashion. Between St Sava and the mobile phone, this is no ordinary student protest.

Two days later – day 106 – there is a vital decision. Early on, the students had formulated three demands. The victories by the Zajedno ('Together') opposition coalition in local-government elections on 17 November (by coincidence, also the starting date of the Prague events in 1989) should be properly recognized, the rector of the university should resign, and the student dean should also go. Milošević conceded the first, main, demand several weeks ago, and Zajedno mayors have already moved into their offices. Today the rector and student dean have offered their resignations. But are these resignations binding or is it a trick? Professors from the law faculty are summoned to explain the legal niceties. Suddenly we're in a law lecture.

Even if the resignations are binding, should the students stop here? Some faculties want to go back to lectures, others to raise new demands. Biljana Dakić, a fourth-year history student who is one of my guides, nods vigorously at a comment by the student chairman. What's he saying? 'He says, "Democracy is when the minority respects the will of the majority."' But then a pale-faced man stands up and shouts, 'This is a provocation! If you accept this, you'll all be fooled!'

Čeda Antić intervenes. If the resignations are definite, he says, they should have a Victory Walk and then go back to lectures; if not, they should call for nationwide elections to a constituent assembly. Back to school or forward to the revolution! 'You see, we have our Robespierres and our Dantons,' Čeda wryly explains afterwards, but he, the Girondin, was trying to outflank them.

Two clichés have been attached to this revolutionary theatre of the Belgrade students, and to the Serbian drama altogether: 'velvet revolution' and 'nationalism'. Neither gets us very far. Certainly some students say things that sound nationalistic to a Western ear. Most seem rather confused in their political views. But is that true only of Serbian students? And who would not be confused if through the most impressionable years of childhood you had seen your country fall apart, in a war which had many Serb victims too, and if, through those years, you were constantly told by state television, radio, your parents, teachers and leading intellectuals that this terrible war was the fault of others: Slovenes, Croats, Muslims, Germans, Americans? 'When I was seventeen,' Momčilo tells me, 'I wanted to go and fight for my fellow Serbs, like my older brother.' Biljana was born in Knin, a city in the Krajina from which the Serbs, including many of her family, were driven out by the Croats' 'Operation Storm' in 1995. Three of her uncles are now refugees in a Serbia which greets its fellow Serbs with far from open arms.

In the circumstances, it is remarkable that these students have produced a protest that has been so relatively peaceful, responsible, wittily inventive and basically democratic. Despite all the propaganda and the poisoned mental environment in which they have grown up since the age of twelve or thirteen, and though many of them have never been to the West, they, like the 'velvet revolutionaries' of Central Europe in 1989, embrace a model of 'normality' which includes the fundamentals of Western democracy. What is more, they are trying to practise it in their own protest. Entirely gentle this was not. At the beginning, stones were thrown and windows broken. Then they reverted to eggs. But some put the eggs in the deep-freeze first, so they came out as hard as stones. Perhaps deep-frozen eggs are the Serb version of velvet.

Against all the virulent denunciations of 'Europe' by Slobo's hacks, the students still write on their placard, 'EURO *polis*, EURO *demok-ratija*, EURO *standard*, EURO *pravo* [law], EURO *vlast* [auth-ority].' We in the rich EURO-Europe hardly deserve such touching faith. Or, again, 'AMERICAN PEOPLE HAVE: Bill Clinton, Stevie WONDER, Johnny CASH and Bob HOPE! SERBIAN PEOPLE HAVE: Slobodan Milošević, no WONDER, no CASH and no HOPE!' But a small wonder this was.

We must also distinguish between nationalism and patriotism. I walk over with Čeda Antić for a coffee at the Hotel Moskva. He, the talented history student, reminds me that the pre-1914 Serbian conspirators of the Black Hand used to meet in this café. Why, perhaps the future assassin of Franz Ferdinand sat in this very corner. But today's Young Serbia is not talking of assassination. Čeda is twenty-two. As a young child, with a Serb father and a Croat mother, he thought he was a Yugoslav. Then he found that he was really a Serb. In his search for identity, he discovered the glorious history of medieval Serbia – and the Orthodox Church. He read the Bible, believed, and was baptized into the Church two years ago. His godfather is a fellow student, active in the protest. Čeda was one of those quietly singing the hymn of St Sava.

Like many people I talk to in Belgrade, he now thinks that Yugoslavia was a mistake from the very beginning. 'It was,' he adds, '*our* mistake' – meaning that of the Serbs who thought their aspirations could best be realized in a larger state of all the southern Slavs. Now the Serbs' historic task is to start again, to build a modern, liberal, democratic Serbian nation state.

It is a travesty to call someone like this thoughtful, idealistic young man a 'nationalist', in the pejorative sense in which that term is now almost universally used. He is a patriot – someone who cares deeply for his country. If it were otherwise, he would not be demonstrating but trying to emigrate, as hundreds of thousands of younger, educated Serbs have already done.

He feels that the students have done what they can for Serbia, their new-old *patria*. Now it is up to the people and the opposition parties, three of which are supposedly united in the Zajedno coalition. The students have carefully kept their demos separate from those organized by Zajedno, so as not to be 'taken over' by any side, but we now walk out to observe the latest opposition demonstration, dedicated to the demand for free media.

I

More flags, more nineteenth-century patriotic hymns, more rousing speeches on Republic Square, before the National Museum. It looks like a scene from 1897 rather than 1997, except that one of the flags says 'Ferrari'. The crowd use their whistles – another hallmark of the Belgrade demos – to blow like crazy at every mention of Milošević. Then off we stroll again, on what I'm told is 'the Media Walk', past the egg-stained state television station, known as 'TV Bastille', past white-haired 'Grandmother Olga', an old lady who became a symbol of the protest, still cheerfully waving from her first-floor balcony, past Radio Belgrade, past the *Politika* newspaper, and so back to Republic Square. On the television in my hotel room I find CNN reporting 'a massive demonstration' with calls for Milošević's resignation. Well, it did not look massive to me, but what CNN says must of course be true.

Seen from outside, through the lens of such Western media coverage, and with the 1989 matrix still imprinted on our retinas, you might think that the Serb story is now 'Zajedno versus Slobo' (like Civic Form versus Husák, or Solidarity versus Jaruzelski) and the question is simply when Slobo will go. Seen from inside it does not look like that at all. Even those parts of the opposition joined in the Zajedno – 'Together' – coalition are still quite untogether in many vital ways. Despite the country's dreadful condition, Milošević and his allies still have many important sources of power, and he has nowhere else to go. Above all, the question of democracy is overshadowed by the still unresolved national question. And that is still, as it was a century ago, about the basic issue of the frontiers of states in relation to those of peoples, including the position of Serbs outside the present Serbian state – especially in Bosnia – and that of other nationalities inside the present Serbian state, especially the Albanians in Kosovo.

I talk to all three leaders of Zajedno – Vesna Pesić of the Serbian

Civic Alliance, Vuk Drašković of the Serbian Renewal Movement and Zoran Djindjić of the Democratic Party – as well as to Vojislav Koštunica, a 'moderate nationalist' whose small but significant Democratic Party of Serbia was briefly in the Zajedno coalition but now stands separately again.

Koštunica – grey-suited, analytical, sober to the point of gloominess – harks back wistfully to the first Yugoslavia, a unitary state under a Serb king, before the dreadful blood-letting between Serbs and Croats during the Second World War confounded British-style nation-building. (Serbs as English, Croats as Scots?) But he thinks Drašković's idea of restoring the monarchy is dotty. Why, the exiled Prince Alexander's Serbian is so poor they have to talk to him in English!

Vesna Pesić – a small, neatly dressed, energetic woman – is the only one with a consistent, impeccable record of commitment to civic, liberal causes, opposition to the war and rejection of nationalism. But – alas! – she also has the smallest following.

Vuk Drašković is the strangest character of them all: a tall, nut-brown, prophetic figure – although his long black locks are now more neatly trimmed and the prophet is cased in a very smart Italian suit. Politically, he is Dr Jekyll and Mr Hyde. When he talks about the past, about the atrocities committed by the Croat Ustasha during the Second World War, he is the old Mr Hyde, the writer whose fiery language helped to inflame Serb nationalist feelings in the 1980s. When he talks about the present, he is a perfect Dr Jekyll, swiftly hitting all the Western piano keys – 'human rights', 'regional cooperation', 'peaceful change', 'right for refugees to return to their home' – but also referring with justifiable pride to his own record of opposition to Milošević's war.

Behind this Jekyll and Hyde there is the unmistakable silhouette of an old '68er, one of that last defining generation of student activists, now to be found in high places all over Europe. To complete the picture there is his equally extraordinary wife, Danica, a tall, dark-skinned, orange-haired woman, bursting out of a gold-threaded designer jacket and skirt. In our short conversation, she lives up to her reputation for verbal extremism by suggesting that the Serbs should really set about getting rid of the communists 'like the Albanians'. (The Albanians are looting army arsenals as we speak.)

Finally, there is Zoran Djindjić, also an old '68er, but now the very model of a modern politician. Neat in suit, white shirt and tie, speaking excellent German (once a pupil of the sociologist Jürgen Habermas, he spent most of the 1980s in West Germany), he sits in his vast office as the new mayor of Belgrade and explains how he can do something from there. In the Balkans, he says, the difference between *pays légal* and *pays réel* is especially large. On paper the city government may have few powers and less money, but in practice it has many properties and concessions (taxi stands, restaurants, bathing places) which can be privatized in an exemplary procedure, as well as other forms of informal power and influence. Also, the Serbs like a big man in power, and the mayor of Belgrade is that. I quote to him the Serb peasant who said, 'I'll vote for the opposition when they are in power.' Exactly so.

For Westerners, the skeleton in the mayor's cupboard is his past support for the Bosnian Serbs and his infamous meeting with Radovan Karadžić in Pale. He defends this vigorously. If he hadn't met Karadžić, he says, the national card would have been left entirely in the hands of Milošević. What is more, the West began to take him seriously only when, helped by this tactical nationalism, the Serb electorate started to take him seriously. Western criticism is so much humbug. (In fact – this is my comment, not Djindjić's – the West is not unlike that Serb peasant, supporting the opposition once it is in power.)

Diverse as they are, all the opposition leaders agree on one thing: they are still weak and divided, while Milošević has many cards to play. Despite recent donations by big businessmen like Karić, now hedging their political bets, the opposition parties are still woefully underfunded and without proper organizations. The deep historical, political and personal differences between the leaders are scarcely papered over by the façade of 'Together'-ness. To give the opposition more time on the state-controlled media, as they demand at the rally, might actually be a clever move for Milošević. The more they talk, the more they will expose their differences, while Milošević can maintain his remote, statesmanlike silence. Though many claim the mantle of 'the Serb Havel', there is no single figure to unite the opposition vote.

2

No one excludes the possibility of a sudden and violent overthrow of Milošević. The comparisons people make here are not with Poland or Hungary, but with Romania (the end of the Ceauşescus), Bulgaria (the parliament besieged) and, of course, Albania. 'Remember,' everyone says, 'this is the Balkans.' The catalyst might be a further, precipitate, worsening of the economy, leading to violent protests by the unemployed or underemployed workers and worker-peasants, rather than just students and city folk. (Vesna Pesić, a sociologist by profession, gives me a small lecture on how the usual social classifications no longer apply to Serbia, but the basic point stands.)

Barring this, however, people expect any peaceful political change to be long-drawn-out and messy. Serbian political scientists struggle to characterize the Milošević regime. It is not simply a dictatorship, says one. It is 'half-legitimate', says another. A third adapts the Latin American term to say *'demokratura'*: a new combination of democracy and dictatorship. Yes, Milošević still has an active secret police, though mainly for collecting information rather than for direct repression. Yes, the army is still vital, although during the demonstrations its commander signalled that it was not available for shooting students. But more important from day to day are the systematic manipulation of public opinion through the media and through the dubiously gained fortunes of business supporters both of Milošević's own Socialist Party of Serbia and of the neo-communist Yugoslav Unity League of his influential wife, Mira Marković, who, in popular mythology, takes the part of Lady Macbeth.

Yes, they tamper with the election results. But, even allowing for electoral fraud, Milošević has won a series of at least formally free elections since 1990. Although Zajedno came out ahead in the local-government elections in November 1996, the government coalition, of his and her parties, still won the more important federal elections held at the same time. According to the official figures, it got 45 per cent of the vote, with a further, alarming, 19 per cent going to the far-right, nationalist party of Vojislav Šešelj, a notorious paramilitary commander in the Bosnian war.

The opposition leaders hope that Milošević's position has since been eroded by the demonstrations and their own arrival in local government, but everyone assumes that he still has significant popular support. For an outsider, this is the great mystery. Consider what Milošević has done for them. Ten years ago there was a country called Yugoslavia 'and I thought it was in Europe', says my friend Ognjen Pribičević, one of Belgrade's brightest political analysts. Economically, they were quite well off compared to the Czechs or Poles. Belgrade looked smarter than Warsaw. Schools and courts functioned more or less normally. They could travel freely. Yugoslavia had a good name in the world.

Now they live in a country known as Serbia, and it is – everyone agrees – not in Europe but in the Balkans. (Before I came out I looked in five popular tourist guidebooks to Europe. Serbia featured in none of them.) Serbia is an international pariah. To be a Serb abroad is like being a German after 1945. Provided, that is, you can even get abroad. You need a visa for almost everywhere. Distinguished professors queue for five hours in the cold, and are then refused.

Physically, the whole place is battered and run-down. Belgrade reminds me of Warsaw in the late 1970s. If you look at the cars, the clothes, the shop windows, you feel that Poland and Yugoslavia have changed places. According to the (unreliable) statistics, average per capita income has shrunk from around $3,000 to less than $1,000. The official unemployment figure is close to 50 per cent. I visit Kragujevac, a town once made prosperous by the large Zastava car, truck and arms factory. The war decimated the production of cars (since parts came from all over the former Yugoslavia), but was good for the arms factory. Now the peace has cut the production of arms. Most of the Zastava factory workers are paid some $20 to $25 a month for doing nothing. They line the streets selling black-market goods: trinkets, Nescafé, chocolate bars, cigarettes smuggled in via Montenegro.

Back in Belgrade, I am taken to a vast black-market bazaar, full of new Western consumer goods, all imported without paying taxes. There is a great double line of people hawking Western cigarettes, but watch out for the 'Marlboros': they are made in Montenegro. Fake Calvin Klein, Versace and Nike clothes adorn the stalls – mainly produced, I am told, in the Sandjak of Novi Pazar.

Crime, corruption and lawlessness are endemic. A notice in the hotel foyer asks you to hand over your personal firearms to the hotel security department. A security man hovers watchfully with a metal detector: does my tweed jacket suggest a local criminal or a Western businessman? I have never seen so many obvious gangsters, not even in Russia. I note that the phrase used about the election fraud is 'when Milošević stole the elections'. Elections are just one of so many things being stolen here.

People don't trust the banks, so they keep their money in cash. Here, as throughout former Yugoslavia, the Deutschmark is the real currency. 'I don't take dollars,' says one small businessman – 'they are too easily forged.' When your money is stolen, you have no redress. Insurance? You're joking. And the courts? A friend is meant, according to the law, to inherit a flat. But to get it he needs to pay DM 10,000 – as a bribe to the judge.

Politics and corruption are deeply intertwined, as in all the post-communist *demokraturas*. The ruling parties run much of the state as a private business; private businesses protect themselves by support-ing the ruling parties. But one would not like to inquire too closely into the finances of opposition parties either. The moral environment is as degraded as the physical one

And what of the Serbs for whom the nationalist standard was supposedly raised: the Serbs in Kosovo, the Serbs 'across the Drina' in Bosnia, the Serbs in Croatia? The Serbs in the Krajina, in Croatia, have been completely expelled. The remaining Serbs in Bosnia, impov-erished and brutalized, wander around the remnants of their tinpot para-state. There are at least 500,000 Serb refugees in Serbia, most of them still without citizenship, let alone economic assistance from the state. In Belgrade, I talk to one woman whose plundered house I visited in the Krajina in 1995. She says, 'I live here like a zombie.'

What a triumphant record of achievement! And yet people still support him. Why? Since I cannot talk individually to 3 million people, I have the usual, frustrating, experience of listening to intellectual, elite explanations of what 'the people' think, supplemented by opinion polls, anecdotes and a few personal encounters. ('Vox pop' in the foreign correspondent's knowingly ironic phrase.) First, this is, after all, a home-grown system, unlike the foreign-imposed regimes of the former Eastern Europe. Second, the intellectuals say, there is a Balkan, backward, authoritarian political culture, which always looks to a strongman in power. (Would they have said that fifteen years ago, in old Yugoslavia?) Third, there is a kind of residual socialist conservatism, fearing the plunge into economic freedom and clinging even to the pittance the Kragujevac worker has, for fear of losing that too. (Milošević talks a lot about privatization, but does relatively little – partly, it is said, because his wife is opposed to it on ideological grounds.) Finally, Milošević has created a national siege mentality, in which everything is blamed on the hostile outside world: the Croats, the Germans, Western sanctions. This has been a perfect self-fulfilling prophecy. He started by telling them that everyone was ganging up against the Serbs – then made it so.

As usual, the generalizations are impossible to prove; and if people soon speak otherwise, through the ballot box or on the streets, that may merely show how things have changed. But I do get a small personal sample of this mental state. A civil servant in one of the ministries, a nice family man and skilled technician, tells me he telephones the private television station BK to complain every time the Pope appears on the screen, 'because he's our greatest enemy'. The Pope, the Germans, the Americans: all against us. A retired major of the Yugoslav National Army – short, fat, bulging out of his grimy trousers – tells me he blames the current misery on what he calls 'the American sanctions' and on the 'immigrants' who come here taking all the jobs and scrounging. But these 'immigrants' are actually the Serb refugees from Croatia and Bosnia.

Sanctions were imposed, he says, because Muslims bombed Muslims in the market place in Sarajevo. And Srebrenica? 'That was also Muslims killing Muslims.' He squats on his sofa like a wary toad. But why on earth would Muslims kill Muslims? Well, the Serbs tried to drive them out and they got frightened, 'so they started killing each other'.

The Zajedno opposition leaders are no good, the retired major continues, because they are not true Serbs: Djindjić was born in Bosnia, Drašković comes from Hercegovina and had a Muslim best man at his wedding. Oh yes, and his father was a communist. But wasn't Milošević once a communist? 'No, he was a banker.' The major doesn't approve of falsifying the local election results, but he's sure Milošević didn't know about that: 'It was the people around him.' Incidentally, he says, apropos of nothing in particular, he'd like me to know that his wife's best friend is Jewish. In fact, his own best friend is Jewish too.

As I rise to leave, his wife – a schoolteacher – rather ceremoniously tells me that the Serbs still like the English, in spite of everything (i.e. everything we English have done to the poor Serbs). She hopes this conversation has given me a better picture of their country.

3

To make a modern, liberal democracy out of this degraded, re-Balkanized society, suffused with national self-pity and psychological denial, would be difficult enough if the Serbs were alone with their problems in a single, clearly defined nation state. But they are not. This is not just a matter of the remaining 'Serbs outside Serbia'. Inside the present rump Federal Republic of Yugoslavia, the Serbs comprise only some two-thirds of the population (or perhaps slightly more if one were to count the Serb refugees). Another 6 per cent are Montenegrins, with their own semi-independent republic within the federation. At least 15 per cent are Albanians – perhaps as many as two million of them, concentrated in the southern province of Kosovo.

As so often before in Balkan and east European history, the unresolved national question cuts across, and frustrates, the attempt to democratize and modernize. As so often before, the Great Powers are called upon to sort out the mess – and end up making it worse. Diplomatic history is present in every conversation. I have never heard the Congress of Berlin mentioned so often. Talk of the frontiers, and people immediately say, 'London Protocol!' The reference is to a secret treaty of 1915. 'In the war . . .' they say, and you don't know if we are in the First World War, the Second World War or the most recent war. In the political imagination, the last 120 years are wired in parallel rather than in series. Dayton (1995) exists simultaneously with the Congress of Berlin (1878). For all its claimed Union, 'Europe' still means Britain, France and Germany. Russia, the Orthodox brother-country, features only at the margin. For real solutions you look to America. That is the lesson they all draw from the agreement signed in Ohio, USA. But can Dayton seriously be described as a solution?

Bosnia features surprisingly little in discussions in Belgrade. The great outstanding national conundrum is now Kosovo. Kosovo is the question the opposition dread, because they have no answer to it. Kosovo reduces even the ebullient students to baffled silence. As all readers of Rebecca West's *Black Lamb and Grey Falcon* know, Kosovo, where the Serbs lost a great battle against the Turks in 1389, has traditionally been regarded by Serbs as the mystical heartland of their great medieval state and national identity. Vuk Drašković repeats to me the familiar description: 'our Jerusalem'. The Serbian-Byzantine monasteries with their exquisite frescos are still there. But 90 per cent of the population is now Albanian. As you drive through the province, you see all around you, dotted across the fields, the unmistakable homesteads of Albanian extended families: several houses and sheds surrounded by a single high brick wall, with a large wooden gate, like a makeshift castle. They have quite literally occupied the land.

In the 1980s, Kosovo was (under Tito's 1974 constitution) an autonomous province, with a largely Albanian administration. Although an Albanian rising in 1981 failed to achieve the status of a full republic, many of the Serbs were still leaving, often being forced out by discrimination and violence. In April 1987, Slobodan Milošević came to Kosovo and told the local Serbs, 'No one should dare to beat you!' With this battle-cry, he mounted the Serb nationalist horse and rode it – ably assisted by politicians of other nationalities, and especially by the Croat Franjo Tudjman – to the bloody destruction of Yugoslavia. Kosovo itself was stripped of autonomy and placed under direct Serb administration. The Kosovar Albanians responded with the declaration of an independent Republic of Kosova (as they spell it) and extraordinary underground elections in which a majority voted for a Democratic League of Kosova. Its leader, Ibrahim Rugova, became 'president of the republic'.

Their headquarters is a large hut in the middle of a dusty bus-park, full of picture-book hawkers and spitters. At the door, I am incongruously met by the 'head of protocol' who ushers me in to see 'the president'. In passable French, Mr Rugova tells me about their extra-ordinary underground state: the 18,000 schoolteachers they fund from unofficial taxes which Kosovar Albanians pay in addition to the official Serb ones; the independent university; the attempt at health care, through an organization named after Mother Teresa. Mr Rugova's immediate demand is merely for an alleviation of the repression. While the Serb police dare not touch him, they regularly harass lower-level activists. He insists on Gandhiesque peaceful means, and has explicitly cautioned his followers against following the example of armed insur-rection across the border in Albania. But on the central goal he is quite unyielding: self-determination for his people, statehood for the republic which he claims already exists.

His main rival, Adem Demaci – sometimes called 'the Albanian Mandela', on account of his twenty-eight years in prison – sits opposite me on a chair in his new party headquarters and, Gandhi-like, pulls up his legs into the lotus position. He might settle for slightly less than Rugova: a republic within a very loose confederation with Serbia and Montenegro. But he wants more dramatic protest actions to achieve it. He has called on his followers to imitate the student and opposition demonstrations in Belgrade.

That is the Kosovar Albanian mainstream. But in the last year there have also been a number of terrorist attacks, with responsibility claimed by a Kosovo Liberation Army. Are these the work of impatient young radicals, like the young Palestinians in Gaza? Or are they secretly encouraged by the Serbian leader? Even sober political observers speculate that a cornered Milošević, faced with total eco-nomic collapse and massive popular calls for his resignation, might in desperation play the Kosovo card, provoking a terrorist assault or armed rising which he could then heroically suppress.

For the time being, no one I speak to thinks the Kosovar Albanians are about to follow the example of their compatriots across the border. And this for one simple reason: even if large quantities of small arms were to be smuggled in from the plundered arsenals of Albania, the heavily armed and professionally trained Serb army could immediately wreak terrible vengeance. 'You see,' both Serbs and Albanians tell me, with chilling matter-of-factness, 'there are some 700 purely Albanian villages. So the people there could all be killed.'

Yet everyone talks of the longer-term possibility of war – and the seeming impossibility of any peaceful solution. The positions are so far apart now, the Serb and Albanian communities so utterly alienated. When a local Albanian leader makes an appointment with my companion, a Serb journalist, he won't even say the name of the street in which he lives – because it's a Serb name. I visit a state school divided by an internal Berlin Wall, so that Serb and Albanian children never meet.

Each side speaks to you out of national martyrologies, underpinned with fantastic historical statistics. I ask the information secretary of the local Serb administration about the ethnic composition of the province. 'In the twelfth century,' he begins, 'the Serbs were 98 per cent of the population'. 'In the 1980s,' says one of Mr Rugova's key aides, 'Kosovar Albanians served a total of 27,000 years in prison.' The mutual stereotypes are equally fantastic. The Albanians portray the local Serbs as cock-a-hoop, triumphantly ruling the roost, whereas I find them, in fact, profoundly depressed and frightened. The Serbs see the Albanians as part of some diabolic conspiracy, *deliberately* having so many children and spreading across the land so as to realize the 'Prizren programme' for a Greater Albania. (The League of Prizren, as readers will doubtless recall, was the Albanian national grouping after 1878.)

What is to be done? Some non-governmental talks between local Serbs and Albanians have started, and are to be continued in New York. The Albanians look to the so-called 'international community'. Like Drašković, they parrot the latest political buzzwords of the West: 'full minority rights', 'regional cooperation'. But 'parroting' is the wrong word. 'Magpieing' would be more like it. For these Western terms are all adapted to their own local purposes, like a pen or pencil-sharpener in the magpie's nest.

From Belgrade, from no less a figure than the novelist Dobrica Ćosić, has come the suggestion of peaceful partition. Serbia should take the main areas of Serb settlement, the mineral resources and the holy places – the patriarchate at Peć, the beautiful monasteries of Gračanica and Dečani. The Albanians should have the rest. Albanian intellectuals have heard of this, of course. They even joke about it, when we talk in a cheerful basement restaurant hidden away beneath the dim, potholed streets of Priština. 'Maximum 15 per cent for the Serbs!' 'No, I'd go to 20 per cent!' For a moment, I feel like the Edwardian British East Europeanist R. W. Seton-Watson, dividing up the Balkans on the back of an envelope. But seriously: the Serb holy places and main settlements are not contiguous to Serbia proper, there are large areas of Albanian settlement along the Serb frontier, and no one knows how it could be done without large movements of people and almost certain bloodshed.

David Owen has suggested an international conference on the Kosovo issue, under the auspices of the Organization for Security and Cooperation in Europe (OSCE). A Vance–Owen plan for Kosovo? But neither the Serb nor the Albanian side is ready for that. For the so-called 'international community', Kosovo is mainly an issue of 'regional stability'. The Nato generals' *cauchemar de Kosovo* is that violent conflict breaks out there and spreads to the large Albanian minority in Macedonia, thus also tearing the fragile Former Yugoslav Republic of Macedonia apart, involving Bulgaria and our Nato ally Greece. Then – hey nonny no! – we have the long-forecast 'third Balkan war'. Assuming, that is, we have not had it already.

For Serb democrats, by contrast, Kosovo is about the future of Serb democracy. One of them puts the case drastically: Serbia can have Kosovo or it can have democracy. But which Serb politician would dare to suggest surrendering the mythical heartland of Serbianness? The leaders of Zajedno all feel it would be political suicide to open themselves to the charge of 'losing Kosovo'. Yet deep down everyone knows that somehow, some day, Serbia must address this issue if it is ever to become a normal, democratic nation state.

Back in Belgrade, I have an extraordinary conversation with Dobrica Ćosić, perhaps the most important intellectual father-figure of Serb nationalism in the 1980s and for a time president of the rump Federal Republic of Yugoslavia, until Milošević cast him aside, as he has so many others when they have served their turn. Ćosić receives me in his large villa in the famous suburb of Dedinje – where Tito used to live – amid ornate wooden furniture and towering bookshelves. A heavy, white-haired man, he speaks a heavy language of portentous national pathos. Yet his message is a surprising one.

It is this. He doesn't like the modern world, with its 'technological civilization' and its dreadful, rootless Americanization. No, he abhors it. But that is the direction History is going. And if Serbia – now a small nation in the Balkans, on the outer edge of Europe – does not want to be left behind, to lose out completely in the great struggle of peoples for survival, then it must go with History. Specifically, then, Serbia should have a democratic and preferably a parliamentary rather than a presidential government (although keeping a federal presidency), a market economy, the rule of law, and a cooperative foreign policy. It must start to rebuild from the ruins. And then he – he of all people – speaks the memorable line 'We cannot live from the myth of Kosovo.'

4

For my last day, I go back to the students. I already have my 'Walker's Passport', with, on the cover, the outline of Serbia filled with a photograph of protesters. (The outline shape includes Kosovo but not Montenegro). Now they give me a badge: 'Room 559: Epicentre of the Resistance'. But Room 559 will soon be returning to its original use, as the departmental lending library for Ancient History.

This has been a long moment of practising democracy; of the new kind of peaceful, self-limiting popular protest that is one of the treasures of late-twentieth-century Europe; of excitement and hope. 'Canada, don't give me a visa,' said one of their placards, 'the victory is near!' (It rhymes – in the language they now call simply 'Serbian'.) But privately their assessments are sober. Biljana wants to go and study in America. Čeda fears a country populated largely by 'old people and refugees', and sees the spectre of fascism in its current politics.

True victory is still a long way off, and the past is such a heavy burden. 'You know, there has been so much blood,' says Aleksa Djilas, sitting in the apartment of his father, the great dissident Milovan Djilas. When I walked with the students a few days earlier, heading up towards Milošević's villa in Dedinje, we were stopped by a line of police just next to a large, new, monstrously vulgar, blue-and-white wedding cake of a building, thrusting out of the hillside. This is the house and headquarters of Arkan, one of the worst Serbian gangster-warlords in Bosnia, but still operating freely here, even appearing on television with his wife and baby child, all dressed up to the nines. Grotesque, utterly grotesque.

One day, in a new Serbian democracy, these young historians will have to address this heavy burden. But, looking at Kosovo, I feel the poisoned cup has still not been drained to the dregs. The tragedy that began on the field of Kosovo may yet end on the field of Kosovo.

Peering deeper into my crystal ball, I can dimly see the shape of a new Serbia. This shape is slightly smaller even than that on the cover of my Walker's Passport. It is the outline of a truncated imperial nation, which overreached itself and then lost, perhaps even more than it deserved to, in the cruel game of international politics. A suggestive comparison is with Russia: the other Orthodox post-imperial nation, now also looking back before the First World War in search of a new-old identity. But a better comparison may be with a closer country of more equal size: modern Hungary, truncated since the 1920 Treaty of Trianon, which gave formerly Hungarian territory to neighbouring states, including Yugoslavia. Like Hungary, this Serbia will be metaphysically depressed, much given to national self-pity, but eventually, slowly, painfully trundling back towards a place in Europe as a more or less liberal, democratic nation state.

Then Momčilo may finally live his 'normal life'. Then Biljana may return from her university in America. Then Čeda may write the true history of a modern Serbia of which he can at last be proud. But how old will they be when that day comes?

For more of Biljana, Čeda, Kosovo and Serbia, see below, pp. 354–75.

1997

2 April. Russia and Belarus sign a treaty providing for even closer ties.

20 April. Fighting between Armenian and Azerbaijani troops in Nagorno-Karabakh.

1 May. The British Labour Party wins a landslide victory at a general election, ending eighteen years of Conservative rule. Tony Blair becomes prime minister.

7 May. The War Crimes Tribunal for the Former Yugoslavia finds Dušan Tadić, a Bosnian Serb, guilty of crimes against humanity. He is subsequently sentenced to twenty years' imprisonment.

25 May. In a referendum, Poles vote for a new constitution.

1 June. Socialists win parliamentary elections in France.

16–18 June. An EU summit in Amsterdam agrees the Amsterdam Treaty, which results from the intergovernmental conference to review Maastricht. It provides for complex but relatively modest steps of further integration.

18–20 June. Amsterdam. Just after the European summit, and the whole city is complaining about the disruption to traffic and everyday life. There is no single hint of pride in the 'Amsterdam Treaty'. In fact, I don't think it's ever mentioned.

20–22 June. A Denver summit of the group of seven leading industrial nations ('G7') is joined by Russia, making it a group of eight.

25 June. Italy is admitted to the Schengen group.

8 July. At a summit in Madrid, Nato agrees to admit the Czech Republic, Hungary and Poland by April 1999.

9 July. Nato signs a security pact with Ukraine.

16 July. The European Commission announces proposals for the EU to open membership negotiations with Poland, Hungary, the Czech Republic, Slovenia, Estonia and Cyprus.

20 July. Warsaw. Lunch with my old friend Adam Michnik, ecstatic about the Nato and EU decisions to admit Poland. He takes me to an extravagant lunch at the Belweder restaurant – proud of being able to pay by credit card – and tells me, 'I feel my life's work is done.' The historic mission of his generation, he now thinks, was to guide

Poland safely and peacefully from East to West, from communism to democracy. Poland could have blown it, like Slovakia under Mečiar. There were many dangers on the way. He still thinks that his dramatic Jeremiah-like warnings about the danger of a clerical nationalist authoritarianism (see above, p. 95) were needed to prevent it becoming a reality. I still disagree. But no matter. The ship is nosing into harbour. Mission accomplished. And even a right-wing prime minister will not throw it off course now.

'Do you know the name of the prime minister of Switzerland?'

'No.'

'Exactly! You see, it doesn't matter . . .'

The Witness Wolf

Some six years ago, I heard 'the world's greatest spymaster', to quote the jacket hype for his newly published autobiography, testify at the trial of one of his former subordinates in a Munich court. The judge started by asking 'the witness Wolf' to give his name, address, age – and then his profession. 'I work as an author,' said Wolf. A titter went round the courtroom, and even the judge could not restrain a smile.

In fact, since he retired in 1986, after thirty-three years as the head of East German foreign intelligence, Markus 'Mischa' Wolf has been equally active and successful as an author. He has also given gainful employment to many other authors. First, in 1989, came *The Troika*, a sentimental memoir of his brother, the film director Konrad Wolf, and three other friends from their shared childhood in Stalinist Moscow. In 1990 there appeared *Markus Wolf: 'I am Not a Spy'* – a title that surely deserves the Kurt Waldheim Prize for Denial. This was a book-length interview with two sympathetic East German questioners. In 1991, Wolf published his second book, called *On My Own Orders*, an edited version of his own notes and diary of the year of wonders, 1989, topped and tailed with a few autobiographical reflections. Two years ago he produced a cookbook with his favourite Russian recipes, predictably named *Secrets of Russian Cuisine*.

Meanwhile, besides a flood of newspaper interviews and television appearances, the now celebrated spy-author has already been the subject of several books by other authors, including one in English by the long-serving Berlin correspondent of the *Financial Times*, Leslie Colitt, entitled *Spymaster: The Real-Life Karla, His Moles and the East German Secret Police*. Initially, Wolf's memoirs were to be published by Bertelsmann, but the West German media giant then pulled out in a fit of morality. Stout-hearted Random House stepped in where Bertelsmann feared to tread, and the American publisher is now orchestrating the worldwide simultaneous publication of an authorized version of his life, with much brouhaha – hindered only by the fact that the United States has so far denied the author a visa, on the grounds that he was implicated in the Stasi's well-documented support for international terrorism.

We must therefore brace ourselves for another torrent of copy-writer's clichés: 'legendary spy chief', 'in from the cold', 'real-life Karla'. Never mind that John Le Carré firmly denies having had Wolf in mind, not just for his Russian Karla but also for a figure more plausibly associated with Wolf: the Jewish intellectual East German intelligence officer Fiedler, bullied by his coarse, anti-Semitic superior Mundt in *The Spy Who Came in from the Cold*. The fact that Mundt was actually called 'Wolf' in an earlier draft of that novel is pure coincidence, Le Carré tells me: he took the name 'Wolf' from his lawnmower. Yet, when I spoke to the real Wolf in Berlin last year, he said that he had read Le Carré's novel soon after it came out in 1963, and had been amazed at the uncanny way in which the novelist had echoed, in the Fiedler–Mundt conflict, the tensions of his own relationship with his superior, Erich Mielke, the minister for state security. He wondered, Was British intelligence *that* good?

So can one, even now, really disentangle fact and fiction, author and spy, Wolf and 'Wolf'?

Man Without a Face is billed as an 'autobiography'.[1] But it is that only in part. A bravura opening chapter describes various attempts to woo Wolf's cooperation by West German, American and even, it seems, Israeli intelligence, in the months between the collapse of the East German communist regime in the autumn of 1989 and formal unification in October 1990. There is a hilarious description of two gentlemen from the CIA appearing at his dacha outside East Berlin, bearing flowers and a box of chocolates for his wife, and offering him a new life in California. He later realized that the costive, fervently non-smoking Mr Gardner A. Hathaway was really after the identity of the Soviet agent at the heart of the CIA. But, while Wolf had heard hints from Soviet comrades, he did not then know the name of Aldrich Ames.

The book then flashes back to a rather perfunctory account of his German childhood as the son of the gifted, womanizing, naturist, communist playwright Friedrich Wolf; his happy, Russian-speaking youth in Moscow in the 1930s (not such a happy place for many others, as he fairly remarks); and his diversion from a dreamed-of career in aeronautical engineering to the Comintern school at Kushnar-enkovo, where he was given the first of many false names. Returning to the Soviet-occupied part of Germany at the age of twenty-three, he became a journalist, covering among other things the Nuremberg trials, and then a diplomat, before joining, at the age of twenty-eight, the fledgling foreign-intelligence service, known initially as the Institute for Economic Scientific Research and later as the *Hauptverwaltung Aufklärung*, or HVA for short.

The story of the service is taken forward more or less chronologically to the building of the Berlin Wall in 1961, but is then broken, for the largest part of the book, into a series of thematic chapters on different aspects of his and the State Security Service's work: the so-called 'Romeo' spies sent to seduce women secretaries in West Germany, double and triple agents, disinformation, terrorism, Cuba. This is to a significant degree the result of further questioning, not to say interrogation, by his co-author, Anne McElvoy, herself the author of an excellent book about communist East Germany, and by his American editors.

The end product is certainly the most substantial piece of Wolf or meta-Wolf literature to date. While he holds to the retired intelligence officer's first commandment, 'Thou shalt not betray thy agents', so many of them have already been exposed that he is able to tell their stories. He adds some interesting details to the story of Günter Guillaume, his man in Willy Brandt's chancellery, whose exposure as an East German agent precipitated Brandt's resignation. For example, he says that the copies of top-secret documents from Brandt's Norwegian holiday retreat, which Guillaume claimed to have sent east, never actually reached him. The messenger took fright and dumped them. On the famous case of Otto John, the first head of West Germany's domestic security service, who turned up in East Berlin one day in 1954, he claims that John did not willingly defect. Rather, he was driven across the border by a man he trusted (who was, in fact, a Soviet agent), at a time when John was depressed about the rehabilitation of former Nazis in the West – and not entirely sober.

While playing down his own direct involvement, he nonetheless catalogues the Stasi's extensive involvement with terrorism. It hosted and supported members of ETA, the IRA, the West German Red Army Faction – to whom it gave further training in how to blow up civilians – and the dreadful Carlos, hanging out in the bar at the Palast Hotel in East Berlin where, fortunately, 'the prostitutes all reported to State Security'. He describes how the Stasi and the KGB helped to finance and support part of the West German peace movement, the so-called 'Generals for Peace'. He is scathing about the CIA, whose agents in the 1980s were, he claims, so bad that the East Germans began to worry that the Americans were not taking them seriously any more. As for the West German foreign-intelligence service, the BND, they had that almost totally penetrated.

He is best on German–German spying, and the larger context in which it took place. 'Germany in the early 1950s', he writes, 'was a huge web of declared and undeclared connections, secret shame, and covert loyalties on both the Right and Left. Nothing was certain, no one could be trusted completely, appearances deceived.' He emphasizes how many subtle gradations of cooperation with the East there were, especially in the period of détente, with its ideology of promoting West–East contacts of all kinds, and how careful his service often was to keep the lines blurred. Thus, for his contacts with a senior West German businessman, Christian Steinrücke, Wolf invented 'a whole alternative family life'. When Steinrücke came to dinner, he took over a small villa where a pretty announcer from East German television pretended to be his wife. Pictures of her children were prominently displayed.

He is interesting about the motives of the people who did become conscious agents. For a start, there were those lonely secretaries in Bonn, frustrated by the acute post-war shortage of men, and then picked up by Wolf's 'Romeos' – a West German journalists' label used in this book, although Wolf told me they never used it in the Ministry at the time. He has some good stories here: for example, that of the West German Margarete, who began to have pangs of conscience, like her namesake in Goethe's *Faust*. Her conscience was assuaged by a Stasi officer masquerading as a Danish priest, who solemnly heard her confession and assured her that to go on passing secrets was no sin. It also leads him to some dry reflections on human nature: 'One thing my job taught me is that women know far more about their husbands than the men think they know.'

Besides sex – or is it love? – there was also what he calls the 'erotic appeal of the East'. Many Westerners were excited by that exotic, dangerous world behind the Wall. Then, very importantly, there was the West German protest generation of 1968, with its revulsion against a Federal Republic which had not 'confronted' the Nazi past, and its hope of 'another republic' of the left. This generation was a rich recruiting ground for his service. A mixture of all these motives seems to have been at work in one of his best agents, Gabriele Gast, a senior analyst with the BND, whose perceptive reports on the state of the Soviet bloc landed both on Chancellor Kohl's desk and on General Wolf's. There were also the usual personal frustrations – the sense of being passed over at work, drink and money problems – which brought two very senior figures in the West German security service to work for the East.

Even if we all along suspected it, the sheer quantity of spying and the degree of interpenetration between East and West Germany are staggering. In the 1950s, he estimates, there were as many as eighty secret-service organizations operating in Berlin, and 'one sometimes had the impression that half of Bonn was employed watching the other'. 'By the end of the Cold War,' he writes, Russian intelligence 'came to the conclusion, which they still hold, that it was impossible to know with certainty which side any German agent was working for.'

Ironically enough, this itself becomes part of his retrospective self-justification. He is sceptical about what intelligence services can ever achieve; you can often learn more, he observes at one point, by a careful reading of the press. But he argues that they did contribute to keeping the peace during the Cold War, precisely because each side was so well informed about the other's military hardware, strategy and real intentions. There is some plausibility in this argument.

His second line of justification is the classic *tu quoque*. 'Our sins and mistakes were those of every other intelligence agency,' he avers on the very first page. 'Crimes were committed by both sides in the global struggle.' In the 1970s and 1980s, the methods used by the East, he argues, were only occasionally more brutal than those used by the West – and less so than those of the CIA in Latin America, or of many secret services in the Middle East. Certainly they used sex, bribery and blackmail, but not, as a rule, torture or what this text racily calls 'wet jobs' (i.e. murder). He, like his counterparts in the West, thought the end justified these means. And he believed in the noble goal which he calls 'socialism' to the bitter end – and even beyond it. The last words of his book are a defiant reaffirmation of faith in Marxism, in the words of another book title: '*À demain, Karl.*'

He does nonetheless ask himself – or is asked by his co-author and editors – whether he feels guilt or remorse. He makes a rather strained distinction between 'responsibility' – a matter of conscience, which he does accept – and 'guilt' – a matter of law, which he does not. This is hardly persuasive, although understandable given that he has spent the last few years in and out of court. He was actually sentenced to six years in prison for 'treason' by a Düsseldorf court in 1993. Pointing out that the German legal term was *Landesverrat* – literally, 'betrayal of country' – Wolf reasonably asks, 'Which country was I supposed to have betrayed?' For the Federal Republic became his country only on 3 October 1990. To its credit, the Constitutional Court accepted the obvious force of this objection and overturned the conviction, but West German prosecutors are reportedly still trying to nail him on lesser charges.

However, at the end of May – as if to coincide with publication of his autobiography – he was given a two-year suspended jail sentence on charges relating to three cases from early in the Cold War: the kidnapping of a Stasi officer who had fled to the West, the abduction of a Nato secretary whom the Stasi hoped to recruit, and the prolonged detention of an East German whom it wanted to involve in a plot to frame Willy Brandt as a Nazi collaborator. I believe this campaign to convict Wolf in the West German courts has been ill-advised, weakening rather than reinforcing the credibility of the 'rule of law' in the newly united country. It beggars belief to suppose that the operatives of Western secret services never did anything of this kind in the tough early years of the Cold War. Yet there is no suggestion of prosecuting them. So much for equality before the law. Many east Germans will be strengthened in the belief that there is one law for westerners and another for them.

The historical and ethical verdict is another matter. He does say he feels remorse about the fate of particular individuals, although this contrasts somewhat with the cold, detached, amused way in which he tells their stories. More substantially, he expresses what in the communist movement used to be called 'self-criticism' for failing to be more critical, sooner, first of Stalinism and then of the Honecker regime. His defence here is that he believed that 'change could only come from the top down' and that nothing would be achieved by East German dissidents like Robert Havemann or protest movements from below. Yet he also acknowledges that in 1980 Poland's Solidarity overturned this conventional wisdom.

The real problem for his claim of moral equivalence between the spies of East and West is the extent to which his foreign-intelligence service was integrated with the vast apparatus of domestic repression. This is a point to which he returns several times, usually in a spirit of denial. 'I did not see the intelligence service as part of a repressive structure,' he says. His work in foreign intelligence was 'a separate and more defensible sphere of activity'. He was 'adamantly against physically violent or dangerous actions'. Of the departments of the Stasi who directly supported terrorists he writes, 'They did their work, I did mine.' However, he admits that there was 'the standard bureaucratic cooperation with counterintelligence', and that 'We were well aware of what was going on, and of counterintelligence's often harsh methods.'

Behind this euphemism is a reality which is by now very familiar to German readers, and which even in the English-speaking world has put 'Stasi' next to 'Gestapo' as a synonym for evil. The methods the Stasi used against its fellow countrymen were not, to be sure, as physically brutal as those of the security services in Latin America or South Africa, although critics of the regime were beaten up, harshly interrogated and incarcerated. In a state where one in fifty people had a direct connection with the secret police – either as full-time employee or part-time collaborator – it did not need much physical brutality. Subtle, detailed plans were worked out to instil fear, sow suspicion, turn a prominent dissident's wife and children against him. East Germany in 1984 was probably as near as we have come in real life to the state of total surveillance that Orwell depicted in *Nineteen Eighty-Four*.

Wolf again insists that none of this domestic repression was his responsibility. Referring to a well-known characterization of East Germany as a 'niche society', in which most people withdrew into some private sphere – a country bungalow, sport, an unpolitical job – he even goes so far as to say that the HVA was his 'niche'.

Now this really will not do. The HVA and the domestic apparatus of the Stasi were not separate services, like the CIA and FBI or the British MI6 and MI5. The HVA was a department of the Stasi; its offices were within the Ministry's main compound. Other Stasi officers to whom I have talked confirm that it was more distinct than other departments and had a somewhat different ethos. But it was much more closely integrated than Wolf now contrives to suggest.

Proof is made more difficult by the fact that most of the papers of the HVA have been destroyed, or in part, it is sometimes suggested, removed to Moscow. Yet there remains ample evidence of the closest day-to-day cooperation in the 111 miles of surviving files from the main body of the Ministry. On my own file, for example, there is a routine instruction for an informer of the HVA to be deployed against me. Wolf himself mentions in passing that 'A former agent of my department named Knut [sic] Wollenberger was infiltrated into Havemann's group of democratic reformers in order to pressure and subvert it.' Some readers may not realize that Knud Wollenberger is one of the most notorious examples of private betrayal to have been revealed since unification. He informed on his own wife from the moment they met. So much for the clean hands of the HVA.

As for the bullying, paranoid Mielke, who was still toasting Stalin into the 1970s: although their relationship was tense, Wolf was one of his deputy ministers and worked with him very closely for more than thirty years. In perhaps the book's strangest revelation, we learn that, when they visited Moscow together, Mielke 'insisted on sharing a room with me because he was lonely – or maybe, given the surroundings, a little afraid. At night my companion would snore violently, which was scarcely a recipe for a relaxing week.' Poor Mischa, deprived of his beauty sleep!

But what of the people whose whole lives were ruined by Mielke's men? What of Knud Wollenberger's horribly betrayed wife and children, not to mention those who committed suicide in the Stasi's prisons? Did Wolf ever stand up to Mielke on any issue other than the conduct of his own service? Not that we hear of either from Wolf or from Mielke. Not that anyone else has ever discovered. Here we come to the moral and psychological heart of the Wolf question: the question of character. This book is called *Man Without a Face* because until 1978 Western secret services did not even know what Wolf looked like. But after the book has been read he remains a man without a face in a deeper sense: partly because of the thematic rather than genuinely autobiographical structure of the book, mainly because he is himself elusive and inconsistent.

Who was he, the real Wolf? Yes, he was a very successful spy chief, methodically and often skilfully exploiting the uniquely advantageous position of a tightly controlled police state trying to penetrate the wide-open, guilt-ridden Western half of the same nation. Yes, he is, when you meet him, intelligent, cultured, charming, witty. But this immediately compels one to ask, how could he stick it out for thirty-five years in that Ministry, with those hams and thugs? His own answer is, unsurprisingly, a romantic rationalization: it was all done for the good of the great cause. On his retirement from the service, he tells us, he quoted a poem by his father, entitled 'Apologies for Being Human':

> And if I hated too much
> And loved too wild, too free.
> Forgive me for being human
> Sainthood was not for me.

One might easily agree with the last line. Yet the whole quotation is testimony to a grandiose delusion. For, while he was attracted and attractive to women, most of his own life, far from being wild and free, was spent working long, grey hours at an office desk in probably the most anal organization in human history.

He himself admits at one point that he lived 'the life of a bureaucrat'. Two former senior officers of his service add that, while the author Wolf praises the lesson of 'civil courage' taught him by his father, the intelligence officer Wolf never showed this in his work. Instead, they say, he was deeply *autoritätsgläubig*: reverential to authority, and given to flattering the thuggish Mielke. For thirty-five years he never spoke up against the horrible, quiet, all-pervasive repression that was being organized from his Ministry – and directly supported by his own department. Was this because of idealism? Well, perhaps a little. But it was also because of conformism, cowardice and – not least – concern for his creature comforts. For the bon viveur Wolf had a very comfortable life in the old GDR: chauffeur-driven car, perks, the nice dacha where he could cook his excellent *pelmeni*. On his retirement in 1986 he 'negotiated a separation package with Mielke' (a wonderful swerve into the language of corporate America). His 'separation package' included a driver, a secretary, an office in the Ministry where he could work on *The Troika*, and a nice flat in the heart of East Berlin, overlooking the river Spree, where he lives to this day.

There he sits, the witness Wolf, articulate, cultured, sophisticated, well dressed and well housed: so unlike all the other bitter, philistine, vulgar former Stasi officers whom I have talked to in their tawdry little bungalows. And yet so very, very like them underneath. Like those petty bureaucratic executors of evil in having behind him a lifetime of conformity, compromise, obedience to authority and dirty hands. Like them, too, in today's hoary patterns of denial: it was not me, it was the other department – 'I did my job, they did theirs.'

Here is the last, best-kept, secret of the legendary spymaster Markus Wolf: he was a sheep in wolf's clothing.

1997

25 August. Egon Krenz, the last communist leader of East Germany, is sentenced to six and a half years' imprisonment for his responsibility for shootings of would-be escapers at the Berlin Wall.
31 August. Diana, Princess of Wales, dies in a car crash in Paris.
21 September. The Solidarity Electoral Alliance wins Polish parliamentary elections.

21 September. Warsaw. The by now traditional election-evening party at the offices of the newspaper *Rzeczpospolita*. Canapés, exit polls and media hullabaloo, just like any election in a Western country. It's as if Poland has been holding free elections for decades. While the Solidarity Electoral Alliance, a coalition of right-wing parties, is the winner, the more centrist, liberal Freedom Union does well too. In spite of everything, there is pleasure at the prospect that two parties emerging from the post-Solidarity tradition can now form the government, albeit under a post-communist president. This will be what the French call '*cohabitation*', but *à la polonaise*.

25–26 September. Şibiu, Transylvania, Romania. Şibiu is now a Romanian town in Romania, but it used to be a German town in Hungary. The Germans had been settled here since the Middle Ages, and they called it Hermannstadt. Even today, it looks like a woodcut illustration to a book of Grimm's fairy tales: Gothic churches, houses with steep-pitched gables, cobbled streets. Yet virtually all the Germans have left. They started leaving under the communist regime. Nicolae Ceauşescu sold them to West Germany for about DM8,000 a head. The rest left after the end of communism.

On the door of the large, handsome German church I find a notice. It says something like this: 'The member of our congregation Gertrud X died on 7 September. Our church bells will ring at the time of the funeral in Munich. The member of our congregation Hans Y died on 18 September. Our church bells will ring at the time of the funeral in Düsseldorf. The member of our congregation Hilde Z died on 24 September. Our church bells will ring at the time of the funeral in Frankfurt.'

For whom the bell tolls? It tolls not just for the Germans of

Transylvania. It tolls for that old Europe where people of different and of multiple nationalities lived mixed up together for generations, in a tense but creative coexistence. Now, having destroyed that world, we set about re-creating it. We call it 'multiculturalism', and artificially nurture it by laws, subsidies and government programmes. The folly of it, Europe, the folly of it!

Bad Memories

The sentence 'We all have bad memories' can be read in two ways: 'We all have memories of things that we found horrible, embarrassing, regrettable' or 'Our faculty of memory is intrinsically weak, leading us to forget or misremember.' The two may be connected, of course. We have a bad memory for bad memories.

In our post-Freudian English, this is usually called 'repression', thus encouraging further wordplay: 'After suffering under a repressive dictatorship, people repress the memory of repression.' To say 'repression', in the psychological sense, implies that the bad memory is the mind's way of handling bad memories. But that is just a theory. Before Freud, there was Nietzsche: ' "I did that," says my memory. "I can't have done that," says my pride and remains adamant. In the end – memory gives way.' And, before Nietzsche, there was Schopenhauer: 'We do not like ruminating on what is unpleasant, at least when it wounds our vanity as indeed is often the case . . . therefore much that is unpleasant is also forgotten.'

Comfort? Repression? Pride? Vanity? The explanations differ, but on the existence of this phenomenon, at least, the sages all agree. As Robert Louis Stevenson put it, we have 'a grand memory for forgetting'. But is 'forgetting' an adequate word? In everyday life, we tend to operate with the binary distinction: remember/forget. And there is an awful lot that we do quite simply forget. Yet there are also many variations in between. There is, for example, the jumbling of memory. And there is the involuntary embroidering of memory. (When you recount an argument you had with somebody, it always sounds as if you won the argument.) Thomas Hobbes drew the most radical conclusion in his *Leviathan*. Discussing memory in a chapter entitled

'Of Imagination', he concluded that 'Imagination and Memory are but one thing.'

Clearly this is a rich field. You may almost feel another little academic specialization coming on. There she goes, the bright young doctoral student heading straight for the Jonathan Aitken Chair of Memory Studies at the University of Westminster, after studying with the fearsome founder of the discipline, Professor Erich Teufelsdonck, Distinguished Professor of *Gedächtnisforschung* at the University of Braunau.

Let the joke die on your lips: the discipline is already here. French historians have been dwelling on this subject for more than a decade. The multi-volume *Les Lieux de mémoire*, edited by Pierre Nora, is a centrepiece of recent French intellectual life. There is even – sure sign of the arrival of another academic sub-sub-discipline – a learned journal, entitled *History and Memory*. Not accidentally, this is based at Tel Aviv University, and centrally concerned with some very bad memories indeed: those of war, occupation and the Holocaust.

By and large, the studies of the French school have been concerned with the history of collective memories. Often this involves a leap from a body of evidence about attitudes to the past – politicians' speeches, films, opinion polls – to a generalization about national memory. Thus, in his very interesting book *The Vichy Syndrome*, Henry Rousso uses the psychological notion of 'repression' to describe the French collective memory of collaboration in Vichy. He even has a 'temperature curve' charting the ups and downs of the syndrome, as if it were a fever. Stimulating though the argument is, these generalizations about some sort of national psyche are as hard to test as old-fashioned generalizations about 'national character'.

As a plodding Anglo-Saxon empiricist, I find it better to start with individual memory. My interest in this subject began – if I remember rightly – with the German memory (or forgetting) of Nazism, as I found it while living in Berlin at the end of the 1970s. The great change of 1989 was another stimulus. Trying to write the history of divided Europe in the Cold War, I found that the end of communism had a remarkable transformative effect on individual memories. As after

1945, everyone suddenly discovered that they had been opposed to the fallen dictatorship. (In *Eichmann in Jerusalem*, Hannah Arendt notes that Dr Otto Bradfisch, head of a Nazi *Einsatzkommando* that shot some 15,000 people, told a German court he was always 'inwardly opposed' to what he was doing.) Meanwhile, politicians in the West suddenly remembered how they had 'always' supported the dissidents and 'said all along' that the division of Europe could not last.

Egon Bahr, the intellectual architect of Willy Brandt's Ostpolitik, now explained that he had always intended this policy to be subversive of communist regimes. Why was there no single record of his ever saying this over the previous quarter-century? Ah, because he could never say this *in public*, for fear that the communists would wake up to what was going on. Not for nothing was he called 'tricky Egon'. Politicians' memories are, of course, made of especially flexible material. But we all do it.

The retrospective rationalization may be half-conscious or even fully unconscious. A fine example is contained in the conversations between members of the German team who had been working on an atom bomb for Hitler, secretly recorded at Farm Hall, the British country house where they were being held. After they heard the news of Hiroshima, the German scientists were trying to work out why the Americans had succeeded where they had failed. 'I believe the reason we didn't do it', ventured Carl-Friedrich von Weizsäcker, 'was because the [German] physicists didn't want to do it on principle. If we had all wanted Germany to win the war we would have succeeded.'

More recently, I have been plunged still deeper into the labyrinth of memory by working on a book about the strange experience of reading my own Stasi file. To read a secret-police file on yourself is a Proustian experience. It brings back to you with incredible vividness many things that you had quite forgotten, or remembered in a different way. There is a day in your life twenty years ago, described minute by minute with the cold, clinical eye of the secret policeman. There are conversations, recorded word for word. There are photographs taken with a concealed camera.

When I went on to talk to the friends, informers and officers who figured in my file, I discovered further veils, wrinkles and tricks of memory. One informer, whom the Stasi gave the code-name 'Michaela', firmly denied ever having been an 'IM', the Stasi abbreviation for 'unofficial collaborator'. But her informer's file, which I subsequently saw, contained handwritten reports signed with the code-name. She asked me, with a remnant of Marxist vocabulary, to 'try to explain the subjective as well as objective conditions' when I wrote about her. 'But,' she added despairingly, 'probably that's impossible. Even I can't really remember now . . .' Another informer, an Englishman code-named 'Smith', told me had tried to talk to the Stasi only about general social and political conditions. In a tragicomic piece of retrospective rationalization, he 'recalled' that by talking to the secret police – and, he fondly hoped, through them to the party leaders – he was trying to substitute for the missing 'civil society'. But his informer's file is full of detailed information on individual people.

As I travelled around with my bag of poisoned madeleines, I saw how people's memories – of events, of each other, of themselves – changed instantly, and then changed and changed again as the revelations sank in. There was no way back, now, to their previous memory of that person or that event. We say 'X or Y jogged my memory' and usually mean simply 'X or Y reminded me.' But these 'jogs' actually change the memory itself, like a digitized picture transformed in a computer: darkening that shadow, lightening this face. Except that, here, the process is involuntary. We are not the operators at the keyboard of memory.

So what we are dealing with, when we try to write history, is nothing less than an infinity of individual memories of any person or event. For these memories are changing all the time. There is, in all normal times, the slow fading that we call forgetting. But there are also the sudden changes that come with a dramatic change of external circumstances, like 1989, or with some new discovery, such as a file. L. P. Hartley famously wrote that 'The past is a foreign country . . .' But the past is much more than another country. It is another universe. The historian is a traveller through endless worlds of individual memory.

As a result, I have become even more sceptical than I was before about the value of *any* retrospective evidence. Yet that is what most historical evidence is. Most recorded history is the history of memories.

What are described as contemporary, primary, sources were usually recorded by an individual some time after the event, even if the interval between action and recording was only a few hours, minutes or even seconds. We know from our own lives that people can have quite different recollections of a conversation or meeting the morning after. (Earlier this year, the leaders of the EU couldn't agree what they had agreed in the last hours of the Amsterdam summit.) For a sobering experience, try comparing ten different newspaper reports of the same event.

The great exceptions to this rule are the tape recorder (overt or covert) and the camera. To be sure, these can lie too. Anyone who has watched a radio editor cutting and splicing a tape will never again believe what they hear. The new digital technology seems to give almost limitless possibilities of photographic manipulation. Still, properly used, they bring us an important step closer to Ranke's 'how it really was'. The television camera can lie, but at least it does not do what all human recorders do: both forget and involuntarily re-remember. That is one reason why the best television documentaries are outstanding works of contemporary history. The television footage gives you not just the words, but the body language which often belies the words, the facial expressions, the atmosphere and telling detail that you can otherwise experience only as a participant or an eyewitness.

For the historian, the lesson is not just about the weakness of human memory but about its fecundity, its infinite creativeness, its ability – no, its elemental compulsion – endlessly to rearrange the past in constantly shifting patterns. Usually, the resulting patterns are more comforting to our self-esteem, pride or vanity, as Nietzsche and Schopenhauer observed. But not always. Sometimes memory tortures people with remorse or guilt more than the circumstances really justify. The awful irony, harrowingly explored by Claude Lanzmann in *Shoah*, his film about the Holocaust, is that most often it is the victims who are cursed by memory, while the perpetrators are blessed by forgetting. Especially if the perpetrators were what the Germans call *Schreibtisch-täter*, 'desk murderers', bureaucratic coordinators of evil, like some of the chilling figures in Lanzmann's film. 'That camp,' said one – 'what was its name? It was in the Oppeln district . . . I've got it: Auschwitz!'

*

Memory, this champion trickster, is thus the great adversary for anyone who tries to establish what really happened, whether as historian, journalist or writer. Martha Gellhorn has written very movingly about this, in relation to her own memories of war, concluding, 'What is the use in having lived so long, travelled so widely, listened and looked so hard, if at the end you don't know what you know?' But there is another set of questions about bad memories faced by all people and countries who have been through terrible experiences: hijacking, imprisonment, torture or – for the collective – occupation, war, dictatorship, genocide. These questions are not about how to reconstruct the past but about what is best for the individual, society, nation or state now and in the future.

And that is the subject of the next essay, 'Trials, Purges and History Lessons' *– see p. 294.*

1997

1 October. SFOR troops in Bosnia take control of Bosnian Serb radio and television transmitters.

15 October. Franjo Tudjman is elected president of Croatia for the third time.

19 October. Milo Djukanović is elected president of Montenegro.

27 October. British Chancellor of the Exchequer Gordon Brown says Britain will not join EMU in January 1999, and sets five economic tests for eventual membership.

October. Major demonstrations by Albanian students in Kosovo.

10 November. Jerzy Buzek of the Solidarity Electoral Alliance becomes prime minister of Poland, with Bronisław Geremek, of the Freedom Union, as foreign minister.

28 November. The Kosovo Liberation Army publicly announces its existence at the funeral of a Kosovar Albanian schoolteacher killed by Serb police.

26–29 November. Prague. Time for a brief visit to Václav Havel, convalescing from serious illness at Masaryk's presidential country house of Lány. He has a glass of beer on the table – 'my medicine'. But one thing seems to be acting as even better medicine: the news of the imminent downfall of the other Václav, prime minister Klaus.

30 November. Czech prime minister Václav Klaus resigns, after more than five years in office.

1 December. Britain is refused permission to attend meetings of the planned council for coordinating the economic policies of European states participating in monetary union – the 'Euro-X'

11 December. Weimar. My favourite town in all of Germany. But now it's a building site, with giant cranes towering over its houses and heavy lorries thundering through its quiet, cobbled streets. Why? Because it's to be 'cultural capital of Europe' in 1999. I fear the delicate balance of its peculiar spirit, at once provincial and cosmopolitan, 'small yet great', may be upset for ever – in the name of culture.

12–13 December. An EU summit in Luxembourg agrees to open negotiations with six new applicants – Poland, Hungary, the Czech

Republic, Slovenia, Estonia and Cyprus – and to consider five others – Slovakia, Romania, Bulgaria, Lithuania and Latvia – in a second wave.

1998

20 January. Václav Havel is re-elected for a second and final five-year term as Czech president.

21–24 January. Milan. I ask an acquaintance if there is a chance of hearing the Nobel Prize-winning anarchist playwright Dario Fo. Well, she says, as a matter of fact he's speaking at Milan University this evening. It's a ceremony to commemorate the death of a student killed by police twenty-five years ago. She says she has to be there anyway.

The large lecture room is packed. Dario Fo is amusing, loquacious and insufferably pleased with himself. Much more interesting is the reason for my acquaintance being here. It turns out that her cousin was a left-wing student leader in the protests we are commemorating. Then he changed tack completely and went into business. He became the right-hand man of a senior industrialist who was deeply implicated in Italy's massive *tangentopoli* bribery and corruption scandal. In fact, her cousin was the man who actually gave the politicians the money. Now he is in prison. But he has been let out on bail for a couple of days, partly to attend this event. That's why she's here – to say hello to him and give him, as it were, moral support. The room is dotted with his cousins and friends.

Later, over dinner, my interpreter tells me that her father is a goldsmith. When the scandal broke, he suddenly found that most of his best clients were no longer coming. His business collapsed.

Ordinary lives, touched and changed by the *tangentopoli*. The human underside of great events.

Trials, Purges and History Lessons

The question of what nations should do about a difficult past is one of the great subjects of our time. Countries across the world have faced this problem: Chile, Argentina, Uruguay, El Savador, Spain after Franco, Greece after the Colonels, Ethiopia, Cambodia, all the post-communist states of central and eastern Europe today. There is already a vast literature on it, mostly written by political scientists, lawyers and human-rights activists rather than historians, and mainly looking at treating the past as an element in 'transitions' from dictatorship to – it is hoped – consolidated democracy. The material for another library is even now being prepared in South Africa, Rwanda, Bosnia and The Hague.

Yet what exactly are we talking about? There is no single word for it in the English language. German, however, has two long ones in regular use: '*Geschichtsaufarbeitung*' and '*Vergangenheitsbewälti-gung*'. These may be translated as 'treating' the past, 'working over' the past, 'confronting' it, 'coping, dealing or coming to terms with' it – even 'overcoming' the past. The variety of possible translations indicates the complexity of the matter in hand. Of course the absence of a word in a language does not necessarily indicate the absence of the thing it describes. But the presence of not just one but two German terms does indicate that this is something of a German speciality.

To be sure, many rivers flow into this ocean, and everyone comes to the subject in his or her own particular way. The lawyer and human-rights activist Aryeh Neier, for example, traces what he calls the 'movement for accountability' back to Argentina in the early 1980s, and there is no doubt that a major impulse did come from Latin America, with its various models of a 'truth commission'. In the years since then there have already been close to twenty truth commissions, although not all were called that.[1] Yet Germany is the only country (so far) to have tried it not once but twice: after Nazism and after communism.

I have come to this subject through the curious experience of reading my own Stasi file, and, more generally, through watching how the countries I know best, in Central Europe, have coped – or not coped – with the communist legacy. Here I shall concentrate on the Central European experience over the eight years since the end of communism. In particular, I want to compare the very special case of Germany with those of its east central European neighbours.

In doing so, I pose four basic questions: *whether* to remember and treat the past at all, in any of the diverse available ways, or simply to try to forget and look to the future; *when* to address it, if it is to be addressed; *who* should do it; and, last but not least, *how*?

I

The answer given to the first question – *Whether?* – in Germany since 1989 has been unequivocal: 'Of course we must remember! Of course we must confront the history of the communist dictatorship in Germany in every possible way!' And Germany has set a new standard of comprehensiveness in the attempt.

The arguments made for tackling the past like this are moral, psychological and political. Interestingly, the moral imperative, the commandment to remember, is often quoted in Germany in forms that come from the Jewish tradition: 'To remember is the secret of redemption.' Then there is the psychological notion, spelled out in an influential book by Alexander and Margarete Mitscherlich, that it is bad for nations, as it is for individual people, to suppress the memory of sad or evil things in their past, and good for them to go through the hard work of mourning, *Trauerarbeit*. Above all, there is the political idea that this will help to prevent a recurrence of the evil. How many times has one heard repeated in Germany George Santayana's remark that those who forget the past are condemned to repeat it?

You can see at once why it is regarded in Germany as politically incorrect, to say the least, to question this received wisdom. After the Holocaust, how dare anyone talk of forgetting? Yet the basic premiss has in fact been rejected in many other times and places. Historically, the advocates of forgetting are numerous and weighty. Just two days after the murder of Caesar, Cicero declared in the Roman senate that all memory of the murderous discord should be consigned to eternal oblivion: '*oblivione sempiterna delendam*'. European peace treaties, from one between Lothar, Ludwig of Germany and Charles of France in 851 to the Treaty of Lausanne in 1923, called specifically for an act of forgetting. So did the French constitutions of 1814 and 1830. The English Civil War ended with an Act of Indemnity and Oblivion.

Even since 1945, there have been many examples in Europe of a policy of forgetting. The post-war French republic was built, after the first frenzy of the *épuration*, upon a more or less conscious policy of supplanting the painful memory of collaboration in Vichy and occupied France with de Gaulle's unifying national myth of a single, eternally resistant, fighting France. In fact, much of post-war West European democracy was constructed on a foundation of forgetting: think of Italy, or of Kurt Waldheim's Austria – happily restyled, with the help of the Allies, as the innocent victim of Nazi aggression. Think, too, of West Germany in the 1950s, where determined efforts were made to forget the Nazi past.

The examples don't stop there. The transition to democracy in Spain after 1975 involved a conscious strategy of not looking back, not confronting or 'treating' the past. The writer Jorgé Semprun speaks of 'a collective and willed amnesia'. To be sure, there was an initial explosion of interest in recent history, but there were no trials of Francoist leaders, no purges, no truth commissions. On the fiftieth anniversary of the beginning of the Spanish Civil War, the prime minister, Felipe González, issued a statement saying that the civil war was 'finally history' and 'no longer present and alive in the reality of the country'.

What is more, we find something similar in Poland after the end of communism. Poland's first non-communist prime minister for more than forty years, Tadeusz Mazowiecki, declared in his opening statement to parliament, 'We draw a thick line [*gruba linia*] under the past.' He has since repeatedly insisted that all he meant by this was what he went on to say in the next sentence: that his government should be held responsible only for what it would do itself. Yet the phrase 'thick line', often quoted in the slightly different form '*gruba kreska*', rapidly became proverbial and was understood to stand for a whole 'Spanish' approach to the difficult past. While this was unfair to the original context in which Mazowiecki first used the phrase, it was not unfair as a shorthand characterization of the general attitude of Mazowiecki and his colleagues.

As I well remember from conversations at that time, their general attitude was: let bygones be bygones; no trials, no recriminations; look to the future, to democracy and 'Europe', as Spain had done. Partly this was because Poland in 1989 had a negotiated revolution, and representatives of the old regime were still in high places – including the government itself. Partly it was because by 1990 they simply could not imagine the post-communist party being voted back into power in free elections. So there seemed to be no pressing political need to remind people of the horrors of the communist past, and many, many more urgent things to do – such as transforming the economy with the so-called Balcerowicz Plan. Yet it also reflected a deeper philosophy – one that Mazowiecki, a liberal Catholic and veteran Solidarity adviser, shared with many from the former opposition movements in Central Europe.

In Germany it was the former East German dissidents who pressed for a radical and comprehensive reckoning. Elsewhere in East Central Europe it was the dissidents – those who had suffered most directly under the old regime – who were often most ready to draw that 'thick line' under the past. Václav Havel in Czechoslovakia was a classic example, and his policy in his first year as president, like that of Mazowiecki, could be described as one of pre-emptive forgiveness. The Hungarian case was rather different. Here the conservative government of József Antall, composed of people who had not been in the front line of opposition to communism, indulged in a vivid rhetoric of reckoning – but their purgative words were not matched by purgative deeds. The sharpest contrast, as so often, was between Germany and Poland.

2

This brings me to my second basic question: *When?* For there is an intermediate position which says, 'Yes, but not yet.' An intellectual argument for this is the neo-Rankean one made against any attempt to write the history of the very recent past: we don't have sufficient distance from the events to understand their meaning; we are emotionally involved, and the sources are not fully available. Better wait thirty years for the relevant official papers to be available in the archives. In post-communist Central Europe, however, the last part of the argument is circular, since those who say 'The sources are not available' are often the same people who are keeping the archives shut.

Beyond this, the arguments are political. What is supposed to strengthen the new democracy might actually undermine it. To examine the difficult past too closely will reopen old wounds and tear the society apart. You need to integrate the functionaries, collaborators and merely supporters of the dictatorship into the new democracy. Thus Hermann Lübbe has suggested that it was precisely the fact that Adenauer's West Germany in the 1950s suppressed the memory of the Nazi past, with both amnesty and amnesia, that permitted the social consolidation of democracy in West Germany. It helped Nazis to become democrats.

Against this it can be argued, I think powerfully, as follows. First, the purely historiographical loss is as large as any gain in evidence or detachment. The witnesses die; others forget or, at least, rearrange their memories; and it is the worst horrors that are often the least well documented in the archives. Second, the victims and their relatives have a moral right to know at whose hands they or their loved ones suffered. Third, delay and suppression have their own psychological and political price. The fact that the torturers or the commanders go unpunished, even remain in high office, compromises the new regime in the eyes of those who should be its strongest supporters. Dirty fragments of the past constantly resurface and are used, often dirtily, in current political disputes.

For France, Henri Rousso has described this vividly as the Vichy Syndrome. He compares it to a chronic fever, an old malaria in the bones of the French body politic. As we have seen in recent years with the revelations about François Mitterrand's Vichy past, it still has not gone away. So also with Germany. In her new book *Politics and Guilt*, the Berlin political scientist Gesine Schwan sensitively explores the political and psychological price paid by the Federal Republic for what she calls the '*Beschweigen*' – that is, the 'deliberately keeping silent about' the crimes and horrors of Nazism – in West German public life, schools and, above all, families, in the 1950s. The systematic academic, journalistic and pedagogic treatment of the Nazi past developed as part of an often angry reaction against the suppression of the 1950s. In fact the portmanteau terms I mentioned at the outset, '*Geschichtsaufarbeitung*' and '*Vergangenheitsbewältigung*', seem to date, in regular usage, only from the 1960s.

Many among the hugely influential West German 'class of '68' also thought the suppression of the Nazi past and the anti-communism of the older generation were two sides of the same coin. In reaction, they produced sympathetic, even rose-tinted, accounts of communist East Germany, with, for example, no mention of the Stasi. There is an interesting if perverse connection here. Their revolt against their fathers' failure to treat fully the past of the previous German dictatorship contributed to their own failure to see clearly the evils of the current one.

In any event, a sense of the high price of that delay in addressing the Nazi past is one reason why the demand for an immediate, comprehensive 'treatment' of the communist past was so swiftly accepted in Germany after 1989.

3

The German case also raises my third question: *Who?* Before the long silence of the 1950s, there had, of course, been the attempt at denazification, carried out by the occupying powers, and the Nuremberg trials, conducted by the victorious Allies. Both Nuremberg and denazification have ever since been basic reference points for all such discussions. To have the business done by outsiders, after a total defeat, does have obvious advantages. There are no domestic political constraints to compare with putsch-happy militaries in Latin America or the still functioning security services in today's Russia. Something gets done. But it also shows the disadvantages. Indeed, one could argue that the suppression of the Adenauer years was itself, in part, a reaction to what had been seen as 'victors' justice' – and victors' history.

In most of post-communist Europe we have the opposite position to that of post-1945 Germany. Far from being newly occupied, most post-communist countries see themselves as newly emerged from occupation. Moreover, only in five countries – Poland, Hungary, Romania, Bulgaria and Albania – is the communist past being faced (or not faced) within the same state boundaries as those in which it occurred. Everywhere else – in the former Soviet Union, the former Yugoslavia and the former Czechoslovakia – you have a number of new, smaller, successor states. Or rather, they might and do say, *not* successors – not heirs to that past. In a country like Lithuania, genuinely emerging from an oppressive occupation, and struggling to build up a new national and state identity, the temptation to say 'That was them, not us' is almost irresistible. Yet even for the Russians there is a large temptation to say, 'That was the Soviet Union, not Russia.'

The German position is, once again, unique. Whereas Poles and Hungarians are, so to speak, alone with their own past, east and west Germans have to work it through together. Disgruntled east Germans, mixing their historical metaphors, talk of an *Anschluss* followed by 'victors' justice'. But this was a voluntary *Anschluss*, voted for by a majority of east Germans in a free election, and the boldest steps of confronting the past were actually pressed for by east Germans. Still, the resentment is understandable. In many cases, west Germans do sit in judgement, whether in courts of law or simply by executive decision, over east Germans.

This extraordinary German self-occupation, or half-occupation, poses in a singular form the issues always raised by outside participation in the process. There is the practical issue of popular acceptance. But there is also the moral issue. What right have we, who never faced the dilemmas of living in a dictatorship, to sit in judgement on those who did? Do we know how we would have behaved? Perhaps we, too, would have become party functionaries or secret-police informers?

So what right have we to condemn? But, equally, what right have we to forgive? 'Do not forgive,' writes Zbigniew Herbert, the great poet of Polish resistance:

> Do not forgive, for truly it is not in your power to forgive
> In the name of those who were betrayed at dawn.

Only the victims have the right to forgive.

4

This is a problem for those inside a country too. Even inside, the question remains: Who has the right to judge? Parliament? Judges? Special commissions or tribunals? The media? Or perhaps historians? At this point, the question of *who* shades into the question of *how*. In my title, I have indicated three main paths: trials, purges or history lessons. (I leave aside here the very important but also very complex issues of rehabilitation, compensation and restitution for the victims or their relatives.)

The choice of path, and the extent to which each can be followed, depends on the character of the preceding dictatorship, the manner of the transition, and the particular situation of the succeeding democracy – if that is what it eventually becomes. Thus, for example, the political constraints in Central Europe are far less acute than in Latin America. But the preceding repression was also very different.

The American writer Tina Rosenberg has put it simply but well: in Latin America, repression was deep; in Central Europe, it was broad. In Latin America, there was a group of people who were clearly victims. They were tortured, murdered or, in that awkward but strangely powerful locution, 'disappeared' by a group of people – army and police officers, members of death squads – who were clearly perpetrators. In Central Europe, since the high-Stalinist period, and with a few major exceptions, the regime was generally kept in power by a much larger number of people exerting less violent or explicit pressure on a much larger number. Many people were on both sides. Society was kept down by millions of tiny Lilliputian threads of everyday mendacity, conformity and compromise. This is a point

Václav Havel has constantly stressed. In these late or post-totalitarian regimes, he says, the line did not run clearly between 'Them' and 'Us', but through each individual. No one was simply a victim; everyone was in some measure co-responsible.

If that is true, it is much less clear who, if anyone, should be put on trial. Havel's implicit answer is: everyone, and therefore no one. Adam Michnik has made this answer explicit. Exceptions to prove the rule are individual cases of abnormal brutality, such as the Polish secret-police officers directly responsible for the murder of the Solidarity priest Father Jerzy Popiełuszko.

The record of trials in post-communist Central Europe is, in fact, a very chequered one. In what was then still Czechoslovakia, two senior functionaries were convicted after 1990 for their part in the repression of anti-regime demonstrations in 1988 and early 1989. In 1993, the Czech Republic's Law on the Illegal Character of the Communist Regime lifted the statute of limitations for crimes which 'for political reasons' had not been prosecuted in the communist period. An Office for the Documentation and Investigation of the Crimes of Communism was established, and brought charges against three former Communist Party leaders for their role in assisting the Warsaw Pact invasion of Czechoslovakia in 1968. In Poland, General Jaruzelski was investigated for ordering the destruction of politburo records and then, more substantially, indicted on charges relating to the shooting of protesting workers on the Baltic coast in 1970–71. A number of senior figures were charged with causing the deaths of striking workers during martial law in 1981–2. But, altogether, the judicial proceedings have been fitful, fragmentary and usually inconclusive.

Germany has, unsurprisingly, been the most systematic. Border guards have been tried and convicted for shooting people who were trying to escape from East Germany. More recently, the country's last communist leader, Egon Krenz, was sentenced to six and a half years' imprisonment for his co-responsibility for the 'shoot to kill' policy at the frontier. Several other senior figures were found guilty with him. Yet, even in Germany, the results are very mixed, to say the least.

The arguments generally made for trials are that they go at least some way to providing justice for the victims; that they help to deter future transgressions by the military or security forces; that they exemplify and strengthen the rule of law; and, finally, that they contribute to public knowledge and some sense of a wider catharsis. The first consideration – justice for the victims – certainly applies in some of these cases; the second applies to a much smaller degree, since, broadly speaking, where such deterrence might still be important (as in Russia) there have been no such trials, and where there have been trials (as in Germany) the deterrence is hardly needed.

Have these trials exemplified and strengthened the rule of law? It is very hard to say that they have. Equality before the law is a fundamental principle; but even in Germany, still more elsewhere, there has been a radical, arbitrary and political selection of the accused. Then there is the familiar problem of trying people for crimes that were not crimes on the statute books of their countries at the time. How to avoid violating the time-honoured principle of *nulla poena sine lege*?

Determined to avoid such a 'Nuremberg' procedure, German prosecutors have therefore tried to identify crimes that were offences in East German law at the time. However, this has involved a highly selective application of East German law, thus violating another basic principle. (Yet, otherwise, the prosecutors should themselves be prosecuted for defaming the East German state, which was an offence under East German law!) And, when the case could still not quite be made to stick, they bridged the gap with an awkward invocation of 'natural law'. Meanwhile, the former minister for state security, Erich Mielke, was convicted not for his heavy responsibility in the regime but for his part in the murder of a policeman as a young street-fighting communist in 1931. The trial of Erich Honecker, the party leader from 1971 to 1989, was finally abandoned on the grounds of his ill health. He then flew off to spend his last months quietly in Chile.

None of this contributed much to any sense of popular catharsis. As for public knowledge: the thousands of pages of legal argument did little to illuminate the true history of the regime, certainly not for the general reader. Nor will future students of communism, I think, use the records of these trials as we do still use those of the Nuremberg trials to understand Nazism.

The Hungarian case is an interesting contrast. Here parliament initially passed a law which, like the Czech one, lifted the statute of limitations for acts of treason, murder and manslaughter during the communist period, but the Constitutional Court struck that down on the grounds that it was retroactive justice. A new law was then passed specifically on Crimes Committed During the 1956 Revolution. This took a different tack, and applied the Geneva and New York conventions on 'war crimes' and 'crimes against humanity' to what happened in 1956. Unlike the German prosecutors, and uniquely in Central Europe, they therefore claimed that some things done in the communist period did qualify for those Nuremberg trial categories – 'crimes against humanity', 'war crimes' – and that these provisions had at least notionally been in force in international law at the time.

The second path is that of purges. Or, to put it more neutrally, administrative disqualification. In this field alone it was not Germany that set the pace. Partly in reaction against Havel's policy of pre-emptive forgiveness, the Czechoslovak parliament passed a draconian law in the autumn of 1991. It laid down that whole categories of people – including high party functionaries, members of the People's Militia, agents and what it termed 'conscious collaborators' of the state security service – should be banned from whole, widely drawn categories of job in the public service. In Czech, the process was called not 'purge' (a somewhat compromised term) but '*lustrace*', a word derived from the Latin and implying both 'illumination' and 'ritual purification'. Thanks to the Czechs, we can therefore revive an old English word: 'lustration'. Among the meanings given by the *Oxford English Dictionary*, with supporting quotations from the seventeenth to the nineteenth centuries, are 'purification *esp*. spiritual or moral' and 'the performance of an expiatory sacrifice or a purificatory rite'.

The Czechoslovak lustration was fully effective in its original form for little more than a year, since Czechoslovakia then broke into two. While the Czech Republic continued with a slightly modified version, Slovakia virtually dropped it. Yet there is no doubt that the law did keep a number of highly compromised persons out of public life in the Czech lands, while such persons remained to do much damage in Slovakia. However, the original legislation was also so crude and procedurally unjust that President Havel publicly expressed deep reluctance to sign the law, and the Council of Europe protested against it. Disqualification by category meant that any particular individual circumstances could not be taken into account. A commission determined, on the basis of a sometimes cursory examination of secret-police and other official records, whether someone had belonged to one of the specified categories. The people thus publicly branded often did not see all the evidence and had only limited rights of appeal. In effect, they were assumed guilty until found innocent.

The German law on the Stasi files is more scrupulous. Employers receive a summary of the evidence on the individual's file from the so-called Gauck Authority – the extraordinary ministry set up to administer the 111 miles of Stasi files, and colloquially named after its head, Joachim Gauck, an east German priest. The employer then makes an individual decision, case by case. Even in the public service, some two-thirds of those negatively vetted have remained in their jobs. The employee can also appeal to the labour courts. Yet here, too, there clearly have been cases of injustice – even when denunciatory media coverage has not ruined the person's life. And the sheer numbers are extraordinary: to the end of June 1996 more than 1.7 million vetting enquiries had been answered by the Gauck Authority. In other words, about one in every ten east Germans has been, to use the colloquial term, 'gaucked'. Here the strict, procedural equality may, in fact, conceal a deeper structural inequality. East German employees are being subjected to tests that west German employees would never have to face.

Yet one also has to consider the cost of not purging. In Poland, that was the original 'Spanish' intent. Within a year, however, the continuance of former communists in high places became a hotly disputed subject in Polish politics. In the summer of 1992, the interior minister of a strongly anti-communist government supplied to parliament summaries of files identifying prominent politicians as secret-police collaborators. Of course the names leaked to the press. This so-called *noc teczek* – or night of the long files – shook the new democracy and actually resulted in the fall of the government. In December 1995, the outgoing interior minister, with the consent of the outgoing president, accused his own post-communist prime minister of being an agent for Russian intelligence. The prime minister subsequently resigned, and the affair still rumbles on. In the latest parliamentary election campaign, this autumn, it was suggested that the current post-communist president of Poland, Aleksander Kwaś-niewski, himself had close contacts with the Russian agent who allegedly 'ran' the former prime minister.

So, in the absence of an agreed, public, legal procedure, Poland has enjoyed not Spanish-style consensus but bitter, recurrent mud-slinging and crude political exploitation of the files. As a long-overdue antidote to all this, the Polish parliament has this year finally passed a carefully drafted lustration law. It obliges people in senior positions in public life, including in the state-owned media, to sign, at the time they stand for elected office or are appointed to the job, a declaration as to whether they did or did not 'consciously collaborate' with the security services in the period June 1944 to May 1990. At the recent parliamentary elections, I saw polling stations plastered with long lists of the candidates, and under each name the appropriate declaration. The admitted fact of collaboration does not in itself disqualify you from standing for public office. Indeed, several candidates on the post-communist list stood admitting their past collaboration. Only if you lie, saying you did not collaborate when in fact you did, are you disqualified for ten years. The declarations of innocence are to be checked, in secret, by a so-called Lustration Court.

Hungary passed a lustration law in 1997, and this is slowly being implemented. There, a commission vets senior figures in public life, but exposes them publicly only if they refuse to resign quietly. Shortly thereafter, the prime minister, Gyula Horn, admitted that he had been negatively assessed in the terms of the law, both on account of his service in the militia assembled to help crush the 1956 revolution and because, as foreign minister, he had been the recipient of secret-police information. However, he declined to resign and said he now regards the matter as closed. In both the Polish and the Hungarian cases, the circle of persons to be vetted is – wisely, in my view – drawn much more closely than in the German case.

Some analysts have taken the argument for purges a step further. Where there was no lustration, they say, as in Poland and Hungary – and elsewhere in eastern and south-eastern Europe – the post-communist parties returned to power. Only where there was lustration, in Czechoslovakia and Germany, did this not occur. Yet to deduce causality from correlation is an old historian's fallacy – *cum hoc, ergo propter hoc*. On closer examination, you find that in eastern Germany the post-communist party has done very well in elections, and one reason for this is, precisely, resentment of what are seen as west German occupation purges and victors' justice. In fact, the number of votes the post-communist PDS received in east Germany at the last Bundestag election, in October 1994, is remarkably similar to the number of people who have been 'gaucked': about 1.7 million in each case. (Not that I would deduce causality from this correlation, but still . . .)

One should by no means simply assume that the return to power of post-communist parties with impeccably social-democratic programmes has been bad for the consolidation of democracy. Yet it is true that, in Poland and Hungary, the new democracy has been shaken by issues arising from the lack of lustration, including the current activities of the security services. And the return to power not just of the post-communist parties but of historically compromised persons within them has furnished the populist, nationalist right with arguments against the working of the new parliamentary democracy altogether. 'If such people are elected, there must be something wrong with elections.'

Finally, there are what I call 'history lessons'. These can be of several kinds: state or independent, public or private. The classic model of a state, public history lesson is that of the 'truth commission', first developed in Latin America and currently being used in South Africa. As José Zalaquett, one of the fathers of the Chilean truth commission, has noted, the point is not only to find out as much as possible of the truth about the past dictatorship but also to see that this truth be 'officially proclaimed and publicly exposed'. Not just knowledge but acknowledgement is the goal. In truth commissions, there is a strong element of political theatre: they are a kind of public morality play. Archbishop Tutu has shown himself well aware of this. He leads others in weeping as the survivors tell their tales of suffering and the secret policemen confess their brutality. The object is not judicial punishment: in South Africa, full confession leads not to trial but to amnesty. It is formally to establish the truth, insofar as it can ever be established; if possible, to achieve a collective catharsis, very much as Aristotle envisaged catharsis in a Greek tragedy; and then to move on. In South Africa, as in Chile, the commission's aims are both 'Truth' and 'Reconciliation'. The hope is to move through the one to the other.[2]

You might think that this model would be particularly well suited to the post-communist world, where the regimes were kept in place less by direct coercion than by the everyday tissue of lies. But, again, only in Germany has it really been tried, and even there they somehow did not dare to use the word 'truth'. Instead, the parliamentary commission, chaired by an east German former dissident priest, was cumbersomely called the 'Enquete Commission in the German Bundestag [for the] "Treatment of the Past and Consequences of the SED-Dictatorship in Germany"' (SED being the initials of the East German communist party). Hundreds of witnesses were heard, expert reports were commissioned, proceedings were covered in the media. We now have a report of 15,378 pages – and a successor Enquete Commission is working on another. There are problems with this report. The language is often ponderous. Some of the historical judgements represent compromises between the west German political parties, worried about their own pasts. Yet, as documentation, it is invaluable. For students of the East German dictatorship this may yet be what the records of the Nuremberg trials are for the student of the Third Reich.

In Poland and Czechoslovakia, by contrast, the national commissions of inquiry concentrated on major crises in the history of the communist state: Solidarity and the Prague Spring. In each case, the focus was on the Soviet connection. Who 'invited' the Red Army to invade Czechoslovakia in August 1968? Who was responsible for martial law in Poland in 1981? In Hungary, too, official inquiries have concentrated on the 1956 revolution, and the Soviet invasion that crushed it. So, instead of exploring what Poles did to Poles, Czechs and Slovaks to Czechs and Slovaks, Hungarians to Hungarians, each nation dwells on the wrongs done to it by the Soviet Union. Instead of quietly reflecting, as Havel suggested, on the personal responsibility which each and everyone had for sustaining the communist regime, people unite in righteous indignation at the traitors who invited the Russians in.

Any explanation for the absence of wider truth commissions must be speculative. Part of the explanation, at least, seems to lie in this combination of two elements: the historically defensible but also comfortable conviction that the dictatorship was ultimately imposed from outside and the uneasy knowledge that almost everyone had done something to sustain the dictatorial system.

Another kind of history lesson is less formal and ritualistic, but requires permissive state action. This is to open the archives of the preceding regime to scholars, journalists, writers, film-makers – and then to let a hundred documentaries bloom. Yet again, Germany has gone furthest, much helped by the fact that the East German state ceased to exist on 3 October 1990. Virtually all the archives of the former GDR are open, and provide a marvellous treasure trove for the study of a communist state. I say 'virtually all' because a notable exception is the archive of the East German foreign ministry, in which are held most of the records of the often sycophantic conversations that West German politicians conducted with East German leaders. In opening the archives, West German politicians have thus fearlessly spared nobody – except themselves.

It has also helped that Germany has such a strong tradition of writing contemporary history. The research department of the Gauck Authority, for example, is partly staffed by younger historians from the Munich Institute for Contemporary History, famous for its studies of Nazism. Theirs are strange careers: progressing smoothly from the study of one German dictatorship to another, while all the time living in a peaceful, prosperous German democracy. The results are impressive. Whereas a West German schoolchild in the 1950s could learn precious little about Nazi Germany, every German schoolchild today can already learn a great deal about the history of communist Germany. Whether they are interested is another question.

Elsewhere in Central Europe, the opening of the archives has been more uneven, partly because of the political attitudes I have described, partly for simple lack of resources and trained personnel. Yet here, too, there have been some interesting publications based on the new archive material, and school textbooks have significantly improved.

In Poland, there has been a lively intellectual and political debate about the nature, achievements and (il)legitimacy of the Polish People's Republic. In Prague, a new Institute for Contemporary History concerns itself with the history of Czechoslovakia from 1939 to 1992. In Hungary, a whole institute has been established solely to study the history of the 1956 revolution. It has roughly one staff member per day of the revolution.

Beyond this, what Germany has uniquely pioneered is the systematic opening of the secret-police files, administered by the Gauck Authority, to everyone – whether spied upon or spying – who has a file and still wants to know its contents. The power is in the hands of the individual citizen. You can choose to read your file, or not to read it. The informers on your file are identified only by code-names, but you can request formal confirmation of their true identity. Then you have to decide whether to confront them, or not to confront them; to say something publicly, just to tell close friends, or to close it in your heart. This is the most deep and personal kind of history lesson.

Maddeningly, the Gauck Authority's statistics do not enable us to say exactly how many people have gone through this experience. But a reasonable estimate is that more than 400,000 people have seen their Stasi files, over 300,000 are still waiting to do so, and more than 350,000 have learned with relief – or was it with disappointment? – that they had no file. I can think of no remotely scientific way to assess this unique experiment. People have made terrible personal discoveries: the East German peace activist Vera Wollenberger, for example, found that her husband had been informing on her throughout their married life. Only they can say if it is better that they know.

There has also been irresponsible, sensationalist media coverage – denouncing people as informers without any of the due caution about the sources or circumstances. In German, such exposure is revealingly called 'outing'. Here is a structural problem of treating the past in societies with free and sensation-hungry media. Against this, however, one has to put the many cases where people have emerged from the experience with gnawing suspicions laid to rest, enhanced understanding, and a more solid footing for their present lives.

Elsewhere in Central Europe, the German experiment was at first strongly criticized and resisted, on the grounds that it would reopen old wounds and unjustly destroy reputations, and that the Polish or Hungarian secret-police records are much more unreliable than the German ones. (This last comment is made with a kind of inverted national pride.) Officers put innocent people down as informers, or simply invented them – the so-called 'dead souls' – in order to meet their assigned plan targets for the number of informers. Many files were later destroyed, others tampered with, and so on. So, instead, the secret-police files have remained in the hands of the current interior ministry or still active security service, and have been used selectively by them and their political masters. Limited access has been given to just a few individual scholars.

Yet, interestingly, this is now changing. Hungary has provided for individuals to request copies of their own file. The precedent is clearly the German one, although the Hungarian rules demand even more extensive 'anonymization' – that is, blacking-out of the names on the copies. The Hungarian Gauck Authority has a simple but rather sinister name: the Historical Office. In sanctioning this access, the Hungarian Constitutional Court drew heavily on the judgements of the German Constitutional Court, notably in using the interesting concept of 'informational self-determination'. In plain English, I have a right to know what information the state has collected on me and, within limits, to determine what is done with it.

The Czech Republic has passed a law which provides for people who were Czechoslovak citizens at any time between 1948 and 1990 to read their own files, under similar conditions. The first applications were accepted in June 1997. Thus far there has been remarkably little debate about individual cases, and few prominent former dissidents have applied to see their files. Perhaps this will change when sensational material is found and published, but at the moment one is told in Prague that there seems to be little public interest. There is a strong sense that the Czechs have already 'been through all this' with the great lustration debate of the early 1990s.

Poland is now following suit. The new post-Solidarity government has committed itself to making the secret-police files accessible to individual citizens. When I was there in mid-November 1997, a lively debate was going on about how best to do this. Frequent reference was made to the German experience. In the parliamentary debate on the government's programme, the Catholic nationalist leader of the Solidarity Electoral Alliance, Marian Krzaklewski, called for a 'lustration archive on the model of the Gauck Authority'.

Altogether, it is remarkable to see how, in this of all areas, Germany has been not just a pioneer but also, in the end, something of a model for its eastern neighbours. Who would have imagined fifty years ago that, when it came to dealing with their own difficult past, the Poles would turn to the Germans for an example?

5

There are no easy generalizations, and certainly no universal laws. So much depends on the character of the preceding regime and the nature of the transition. Even my first, basic, question – *Whether?* – does not have a simple answer. The ancient case for forgetting is much stronger than it is comfortable for historians to recall. Successful democracies have been built on a conscious policy of forgetting – although at a cost, which often has not appeared until a generation later.

In Central Europe after communism, Germany's policy of a systematic, unprecedentedly comprehensive 'treatment' of the past contrasted with Poland's initial policy of drawing a 'thick line' between the past and the present. But the Polish attempt to follow the Spanish example did not work as it had in Spain. Within a year, the issue of the communist past had come back to bedevil Polish politics, and continues to be used in a messy, partisan way, with ill-documented accusations being made about past collaboration with the communist authorities. My conclusion is that if it is to be done it should be done quickly, in an orderly, explicit and legal way. This also has the great advantage of allowing people then to move on – not necessarily to forget, perhaps not even to forgive, but simply to go forward with that knowledge behind them.

If the questions '*Whether?*' and '*When?*' are thus closely connected, so are the questions '*Who?*' and '*How?*' In Germany, the process has been made both easier and more difficult by west German participation: easier administratively; more difficult psychologically. Yet, doing it among themselves, Hungarians, Poles, Czechs and Slovaks have all too humanly been inclined to focus on the responsibility of others rather than their own.

There are places in the world where trials have been both necessary and effective. In Central Europe, trials have been – with a few important exceptions – of only questionable necessity and even more dubious efficacy. The attempt to use existing national laws has been contorted and selective, and often ended in simple failure. It has hardly exemplified or strengthened the rule of law. This is one area in which the international component may be a real advantage.

Difficult though it is, the least bad way forward must be to try to establish a firm international framework of law on 'crimes against humanity' or 'war crimes'. Building on the Hague tribunals for Bosnia and Rwanda, we need to move towards the permanent international criminal court for which Aryeh Neier, Richard Goldstone and others have eloquently argued – a court to which all dictators, everywhere, should know that they may one day have to answer. Meanwhile, the Hungarian path of writing the existing international law into domestic law is an interesting precedent. It was, however, confined to just one event, the Hungarian revolution of 1956, now more than forty years past, and its implementation has been plagued by all the problems of evidence that we know so well from the trials of Nazi criminals in recent decades.

As for purges, there is probably no such thing as a good purge, even if it is politely called lustration. The Czechoslovak lustration was prompt and crudely effective, but deeply flawed by procedural injustice. The German 'gaucking' has been procedurally more just: careful, individual, appealable. But it has sometimes been perverted by media abuse, and it has suffered from elephantiasis. Did postmen and train-drivers really need to be gaucked? Again we come back to the question of who is doing it, for would the west Germans ever have done this to themselves?

Yet Poland has shown the price of not purging. The Hungarians, with their nice habit of taking the German model and then improving on it, came up with a defensible refinement: it would apply careful individual scrutiny only to those seeking senior positions in public life. But this was seven years late. Now Poland has finally followed suit, with a law that is probably the most scrupulous of them all.

I believe the third path – that of history lessons – has been the most promising in Central Europe. Much of the comparative literature comes to a similar conclusion for other countries: what is somewhat biblically called 'truth-telling' is both the most desirable and the most feasible way to grapple with a difficult past. This is what West Germany did best in relation to Nazism, at least from the 1960s on. What united Germany has done in this regard since 1990 has been exemplary: the parliamentary commission, the open archives, the unique opportunity for a very personal history lesson given by access to the Stasi files.

To advocate the third path does, of course, assign a very special place to contemporary historians. In fact I do think that if you ask 'Who is best equipped to do justice to the past?' the answer is, or at least should be, historians. But this is also a heavy responsibility. Truth is a big word, so often abused in Central Europe during the short, rotten twentieth century that people there have grown wary of it. Studying the legacy of a dictatorship, one is vividly reminded how difficult it is to establish any historical truth. In particular, across such a change of regime, you discover how deeply unreliable is any retrospective testimony.

Yet studying this subject also strengthens one's allergy to some of the bottomless, ludic frivolities of postmodernist historiography. For this is too serious a business. Carelessly used, the records of a state that worked by organized lying, and especially the poisonous, intrusive files of a secret police, can ruin lives. To interpret them properly tests the critical skills that historians routinely apply to a medieval charter or an eighteenth-century pamphlet. But, having worked intensively with such records, and read much else based on them, I know that it can be done. It is not true, as is often claimed, that this material is so corrupted that one cannot write reliable history on the basis of it. The evidence has to be weighed with very special care. The text must be put in the historical context. Interpretation needs both intellectual distance and the essential imaginative sympathy with all the men and women involved – even the oppressors. But, with these old familiar disciplines, there is a truth that can be found. Not a single, absolute Truth with a capital T, but still a real and important one.

1998

January–February. Parts of the Drenica area in Kosovo are claimed as 'liberated' by the Kosovo Liberation Army.

28 February–March. Violent repressive action by Serb forces against the extended families of Kosovo Liberation Army activists sparks large-scale armed insurrection in Kosovo.

12 March. Leaders of the eleven states recognized as candidates to join the EU meet with EU leaders in London to launch enlargement. Turkey, not being so recognized, refuses to attend.

25 March. The European Commission declares that eleven member states have met the Maastricht criteria for monetary union and wish to go ahead. Greece does not qualify; Britain, Denmark and Sweden do not wish to join at this stage.

The Case for Liberal Order

There is Europe and there is 'Europe'. There is the place, the continent, the political and economic reality, and there is Europe as an idea and an ideal, as a dream, as project, process, progress towards some visionary goal. No other continent is so obsessed with its own meaning and direction. These idealistic and teleological visions of Europe at once inform and legitimate, and are themselves informed and legitimated by, the political development of something now called the European Union. The very name 'European Union' is itself a product of this approach. For a Union is what it's meant to be, not what it is.

European history since 1945 is told as a story of unification; difficult, delayed, suffering reverses, but nonetheless progressing. Here is the grand narrative taught to millions of European schoolchildren and accepted by Central and East European politicians when they speak of rejoining 'a uniting Europe'. Meanwhile, West European leaders have repeatedly reaffirmed the goal of 'ever closer union' since it was first solemnly embraced in the Treaty of Rome.

A classic example of this European self-interpretation is the French historian Jean-Baptiste Duroselle's *Europe: A History of its Peoples*, published simultaneously in several European languages in 1990. Discussing different ways of viewing the post-1945 history of Europe, he writes, 'One may, finally, see this phase of history in a European light' – by implication, the other lights must be un-European – 'and observe how many objective factors have combined with creative acts of will to make possible the first step towards a united Europe.'

The next chapter in this grand narrative is even now being written by a leading German historian, Dr Helmut Kohl. Its millennial culmination is to be achieved on 1 January 1999, with a monetary union that will, it is argued, irreversibly bind together some of the leading states of Europe. This group of states should in turn become the 'magnetic core' of a larger unification.

European unification is presented not just as the work of visionary leaders from Jean Monnet and Robert Schuman to François Mitterrand and Helmut Kohl, but also as a necessary, even an inevitable, response to the contemporary forces of globalization. Nation states are no longer able to protect and realize their economic and political interests on their own. They are no match for transnational actors like global currency speculators, multinational companies or international criminal gangs. Both power and identity, it is argued, are migrating upward and downward from the nation state: upward to the supranational level; downward to the regional one. In a globalized world of large trading blocs, Europe will be able to hold its own only as a larger political-economic unit. Thus Manfred Rommel, the popular former mayor of Stuttgart, declares, 'We live under the dictatorship of the global economy. There is no alternative to a united Europe.'

It would be absurd to suggest that there is no substance to these claims. Yet, when combined into the single grand narrative, into the idealistic-teleological discourse of European unification, they result in a dangerously misleading picture of the real ground on which European leaders will have to build at the beginning of the twenty-first century. Here I shall make what many Europeans will regard as the heretical argument that unification is the wrong paradigm for European policy in our time. And I shall suggest a better one: that of liberal order.

I

In the index to Arnold Toynbee's *A Study of History*, we read, 'Europe, as battlefield', 'Europe, as not an intelligible field of historical study' and, finally, 'Europe, unification of, failure of attempts at'.

Toynbee is an unreliable source, but he raises important questions about the long sweep of European history. The most fundamental point is, of course, his second one. Is the thing to be united actually a cultural-historical unit? If so, where does it begin and end? It is,

Toynbee claims, a 'cultural misapplication of a nautical term' to suggest that the Mediterranean Ancient History of Greece and Rome and modern Western history are successive acts in a single European drama. He prefers the Polish historian Oskar Halecki's account, in which a Mediterranean Age is followed by a European Age, running roughly from AD 950 to 1950, which in turn is succeeded by what Halecki called an Atlantic Age. Today we might refer to our period simply as a global age.

Yet, even in the European Age, the continent's eastern edge remained deeply ill-defined. Was it the Elbe? Or the dividing line between Western and Eastern Christianity? Or the Urals? Europe's political history was characterized by the astounding diversity of peoples, nations, states and empires, and by the ceaseless and often violent competition between them.

In short, no continent was externally more ill-defined, internally more diverse or historically more disorderly. Yet no continent produced more schemes for its own orderly unification. So our idealistic-teleological or Whig interpreters can cite an impressive list of intellectual and political forebears, from the Bohemian King George of Podebrady through the Duc de Sully and William Penn (writing already in America) to Aristide Briand and Richard Coudenhove-Kalergi, the prophet of Pan-Europa.

The trouble is that those designs for European unification that were peaceful were not implemented, while those that were implemented were not peaceful. The reality of unification was either a temporary solidarity in response to an external invader or an attempt by one European state to establish continental hegemony by force of arms, from Napoleon to Hitler. Yet the latter, too, failed, as Toynbee's index drily notes.

2

The attempt at European unification since 1945 thus stands out from all earlier attempts by being both peaceful and implemented. An idealistic interpretation of this historical abnormality is that we Europeans have at last learned from history. The 'European civil war' of

1914 to 1945 – that second and still bloodier Thirty Years War – finally brought us to our senses.

Yet this requires a little closer examination. For only after the end of the Cold War are we discovering just how much European integration owed to it. First, there was the Soviet Union as negative external integrator. West Europeans pulled together in face of the common enemy, as they had before the Mongols or the Turks. Second, there was the United States as positive external integrator. Particularly in the earlier years of the Cold War, the United States pushed very strongly for West European integration, making it almost a condition for further Marshall Aid. In later decades, the United States was at times more ambivalent about building up a rival trading bloc, but in broad, geopolitical terms it certainly supported West European integration throughout the Cold War.

Third, the Cold War helped, quite brutally, by cutting off most of central and eastern Europe behind the Iron Curtain. This meant that European integration could begin between a relatively small number of nation states – bourgeois democracies at a roughly comparable economic level, and with important older elements of common history. As has often been observed, the frontiers of the original European Economic Community of six were roughly coterminous with those of Charlemagne's Holy Roman Empire. The EEC was also centred around what historical geographers have nicely called the 'golden banana' of advanced European economic development, stretching from Manchester to Milan, via the Low Countries, eastern France and western Germany. Moreover, within this corner of the continent there were important convergences or trade-offs between the political and economic interests of the nations involved. The crucial trade-offs were between France and Germany.

None of this is to deny a genuine element of European idealism among the elites of that time. But, the more we discover about this earlier period, the more hard-nosed and nationally self-interested the main actors appear. Contrary to the received view, the idealists are more to be found in the next generation: that of Helmut Kohl rather than Konrad Adenauer. There is no mistaking the genuine enthusiasm with which Helmut Kohl describes, as he will at the slightest prompting, the unforgettable experience of lifting the first frontier barriers between France and Germany, just a few years after the end of the war.

To be sure, the national interests were still powerfully present in the 1970s and 1980s. Britain, most obviously, joined the then still European Economic Community in the hope of reviving its own flagging economy and buttressing its declining influence in the world. In a book of 1988 entitled *La France par l'Europe*, none other than Jacques Delors wrote that 'creating Europe is a way of regaining that room for manoeuvre necessary for "a certain idea of France"'. The phrase 'a certain idea of France' was, of course, de Gaulle's. In my book *In Europe's Name* I have shown how German enthusiasm for European integration continued to be nourished by the need to secure wider European and American support for the vital German national interest of improving relations with the communist East and, eventually, for the reunification of Germany. Besides this mixture of genuinely idealistic and national-instrumental motives, there was also a growing perception of real common interests.

As a result of the confluence of these three kinds of motive, and those three favourable external conditions, the 1970s and 1980s saw an impressive set of steps towards closer political cooperation, and economic and legal integration. Starting with the Hague summit of December 1969, they included direct elections to the European Parliament, the founding of the European Monetary System, the Single European Act and the great project of completing the internal market in the magic year of '1992'.

This dynamic process, against a background of renewed economic growth and the spread of democracy to southern Europe, contributed directly to the end of the Cold War. One of the reasons behind Mikhail Gorbachev's 'new thinking' in foreign policy was Soviet alarm at the prospect of being left still further behind by a 'Europe' that was seen as technologically advanced, economically dynamic and integrating behind high protective walls.

How much more was this true of the peoples of East Central Europe, who anyway felt themselves to belong culturally and historically to Europe – felt this with the passion of the excluded – and for whom the prosperous Western Europe they saw on their travels now clearly represented the better alternative to a discredited and stagnant 'real

socialism'. Accordingly, one of the great slogans of the 'velvet revolutions' of 1989 was 'the return to Europe'. In this sense one could
argue, in apparent defiance of historical logic, that '1992' in Western
Europe was one of the causes of 1989 in Eastern Europe.

The idealistic-teleological or Whig interpretation of recent
European history, so widely taught and accepted in the 1980s, might
not face the music of historical facts. But the very prevalence and
wide appeal of this interpretation was itself a major historical fact.
1989 seemed to be the ultimate confirmation of its rightness. Yet the
end of the Cold War also ended a historical constellation that was
especially favourable to this particular model of West European integration.

3

What have we witnessed since? It is possible to construe the 1990s as
one more chapter, even a decisive one, in the pilgrim's progress to
European unification. The Community has been renamed a Union.
The major states of Western Europe have devoted extraordinary
efforts to readying themselves for the unprecedented step of uniting
their currencies. At the same time, preparations have been made to
enlarge the Union. Serious negotiations have started with five new
post-communist democracies and Cyprus, slightly less serious ones
with five other post-communist states. Certainly, there have been
difficulties along the way; but never in its history has Europe been so
close to the peaceful achievement of unity.

Against this optimistic, even Panglossian, view, we have to enter a
number of objections. For a start, in this same period war has returned
to the European continent: war and, in former Yugoslavia, atrocities
such as we had not seen in Europe since 1945. Even in core states of
the old European Community, we have seen a popular reaction against
the technocratic, elitist model of 'building Europe from above' epitom-
ized by the impenetrable detail of the Maastricht Treaty. The French
referendum vote on the Maastricht Treaty, so narrowly won, was a
telling symptom of this. And the Amsterdam Treaty of 1997 was no
more accessible or popular. This popular resentment, and a sense

that the institutions of the European Union are perilously short on democratic legitimacy, still persists.

While these years have seen further incremental diminution in the effective powers and sovereignty of established nation states, they have also seen the explosive emergence of at least a dozen new nation states. Indeed, there are now more states on the map of Europe than ever before in the twentieth century. In the former Yugoslavia, these new states emerged through ethnic cleansing and the violent redrawing of frontiers. In the former Czechoslovakia, the separation into two states was carried out peacefully, by negotiation. In the former Soviet Union, there were variations in between.

I do not suggest that these de-unifications reflected some deeper historical necessity. The specific aetiology is different in each case, but very often rooted in the conduct of post-communist politicians, making manipulative use of nationalist agendas to gain or maintain power for themselves. Yet the logic of de-unification is by no means always anti-democratic. It can be closely related to that of democracy. Democracy requires trust. It requires that the minority is prepared to accept the decision of the majority, because the minority still regards the state as fundamentally 'theirs'. The argument is hardly original – you find it already in John Stuart Mill's *Considerations on Representative Government*. 'Among a people without fellow-feelings,' writes Mill, 'especially if they read and speak different languages, the united public opinion necessary to the working of representative government cannot exist.'

Nor is this phenomenon of de-unification confined to the post-communist half of Europe. The cliché of 'integration in the west, disintegration in the east' does not bear closer examination. It is surprising, for example, to see the progressive dis-integration of Belgium cited as evidence of the decline of the nation state and the rise of regionalism. For the tensions that are pulling Belgium apart would be entirely familiar to a nineteenth-century liberal nationalist. Each ethno-linguistic group demands a growing measure of self-government. Britain has for decades been an unusual modern variation on the theme of the nation state: a nation composed of four nations – or, to be precise, three and a part. But now the constituent nations, especially

Scotland, are pulling away towards a larger measure of self-government.

And what of Europe's central power? It would be hard to dispute the simple statement that since 1989 Germany has re-emerged as a fully sovereign nation state. In Berlin, we are witnessing the extraordinary architectural reconstruction of the grandiose capital of a historic nation state. Yet, at the same time, Germany's political leaders, and above all Helmut Kohl, are pressing ahead with all their considerable might to surrender that vital component of national sovereignty – and, particularly in the contemporary German case, also identity – which is the national currency. There is a startling contradiction between, so to speak, the architecture in Berlin and the rhetoric in Bonn.

I do not think this contradiction can be resolved dialectically, even in the homeland of the dialectic. In fact, Germany today is in a political-psychological condition that can only be described as Faustian: '*Zwei Seelen wohnen, ach, in meiner Brust*' ('Oh, two souls live in my breast'). After monetary union has gone ahead and the German government moves to Berlin, then the country will wake up in its new bed on 1 January 2000, scratch its head, and ask itself, 'Now, why did we just give up the Deutschmark?'

What is the answer? Of course there are economic arguments for monetary union. But monetary union was conceived as an economic means to a political end. In general terms, it is the continuation of the functionalist approach adopted by the French and German founding fathers of the European Economic Community: through economic integration to political integration. But there was a more specific political reason for the decision to make this the central goal of European integration in the 1990s. As so often before, the key lies in a compromise between French and German national interests. In 1990, there was at the very least an implicit linkage made between François Mitterrand's anxious and reluctant support for German unification and Kohl's decisive push towards European monetary union. 'The whole of Deutschland for Kohl, half the Deutschmark for Mitterrand,' as one wit put it at the time. Leading German politicians will acknowledge privately that monetary union is the price paid for German unification.

Yet, to some extent, this is a price that Kohl himself wants to pay. For he wants to see the newly united Germany bound firmly and, as he himself puts it, 'irreversibly' into Europe. Even more than his mentor Konrad Adenauer, he believes that it is dangerous for Germany, with its erratic history and its critical size – 'too big for Europe, too small for the world', as Henry Kissinger once pithily observed – to stand alone in the centre of Europe, trying to juggle or balance the nine neighbours and many partners around it. So Dr Kohl's ultimate, unspoken, answer to the question 'Why did we just give up the Deutschmark?' will be 'Because we can't trust ourselves.'

To which a younger generation will say, 'Why not?' Many of them see no reason why Germany needs to be bound to the mast like Odysseus, to resist the siren calls of its awful past. They think Germany can be trusted to keep its own balance as a responsible, liberal nation state inside an already close-knit community of other responsible, liberal nation states. Certainly Kohl's implicit argument will not convince the man in the Bavarian beer tent, especially when Kohl himself is no longer there to make it. In opinion polls, a majority of Germans still do not want to give up the Deutschmark for the euro. So Germany, this newly restored nation state, will enter monetary union full of reservations, doubts and fears.

4

Economists differ, and a non-economist has to pick his way between their arguments. But few would dissent from the proposition that European monetary union is an unprecedented, high-risk gamble. As several leading economists have pointed out, Europe lacks vital components that make monetary union work in the United States. The USA has high labour mobility, price and wage flexibility, provision for automatic, large-scale budgetary transfers to states adversely affected by so-called 'asymmetric shocks', and, not least, the common language, culture and shared history in a single state that make such transfers acceptable as a matter of course to citizens and taxpayers.

Europe has low labour mobility and high unemployment. It has relatively little wage flexibility. The EU redistributes a maximum of

1.27 per cent of the GDP of its member states, and most of this is already committed to schemes such as the Common Agricultural Policy and the so-called 'structural funds' for assisting poorer regions. It has no common language, and certainly no common state. Since 1989, we have seen how reluctant west German taxpayers have been to pay even for their own compatriots in the east. Do we really expect that they would be willing to pay for the French unemployed as well? The Maastricht Treaty does not provide for that, and leading German politicians have repeatedly stressed that they will not stand for it. The minimal trust and solidarity between citizens which is the fragile treasure of the democratic nation state does not, alas, yet exist between the citizens of Europe. For there is no 'united public opinion', to recall Mill's phrase. There is no European *demos* – only a European *telos*.

Against this powerful critique, it is urged that 'asymmetric shocks' will affect different regions within European countries, and the countries themselves do make provision for automatic budgetary transfers. In France, it is very optimistically suggested that reform of the Common Agricultural Policy and 'structural funds' will free up EU resources for compensatory transfers. (But, if we are serious about enlargement, some of these resources will also be needed for the much poorer new member states.) More economically liberal Europeans argue that monetary union will simply compel us to introduce more free-market flexibility, not least in wage levels. Yet none of this adds up to a very persuasive rebuttal, especially since different European countries favour different kinds of response.

The dangers, by contrast, are all too obvious. EMU requires a single monetary policy and a single interest rate for all. What if that rate is right for the German economy but wrong for Spain and Italy, or vice versa? And what if French unemployment continues to rise? As elections approach, national politicians will find the temptation to 'blame it on EMU' almost irresistible. If responsible politicians resist the temptation, then irresponsible ones will gain votes. And the European Central Bank will not start with any of the popular authority that the Bundesbank enjoys in Germany. It starts as the product of a political-bureaucratic procedure of 'building Europe from above' which is even now perilously short of popular support and democratic legitimacy.

In fact, received wisdom in EU capitals is already that EMU will sooner or later face a crisis: perhaps after the end of a pre-millennium boom, in 2001 or 2002 (just as Britain is preparing to join). Euro-optimists hope this crisis will catalyse economic liberalization, European solidarity and perhaps even those steps of political unification that historically have preceded, not followed, successful monetary unions. A shared fear of the catastrophic consequences of a failure of monetary union will draw Europeans together, as the shared fear of a common external enemy (Mongols, Turks, Soviets) did in the past. But it is a truly dialectical leap of faith to suggest that a crisis which exacerbates differences and tensions between European countries is the best path to uniting them.

The fact is that at Maastricht the leaders of the EU put the cart before the horse. Out of the familiar mixture of three different kinds of motive – idealistic, national-instrumental, and perceived common interest – they committed themselves to what was meant to be a decisive step to uniting Europe, but now seems likely to divide even those who belong to the monetary union. At least in the short term, it will certainly divide those existing EU members who participate in the monetary union from those who do not: the so-called 'ins' and 'outs'.

Meanwhile, one consequence of monetary union has been seen even before it has happened. Such massive concentration on this single project has led to neglect of the great opportunity that arose in the eastern half of the continent when the Berlin Wall came down – an opportunity best summed up in George Bush's phrase about making Europe 'whole and free'. The Maastricht agenda of internal unification has taken the time and energy of West European leaders away from the agenda of eastward enlargement. To be sure, there is no theoretical contradiction between the 'deepening' and the 'widening' of the European Union. Indeed, widening requires deepening. If the major institutions of the EU, originally designed to work for six member states, are still to function in a community of twenty-six, then major reforms, necessarily involving a further sharing of sovereignty, are essential. But these changes are of a different kind from those required for monetary union. While there is no theoretical contradiction, there has been a practical tension between deepening and widening.

To put it plainly: our leaders set the wrong priority after 1989. We were like people who for forty years had lived in a large, ramshackle house divided down the middle by a concrete wall. In the western half we had rebuilt, mended the roof, knocked several rooms together, redecorated, and installed new plumbing and electric wiring, while the eastern half fell into a state of dangerous decay. Then the wall came down. What did we do? We decided that what the whole house needed most urgently was a superb, new, computer-controlled system of air-conditioning in the western half. While we prepared to install it, the eastern half of the house began to fall apart and even to catch fire. We fiddled in Maastricht, while Sarajevo began to burn.

The best can so often be the enemy of the good. The rationalist, functionalist, perfectionist attempt to 'make Europe' or 'complete Europe' through a hard core built around a rapid monetary union could well end up achieving the opposite of the desired effect. One can all too plausibly argue that what we are likely to witness in the next five to ten years is the writing of another entry for Toynbee's index, under 'Europe, unification of, failure of attempts at'.

Some contemporary Cassandras go further still. They suggest that we may even witness the writing of another entry under 'Europe, as battlefield'. One might answer that we already have, in former Yugoslavia. Yet the suggestion that the forced march to unification through money brings the danger of violent conflict between states in the European Union does seem drastically overdrawn. For a start, there is the powerful neo-Kantian argument that bourgeois democracies are unlikely to go to war against each other. Unlike pre-1945 Europe, we also have a generally benign extra-European hegemon in the United States. And to prophesy such conflict is to ignore the huge and real achievement of European integration to date: the unique, unprecedented framework and deeply ingrained habits of permanent insti-tutionalized cooperation which ensure that the conflicts of interest that exist, and will continue to exist, between the member states and nations, are never resolved by force. All those endless hours and days of negotiation in Brussels between ministers from fifteen European countries, who end up knowing each other almost better than they know their own families: that is the essence of this 'Europe'. It is an economic community, of course, but it is also a security community

– a group of states that do find it unthinkable to resolve their own differences by war.

5

Now one could certainly argue that Western Europe would never have got this far without the utopian goal or *telos* of 'unity'. Only by resolutely embracing the objective of 'ever closer union' have we reached this more modest degree of permanent institutional cooperation, with important elements of legal and economic integration. Yet as a paradigm for European policy in our time the notion of 'unification' is fundamentally flawed. The most recent period of European history provides no indication that the immensely diverse peoples of Europe, speaking such different languages, having such disparate histories, geographies, cultures and economies, are ready to merge peacefully and voluntarily into a single polity. It provides substantial evidence of a directly countervailing trend: towards the constitution – or reconstitution – of nation states. If unity was not attained among a small number of West European states, with strong elements of common history, under the paradoxically favourable conditions of the Cold War, how can we possibly expect to attain it in the infinitely larger and more diverse Europe – the whole continent – that we have to deal with after the end of the Cold War?

'Yes,' replied Pierre Hassner, the brilliant French analyst of international politics, when I made this case to him, 'I'm afraid you're right. Europe will not come to pass.' 'But, Pierre,' I exclaimed, 'you're in it!' Europe is already here – and not just as a geographical expression. There is already a great political achievement that has taken us far beyond de Gaulle's *Europe des Patries* or Harold Macmillan's vision of a glorified free-trade area. Yet, to a degree that people outside Europe find hard to comprehend, European thinking about Europe is still deeply conditioned by these notions of project, process and progress towards unification. (After all, no one talks hopefully of Africa or Asia 'becoming itself'.) Many Europeans are convinced that, if we do not go forward towards unification, we must necessarily go backward. This view is expressed in the so-called 'bicycle theory' of

European integration: if you stop pedalling, the bicycle will fall over. Actually, as anyone who rides a bicycle knows, all you have to do is to put one foot back on the ground. And, anyway, Europe is not a bicycle.

If we Europeans convince ourselves that not advancing further along the path to unity is tantamount to failure, we risk snatching failure from the jaws of success. For what has been achieved already in a large part of Europe is a very great success, without precedent on the European continent or contemporary equivalent on any other continent. It is as if someone had built a fine if rather rambling palace and then convinced himself that he was an abject failure because it was not the Parthenon. Yet the case is more serious and urgent than this. For today it is precisely the forced march to unity – across the 'bridge too far' of monetary union – that is threatening the very achievement it is supposed to complete.

But what is the alternative? How else should we 'think Europe' if not in terms of this paradigm of unification that has dominated European thinking about Europe for half a century? How can we characterize positively what we have already built in a large part of Europe, and what it is both desirable and realistic to work towards in a wider Europe? I believe the best paradigm is that of *liberal order*. Historically, liberal order is an attempt to avoid both of the extremes between which Europe has unhappily oscillated through most of its modern history: violent disorder, on the one hand, and hegemonic order, on the other – hegemonic order that itself was always built on the use of force and the denial of national and democratic aspirations within the constitutive empires or spheres of influence. Philosophically, such an order draws on Isaiah Berlin's central liberal insight that people pursue different ends that cannot be reconciled but may peacefully coexist. It also draws on Judith Shklar's 'liberalism of fear', with its deeply pessimistic view of the propensity of human beings to indulge in violence and cruelty, and the sense that what she modestly called 'damage control' is the first necessity of political life. Institutionally, the European Union, Nato, the Council of Europe and the Organization for Security and Cooperation in Europe are all building blocks of such a liberal order.

Liberal order differs from previous European orders in several vital ways. Its first commandment is the renunciation of force in the resolution of disputes between its members. Of course, this goal is an ancient one. We find it anticipated already in King George of Podebrady's great proposal of 1464 for 'the inauguration of peace throughout Christendom'. There we read that he and his fellow princes 'shall not take up arms for the sake of any disagreements, complaints or disputes, nor shall we allow any to take up arms in our name'. But today we have well-tried institutions of bourgeois internationalism in which to practise what Churchill called 'making jaw-jaw rather than war-war'.

Liberal order is, by design, non-hegemonic. To be sure, the system depends to some extent on the external hegemonic balancer, the United States – 'Europe's pacifier', as more than one author has quipped. And, of course, Luxembourg does not carry the same weight as Germany. But the new model order that we have developed in the European Union does permit smaller states to have an influence often disproportionate to their size. A key element of this model order is the way in which it allows different alliances of European states on individual issues, rather than cementing any fixed alliances. Another is the framework of common European law. If the European Convention on Human Rights were incorporated into the treaties of the Union, as Ralf Dahrendorf has suggested, the EU would gain a much-needed element of direct responsibility for the liberties of the individual citizen.

Liberal order also differs from previous European orders in explicitly legitimating the interest of participating states in each others' internal affairs. Building on the so-called 'Helsinki process', it considers human, civil and, not least, minority rights to be a primary and legitimate subject of international concern. These rights are to be sustained by international norms, support and, where necessary, also pressure. Such a liberal order recognizes that there is a logic that leads peoples who speak the same language, and share the same culture and tradition, to want to govern themselves in their own state. There is such a thing as liberal nationalism. But it also recognizes that in many places a peaceful, neat separation into nation states will be impossible. In such cases it acknowledges a responsibility to help sustain what may variously be called multi-ethnic, multicultural or multinational democracies, within an international framework. This is what we disastrously failed to do for Bosnia but can still try to do for Macedonia or Estonia.

Missing from this paradigm is one idea which is still very important in contemporary European visions, especially those of former Great Powers such as France, Britain and Germany. This is the notion of 'Europe' as a single actor on the world stage – a world power able to stand up to the United States, Russia or China. In truth, a drive for world power is hardly more attractive because it is a joint enterprise than it was when attempted – somewhat more crudely – by individual European nations. Certainly, in a world of large trading blocs we must be able to protect our own interests. Certainly, a liberal order also means one that both gives and gets as much free trade as possible. Certainly, a degree of power-projection, including the coordinated use of military power, will be needed to realize the objectives of liberal order even within the continent of Europe, and in adjacent areas of vital interest to us, such as North Africa and the Middle East. But, beyond this, just to put our own all-European house in order would be a large enough contribution to the well-being of the world.

Some may object that I have paid too much attention to mere semantics. Why not let the community be called a 'Union' and the process 'unification', even if they are not that in reality? Václav Havel seems to come close to this position when he writes, 'Today, Europe is attempting to give itself a historically new kind of order in a process that we refer to as unification.' And of course I do not expect the European Union to be, so to speak, dis-named. After all, the much looser world organization of states is still called the United Nations. But the issue is far from merely semantic.

To consolidate Europe's liberal order and to spread it across the whole continent is both a more urgent and, in the light of history, a more realistic goal for Europe at the beginning of the twenty-first century than the vain pursuit of unification in a part of it. Nor, finally, is liberal order a less idealistic goal than unity. For unity is not a primary value in itself. It is but a means to higher ends. Liberal order, by contrast, directly implies not one but two primary values: peace and freedom.

1998

10 April. A multi-party agreement is signed on the future of Northern Ireland – the 'Good Friday Agreement'.

24 April. Russian president Boris Yeltsin's youthful candidate for prime minister, Sergei Kiryenko, is accepted by the Duma at the third attempt.

April–May. Armed conflict between Serb forces and the Kosovo Liberation Army escalates in Kosovo.

1–3 May. A special EU summit in Brussels announces that monetary union will be launched on 1 January 1999 with eleven countries participating.

22 May. In a referendum, voters in Northern Ireland approve the 'Good Friday Agreement'.

31 May. A coalition led by President Milo Djukanović, a critic of Serbian president Slobodan Milošević, wins parliamentary elections in Montenegro.

1 June. An international aid package is announced in response to financial crisis in Russia.

8 June. Threatening a strong Western response to Serb actions in Kosovo, British foreign secretary Robin Cook says, 'I hope Milošević is listening. This is the last warning.'

20 June. All EU ambassadors are withdrawn from Belarus in protest at President Lukashenka's attempt to evict them from their embassies.

25 June. Voting in Northern Ireland to elect a new assembly.

7 July. Former Italian prime minister Silvio Berlusconi is sentenced to two years and nine months' imprisonment for bribing tax officials.

8 July. Viktor Orbán of the 'Young Democrats' (FIDESZ) becomes prime minister of Hungary.

8–9 July. Gdańsk, Poland. I visit the former Lenin Shipyard, birthplace of Solidarity. It is now almost an industrial archaeology site, with head-high weeds, rusting hulls and only a couple of ships being built this year. One of the shipyard halls has been converted into a techno-rock discothèque. Lech Wałęsa tells me he feels a kind of 'moral hangover' when he looks at the shipyard now. Certainly, all the radical, neo-liberal changes to a free-market economy were essential. There was no other way. But he feels that somehow they should have done more for this place.

9 July. A new Czech government is formed under Social Democrat prime minister Miloš Zeman, based on a pact with the centre-right Civic Democratic Party of former prime minister Václav Klaus.

28 July. Mališevo, unofficial capital of the Kosovo Liberation Army, is retaken by Serb forces.

August. Financial 'melt-down' in Russia.

15 August. A terrorist bomb kills twenty-eight people in Omagh, Northern Ireland.

23 August. President Yeltsin sacks his cabinet for the second time in five months, and replaces prime minister Sergei Kiryenko with Victor Chernomyrdin.

26 August. The Russian rouble loses 40 per cent of its value against the Deutschmark after trading in dollars is suspended.

9−11 September. Slovenia. A long conversation with President Milan Kučan, eloquent about his country's new-old location in Central Europe. Referring to the Serbs' view of Kosovo as the historic cradle of their nation, he says, 'Our Kosovo is in Austria.' He means Carinthia, the medieval duchy or Civitas Carantania, back to which the Slovenians trace their historic nationhood.

I assume that, as the man who led the first former Yugoslav republic to fight for its independence from Milošević's Serbia, he might support the Kosovar Albanians in their struggle for independence from Milošević's Serbia. But no. A lawyer by training, he insists that Kosovo was always part of the Republic of Serbia, not a constituent part of Yugoslavia, and therefore does not have the right to secede. Altogether, he shows remarkably little sympathy for the Kosovar Albanians, whom he describes as a 'rural patriarchal society' with an insatiable appetite for land. He speaks like a Central European contemplating some remote, slightly barbaric part of the Balkans. Yet ten years ago, they were part of the same country.

11 September. Post-communist Yevgeny Primakov becomes the Russian prime minister.

22 September. The Polish parliament votes to give people access to their own secret-police files from the communist period.

23−26 September. Poland, for publication of the Polish edition of my book about the Stasi files, *The File*. A young presenter on breakfast television interviews me about my experiences with the Stasi. Afterwards he says, 'But one thing I didn't understand. These people who informed on you. You write that they were afraid. But what did they have to be afraid of?' So swift is the forgetting, even in Poland.

25 September. Vladimír Mečiar is defeated in parliamentary elections in Slovakia.

27 September. Bundestag elections in Germany.

Goodbye to Bonn

'This is a historic moment,' a stalwart German Christian Democrat whispered to me as the familiar giant figure of Helmut Kohl mounted the stage at party headquarters in Bonn, shortly before seven o'clock on the evening of Sunday 27 September 1998. As if it needed saying! Given the scale of the Christian Democrats' electoral defeat, we all guessed that, after a staggering sixteen years in power, the chancellor of German and European unification would be stepping down. When the cries of 'Helmut! Helmut!' had finally abated, he gave a dignified short speech. He congratulated the Social Democrat Gerhard Schröder on his victory and wished him 'a happy hand for our land'. As for himself, he would now also retire as party leader. It felt as if the Alps had suddenly announced their departure.

As the twentieth century draws to a close, we can safely say that Helmut Kohl is its last great European statesman. Watching him leave the stage, I thought of a memorable conversation we had a few years ago. At one moment he took my breath away. 'Do you realize', he said, 'that you are sitting opposite the direct successor to Adolf Hitler?' The point of this startling, even shocking, remark was that he – the first chancellor of a united Germany since Hitler – was going to do everything quite differently. Whereas Hitler had tried to put a German roof over Europe, he was determined to put a European roof over Germany. This amazing sally encapsulated several ingredients of Kohl's greatness: his acute instinct for power, his historical vision, and the bold simplicity of his strategic thinking. Add tactical adroitness, tireless attention to party-political details, and vast physical presence and stamina – the result is a provincial politician who changed the world.

The election of Sunday 27 September was not just the end of 'the Kohl era'. It marked several other ends – and new beginnings. This is the last federal election in which the parties' election expenses will be calculated in Deutschmarks. Next time round, in 2002, the Deutschmark, that totem of post-war West German prosperity, stability and identity, will be no more. Everything will be done in euros. It was also the last election for which we will go to Bonn. Next year, parliament and government move to Berlin. As Christopher Isherwood didn't write, 'Goodbye to Bonn.'

Walking up the modest highway which is the spine of that dank Rhineland city, with cheerful crowds thronging the pavements, their attention soon turning back from the election to a rock band, beer, and the Formula One championships just up the road, I felt a pang of regret. Bonn is a dull place, but what came to be known as 'the Bonn republic' has been a good Germany – perhaps the best Germany we have ever had. In this election, it proved the maturity of its carefully constructed, quiet, civil democracy. Although the country has 4 million unemployed, German voters once again rejected the extremes of left and right. The old saying 'Bonn is not Weimar' – that is, its democracy will not be torn apart by a flight to anti-democratic extremes, as in the Weimar republic – can now be adapted to a definitive, final form: 'Bonn was not Weimar.'

I

We knew we were saying goodbye to Bonn and the Deutschmark. We thought we would be saying goodbye to Kohl. What we didn't expect was a landslide that changes the whole political face of Germany. All the public-opinion polls except one showed Kohl closing the gap on Schröder. Electoral arithmetic based on these polls suggested the likelihood of a 'grand coalition' in which Schröder's Social Democrats would govern together with the Christian Democrats, the latter under a new leader. This seemed about right for the Bonn republic's style of gradual, consensual change. It is a remarkable fact that, in the whole previous history of the Federal Republic, the government has never completely changed as a direct result of the popular vote. Either the governing coalition has changed between elections or, in the rare event of it changing at an election, one previous coalition partner has remained in power.

This time the voters decided otherwise. As if to show that, after half a century, German democracy has fully come of age, they produced a result which means that the Social Democrats replace the Christian Democrats as the senior partner, and the environmentalist Greens replace the Free Democrats as the junior partner. In this so-called 'red–green coalition', all the faces will be new.

Why was the vote so decisive? I saw three main reasons. First, and most important, after sixteen years people simply felt it was 'time for a change'. That was the answer that came again and again in my own conversations and those reported elsewhere. The old man and his team had run out of energy and ideas. Voters were plain bored of those same old faces. Boredom is an underrated factor in politics.

This was exactly what happened in Britain, after eighteen years of Conservative rule. A Conservative candidate in that 1997 election told me that when people asked him 'Isn't it time for a change?' he simply had no answer. In his heart of hearts, he thought it was too. So also here. Contrary to some predictions, the crises in Russia and Asia did not make voters feel that it was better to stick with the experienced statesman.

Second, the 'Clintonblair' Schröder was a smooth, telegenic, attractive candidate, with an unusually well-disciplined Social Democratic Party behind him, led by his colleague and rival Oskar Lafontaine. Post-election research shows that the main component of the swing was straightforward: people who voted Christian Democrat last time voted Social Democrat this time. Among them were many pensioners, whose pensions Kohl had trimmed and Schröder promises to restore.

Third, there was the east. Back in the historic spring of 1990, Helmut Kohl won a crucial election in what was still East Germany by promising to create 'blooming landscapes' out of the post-communist wasteland. That vote meant East Germany became just east Germany: the eastern part of a larger Federal Republic. By the time of the last federal election, in 1994, with old communist factories rusting all around, and their workers on the dole, 'blooming landscapes' had become a bitter joke. I saw people holding up placards at Kohl's election rallies saying 'Where are the blooming landscapes?' or simply 'Blooming landscapes!' But enough people still had enough confidence in Kohl to give the CDU the largest share of the vote.

This time, I spent much of the pre-election week in the east. In the city of Schwerin, I watched disillusioned youngsters, many of them unemployed, heckle the chancellor as he spoke glowingly of growth and jobs. They held up a satirical banner proclaiming, 'Helmut: You are the Way, the Truth and the Light.' Then, on the hustings at a village on the outskirts of east Berlin, I was amazed to see a poster proclaiming, 'Vote for Blooming Landscapes – CDU.' The left-wing cartoonist Klaus Staeck was not amused. 'That was my *joke*,' he protested. And a joke in the end it proved to be, since the CDU vote in the east plummeted from more than 38 per cent in 1994 to just over 27 per cent. In the west it fell less than half as much, from just over 33 per cent to just under 28 per cent. It was the east that turned a defeat into a rout.

There's a deep irony here. For Kohl has been voted away at a time when large parts of that eastern landscape actually are beginning to 'bloom'. Travelling around, I still found large patches of desolation, rust, unemployment and the accompanying mixture of apathy among the old and often xenophobic anger among the young. But I also found impressive areas of large-scale construction, new jobs, energy and hope.

Nowhere else in post-communist Europe does one see such vistas of shining new steel, glass and concrete. Hardly surprising, given that west Germany has pumped more than DM 1,000,000,000,000 into the east over the last eight years. And there is massive private investment too. The mayor of one community in the so-called 'bacon belt' of prosperous commuter villages around Berlin showed me the newly made streets and fire station, the freshly renovated school, and a whole estate of detached, private houses, built by local people on savings and building loans. The old kingdom of Saxony in the south is booming, under its Christian Democratic 'king', Kurt Biedenkopf. Even in the poor northern province of Mecklenburg-Vorpommern, which has more than 17 per cent unemployment, every village I drove through had some new building projects.

Still more important is the mental architecture. The picture you get from the British or American press is one of almost universal resignation and resentment. Yet I found people hungrily participating in a democracy that is still new to them. This was the liveliest campaign in the east since that vote for unification back in 1990. Walls were plastered with posters. Meetings were packed. More than 80 per cent of those eligible turned out to vote, compared with 72 per cent four years ago. And such civic activism is not confined to election time. The mayor of that 'bacon belt' village tells me she is deluged with petitions and 'citizens' initiatives'. Many are dedicated to protecting the selfish interests of the new middle class. For example, the residents of that new private housing estate protest about being asked to contribute to the cost of a local 'cycleway'. This is 'civil society' emerging, but civil society less as the Central European dissidents dreamed of it than as Karl Marx analysed it – the self-defence of the bourgeoisie!

A comparison is sometimes made between the German east after unification and the American south after the Civil War. This is quite misleading. East Germany was always an artificial unit: the Soviet Zone of Occupation turned into a state. The flourishing southern *Länder* of Thuringia and Saxony now feel themselves closer to Bavaria than to Mecklenburg. East and west Berlin are slowly but surely getting mixed up together. The arrogance, condescension and incomprehension that many west Germans display towards their eastern compatriots is still a big problem. It was rightly said after 1990 that Germany had been united, the Germans had not. But even that is beginning to happen. In the early 1990s there continued to be a mass emigration of east Germans to the west. Last year, for the first time, almost as many west Germans came to live in the east.

All just as Kohl promised – though a lot more slowly, more painfully, and more expensively. Yet those ungrateful easterners have bitten the hand that fed them. So now Helmut Kohl will retire to his modest house in the small western town of Oggersheim, while Gerhard Schröder will move into the grand new chancellery in the big, raw, eastern city of Berlin. A half-century of the Bonn republic has suddenly and decisively ended.

2

New government, new capital, new currency. As New Britain's Tony Blair likes to say, everything is new, new, new. But what can we say, or guess, about this New Germany?

It is already being called 'the Berlin republic'. Some German federalists object to the term. The Federal Republic, they argue, will still be a decentralized state. The business weekly *Wirtschaftswoche* ran a major article in election week arguing that Frankfurt, which narrowly failed to become the federal capital in 1949, and was again a candidate after unification, will remain the undisputed economic capital of Germany. Major newspapers are still in Hamburg, the Constitutional Court still in Karlsruhe. For all that, I think it will be 'the Berlin republic', because I think the move to Berlin will have a profound psychological impact on the politicians and hence the politics of Germany.

Berlin is a city full of ghosts – Prussian militarist, Wilhelmine, Nazi and communist, as well as the more attractive ghosts of Prussian intellectual life, Weimar culture and anti-Nazi resistance. Amid these ghosts, vast, impressive new government buildings are thrusting up. These buildings do not speak of a nation that is proposing to surrender its only recently recovered sovereignty to a European superstate. Berlin is a metropolis, with many foreigners living there. Berlin is in the middle of east Germany, close to all the problems of the transition from communism. Berlin is just forty minutes' drive from the Polish frontier.

The Berlin republic, it is suggested, will be not only more eastern but perhaps also more Protestant than a Bonn republic shaped by the Catholic Rhineland tradition from which both Konrad Adenauer and Helmut Kohl came. Even in a highly secularized society, this matters. The Israeli political scientist Shlomo Avineri has observed that a Jewish atheist and a Christian atheist are not the same thing: they disbelieve in a different God. The same may be said of Catholic atheists and Protestant atheists.

Into this new setting moves a new generation of politicians, most in their fifties, some in their forties. Many of them, including Gerhard

Schröder and the likely Green foreign minister, Joschka Fischer, are classic '68ers, shaped by that distinctive moment of student protest across the western world. Others were formed by the protest movements of the 1970s and 1980s: feminist, ecological, against nuclear weapons and against nuclear power. As always in German politics, another formative influence is their diverse experience of policy-making in coalition governments in the federal states. Meanwhile, years of schooling themselves for power at the national level have made them adepts of the sound-bite.

In theory, this red–green coalition will be able to stamp its mark on the new republic. Not only does it have a clear majority in the Bundestag, the lower house of parliament, it also has a majority in the Bundesrat, the upper house composed of representatives of the federal states. The coalition will be able to propose its candidate for federal president, and to start nominating judges to the Constitutional Court. By the year 2000, all the key institutions of the republic might therefore be coloured 'red–green'. They could even choose a president of the Bundesbank, although that is to be supplanted by the European Central Bank.

In opposition, the Christian Democrats, like the British Conservatives, will take some time to pull themselves together again, in alliance with the Bavarian Christian Social Union. Their new leader is Wolfgang Schäuble. When I spoke to the wheelchair-bound Schäuble, one of the most thoughtful and impressive figures in German politics, he was clearly looking forward to the task of regenerating a broadly based party – what in German is called a *Volkspartei* – that would, among other things, prevent disgruntled voters breaking away to the nationalist right. Yet German Christian Democracy will have to redefine itself in circumstances where its three traditional unifying forces have either disappeared or faded: anti-communism, Christianity and a shared commitment to further steps of European integration. The last-mentioned is most plainly challenged by the Bavarian premier, Edmund Stoiber, sometimes jokingly called Edmund Thatcher.

Meanwhile, in opposition from the left there is the ex-communist Party of Democratic Socialism, which just scraped over the 5 per cent hurdle to get its full complement of members of parliament. While its electorate is still overwhelmingly in the east, it is now setting out to establish itself as a party of the 'socialist left' in the whole Federal Republic.

For the time being, however, the coalition's main problems will be not with the opposition, but within its own ranks. For this will be a coalition of coalitions. Schröder may be chancellor, but Oskar Lafontaine is the Social Democrats' party leader. They appeared together at virtually all the post-election meetings. Some even say 'Lafontaine makes policy and Schröder sells it.' Lafontaine is an opportunist, but an opportunist with close ties to the old left. And that old left is much more strongly represented among the Social Democrats than it is in Tony Blair's purged New Labour. Meanwhile, the Greens remain the most diverse and even chaotic of parties, with a strong pacifist wing.

What of Schröder himself? Though his rugged features are sharply cut, they are the sharpest thing about him. Except, perhaps, his suits. He looks very good on television. Indeed, he seems slightly more real on television than when you meet him in person. He is the epitome of the fifty-something, smooth, flexible, professional politician. But someone who knows him quite well told me that, unlike Clinton or Blair, he does not have any religious attachments (albeit, in the case of Clinton, honoured in the breach) or perceptible value system. So he's a sort of Clinton without the principles.

He has never, this colleague pointed out, taken a courageous independent stand on any issue. In the past, he has embraced left-wing positions – opposing the deployment of Nato's cruise and Pershing missiles in the early 1980s, for example – and positions more associated with the right – for instance, last year he was suggesting the postponement of European monetary union. In each case, he has gone with the wind. In the public-opinion polls, more of those asked thought he would be a competent chancellor than thought Helmut Kohl would be. But my private opinion polls suggest that a lot of people, including some Social Democrats, share the doubts expressed on a recent *Economist* cover: 'Would you buy a used car from Gerhard Schröder?' The polite word is 'pragmatist'.

The elementary point of this catalogue of observations is that the Berlin republic begins with a whole series of unknowns. And a combination of unknowns is a larger unknown. In fact, the Germans have got more than they bargained for. They voted for a change, yes. But there was little of the popular enthusiasm for a new beginning that accompanied Willy Brandt's appointment as chancellor in 1969, with his famous slogan 'Risk More Democracy.' Instead, Schröder actually used the conservative Konrad Adenauer's motto 'No Experiments'. An experiment is what Germany has got, all the same.

3

This being so, all predictions are more than usually risky. But let me venture three guesses. My first guess is an optimistic one. It has to do with so-called 'foreigners' living in Germany. The only disturbing element in this campaign was the popular hostility to these 'foreigners' that was revealed. This was particularly true in east Germany, where one in five young men say they could imagine voting for a party of the far right. On the streets of Berlin, the posters of one of these parties proclaimed 'Criminal Foreigners Out!' The hostility extends not just to blacks and Turks but to the Poles they call *'Pollacken'*. And it reaches well into the Christian Democrat electorate. I saw Christian Democratic politicians receiving tumultuous applause whenever they said that foreigners 'should not abuse our hospitality' or 'must respect our laws and ways'.

This is a problem that Germany has made for itself, since it has been very liberal in taking people in, but very restrictive in granting German citizenship. The result is that a staggering 7 million people, out of a total population of 80 million, live as 'foreigners' in Germany. Until quite recently, the main qualification for citizenship was to have German blood. Although the Christian Democrats changed the law to make it possible to gain citizenship after fifteen years' residence, they held out firmly against dual citizenship for, say, long-time Turkish residents in Germany. (Yet Germany itself is quite happy to grant dual citizenship to ethnic Germans living in Poland.) With a red–green government this should change, giving the country a normal, liberal citizenship law, more comparable with that in Britain and America. Altogether, it should encourage a more welcoming attitude to immigrants, and to the whole idea of Germans of different ethnic and cultural backgrounds.

My second guess is more pessimistic – for Germany, though perhaps not for its competitors. Helmut Kohl probably did larger things for his country than Margaret Thatcher did for hers. (To be fair, larger things needed doing. The United Kingdom did not need to be reunited.) But Kohl failed to do precisely those big things that Thatcher did: reducing the power of the trade unions, privatization, deregulation, lowering direct taxation, cutting public spending, and so on. In Britain, this is the foundation that Tony Blair can build on. Now Gerhard Schröder fought a campaign of Blair-like discipline and razzmatazz. But, to be a Blair in office, you need first to have had your Thatcher.

Virtually all German business leaders argue that, if Germany is to remain competitive and to create new jobs, it needs some of that medicine. It needs Thatcherism with a human face. But can this new government deliver it? Schröder says economic and social reform is his top priority. He is famously close to business leaders, and was on the board of Volkswagen. He understands some of what needs to be done. On the other hand, he was recently involved in a spectacular state bail-out of a failing steelworks. The state of which he has been premier, Lower Saxony, has run up a large public debt. Moreover, he has promises to keep: that promise to restore pensions, for example. He also promised to defend the welfare state, promote 'social justice', and finance job creation.

His own party, under Oskar Lafontaine, will surely try to keep him to that. Indeed, the Social Democrats actually favour a higher top rate of income tax than the Greens do: 49 per cent, against the Greens' proposed 45 per cent. But the Greens have their own pet scheme: a rapidly increasing tax on petrol. German industry does not think that will help its competitiveness. If you add up the chancellor's track record and promises, his coalition of coalitions, the strength of the trade unions and the whole post-war German tradition of change by consensus, you do not get a recipe for rapid implementation of the reforms that German business leaders think essential.

Finally, a guess about foreign policy, in which Schröder has promised 'continuity'. This promise is credible, but I suspect the character of this continuity will be 'the same, only less so'. The Greens and the Social Democratic left have a record of anti-Nato protest. A Green foreign minister may be bad for Nato military actions 'out of area', since, whatever his personal convictions, he will have to pay some attention to his own party's pacifists. The outgoing defence minister, Volker Rühe, an outspoken advocate of both Nato enlargement and Nato intervention in Kosovo, told me he fears that the close partnerships for effective action that he has built up, especially with the United States, may be imperilled.

In the European Union, Schröder signalled continuity by paying his first foreign trip to Paris. Despite his past reservations about European monetary union, he'll try to make it work. But, like most of his generation, he will, I believe, be cooler and more hard-nosed about any further steps of European integration than were the post-war Euro-enthusiasts such as Helmut Kohl. Even if the inaugural speeches contain the usual visionary Euro-rhetoric, he won't in fact be pursuing any personal vision of ever closer union.

This will make him a more congenial partner for Britain. He has talked in the past of turning the Franco-German axis into a Franco–German–British triangle. On the other hand, there is at least one mighty argument ahead: about Germany's desire to reduce its outsize contribution to the EU budget. And cost will also be a problem when it comes to detailed negotiations about eastward enlargement of the Union. Sitting in Berlin, the new government will see more clearly the necessity but also the difficulties of bringing in the neighbours just up the road. In this regard, too, we may expect more cool pragmatism, with close attention to both national interest and public mood.

There are my three guesses. But they are just guesses. What has been extraordinary about Germany in the 1990s has been the great continuity of its policies, despite the fact that the country's shape, size, internal composition and geopolitical position have all changed with unification. This continuity was due to Helmut Kohl, the Deutschmark and the Bonn republic. Now it's goodbye to all that. Like it or not, the Berlin republic may be more interesting.

1998

September. Atrocities are committed by Serb forces in Kosovo. Nato responds with threats of air strikes against Serbia.

12 October. An agreement between US envoy Richard Holbrooke and Serbian leader Slobodan Milošević provides for 2,000 OSCE 'verifiers' in Kosovo, Nato air surveillance, and negotiations for a political settlement.

16 October. Twentieth anniversary of the election of Pope John Paul II.

October. New German chancellor Gerhard Schröder indicates that eastward enlargement of the EU may depend on Germany getting a satisfactory reduction in its contribution to the EU budget.

'Be not Afraid!'

Brezhnev, Carter, Deng Xiaoping, Callaghan, Schmidt: where are they now? These were the 'world leaders' back in October 1978, when a little-known Polish cardinal stepped out on to St Peter's Square as the new pope and proclaimed his electrifying message: 'Be not afraid!' Twenty years on, those worldly leaders are long since retired or dead, but the 'servant of the servants of God' is still with us, still travelling the world, still tirelessly proclaiming the same urgent, universal message to all humankind.

At seventy-eight, he is frail and bent now. That rugged, athletic figure has been worn down by Parkinson's disease, by the assassin's bullet that tore through his intestines in 1981, and by two decades of ceaseless toil. He used to ski for hours; now he leans on his old ski-sticks for support while taking undemanding walks. His voice used to be so powerful and clear, with a skilled actor's delivery that John Gielgud once described as 'perfect'. Now it is often slurred. His broad, smiling face used to radiate human warmth for a hundred yards around – a quality he shared with his 'fellow Slav' Mikhail Gorbachev. Now the face is half-frozen with Parkinson's. His left hand trembles uncontrollably.

Yet still you glimpse flashes of the old magic, as the distant figure, all in white, draws a whole crowd to him with a characteristic gesture: gently but repeatedly lifting two outstretched open hands. Then he speaks to half a million people as if he were talking to one person. It's the magic that I saw in communist Poland, where he dissolved the fear instilled by all Brezhnev's divisions with one wave of that now trembling hand. And still he goes on admonishing the rulers of this world, whatever their political colour, whether Castro or Clinton.

Still he offers succour to the poor, the weak, the sick, the oppressed in every land.

You might think from this opening hymn of praise that I'm a Catholic, even a papal groupie. Far from it. Indeed, if I were a Catholic, I might be much less enthusiastic. His fiercest critics are among his own flock. I leave it to them to argue about his restoration of a 'monarchical' papacy and the stifling of debate inside the Church. As an agnostic liberal, albeit one rooted in a rich humus of Christianity, my concern is not with the Church but with the world. And I want to argue that Pope John Paul II is simply the greatest world leader of our times.

I say this not just because of what I saw him do in Poland, although of course that counts. Nor is it simply because I have experienced the force of his personality in a small gathering, although that was unforgettable. Over these twenty years I have had the chance to talk with several credible candidates for the title of 'great man' or 'great woman' – Mikhail Gorbachev, Helmut Kohl, Václav Havel, Lech Wałęsa, Margaret Thatcher – but none matches Karol Wojtyła's unique combination of concentrated strength, intellectual consistency, human warmth and simple goodness.

Yet my case rests on his public record. No one has conveyed a better message, more effectively, to more people. What is this message? When he arrived on St Peter's throne, it was all there, fully formed, ready to go. He immediately wrote it down, in longhand, for his first encyclical, *Redemptor Hominis* ('The Saviour of Man'). But there's a problem here. A philosopher, poet and playwright as well as a pastor, he writes in a dense, difficult linguistic blend of Thomism (the philosophy based on the teachings of Thomas Aquinas), phenomenology and Polish Marian mysticism. After tackling his book *The Acting Person*, an American philosopher mildly observed, 'I could not quite decide what the author was up to.' Yet in conversation, or on his travels, he can say what he means with stunning simplicity.

One common mistake is to suggest that he looks at the whole world through a Polish prism. Of course he is profoundly Polish. If you ever doubt that – and he hardly conceals it! – just listen to him speaking directly to the Virgin Mary before the great monastery of Częstochowa, emotionally addressing her as 'Queen of Poland'. (It's also deeply moving, for he really is like a man talking to a much loved mother. His own mother died when he was eight.) But when I once had dinner with him, in a circle of Polish friends, speaking Polish, I was struck by the very opposite impression. Here was a man who, far from looking at the world through Polish lenses, looked even at Poland through the prism of his global experience, faith and mission.

The other common mistake is to interpret him in conventional political categories, such as 'left' and 'right'. Many in the West see him as just an old, dyed-in-the-wool reactionary. Gorbachev, by contrast, says the Pope is a man of the left. In fact, he has always been fiercely critical of both capitalism and communism. But, as he insists in one of his encyclicals (*Solicitudo Rei Socialis*), the Church's doctrine is 'not a "third way" between liberal capitalism and Marxist collectivism'. Tony Blair and Bill Clinton please note. Rather it is 'a category of its own'. It is not ideology but theology. On the plane out to Poland for his first, great pilgrimage in 1979, he told journalists that the differences between communism and capitalism are superficial: 'Underneath is where the people are.'

His first concern is with what he believes to be the presence of God and Christ in the world. But, translated into the language of secular politics, his message becomes a set of demands to those who wield political, economic or cultural power – demands on behalf of the people 'underneath'. And a matching set of appeals to those individual people. At the centre is always what he calls 'the human person' (comprising, in Catholic teaching, body, reason and soul). He insists that each and every individual human being has an ineradicable dignity and inalienable rights – the poorest child in the worst barrio in Mexico City no less than the richest man in New York. John Paul II's passionate embrace of the language of human rights, previously associated with the heirs of the Enlightenment, was little short of revolutionary. And he preaches this gospel of human rights to one and all. He told Fidel Castro to respect his citizens' human rights, but also General Stroessner in Paraguay.

Everywhere, he takes the part of the poor. He may condemn 'liberation theology', but his own Latin American homilies have been full of the liberation theologians' concerns for the structurally oppressed.

His demands for 'social justice' make pure neo-liberal free-marketeers squirm. The right to work belongs to his core notion of human dignity. Again and again, he has denounced the evil of unemployment in capitalism, as well as that of 'senseless work' in command economies.

Another great theme is tolerance and mutual respect between different peoples and faiths. He grew up with Jewish schoolfriends in pre-war Poland, and reconciliation between Christians and Jews is very close to his heart. He has not gone as far as some Jewish leaders would like in acknowledging the Catholic church's own historical responsibility for anti-Semitism, but he has gone further than any of his predecessors. He also reaches out to Islam. Visiting Zagreb, he ordered Catholic Croats to respect the 'outstanding presence' of muslims in the Balkans. If the Harvard political scientist Samuel Huntington is right that the next great world conflict will be 'the clash of civilizations' (which, by the way, I don't think he is), it will certainly be no fault of this pope.

Everywhere, too, he preaches peace. On this he has been utterly consistent. Even in Nazi-occupied Poland, he refused to support armed resistance. 'Prayer is the only weapon that works,' he told a friend. In Japan, he cried, 'Never again Hiroshima! Never again Auschwitz!' In Ireland, he told the IRA to abandon the violence that would 'ruin the land you claim to love and the values you claim to cherish'. In Britain, he criticized the Falklands War. And he opposed the Gulf War too. All peoples have a right to justice and sovereignty, he says, but these may be achieved only by non-violent means. As he told his fellow-Poles in 1983, when General Jaruzelski had tried to dash their hopes with tanks, 'You must defeat evil with good.'

Not only has he kept saying these things on eighty-four foreign trips, from Argentina to Yamoussouka. He has also dramatized them, with the skills of the professional actor he once nearly became. He has, as Princess Diana had, the ability to present compassion in a single photogenic image: the gentle embrace of a crippled child, the head bowed in sadness at a place of horror. Yet he can also make the mighty tremble. Literally so in the case of General Jaruzelski, whose knees we could see visibly shaking before he met John Paul II in 1983: 'But only at the beginning,' the Pope commented kindly.

*

It's magnificent, but has it been effective? This is much harder to judge than in the case of ordinary politicians. For how can you measure the effects of small changes in millions of human hearts? His old friend Father Józef Tischner said that the Solidarity movement in Poland was 'a forest of awakened consciences'. But such forests are usually invisible.

Politically, his most obvious contribution was to the end of communism. Gorbachev himself says, 'Everything that happened in Eastern Europe would have been impossible without the presence of the Pope.' I would add 'including Gorbachev'. My argument is in two stages. First: without the Pope, no Solidarity in Poland. His great pilgrimage in 1979 broke the barrier of fear and created the solidarity that paved the way for Solidarity. This was far more important than anything in his biographer Carl Bernstein's overexcited tale of a 'secret alliance' between the Vatican and the CIA.

Second: without Solidarity, no Gorbachev. I don't mean, of course, that Gorbachev would not have emerged as Soviet leader. I mean that he would not have made his seminal revision of Soviet policy towards Eastern Europe unless the persistence of Solidarity – despite Jaruzelski's tanks – had shown him that the Soviet Union just could not carry on in the old way. When Gorbachev gave an inch, the Poles took a mile. Here is the specific chain of causation that goes from the election of the Polish pope in 1978 to the end of communism, and hence of the Cold War, in 1989.

If this was his clearest positive contribution to world history, then his largest negative contribution has been his opposition to all forms of artificial contraception. Here, too, he has been nothing if not consistent. He came to this position after thinking deeply about love, marriage and sexuality as a young priest. He personally encouraged Paul VI to take his stand against the pill in the fateful 1968 encyclical *Humanae Vitae* ('On Human Life'). He once said to a friend who challenged him on the subject, 'I can't change what I've been teaching all my life.' But the result has been much needless, avoidable suffering, as poor women in the Third World, denied contraceptives or proper education on birth control, have brought unwanted children into lives of misery. Yes, that very poverty and misery against which his own heart cries out.

After seeing off communism in the 1980s, he has spent the 1990s attacking the evils of unbridled capitalism. He tells us, far more robustly than any of the supposedly left-wing parties which again rule in much of Europe, that the rich still exploit the poor and the North damages the South. He says we are caught up in the pursuit of 'having' at the expense of 'being'. He says consumerism is 'a web of false and superficial gratifications'. Turning red in the face with anger, he rails against liberty decayed into licence, sexual promiscuity, alcoholism, drugs, relativism and postmodernism. Most people, even in his native Poland, ignore the old man's warnings. But are we really so sure there is no truth in what he says about our world – a world more free than it has ever been before?

As I write, I have before me a little book, some five inches by three. A miniature anthology of the Pope's teaching, it's called *Agenda for the Third Millennium*. Who else would dare such a title? I can't get anywhere with half of it, because I, like most of humankind, no longer believe. But there are things in the other half that I find magnificent, rich and true. And important, too, for the next twenty years – never mind the next thousand. It may not be *the* agenda for our time. But do any of us have a better one?

1998

21 October. Former communist Massimo D'Alema becomes prime minister of Italy, forming the fifty-sixth Italian government since 1945. 21 November. New German foreign minister Joschka Fischer provokes controversy by suggesting that Nato should adopt a doctrine of 'no first use' of nuclear weapons.

Cry, the Dismembered Country

Once upon a time there was a country called Yugoslavia. It was a medium-size country in the south-east of Europe, and more than 23 million people lived there. It was not democratic, but it had a fair name in the world. Its king was called Tito. Being both largely rural and socialist, this country was not rich. But it was getting a little richer. Most of its children grew up thinking they were Yugoslavs. They had other identities, too, and strong ones. Slovenes already talked of the 'narrower homeland', meaning Slovenia, and the 'wider homeland', meaning Yugoslavia. Its Albanians were always Albanians. But, still, it was a country.

In the last decade of the twentieth century, this European country has been torn apart. At least 150,000 and perhaps as many as 250,000 men, women and children have died in the process. And how they have died: with their eyes gouged out or their throats cut with rusty knives, women after deliberate ethnic rape, men with their own severed genitalia stuffed into their mouths. More than 2 million former Yugoslavs have been driven out of their homes by other former Yugoslavs, and many deprived of everything but what they could carry in precipitous flight.

In this former country, the grotesque spectacle of a whole village burned, looted and trashed has become an entirely normal sight. 'Yeah, the usual story,' says the journalist, and drives on. A few have grown rich: mainly war profiteers, gangsters and politicians – the three being sometimes hard to distinguish. The rest, save in Slovenia, have been impoverished, degraded and corrupted too. Real wages in Serbia are estimated to be at the level of 1959 – in the rare event of your actually being paid a wage. In Kosovo, the killing, burning, plundering and expelling went on throughout the summer of 1998, even as West Europeans took their holidays just a few miles away. It went on though the leaders of the West had all repeatedly declared it would never, ever, be allowed to happen again. Not after Bosnia.

If you look at a current political map of Europe, you may conclude that the former country is now five states: Slovenia, Croatia, Bosnia, Macedonia and the Federal Republic of Yugoslavia (known to diplomats as the FRY, pronounced as in 'French fries'). But the reality on the ground is at least nine parts. Bosnia is still divided between a 'Serb Republic' (Republika Srpska) and a Croat–Bosniak Federation, which itself is effectively divided between Croat-controlled and Bosniak- (or 'muslim'-) controlled areas. The FRY is divided between what may loosely be called 'Serbia proper', Kosovo, and the increasingly independent-minded republic of Montenegro. But even 'Serbia proper' should be disaggregated to notice the northern province of the Vojvodina, with its large Hungarian minority, and – oh, delight to the diplomatic historian! – the still partly muslim-settled Sandjak of Novi Pazar. Perhaps one should also distinguish the Albanian-settled areas from the rest of Macedonia. That makes twelve ethnically defined parts, to be going on with.

It's not just we in the West who are largely indifferent. Most inhabitants of most of these dismembered parts themselves live in growing indifference or active antipathy to each other. In Ljubljana, a cultured Slovene woman tells me sadly that her children cannot enjoy the wonderful work of Serbian writers, because they no longer read the Cyrillic alphabet. Why, she exclaims, they don't even understand Croatian! In Sarajevo, a local veteran of the siege says, 'You know, if I'm honest, we watched the television pictures from Kosovo this summer much as I suppose Westerners watched the pictures from Sarajevo.' But the feeling is reciprocated. In Priština, the capital of Kosovo, a leading representative of the mainly muslim Albanians tells me, 'We don't feel any fellowship with muslims in Bosnia, because they are Slavs.' In fact, the two groups have diametrically opposed goals: Bosnian 'muslims' want to keep together a multi-ethnic state, Kosovar Albanian 'muslims' want ethnic separation.[1]

Across this landscape of extraordinary ethno-linguistic-religious-historical-political complexity crawl the white-and-orange vehicles of an international presence which, in its different, political-bureaucratic, way, is just as complicated. SFOR, OHR, UNHCR, MSF, CARE, OSCE, USKDOM, EUKDOM, RUSKDOM: international alphabet soup poured over Balkan goulash. Americans may be the new Habsburg governors here, but French deputies tussle with British ones for priority at court, while earnest Scandinavians get on with laying the phone lines. At Sarajevo Airport, I sit next to a man whose shoulder-badge proclaims 'Icelandic Police'. Perhaps that Icelandic policeman will now be sent to Kosovo, to keep peace among the dervishes of Orahovac.[2]

Faced with such complexity, it's no wonder newspaper and television reports have largely stuck to a few simple, well-tried stories: bang-bang-bang, mutilated corpse, old woman weeps into dirty handkerchief, ruined mosque/church/town, US envoy Richard Holbrooke meets Serbian leader Slobodan Milošević, NATO bombers at Italian airbase, preparing not to bomb. Yawn. In truth, it needs a whole book to do justice to each single part. Here, I shall confine myself to reporting some of what I saw, in winter 1998, in just three closely related parts of the post-Yugoslav jigsaw: Kosovo, Macedonia and Belgrade. But then I shall draw a few larger conclusions.

I

KOSOVO

The fresh red blood on the fresh white snow looks unreal, like a new avant-garde exhibit at the Tate Gallery in London. But it is entirely real. This is the blood of two dead Serb policemen, shot at dawn, almost certainly by the soldiers of a tough local commander of the Kosovo Liberation Army (KLA), violating the October ceasefire. The blood lies, symbolically, just beneath a ruined mosque, in the middle of an Albanian village which those Serb forces have systematically destroyed. Now the women of one of the few Albanian families daring to remain here are telling us how the Serb police beat them up after the assassination.

Earlier, we drive through the town of Mališevo, which has been called 'the most dangerous place in Europe'. This summer it was the bustling unofficial capital of the KLA's 'liberated' heartland of Drenica. They even had their own KLA number plates. Now Mališevo is completely ruined and deserted, its shopping centre reduced to rubble and pulverized glass. The only people visible are heavily armed Serb police, behind their sandbags in a makeshift, fortified police station. Instead of shoppers, there are large packs of dogs scavenging, as many as twenty together, presumably domestic animals gone feral. You see these dogs all over the province, and their corpses lying on the roads.

Further down the empty highway, we find a solitary Albanian farmer trying to rescue his car. As we stop to help him, we face a surreal sight. A large, orange-painted armoured car, of the American type known colloquially as a Humvee, slowly and silently approaches. Right behind it trundles a long convoy of blue-painted armoured vehicles, packed with heavily armed Serb police in their blue combat uniforms. In the middle of the convoy there are some very nasty-looking men in an unmarked white jeep. The farmer is terrified: 'If the Americans weren't there, the police would beat us up.'

Later, he shows us his farmstead. Behind the high rough walls with which the Albanians surround the property of an extended family, we find two substantial houses, both blown up and looted. The families huddle together in one small basement room. 'We can't come back here while the Serbs are in the police station,' they say. 'We can't live under Serbia.'

Further on, we turn into the village of Dragobilje. Just a hundred yards off the main road patrolled by the Serb police, we find the KLA in their brown-and-green camouflage gear. A thickset, bearded man, with hand grenades slung in a belt round his chest, speaks with us on behalf of the '122nd Brigade'. When we ask his identity, he gives his code-name: 'Journalist'. He explains that he actually was a journalist in Priština before the war. They are currently respecting the ceasefire, he says, but they are ready to fight again at any time, for a free Kosovo. Meanwhile, several carloads of men in KLA uniforms come bucking down the muddy back lane, dodging the horned cattle and the tractor trailers carrying old men wearing traditional white caps. It's their own local version of a Ho Chi Minh trail.

As we drive out of Dragobilje, we see the same orange-painted

Humvee halted at the roadside. Beside it, a burly American monitor is talking to a local leader. 'Don't let your guys in uniform be visible from the main road, because that will provoke them [i.e. the Serbs],' says the monitor. When the local leader starts talking about the bitter past, this quiet American says, 'All you can do is look ahead – just look ahead.' And he offers help to get their school and hospital open again. 'What do you need? Plastic? Just tell us what you need.'

Another day, another ruined village in the snow, another guerrilla stronghold: Lauša to the Serbs, Llaushe for the Albanians. This was where the KLA first showed its face in public, on 28 November 1997, when two uniformed soldiers unmasked themselves and delivered a liberation speech at the funeral of a local schoolteacher shot by the Serbs.[3] Now two of the Geci brothers contemplate their devastated homestead. It was once home to seven brothers and their families – some thirty-five people in all. Most are now refugees in Albania. Those who remain are living on aid. Their own crops have been burned; their cattle killed or lost. 'The KLA is our self-defence,' they say. 'The soldiers are all local people.' Can they imagine ever again living together with Serbs in Kosovo? The grandmother gestures to a bare wire dangling from the ceiling: 'How can you live with those who hang people from light fittings?'

Our knowledge of the KLA is still fragmentary, partly because this guerrilla army is itself quite fragmentary. It has, as one Western military observer politely puts it, a 'rather horizontal' command structure. Each region is different, and regional commanders behave like local bandit chiefs. Nonetheless, we can establish a few significant things about its history, leaders and support.

First and foremost, its emergence is the result of Kosovar Albanians despairing of the non-violent path which they adopted after the province was robbed of its autonomy by Milošević in 1989, and Yugoslavia began to fall apart in 1990–91. Under their unofficially elected 'president of the Republic of Kosova', Ibrahim Rugova, they organized an extraordinary alternative state, with its own taxes, parliamentary committees, private health service and, most impressive, unofficial education system, from primary school to university. To the frustration of Western policy-makers, Rugova was unbending in his commitment to the goal of independence. To their relief, he was equally unbending in his attachment to non-violent means. How did he propose to square the circle? By the 'internationalization' of the Kosovo problem.

Even in the early 1990s, there were those who thought change would come only with the help of more traditional methods. Many Albanians from this region go to Western Europe for training and to earn money to send home. So did they. Ramush Haradinaj, the local commander almost certainly responsible for that blood in the snow, went off to get his military training in the French Foreign Legion. In Priština, people recall first hearing of a KLA in 1993. But then it was something like one of the terrorist splinter groups from the West European student movement of 1968. One of the KLA's more important current political leaders, Hasim Thaqi, code-name 'Snake', was a student activist in Priština who then went to study in Albania and to raise funds in the West. But most of the political activists who came from three generations of formative student political protest – in 1968, 1981 and 1990–91 – were still for non-violence.

What changed the balance? The startling answer I am given is: 'Dayton.' I'm told this by the veteran political prisoner Adem Demaci, who is now the KLA's political representative. He dates the true emergence of the KLA to spring 1996, just a few months after the November 1995 Dayton agreement on Bosnia. I'm also told this by Veton Surroi, a favourite source for visitors from the West, whose influential daily newspaper nonetheless supported (some even say inflamed) the armed struggle. And by several others.

They say they drew two lessons from Dayton. After more than five years of their Gandhiesque struggle for independence, the United States made a deal with Milošević over Bosnia without securing even a restoration of mere autonomy for Kosovo. So, lesson one: non-violence wasn't working. Meanwhile, in Bosnia itself, the Dayton agreement went a long way towards recognizing ethnic realities created by force. Lesson two: force pays.

There's an element of retrospective rationalization in this account. This is not what these same people were telling me in Priština in March 1997.[4] But there is also an uncomfortable element of truth. So long as Rugova kept the lid on his own people, and so long as we felt we had to deal with Milošević over Bosnia, we weren't going to push him on Kosovo.[5]

The armed rising then grew from two further developments: the looting of arsenals during the violent implosion of Albania in spring 1997, which gave the KLA access to Kalashnikovs galore, and the brutality of Serbian 'reprisals' against whole extended families and villages, starting in February 1998. As always, an oppressive army and police were the best recruiting sergeants for the guerrillas.

At each stage, more individuals from the peaceful resistance went for the gun. Thus the KLA's spokesman, Jakup Krasniqi, had previously studied at the underground Pedagogical Higher School in Priština. 'Un bon étudiant,' says his charming, francophone professor, Abdyl Ramaj, as he shows me round the tatty bungalow which is the school's temporary home. Most intriguing, most sobering, is the case of Shaban Shala. Until the spring of this year, Shaban Shala was the vice-chairman of the Council for the Defence of Human Rights and Freedoms, a human-rights monitoring group supported by several Western foundations. Now he is a guerrilla commander in the hills of his native Drenica. 'Well, in a way he's still fighting for human rights,' says an embarrassed employee of the Council. Well, in a way.

Though it's dangerous to generalize, those who joined or actively support the KLA often have three things in common. First, many of them were political prisoners in former Yugoslavia: Demaci for a record twenty-eight years, Shaban Shala for a pretty standard nine. Second, they often come from the worst-hit rural areas. In the countryside, extended family and clan loyalties are still very strong. And, in villages like Llaushe, the KLA is now the local community in arms. Third, they are fiercely critical of what they see as the inflexible, authoritarian but also weak leadership of Rugova.

These, then, are the fighters for national liberation – or 'terrorists', according to the Serb authorities – who have completely transformed the situation here. Western military observers are pretty contemptuous of their ragtag army, just as they used to be of the Bosniak army in Bosnia. They say it was wildly irresponsible of the KLA, in the liberation euphoria of the summer, to take over larger towns such as Orahovac, which they could not seriously defend. When the Serbs came back, 'they just ran'. They must have known that the Serbs would then wreak vengeance on innocent civilians like the family I visited. (In all, some quarter of a million people were made homeless in this summer of war.)

This is true. But it's also true that the KLA are heroes to most Kosovar Albanians. Their exploits are already the stuff of legend, ready to enter the history books beside the doubtless equally mythologized deeds of the *kaçak* rebel fighters against the Serbs eighty years ago. (Drenica was their stronghold too.) Whatever its military weakness, the KLA has growing political strength. Teasing out a comparison with Ireland's 1916 Easter Rising that certainly occurs to an Englishman, Veton Surroi says, 'We now need a Michael Collins.' They need a political Sinn Fein to partner their IRA.

Moreover, the KLA in practice holds a large part of the land. The division is roughly this. The Serb forces still patrol the main towns, the main roads, and the borders with Albania and Macedonia; the KLA has most of the countryside in between. In places, the two sides are barely fifty yards apart. This is not peace. It is frozen war. The war is frozen by the heavy snows that came down suddenly in mid-November, although this has not prevented some serious fighting going on. It is also frozen, even less effectively, by the presence of international monitors.

There have been diplomatic monitors officially accepted here since July. Following the agreement reached by Richard Holbrooke with Slobodan Milošević on 12 October, under the threat of Nato bombing, they are becoming part of a much larger team of 2,000 unarmed 'verifiers' under the novel auspices of the Organization for Security and Cooperation in Europe (OSCE). At the moment, they are trying to 'verify' compliance with the ceasefire, and some rather unclear supplementary agreements on Serb police and army numbers and locations. But the idea is that early in 1999 they should start 'verifying' the implementation of a political agreement.

Since October, the United States' impressive ambassador to Macedonia, Christopher Hill, has been engaged in exhausting rounds of shuttle diplomacy to produce an outline for that new masterpiece of fudge. This has to reconcile the virtually unanimous insistence of Kosovar Albanians that they can no longer live 'under Serbia', and that after a transitional period a door must clearly be open to independence, with the insistence of Milošević – but also of most other Serb politicians – that Kosovo must remain in Serbia, with the independence door firmly closed. Hill deals with a frustratingly disunited array of Kosovar Albanian leaders, including what he calls 'the KLA guys'. On the Serb side, he deals with Milošević.

The local Kosovo Serbs fear Milošević will sell them down the river. They are a nervous, sad bunch, hunched over their beers in tatty, dim-lit pubs, while the Albanians take you to smart new cafés. (The Serb-run Grand Hotel magnificently lives down to its reputation as the worst five-star hotel in the world.) How many Serbs are left in this medieval cradle of Serbianness? The 1991 census showed just over 200,000. Some have since given up and left. But Serb refugees from other parts of former Yugoslavia have been resettled here, in prefabricated single-home settlements that stand out amid the sprawling high-walled Albanian farmsteads.

Momčilo Trajković, leader of the so-called Serb Resistance Movement, says that a further 20,000 Serbs have left the province since March. Pathetically, he now talks of their desire for a 'multicultural, multi-ethnic' Kosovo. 'Multicultural, multi-ethnic!' he intones, almost like a Sarajevan. What would the local Serbs do if Kosovo became independent? Some would fight, he says. Some would flee. Pause. 'I think most would flee.'

2
MACEDONIA

'We all support the UCK,' says the burly student, using the Albanian initials for the KLA. 'All Albanians here are UCK.' We are sitting in the 'Queen's Club' café, in the largely Albanian town of Tetovo, in western Macedonia. Nearby, behind the closed metal doors of seemingly half-finished red-brick private houses, I have seen classrooms packed with students of the unofficial Albanian University of Tetovo.

'Yes,' agrees that student's professor, Zamir Dika, a lean, intense, black-bearded man, 'there is total support for the KLA. We are one nation.' But there's still a last chance to realize equal rights for

Albanians peacefully, inside the present Macedonian state. And the political party he represents, the Albanian Democratic Party, proposes to seize that chance as a member of the new Macedonian coalition government. His party demands the legal recognition of Tetovo University, the release of political prisoners, ethnic Albanians' participation in public service proportional to their numbers, and, finally, that the Albanians be recognized in Macedonia as what is called a *drzavotvorna nacija* – literally, a 'state-creating nation'. (This is a piece of Yugoslav ethno-constitutionalist jargon that presumably derives ultimately from Fichte's notion of a nation capable of creating a state.)

Later, I talk to his party leader, Arbën Xhaferi, a brooding, steely, black-bearded man, in a small, dark room in a headquarters festooned with the black double-headed Albanian eagle on a red background. He says people chant 'UCK' at his rallies, not the name of his party. His own support for the Kosovar armed struggle is passionate – which is not surprising, since he spent most of his adult life as a journalist in Priština. (He was a colleague of 'Journalist'.) Kosovo is the cradle of Albanian nationhood, he lectures me, scene of 180 Albanian risings against Turkish rule. The Albanians are not peaceful people by nature. They are warriors. Sooner or later Kosovo will win its right to self-determination, even though Americans try to put it 'in a strait-jacket'. Altogether, he informs me in a mesmerizing disquisition, the whole direction of European history is towards the separation of ethnic groups into their own states. He personally wouldn't at all mind the Serbs annexing their 'Serb Republic' part of Bosnia, if they give up Kosovo in exchange.

As for Macedonia, well, he accepts what he calls the 'international framework'. He knows the West jumps nervously at the merest whisper of secession for the Albanian part of Macedonia, fearing that its neighbours Bulgaria (which says that the Macedonian language is really a dialect of Bulgarian) and Nato member Greece (which obstinately insists that the state can't call itself 'Macedonia' because Macedonia is in Greece) might then become involved, leading to a bad case of Balkan dominoes, even to another Balkan war. An interesting gloss is added by Bejtulla Ademi, a local politician from the other Albanian party, who himself served nine years as a political prisoner, together with several present leaders of the KLA. There was, he says, a coordinating body of Albanian political parties in the former Yugo-slavia which, after playing with much more radical variants, decided in 1992 that the Albanians in Kosovo should go for independence, the Albanians in Macedonia should aim for equal rights as a 'state-creating nation' in the new state, while the Albanians in Montenegro and Serbia would have to settle for plain citizenship rights.[6] One step at a time.

Next day, I watch Xhaferi at a press conference to present the new Macedonian government in the capital, Skopje, together with the prime minister-elect, the fresh-faced Ljubco Georgievski, and the likely next candidate for president, a tubby old fox called Vasil Tupurkovski, formerly of the Yugoslav communist politburo. All three leaders privately assure me they didn't need the pressure exerted by the United States in order for the Albanians to be included in the new government. All agree that the Macedonian nationalists of Georgievski's party have become more moderate and pragmatic.

The Macedonian tragedy today, Prime Minister-elect Georgievski tells me in a subsequent conversation, is no longer foreign occupation, whether Turkish, Serbian, Bulgarian or communist Yugoslav. It is poverty. The country has 30 per cent unemployment. To revive the economy, they need to work constructively with Greece and Bulgaria. The challenge, says Tupurkovski, is simply to make a viable state. To do that, they must have the Albanians on board. And a lot of help from the West too. Last year, the country got just $6 million in foreign investment.

In the short term, things look moderately encouraging for this fragile new state of just 2 million people. Macedonia's Albanian leaders are not about to lead their people in an armed uprising. But in the long run? Young Macedonian Albanians tell you they are 'all KLA'. Talking to Arbën Xhaferi I am reminded of Walter Scott's haunting romantic insurrectionary Redgauntlet. Indeed, the Albanians here may never need to reach for the gun. All they need to do is what they do anyway: have many, many children. Albanians are now at least one-quarter of the Macedonian population. On current birth rates, they will be a majority in about 2025. And doesn't democracy mean rule by the majority?

3
BELGRADE

'I will lead a movement of one million Serbs to liberate Kosovo,' Vuk Drašković tells me. 'My party is organized like an army. We will fight.' Fight Nato? 'There is no Serbia without Kosovo. I cannot betray it. I cannot betray Jesus Christ.' And the leader of the Serbian Renewal Movement pulls from his inside pocket a map marking all the Serbian Orthodox churches across the province. This from the man who early last year was still part of the Zajedno ('Together') coalition that was supposed to bring democracy to Serbia.

But Kosovo upsets more than just the ranting Drašković. I tell the wife of an eminently liberal friend how in Kosovo I visited the medieval Serbian monastery of Dečani. It looked indescribably beautiful in the snow. But it is now occupied by soldiers. Suddenly her eyes are full of tears. She has such happy childhood memories of visiting her grandparents in the nearby town of Peć, of a Christmas with the nuns, of a magical cave where water runs uphill . . .

I explain to Biljana Dakić, one of my student guides through the great Belgrade demonstrations of 1996–7, that I think Kosovo will become a kind of Western protectorate. 'You know,' she says, 'my stomach really churns when you say that. It's such an emotional thing.' Kosovo is somehow closer to her heart even than the fate of the Serbs beyond the River Drina, in Bosnia and formerly in the Croatian Krajina, although her own family comes from there. Čeda Antić, a patriotic and religious young Serb whom I got to know as a leader of last year's student demonstrations, still uses the official Serb name for the province, 'Kosovo and Metohija', Metohija being the historic lands of the Serb Orthodox Church. He is equally dismayed to contemplate its loss.

Never mind that their history of Kosovo, like the Albanians', is partly myth.[7] Never mind that they haven't been to Kosovo for years, and would not dream of living there. Never mind that they know, in their heads, that the Albanians have already won, simply by multiplying and occupying the land. The prospect of losing Kosovo is so painful because it comes on top of many other bitter blows. The former

Yugoslav metropolis of Belgrade is so impoverished and depressed. Its population has been swollen by Serb refugees from the parts of former Yugoslavia that Milošević's adventurism has already lost, but diminished by the emigration of much of the elite. Biljana tells me that 70 per cent of her high-school classmates have left. Those that remain live in a cage, with only limited information from a few independent radio stations and newspapers, and great difficulty in obtaining visas to travel to the West.

My Serb friends feel – and they are surely right – that even sophisticated men and women in the West no longer distinguish sufficiently between the Serbian people and their regime. To be a Serb in the world today is like being a German in 1945. They also fear – and in this they are probably also right – that, just as the Germans were the last victims of Adolf Hitler, so the Serbs will be the last victims of Slobodan Milošević.

I find that, if pressed, more and more people in Belgrade see partition as the least bad solution for Kosovo. But generally they prefer to talk about the prospects of political change in Serbia proper, rather than about Kosovo. 'Democratization in Serbia' is, they insist, the key to progress in the whole of former Yugoslavia. But what chance of that? At the moment, things look worse than ever. Veran Matić, the forceful head of the independent Radio B92, sees a familiar pattern: when Milošević makes concessions externally (over Kosovo, as previously over Bosnia) he cracks down internally. This autumn saw the universities stripped of their autonomy and the passing of a draconian 'information law' that threatens critical newspapers with confiscation of their assets. This has already happened, in a flagrant example of political justice, to the semi-tabloid *Dnevni Telegraf*, after its owner turned sharply against the regime.

How might change for the better come? Milošević's regime is an extreme post-communist example of what has been called a *demokratura*: formally democratic, substantially authoritarian. These post-communist *demokraturas* maintain their power through control of state television, the secret police, and the misappropriation of large parts of the formerly state-owned economy. Such regimes may be overthrown peacefully, but this requires a grand coalition of virtually all the forces opposed to them. I come to Belgrade from Slovakia, where the *demokratura* of Vladimír Měciar has just been overthrown, at the ballot box, by just such a 'coalition of coalitions': opposition parties, non-governmental organizations, independent media, trade unions, parts of the Church.

In 1997, with the 'walking revolution' and the 'Together' coalition, it looked as if that might just be happening in Serbia. But the West gave little effective support, and 'Together' soon fell apart disastrously. Drašković's partners reneged on their promise to support his candidacy for the Serbian presidency, and he then made a shocking tactical alliance with the regime, being rewarded with the ample spoils of running the Belgrade city government. Now he and his former ally Zoran Djindjić speak more bitterly of each other than they do of Milošević. Djindjić is trying to build a broad democratic alternative again, helped by Čeda Antić and other former student activists who have joined his Democratic Party. But their current public support is small, and the necessary 'coalition of coalitions' seems more remote than ever.

Another recurrent idea is that the Milošević regime might crumble from within, perhaps being supplanted by a military coup. A recent bout of sackings, including the heads of the army and the secret police, and their replacement with confidants of Milošević's wife, Mira Marković (a.k.a. Lady Macbeth), has fuelled such speculation. Romania is close, and people wistfully recall how Nicolae and Elena Ceauşescu met their end. But do these purges actually weaken Milošević or strengthen him? I, at least, don't know anyone who can really tell me what is going on behind the closed doors of this messy, embattled, yet horribly durable regime.

But I will venture one guess about the social psychology around it. There is a kind of chemical solution that is both deeply inert and highly unstable. It's not bubbling at all, but one tap on the test tube and – bang! – up it goes. Serbian society today may be like that. What could the tap be? Many serious observers agree that Western sanctions against Serbia produced a certain defiant popular solidarity with Milošević, while this autumn's Nato bombing threat occasioned a wave of xenophobia. Could concessions by Milošević over Kosovo, in the middle of an economically difficult winter, have an opposite effect? Might that be the final tap?

Yet, even if that were so, it is possible – even likely – that power would at least initially be seized by radical nationalists like Vojislav Šešelj rather than by conciliatory democrats. Things could get even worse before they finally get better. The tragedy of former Yugoslavia is in its sixth or seventh act. Many have observed that 'It began in Kosovo and may end in Kosovo.' Perhaps it is more accurate to say that it began in Belgrade, with Milošević's cynical exploitation of the Kosovo issue. And so the last act, too, may be in Belgrade, as Kosovo comes back to haunt him.

4

What have we learned from this terrible decade in former Yugoslavia? And what is to be done? We have learned that human nature has not changed. That Europe at the end of the twentieth century is quite as capable of barbarism as it was in the Holocaust of mid-century. That, during the last decades of the Cold War, many in Europe succumbed to fairy-tale illusions about the obsolescence of the nation state and war being banished for ever from our continent. That Western Europe has gone on living quite happily while war returned almost every summer to the Balkans. And we have learned that, even after the end of the Cold War, we can't manage the affairs of our own continent without calling in the United States. Wherever you go in former Yugoslavia, people say, 'the international community – I mean, the Americans . . .'

Our Western political mantras at the end of the twentieth century have been 'integration', 'multiculturalism' or, if we are a little more old-fashioned, 'the melting pot'. Former Yugoslavia has been the opposite. It has been like a giant version of the machine called a separator: a sort of spinning tub which separates out cream and butter, or liquids of different consistency. Here it is peoples who were separated out as the giant tub spun furiously round. Even half-formed nationalities (Macedonian, Bosnian) were solidified by the separator, while blood dripped steadily from a filter at the bottom. But, when separation was almost complete, the West finally stepped in to try to halt the bloody process: in 1995 in Bosnia, in 1998 in Kosovo. In

Bosnia, we now have a Western quasi-protectorate. Soon we may have another in Kosovo.

At this point, I will make an argument that departs from the received wisdom of the West and political correctness. I believe that, if it were possible, probably the least bad framework in which the peoples of former Yugoslavia might now start their slow journey to join a civilized, liberal, democratic Europe would be as a group of small nation states with clear ethnic majorities. (By that I mean, as a very crude rule of thumb, with at least 80 per cent belonging to one nationality.) I am definitely not arguing that separating out into such nation states was the inevitable result of 'ancient tribal hatreds' in the Balkans. Buried hatreds there surely were, but to revive, exacerbate and exploit them was the culpable responsibility of bad leaders: Milošević above all, but also Franjo Tudjman of Croatia. Nor am I arguing that earlier, more forceful Western intervention could not have created different possibilities. I am simply arguing that now, after all that has happened, peaceful separation, where it is possible, might be a lesser evil. To adapt Shakespeare to the Balkans, 'Journeys end in haters parting.'

If peoples really cannot live peacefully together, it is better that they should live apart. To be sure, there is always a loss – cultural, economic and political – in descending from the larger to the smaller state. And there is a human cost. I think of Violeta, a plucky Priština journalist from a mixed Serb–Albanian marriage. What is she supposed to do? Cut herself in half?

But good fences might eventually make good neighbours. It is clear to every thinking person that this array of small and tiny states on the Balkan peninsula will sooner or later have to start cooperating again out of pure economic self-interest, if for no other reason. (One thing they already have, in practice though not in theory, is a common currency: the Deutschmark. I suppose when the DM disappears in 2002 they will have to start using the euro.) Some talk dreamily of getting together again inside the European Union. A faint hope, seeing the current pace of EU enlargement. Others, more realistically, would start with a Balkan customs union. Adem Demaci preaches a confederation that he calls 'Balkania'.

We are looking at an almost Hegelian dialectic here: separation as the path to integration. But is this dialectic so unfamiliar? After all, we in Western Europe have long since been moulded into nation states, in a process that lasted from the Middle Ages to the early twentieth century. There are a few exceptions, to be sure, but even those exceptions – such as Belgium, increasingly divided between its French- and Flemish-speaking parts, or Scotland in Britain – are now proving difficult to sustain. (Yes, I know, there's still tri-national Switzerland, God bless her.) It's precisely on this basis of clear separation into nation states that we have been getting together in the European Union, as well as becoming more ethnically mixed again, through immigration.

In Central Europe, the process happened later, in the mid twentieth century, through war, genocide, ethnic cleansing and the redrawing of frontiers. In the early 1990s, the process was completed by the peaceful 'velvet divorce' of Czechs and Slovaks. In each case, it is a sad, hard truth that the resulting relative ethnic homogeneity has, in the medium term, helped the country's return to the civilized, democratic community of states. And now the small new nation state of Slovakia is following suit. Again, I am not saying that history had to go this way. I am not peddling a philosophy of history. I am merely saying that this is the way European history seems to have gone. But, if that is true, then what we are proposing to do in our Balkan quasi-protectorates is not just to freeze war. It is also to freeze history.

The trouble is this. Intellectually we may – although many Western policy-makers still do not – see the case for separation, as a dialectical stepping stone to integration. But the modern liberal conscience rightly recoils from the means used throughout most of European history to achieve it – namely war, partition, forced assimilation and ethnic cleansing. Yet where in former Yugoslavia can it happen without them?

The former Yugoslav republic of Slovenia was fortunate not only in being the most northern and economically advanced, but also in having a clear ethnic majority. As a result, it is today well on track to join the EU in the first wave of its eastward enlargement. In Croatia, we did in fact condone ethnic cleansing. We let Tudjman 'cleanse' the Krajina of more than 150,000 Serbs in 1995, while his troops went on to do what we wanted them to do in Bosnia. (Yes, we protested, but very feebly.) The result is that Tudjman no longer has an ethnic 'enemy within' to blame for the country's woes, and I believe the days of his nasty little *demokratura* are numbered. Here the West just has to work to hasten the advent of real democracy, as in Slovakia. Having got away with murder, Croatia, as a well-defined new nation state, can then start its progress back to Europe. It may then also be more cooperative in respect of the Croat-controlled parts of Bosnia.

Some argue that Serbia without Kosovo would still be liable to further disintegration, with Montenegro, the Sandjak and even the Vojvodina pulling away. This may yet happen, if Milošević carries on as he is, starting with the incremental secession of Montenegro. But a Serbia without Kosovo and without Milošević would have a reasonable chance of consolidating itself as a democratic federal republic. In this state, Serbs would constitute a clear majority.

In its policy towards Serbia, the West now has to work simultaneously with and against Milošević. This is a difficult trick that we nonetheless managed in relations with the leaders of Eastern Europe in the last half of the Cold War. We have to work with Milošević to some extent, because of his direct power over Kosovo and his spoiling power in Bosnia. But we also have to work against him, to encourage much more energetically such fragmentary positive forces for change as there are in Belgrade. For, as Madeleine Albright rightly insists, Milošević is the single person most responsible for all the bloody dissolution of former Yugoslavia. When he finally goes, I'm sure the British government will be delighted to welcome him to the VIP lounge at Heathrow Airport, as it recently did General Pinochet. And then, over a glass of dry sherry, the Hague tribunal can present him with its sealed indictment.

In Kosovo, the intricate details of successive drafts of what has come to be known as 'the Hill plan' are still fiercely disputed between Serbs and Albanians. But its basic elements are now clear. It would restore the far-reaching autonomy of which the province was robbed in 1989, but not explicitly remove Kosovo from Serbia. It would devolve much power to local communes, thus allowing purely Albanian areas to have Albanian authorities and police, while mixed areas would supposedly have mixed ones. It foresees direct international involvement, especially in the reconstruction of the police and the conduct of new elections within six to nine months. And the whole arrangement should be subject to 'comprehensive review' in three years' time.

The hope is to move forward early in 1999 to direct negotiations between the Serbian and Kosovar Albanian sides, with American and EU negotiators present to help things along. But it is very far from certain that this will produce an agreement, even after deploying the political cruise missile called Richard Holbrooke. If the negotiations fail, fighting in Kosovo will surely escalate around our unarmed 'verifiers', especially when the snows melt in the spring. It will only be a matter of time before we need to activate the French-led Nato 'Extraction Force' (jokingly known as 'the dentists') recently deployed in northern Macedonia, in order to extract an imperilled verifier. However fleetingly, Nato will then have invaded Serbia.

If negotiations succeed, we will have another Western quasi-protectorate. A conversation with Ambassador William Walker, the American head of the OSCE mission in Kosovo, makes it clear that he proposes to give a new dictionary meaning to the word 'verifying'. The OSCE will mediate and supervise. In effect, the police will be OSCE-trained police, the elections will be OSCE-run elections, election-time television will be OSCE television. But what happens then?

I believe Kosovo is a case where we can and should think of working towards peaceful separation. The Albanians are more than 90 per cent of the population in a well-defined territory. They have not achieved this preponderance by ethnic cleansing, as happened in Bosnia, so we would not be 'condoning ethnic cleansing'. By their conduct in the province over the last decade, the Serbs have seriously diminished their own moral right to rule. There is at least some legal basis for arguing that Kosovo was a constituent part of former Yugoslavia, and therefore could be recognized on a similar basis to the other successor states.[8] Anyway, this is a special case, not an international precedent for ethnic self-determination.

Yet certainly this process would have to be managed very carefully over a number of years, with a major international presence. Those magnificent Serb monasteries do need a special status. More seriously, there is a real danger of another panic flight of innocent local Serbs. I ask an Albanian civil-society activist in Priština, a sophisticated woman speaking excellent English, what should be done about the Serbs in a free Kosovo. She slowly exhales the smoke from her cigarette and smiles at me. 'Kill them all?' she says. A joke, you understand. Just a joke. But the hard men in the hills are not joking. Without firm preventive action, we will again be party to ethnic cleansing by terror.

Macedonia's Albanian leaders tell me that independence for Kosovo would stabilize the situation in Macedonia. In the short run, this may be right, since few things could be more immediately dangerous than those young Albanian Macedonians joining a renewed war in Kosovo. But in the long run I don't believe it. History suggests that a contemporary European state with a less than 80 per cent ethnic majority is inherently unstable. If the large and growing minority happens to be Albanian, and contiguous to the motherland, it is even more so. Albanians in former Yugoslavia have been victims, there is no doubt of that. But there is also complex, patient, but stubborn Albanian nationalism. Without continued American and West European involvement in both Macedonia and the anarchic state of Albania itself, and in coaxing along their relations with their neighbours, the last act in Belgrade may not be the last one after all.

Finally, there is insoluble Bosnia. My Sarajevan friends are delighted with the 10,000 foreigners living there, and the $9 billion being spent on the country every year. They tell me that Sarajevo has actually never in its history been so genuinely cosmopolitan. The new cafés are pulsating. Increasingly, the Office of the High Representative, headed by the Spanish diplomat Carlos Westendorp, rules like a colonial administration. It's tempting to say that Bosnia-Hercegovina has again become an Austro-Hungarian protectorate, as it was after the Congress of Berlin, with the Americans as the Austrian Habsburgs and we West Europeans as the Hungarian junior partner (although picking up most of the bill). But it's not a real protectorate. Rather, it's a bizarre novelty in international relations. We have had protectorates before. We have had partitions before. This is half-protectorate, half-partition.[9]

The official ideology of all Western agencies in Bosnia is that the unitary state is being pulled together again. It's just taking rather a long time. Alas, I don't think this is true. I fear all the king's horses and all the king's men will not put Humpty-Dumpty together again.

But final partition would be an even less acceptable option. For the Bosniaks to have a serious, viable state, you would need to give them at least part of the western half of the 'Serb Republic'. That would almost certainly mean more bloodshed, and tens of thousands more people driven from their homes. If, on the other hand, you allowed the Serb- and Croat-run parts to secede as they are, you would be left with a landlocked rump Bosniak state. Bosniaks warn that this could turn their people into muslim-fundamentalist nationalists. The result would be a 'Gaza strip in the middle of Europe'.

In fact the Bosniaks hold the conscience of the West in a powerful moral half nelson. In effect, they say, 'We are the Jews of the Balkans *and* the Palestinians of the Balkans!' The Jews, because no people in Europe has suffered something as close to genocide since the Jews in the Holocaust. So how could we abandon them? The Palestinians, for the reasons already given. I very much doubt that a rump Bosnia would actually become a muslim-fundamentalist state. But in a sense this doesn't matter. Earlier this autumn, the former German defence minister Volker Rühe told me that the deepest issue in Bosnia and Kosovo was 'whether the West sees a place for Islam in Europe'. Powerful Islamic countries agree. Faced with these complementary perceptions of the powerful, the local truth is largely irrelevant.

So, in some parts of former Yugoslavia, violent separation has already happened. In Kosovo, there remains a difficult but still Humvee-navigable dirt road to peaceful separation. That road we should take. Elsewhere, in Bosnia, but in a different way also in Macedonia, I see no morally acceptable alternative to a direct Western involvement lasting many years, probably decades. Even if, intellectually, we will the end of separation, we cannot will the means.

But why on earth should Americans be the new Habsburgs? Why should American diplomats enter the twenty-first century trying to solve problems left over from the dissolution of the Ottoman empire at the end of the nineteenth? Why should sons of Kansas and daughters of Ohio risk their lives in these perilous, snow-covered mountains ('What do you need? Plastic?') to stop Europeans fighting over obscure patches of territory? After all, the great-grandparents of some of these Americans probably fled these very mountains to escape just these insoluble squabbles.

The vital national interest is indeed hard to see. The new catch-all bogey of 'regional instability' hardly compares with the old fear of the Soviet Union getting the upper hand in the Cold War. But empires – especially informal, liberal empires – are like that. You muddle in; then somehow you can't quite muddle out. Somalia could never apply the moral half nelson that Bosnia has. For the Balkans, this has been a decade of Western bluster. First, we had the Western bluster of intervention. Now we have the Western bluster of withdrawal. I don't believe this bluster either. I think the sons of Kansas and the daughters of Ohio will be here for a good, long time.

'Take up the White Man's burden,' Rudyard Kipling wrote a hundred years ago, welcoming the United States' willingness, in the Philippines, 'To wait in heavy harness/ On fluttered folk and wild'. There, and elsewhere, he prophesied, Americans would reap only 'The blame of those ye better,/ The hate of those ye guard'. Today, some of the finest white men are, of course, black. And the local savages are Europeans.

Long Live Ruthenia!

Whence they came, no one can tell. No one knows exactly who, how many or where they are. They live in six states and in none. They are loyal to each of these states, and to none of them. Their language is written in five different versions; in the Cyrillic alphabet, but also in the Latin. Some regard themselves as Ukrainians, others as Slovaks, others again as Poles. Or Romanians. Or Hungarians. Or Yugoslavs. But many insist they are 'Rusyns', or 'Carpatho-Rusyns', or '*rusnatsi*'. Or they throw up their hands and give the ancient answer of the peasant from Europe's Slavic borderlands: 'We're just from here.'

Yet now they have a provisional government that wants to form a new nation state. A state called Ruthenia.

And here I am, talking to the prime minister. We are sitting in the office he occupies as a pharmacologist at a large hospital in Užhorod, capital of what Ukrainians call Transcarpathian Ukraine but he insists is Sub-Carpathian Rus'. Professor Ivan Turyanitsa is a stout, cheerful, energetic man, with a shock of black hair, bright eyes and the gift of the gab. He is dressed in what I find to be the current style among the Ruthenians: synthetic sports jacket above, pinstriped trousers below. He has just introduced me to the foreign minister, who has come specially from Slovakia, and the justice minister, who is a surgeon in the same hospital. 'But', he hastens to add, 'only two of the cabinet work here.'

While the justice minister – still wearing his medical white coat – makes me a cup of tea from a kettle in the corner, the prime minister expounds. In the December 1991 referendum on Ukrainian independence, he says, 78 per cent of the people in this region voted for greater autonomy from the rest of Ukraine, on the far side of the high

Carpathian mountains. But what he calls 'the Ukrainian national fascist regime' ignored this popular wish. So in May 1993 he and his colleagues formed the provisional government of Sub-Carpathian Rus' – or, in English, Ruthenia.

How did the Ukrainian authorities react?

'*Normalnie!*' he replies. (As befits this transfrontier folk, we are speaking a mixture of Slovak and Polish.) 'In the normal way. They arranged a car crash for me.' Later, he takes me outside to show me the damaged car. At present, he says, he and his colleagues are tolerated, but given no access to the media.

They want their own state, in the boundaries of the present Trans-carpathian *oblast* of Ukraine, but with close ties to fellow Ruthenians in Slovakia and Poland. As responsible politicians, they will leave defence and what they call 'global' foreign policy to the Kiev government. Everything else – including 'local and European' foreign policy, education, health and so on – would be their domain. They would have their own currency, 'though it could be called the same'. Professor Turyanitsa hands me a lapel badge showing their national symbol: yellow and gold stripes, with a red bear, prancing. Rather handsome.

Do they have a national anthem? Yes, of course. Could I see the text? Well, er, um, they don't seem to have a copy to hand. 'But,' says the foreign minister helpfully, 'we could sing it for you!' Yes, please! Unfortunately they then get bashful, and instead of singing they dig around until they do find the words, written by Aleksander Dukhnovych, a nineteenth-century priest regarded as the father of the nation. 'Subcarpathian Rusyns,' the anthem begins, 'Arise from your deep slumber.'

It's tempting to dismiss this all as a joke. Ruthenia even sounds like something out of a Tintin book; perhaps a neighbour to Ruritania. And the provisional government is certainly good for a laugh. Yet the Ruthenian Question takes you to the heart of one of the most important problems of international politics in our time. For, in the decade since the end of the Cold War, in the new freedom, these suppressed or sometimes only half-formed nationalities have re-emerged and formulated political aspirations all over Europe.

To understand the Ruthenians' case, you need first to swallow a little potted history. The Ruthenians are a part of the family of east Slavic peoples, like the Russians, Belarussians and Ukrainians, all of whom were at one time or another described as part of Rus'. One scholar wanted to call them 'Rus'ians' as opposed to 'Russians', but you can see why the fine distinction did not catch on. Everything about their origins, culture, language and politics is disputed.

For most of their modern history, most of them lived in the Austro-Hungarian empire. They were mainly farmers or woodcutters in the heavily forested Carpathian foothills. (You still see peasant wood-cutters at work in mountain villages that look like pictures by Chagall.) It was the Habsburgs who christened them *Ruthenen*; the English word derives from the German. When the empire was broken up after the First World War, they found themselves scattered between Poland, Hungary, Romania, Yugoslavia and what would shortly become the Soviet Union, but the greatest concentration was in the new state of Czechoslovakia.

Czechoslovakia – the most democratic and liberal of those successor states – gave them considerable autonomy, in a province it called Sub-Carpathian Rus'. The book in which they found me the words of the national anthem was actually published in pre-war Czechoslovakia. In those golden days of freedom, there was a great debate between Ukrainophiles, who argued that the Ruthenians were really Ukrainians, Russophiles, who thought they were closer to Russians, and Rusynophiles, who said they were altogether different. Today, the debate has revived as freedom has returned. In Slovakia, I visit two rival organizations: the Union of Rusyno-Ukrainians, who insist that they are just a kind of Ukrainian, and Ruthenian Renaissance, whose spokeswoman tells me it's impossible to be both Ruthenian and Ukrainian.

The autonomy of Sub-Carpathian Rus' reached a perilous height after Britain and France agreed to the dismemberment of Czechoslo-vakia at Munich in 1938. For six months it was a separate unit in a rump federal Czechoslovakia. The official English name for this unit was Ruthenia. Then, as the Nazis marched into Prague, Ruthenia was gobbled up by Hungary. But that didn't last long either. At the end of the Second World War, Stalin seized it for the Soviet Union. When the Soviet Union collapsed, it became part of Ukraine.

Through all this, the Ruthenians went on chopping their wood. Professor Turyanitsa tells me the classic east European joke about the old man who says he was born in Austro-Hungary, went to school in Czechoslovakia, married in Hungary, worked most of his life in the Soviet Union, and now lives in Ukraine. 'Travelled a lot, then?' asks his interviewer. 'No, I never moved from Mukachevo.'

One of the big questions that little Ruthenia prompts is whether the ethnically chequered successor states of the former Soviet Union might yet go the bloody way of former Yugoslavia. Are the Ruthenian rumblings an exception, inspired by the relatively recent experience of autonomy in pre-war Czechoslovakia? Or are other suppressed nationalities even now forming provisional governments in remote hospital offices?

Perhaps as many as 1 million Ruthenians live in Ukraine. There are another 100,000 or so in Slovakia, some 60,000 in Poland (where they are called 'Lemkos') and smaller numbers in Romania, Hungary and the Vojvodina province of rump Yugoslavia. (They also have one vital asset for any would-be nation: a large community in the United States.) So they live across half a dozen frontiers. One dramatic way in which they describe themselves is as 'the Kurds of Central Europe'.

Moreover, these are not just any old frontiers. Samuel Huntington argues in his influential book *The Clash of Civilizations* that the great dividing line in Europe, after the end of the Iron Curtain, is that between western (Catholic or Protestant) Christianity and eastern (Orthodox) Christianity or Islam. Here, according to Huntington, is the new eastern boundary of Europe and of 'Western civilization', no less. The Ruthenians, true to form, cut right across it. They worship in both the Orthodox and the Uniate (or Greek Catholic) church, which uses the eastern rite but acknowledges the authority of the western Pope. If you drive through the Ruthenian mountain villages of eastern Slovakia, you often see two churches side by side: an old wooden-built one, which is Uniate, and a new Orthodox one. The original wooden churches were illegally given to the Orthodox by the communists after 1945, then returned to the Uniates after the end of communism, whereupon the Orthodox congregations stormed off and built their own churches next door.

More immediately, the Ruthenians will soon straddle the new

eastern frontier of Nato. That will be true when Poland joins Nato in March 1999, and even more so if a now rapidly reforming Slovakia enters the Western alliance in a few years' time. Then you will have significant numbers of Ruthenians on both sides of the West's front line. The foreign minister tells me confidentially that his government is 'delighted to see Nato coming closer to us'.

The Ruthenian story is, in every respect, a quintessentially east European one, and those of us with the perverse taste for such things may love it for its own sake. But it's not just an east European question. In western Europe, too, we have nationalities, in varying degrees of formation, striving for anything from autonomy to statehood. Think of Scotland and Wales in Britain, or Catalonia and the Basque country in Spain.

And it's not just in Europe. When I ask the prime minister if his government has achieved international recognition, he proudly declares, 'Yes, we've been accepted into UNPROFOR.'

'UNPROFOR? But that was the military force in Bosnia!'

'Sorry, I mean UNPRO.'

Finally, we establish that it's UNPO – the Unrepresented Nations and Peoples Organization. On my return, I visit UNPO's web site and find a list of more than fifty members, starting with Abkhazia, Aboriginals in Australia, Alcheh/Sumatra, then on to East Timor, Kurdistan, Nagaland and Tibet. And, in the middle, Kosova – the Albanian spelling of Kosovo.

All over the world there are these peoples who would be states. Or at least recognized political units. This is a problem in dictatorships, when established identities are brutally suppressed, as in Tibet or East Timor. It's also a problem in liberal democracies, when people wish to be governed by those who they feel speak the same language or are of the same kind. Perhaps most of all, it's a problem at the fragile halfway stage between dictatorship and democracy. So often the road that begins with an UNPO ends in the need for an UNPROFOR.

The Ruthenians are still far from being Kurds or Kosovars. For now, their 'representatives' want some basic minority rights, like education in their own language. Improvements in Slovakia will increase the calls for change in Ukraine. They demand that Ruthenian nationality should be an option in the Ukrainian census scheduled for 2001, and that Ukrainian state forestry companies should stop the mechanized stripping of the trees from their beloved hills. Those forests are their national heritage. They hope to prevent the Transcarpathian *oblast* being incorporated into a new, enlarged province ruled from Lviv, in a planned reform of public administration for which, they tell me, the International Monetary Fund has been pressing. And they look for more cooperation across the frontiers, in what is already the Carpathian Euro-region.

That's a long way short of statehood. But Professional Turyanitsa is a gifted demagogue. If the circumstances were right, and he was given access to the media, I could see him – or someone like him – persuading an audience of Ruthenian hill-farmers, woodcutters and impoverished town-dwellers that they are heirs to a great tradition; that they were more prosperous and free as part of Czechoslovakia before the war; that the Ukrainian 'national chauvinists' – a phrase he repeats often and with relish – are to blame for all their troubles; in short, that they'd be much better off governing themselves. As we speak, rainwater is pouring down from the Carpathians and flooding the lowlands on the border with Slovakia, Hungary and Romania. 'You see,' he exclaims, 'the very waters are pushing us to the West.'

Absurd as it may sound, I have a strange hunch that one day we will again see the name 'Ruthenia' on the map, if not as a sovereign state, then at least as some sort of autonomous province. When that day comes, remember: you read it here first.

1998

19 November. President Bill Clinton is impeached for lying under oath.

16–20 December. The USA and Britain bomb military installations in Iraq. The USA proclaims removal of Saddam Hussein to be a policy objective.

December. Major ceasefire violations in Kosovo by both Serb forces and the Kosovo Liberation Army.

1999

1 January. Monetary union comes into force between eleven member states of the EU. Only Britain, Sweden, Denmark and Greece do not participate.

4 January. The Euro makes a strong start on its first day of trading.

14 January. The European Parliament votes on a resolution to sack the whole European Commission, because of corruption in two commissioners' areas of responsibility.

15 January. Serb forces massacre forty-five Kosovar Albanian civilians in the village of Raçak.

29 January. The Contact Group on former Yugoslavia issues ultimatum to the Serbian regime and Kosovar Albanian rebels. If they have not agreed an interim political framework in three weeks, Nato will take military action against both sides.

6 February. Negotiations jointly chaired by the French and British foreign ministers begin in Rambouillet between Kosovar Albanian and Serbian government delegations.

17 February. Kurds protest across Europe after the arrest of Addullah Ocalan by Turkish special forces.

23 February. The Rambouillet talks end inconclusively with provisional agreement by the Kosovar Albanian delegation to an autonomy deal. Tony Blair announces plans for the 'changeover' from pound to euro.

Where is Central Europe Now?

'I'm delighted', said Henry Kissinger, 'to be here in Eastern, I mean *Central* Europe.' And for the rest of his talk he kept saying, 'Eastern, I mean Central Europe'. The place was Warsaw; the time, summer 1990; and this was the moment I knew Central Europe had triumphed.

For nearly forty years after 1945, the term was almost entirely absent from the political parlance of Europe. Hitler had poisoned it; the Cold War division into East and West obliterated it. In the 1980s, it was revived by Czech, Hungarian and Polish writers such as Milan Kundera, György Konrád and Czesław Miłosz, as an intellectual and political alternative to the Soviet-dominated 'Eastern Europe'. At that time, I wrote a sympathetic but also sceptical essay entitled 'Does Central Europe Exist?'[1]

In the 1990s, Central Europe has become part of the regular political language. To mark the shift, both the US State Department and the British Foreign Office have Central European departments. Although people still privately tend to say 'Eastern Europe', every greenhorn diplomat knows that one should refer to the whole post-communist area as 'Central and Eastern Europe' – a phrase so cumbersome it is often reduced to an abbreviation: CEE in English, MOE (*Mittel- und Osteuropa*) in German. Even Queen Elizabeth II has spoken of 'Central Europe', in the Queen's Speech to Parliament. So that's official. If the Queen and Henry Kissinger say it exists, it exists.

Just one problem remains: where is it? 'Central Europe', wrote the US secretary of state Madeleine Albright in a newspaper article in 1998, 'has more than 20 countries and 200 million people.'[2] Yet we often find the term used to mean just the countries who are joining Nato this spring – Poland, Hungary and the Czech Republic – or the 'first wave' of post-communist states negotiating to join the EU – the same three, plus Estonia and Slovenia.

Such disagreement is nothing new. In an article published in 1954, the geographer Karl Sinnhuber examined sixteen definitions of Central Europe. The only part of Europe that none of them included was the Iberian peninsula. The only areas they all had in common were Austria, Bohemia and Moravia.[3] Tell me your Central Europe and I will tell you who you are.

In the first half of the twentieth century, the debate about who did or did not belong to Central Europe had real political significance. So it has today. For to be 'Central European' in contemporary political usage means to be civilized, democratic, cooperative – and therefore to have a better chance of joining Nato and the EU. In fact, the argument threatens to become circular: Nato and the EU welcome 'Central Europeans', so 'Central Europeans' are those whom Nato and the EU welcome.

The rival definitions are based on arguments from geography, history, culture, religion, economics and politics. There are also major differences between how countries see themselves and how others see them. Since countries are not single people, and there are many 'others', one has to generalize dangerously from a whole kaleidoscope of national and individual views. I am mainly concerned here with the way the concept is deployed in what we still often call 'the West' – meaning primarily policy-makers and opinion-formers in the United States, Britain, France, Germany, Italy and other members of Nato and the EU.

Since Central Europe is, by definition, somewhere in the centre, every one of its boundaries is disputed: northern, western, southern and eastern. By the same token, in delineating Central Europe we also delineate the other major geopolitical regions of Europe today.

I

Interestingly, and encouragingly, the boundary that was most hotly disputed at the beginning of the twentieth century is largely uncontroversial at its end: the western one. The idea of 'Central Europe' exploded during the First World War as a furious argument between those, like the German liberal imperialist Friedrich Naumann, who envisaged a German- and Austrian-ruled *Mitteleuropa*, and those, like Tomáš Garrigue Masaryk, the future president of Czechoslovakia, who were fighting for a Central Europe of small states liberated from German, Austrian and Russian imperial domination. This argument between visions of *Mitteleuropa*, on the one side, and of *Střední Evropa* or *Europa Środkowa*, on the other, continued throughout the 'Second Thirty Years War' from 1914 to 1945. It culminated in the Austrian-German Adolf Hitler's attempt to impose his own grotesque version of *Mitteleuropa* on Germany's eastern neighbours.

So, when the term was revived in the 1980s, there was understandable nervousness both among Germany's neighbours and in Germany itself. Many German writers preferred to use the less historically loaded term *Zentraleuropa*. But recent years have been reassuring. After some discussion, the Masaryk of the 1990s, Václav Havel, invited President von Weizsäcker of Germany to attend regular meetings of 'Central European presidents', and the German president has done so ever since. Most German policy-makers now accept that the reunited country is both firmly in Western Europe and in Central Europe again. As Havel once put it to me, Germany is in Central Europe 'with one leg'.

Of course, there have been tensions between Germany and its eastern neighbours – especially between Germany and the Czech Republic. And there will be more as the enlargement of the European Union slowly approaches, with Germans fearing that Poles and Czechs will take their jobs, and Poles and Czechs fearing the Germans will buy up their land. (The latter fears are especially pronounced in the formerly German western parts of Poland and in what used to be the Sudetenland, in the Czech Republic.) Yet no one could now argue that there is any fundamental political difference between what a mainstream German politician means by *Mitteleuropa* and what a Czech leader means by *Střední Evropa* or a Pole by *Europa Środkowa*. Increasingly, they are just different words for the same thing. This is a tribute to wisdom on both sides, and one of the bright spots on the map of Europe at century's end.

Meanwhile, the Austrians quietly pursue their own dream of Central

Europe, by which they mean nothing more nor less than the area of the former Austro-Hungarian empire. Symbolically, Austria celebrated its first presidency of the European Union with a 'Festival of Central European Culture'. More practically, flying Austrian Airlines is now the best way to get around the former Austro-Hungarian empire, and a new Central European Air Traffic Control centre will be located in Vienna. At the same time, Austrians are even more hostile than Germans are to the idea of people from their former empire actually coming to live in their country and competing for their jobs.

For completeness, one should add the eastern parts of Italy that have very special ties with Slovenia, Croatia and Austria – special ties consisting partly in the fact that Italy contains a small, still largely German-speaking piece of what used to be Austria (the South Tirol or Alto Adige), while Slovenia and Croatia have a little bit of what used to be Italy (eastern Friuli, the area around Trieste and the Istrian peninsula). Some would also include Liechtenstein and German-speaking Switzerland, although the Swiss generally hold themselves above this kind of thing. In all these cases, the historical legacy is still being played out in a hundred intricate ties and tensions. As I write, I have before me a purely hedonistic *Guida alla Mitteleuropa*, published in Florence in 1992, which maps an Italian '*Mitteleuropa*' from Milan via St Moritz, Vaduz and Bayreuth to Prague, then back through Vienna, Budapest and Zagreb to Trieste, Venice and Verona.

I find it useful to distinguish between West Central Europe – meaning mainly Germany, but also Austria and that corner of Italy – and East Central Europe. But when people say 'Central Europe' in English, they usually mean just the latter. As Poland, Hungary and the Czech Republic become Western-style capitalist democracies, join Nato and (eventually) enter the EU, so the line between Central and Western Europe becomes increasingly blurred. Far from being dismayed, those who revived the terms in the 1980s should be delighted by this merging.

The frontier that need trouble us least is the northern one. In his anxiety to gather all the same nations under the flag, Masaryk included in his Central Europe everyone from Laplanders in the north to Greeks in the south. The region stretched, he implausibly suggested, from 'the North Cape to Cape Matapan'. But Scandinavia has a quite distinct identity. To be sure, the Baltic states are an important borderline case. Lithuanians, in particular, will tell you their country belongs both to the Nordic or Baltic area and to Central Europe. Lithuania, they argue, is a bridge between the two. Since, however, Scandinavia is part of the Western capitalist democratic world, and the Baltic states are small, their in-between position is not in itself a political problem, although Russia's objections to their membership of Nato and the status of the Russian exclave of Kaliningrad will be.

The major political argument now is about the eastern and southern edges. As revived by Kundera and others, the idea of Central Europe was directed against the East (with a large E), and specifically against Russia. Central Europe, Kundera suggested, was the 'kidnapped West'.[4] Until 1945, it had participated fully in all the great cultural movements of the West, from western Christianity, the Renaissance and the Enlightenment to Expressionism and Cubism. But politically it was now imprisoned in the East. Out of a cultural canon he made a cannon – firing against the East. As Joseph Brodsky pointed out, this was quite unfair to Russian culture. But politically it was justified and effective as an antidote to the even more misleading notion of a single 'Eastern Europe'.

In the 1990s, the cultural ca(n)non has been directed against the south more than the east. The new democracies of Poland, Hungary and Czechoslovakia set out early in the decade to pursue Central European cooperation, symbolized by the 'Visegrád group' established in February 1991. They did this partly because they believed in the idea, which Havel and the new Hungarian president Árpád Göncz had preached in the 1980s, and wished to preclude any return to the petty nationalisms of the inter-war years. But it was also because this right, tight little regional cooperation would win their countries favour in the West. Which it did.

They had little trouble distinguishing themselves from the new eastern (with a small e) Europe: Belarus, Ukraine and European Russia. More difficult was the south. Romania tried to join the group at an early stage. The door was firmly closed in its face. A good reason for this was that Romania was at that time an undemocratic mess. A less good reason was that Polish, Hungarian and (then still) Czechoslovak leaders thought they had a better chance of entering or (as the Central

European ideology prescribes) 'rejoining' the West in a smaller, more homogeneous group. Which they did.

Then came the bloody collapse of the former Yugoslavia. This revived another previously dormant geopolitical nation, 'the Balkans', with connotations as negative as those of 'Central Europe' were now positive. For politicians everywhere, and especially for Polish, Hungarian and Czech politicians, the Manichaean contrast between 'Central Europe', bathed in light, and 'the Balkans', drenched in blood, was irresistible.[5]

To cap it all, the Harvard political scientist Samuel Huntington made his influential argument that the new cleavages of world politics would be based on 'the clash of civilizations' – civilizations being defined mainly by their religious origins.[6] The Kunderaesque view of Central Europe, arguing as it does from culture to politics, fits perfectly into the Huntingtonian scheme, and it's no surprise to find Huntington enthusiastically adopting the term. But he goes further, suggesting that the eastern and southern boundary of Central Europe is simultaneously the frontier of Europe and 'Western civilization'.

What is this boundary, more fundamental even than the post-1945 Iron Curtain? According to Huntington, it is the dividing line between western (Catholic or Protestant) Christianity, on the one side, and eastern (Orthodox) Christianity or Islam on the other. This line has been in roughly its present position for about 500 years, and its origins go back as far as the division of the Roman empire in the fourth century. Huntington even suggests that, because they are on the wrong side of the line, Turkey and Greece may not remain full members of Nato and, in the case of Greece, the EU. Note, however, that the Baltic states, most of western Ukraine, half of Romania, all of Croatia and even small parts of Bosnia and Serbia (i.e. the formerly Hungarian province of Vojvodina) fall on the 'western' side.

At worst, the result has been an extreme cultural determinism. I call it Vulgar Huntingtonism, by analogy with Vulgar Marxism. It says: If your heritage is western Christianity, the Renaissance, the Enlightenment, the German or Austro-Hungarian empires, Baroque architecture and coffee with *Schlagobers*, then you are destined for democracy. But eastern (Orthodox) Christianity or Islam, the Russian or Ottoman empires, minarets, *burek* and Turkish coffee? Doomed to dictatorship! Of course this is crude to the point of parody. But the way political ideas get used in real politics is very crude. And it has not been in the interest of the 'Central Europeans' to restore any confusing nuances.

Yet this extreme cultural determinism curiously coexists with an equally extreme political voluntarism. For, in the political usage of the West, countries seem to jump in and out of 'Central Europe' according to their current political behaviour. The best example of this is Slovakia, and it's worth dwelling on for a moment.

2

In 1990, few people doubted that Slovakia belonged to Central Europe. It joined the Visegrád group as part of Czechoslovakia; and being in the same state as the Czech lands was certainly a help. Yet Slovakia had many of the historical qualifications in its own right, being geographically central, overwhelmingly Catholic, formerly part of the Austro-Hungarian empire, and with a capital that was once – though as Pressburg or Pozsony rather than as Bratislava – a cosmopolitan Central European city.

At the same time, its politicians were looking for more autonomy from Prague and a better deal in the Czecho-Slovak federation. These nationalist demands escalated under the demagogic populist Vladimír Mečiar, until the new Czech prime minister Václav Klaus suddenly gave more than most Slovaks (and probably Mečiar himself) wanted: full independence as a sovereign state, from 1 January 1993. A headline in a Czech newspaper encapsulated the Klaus view. It said, 'Alone to Europe or with Slovakia to the Balkans?'

For nearly six years thereafter, with one six-month intermission, Mečiar ran a corrupt, nationalist, semi-authoritarian regime of the kind that has been called, adapting a Latin American term, *demokratura*. It had more in common with the Tudjman regime in Croatia or even the Milošević regime in Serbia than it did with politics in the Czech Republic. The two parts of the former country – Masaryk's country – grew apart at extraordinary speed. ('Yes, we occasionally look at Czech television,' a Slovak friend told me. 'We watch it as we used to watch Austrian television in the communist times.')

The three pillars of Mečiar's *demokratura*, as of Tudjman's and Milošević's, were state television, the secret police and the misappropriation of the formerly state-owned economy by regime members and supporters.[7] Television was grotesquely biased and manipulated. The secret police, called the Slovak Information Service (hence SIS, but not to be confused with the British Secret Intelligence Service), bugged, burgled and intimidated Mečiar's opponents. SIS officers were almost certainly implicated in kidnapping the son of the country's president, Michal Kováč, Mečiar's most prominent critic, and the subsequent murder of someone trying to spill the beans on their involvement in the crime. 'Privatization' was a polite word for misappropriation. And then there was nationalist scapegoating of ethnic Hungarians, some 11 per cent of the new state's population. They were denied basic minority rights, such as having street signs in their own language, and ranted against by Mečiar in what one Slovak democrat described to me as 'hate hours'. Relations with Hungary were abysmal.

In this fashion, Slovakia ejected itself from Central Europe. It fell off the 'first wave' list of candidates for Nato and the EU. The Czechs, despairing of their former partner, took up instead with Slovenia, as that most northern, prosperous and peaceful of the former Yugoslav republics successfully sold itself as a Central European state. (There were even quips about Czecho-Slovenia.) Early in 1998, Madeleine Albright – herself of Czech origin – warned that Slovakia could become 'a hole on the map of Europe'. As late as August, Milan Šimečka, one of the country's leading independent journalists, wrote to me, 'The situation here is worse and worse. Yesterday happened something bad in the private TV Markiza, Mečiar is going to take it. He learns from Milošević and Tudjman.'

Then, suddenly, everything changed. In September 1998, Mečiar lost the election. He was peacefully and decisively defeated by a grand coalition of opposition parties, supported by non-governmental organizations, trade unions, independent media and parts of the Catholic Church. When I visited Bratislava in November, there was a real sense of liberation. Slovakia did not have much of a popular 'velvet revolution' in 1989, and the sociologist Martin Bútora suggested to me that this peaceful overthrow of Mečiar was 'our delayed velvet revolution'. In previous years, people who joined in the 28 October manifestation to mark the founding of Czechoslovakia looked around nervously, fearing Mečiarite surveillance or provocation. This year it was all smiles and celebration. The head of the private Radio Twist told me he used to spend three-quarters of his time defending it against regime harassment: licences revoked, punitive taxes, power lines cut. Now he jokes that he has so much free time he doesn't know what to do with it.

In parliament, I watched the dismantling of two pillars of the *demokratura*, as deputies installed a new supervisory board for state television and a new head of the security service. One deputy prime minister told me how the new government was going to build a true market economy. Another, himself a Hungarian, explained how the rights of the Hungarian minority would be respected.

The governing coalition is a fragile one, but thus far it has made all the right noises. And the West has responded in kind. Madeleine Albright told the new foreign minister in January that 'if Slovakia continues these reforms and keeps improving its relations with its neighbours' then it would be 'a strong candidate' for the next round of Nato enlargement. The French foreign minister encouraged him to believe that the EU might start negotiations with Slovakia before the end of 1999. As if by magic, Slovakia is back in Central Europe again!

If you ask 'Why did it fall out?' you can find several answers. One is the presence of a substantial ethnic minority, who could be made scapegoats – especially because the Hungarians are widely seen as a former oppressor. (Slovakia was part of Hungary until 1918, and subjected to 'Magyarization'.) It has been something close to a rule in the 1990s that the greater the ethnic mix in a post-communist country, the more likely the country has been to take a nationalist authoritarian rather than a liberal democratic path. Those that have done best are also those that are ethnically most homogeneous: Poland, the Czech Republic, Hungary and, yes, Slovenia. (Like all rules, this one has exceptions to prove it, such as Estonia, with its large ethnic Russian population.)

There's a great irony here so far as the Central European debate is concerned. The 1980s revival of the Central European idea involved a celebration of the region's pre-war ethnic and cultural mélange: mixed cities, like Prague or Czernowitz or Bratislava before it was called Bratislava, where people habitually spoke three or four languages; large minorities, especially Jewish and German ones; multi-culturalism *avant la lettre*. Yet it seems that one of the preconditions for being seen as part of the political Central Europe in the 1990s was precisely *not* to be Central European in this earlier sense. Or, to put it another way, Slovakia's problem was that it was still a bit too Central European, in the older sense.

Other reasons offered for Slovakia's falling away include the weakness of its pre-1989 opposition. 'There were really only two dissidents in Bratislava before 1989,' the former dissident Miroslav Kusý reminded me. (The other was Milan Šimečka, father of the independent journalist.) This meant there was no liberal counter-elite to take power after the communists fell, leaving the door open for a skilful populist thug like Mečiar. Then there was the fact that Slovakia's only previous experience of nation-statehood was the clerical-fascist state of Monsignor Jozef Tiso, established under licence from Hitler during the Second World War. And this was an agrarian society, with a relatively small bourgeoisie. In other words, Slovakia was missing some vital elements on the 1980s Central European checklist.

But then you have to ask why it succeeded in bouncing back again. Well, there was the proximity to better examples: Slovakia is sandwiched between Poland, Hungary and the Czech Republic, while Bratislava is an hour's bus ride from Vienna. And there was significant pressure from the West – both active criticism and what has been called the 'passive leverage' of Nato and the EU (i.e. if you don't do X and Y, we simply won't let you in).[8] But perhaps most important was another key item on the 1980s checklist: civil society.

Even in the worst moments of Mečiarism, Slovakia had a vibrant civil society – or what Slovaks call 'the third sector'. There was the powerful Catholic Church. (Although its leaders were rarely outspoken in criticizing Mečiar, prominent lay Catholics were.) There were independent radio stations, magazines and the private television channel Markiza. And there were numerous non-governmental organizations. Some sixty of these got together before the elections in a countrywide campaign to persuade people to turn out and vote, starting in the remotest mountain villages and working down towards Bratislava. There were mass meetings, posters, pamphlets, T-shirts, buttons, baseball caps and 'Rock the Vote' concerts. Arguably this swung the election. The number of votes cast for Mečiar's party actually increased marginally from the previous election in 1994, but, at least partly thanks to this campaign, the electoral turnout went up much more – from 75 per cent to 84 per cent. It was these new voters who did for Vladimír the Terrible. When I described this civic campaign to opposition friends in Serbia a week later, they threw up their hands in envious despair. So perhaps this was a triumph for Central Europe, in yet another sense.

In sum, the phenomenon of Mečiar shows that a positive political outcome (in shorthand, 'democracy') is not culturally predetermined by a Central European heritage. But the circumstances of his ousting do suggest that it helps.

3

Geopolitical boundaries are not just lines drawn on maps by officials in gilded conference chambers. If they are real, then things change when you cross them on the ground. The Iron Curtain was like that: walk ten yards from Checkpoint Charlie and you were in a different world. If you want to experience such a dividing line in today's Europe, then I suggest you go by foot, as I did on a cold November evening, through the border crossing between Vyšné Nemecké in Slovakia and Užhorod in Ukraine.

The shock is instantaneous. Well-made asphalt roads give way to potholes and cobblestones. The Ukrainian border post seems to have been overrun by shaven-headed, thickset men, dressed in black boots, black jeans, black sweaters and bulging black leather jackets – the uniform of the post-communist mafiosi. I watch them taking customs officials by the elbow for a quiet word in a dark corner. I can almost hear the word 'corruption' hiss through the freezing fog. Murmuring into their mobile phones, they jump into dirty black Volvos – of the latest, most powerful, model – and screech off down the road.

Pausing only to set our watches forward one hour from Central to East European Time, my companion and I proceed, more sedately, past large, extravagant villas, with giant satellite dishes, security cameras, high walls and metal gates. 'New Ukraine!' exclaims our guide, a professor at Užhorod University, whose own salary is barely $50 a month – and he hasn't been paid for three months. He accepts the hard currency that I give him for a day's guiding services (the equivalent of a month's salary) with a mixture of gratitude and wounded pride, while we both desperately try to keep up the pretence that this is just normal academic collaboration between two of the world's great universities, Oxford and Užhorod.

The hotel demands payment in advance – cash only – and remember to lock your door from the inside. A friend tells how his father-in-law had a small collision with one of those black Volvos. Four men in black jumped out: 'This will cost you $4,500. Cash. We come to your office tomorrow morning.' He rang the police, gave them the Volvo's licence number, and they promised to check it out. An hour later the police rang back. They said, 'When those men call tomorrow, you pay.' This is a different world. Its essential qualities, as in Serbia, are habitual corruption, arbitrariness supported by violence, and a state that either cannot protect you or is itself criminal.

Today, the boundary between Central and eastern Europe – Ukraine, Belarus and European Russia – is clear and deep and real. I've made the case anecdotally, almost flippantly, but one could do so systematically and at length, with supporting statistics and graphs. This is emphatically not to argue cultural predestination. The Huntington line, our new successor to the Curzon line, runs many miles east of here. The line you cross at Užhorod is the western frontier of the former Soviet Union, not the eastern frontier of western Christendom. Nor am I suggesting that these countries are eternally doomed to corruption, chaos and poverty. Indeed, there is a real possibility that western Ukraine and western Belarus, which, like the Baltic states, were part of the Soviet Union for only two generations rather than three, might recover more quickly than the rest. But both the quality and the sheer scale of the problems of post-communism in the states of the eastern Slavs make for a political dividing line that will probably last for at least another decade. Today, the eastern frontier of the West runs no longer along the river Elbe, nor along the Oder and Neisse, but along two rivers most people have never heard of: the Bug and the Už.

The crossings to the south, by contrast, between Central Europe and what we again call the Balkans, are much less sharp. To walk from Hungary into northern Romania is not to enter a different world. Partly that is because Hungarians live on both sides of the frontier. Both Transylvania and the Banat, which between them comprise more than a third of Romania, are positively marked by the Austro-Hungarian heritage. But even if you take the southern parts of Romania that belonged to the Ottoman empire, the differences in society, politics and economics between Hungary and Romania are nothing like as marked as those between Slovakia and Ukraine.

If you go from the Slovenian part of Istria to the Croatian part, you hardly notice the difference at all. As my *Guida alla Mitteleuropa* rightly suggests, Catholic, formerly Habsburg Croatia clearly qualifies historically as part of Central Europe. Politically, in the 1990s, Croatia has been part of the Balkans. But there is a good chance that it will come back, with Tudjman's *demokratura* crumbling either before or after his death. A new ethnic homogeneity – achieved by ethnic cleansing while the West looked the other way – provides favourable conditions for a return to Central Europe.

There is work for at least another ten years ahead before all those states which have a credible claim to belong to Central Europe by virtue of geography, history and culture will also be part of Central Europe, in the 1990s sense, on account of their current politics and the way they are viewed in the West. It will be longer still before this Central Europe becomes just central Europe, another region of Western Europe, as northern Europe and southern Europe are today. Meanwhile, countries like Ukraine may lift themselves up, especially if the West does more to help them.

Yet Central Europe does have to stop somewhere. To have a purely political, voluntarist definition of it is as absurd as it is to have a purely cultural-determinist one. It has been reasonable enough for the West to make political behaviour the prime criterion of acceptance, saying, in effect, 'Central European is as Central European does.'

But you can't go on for ever suggesting that whichever among the post-communist states exhibits the rule of law, democracy, tolerance, respect for minority rights and interest in peaceful international cooperation will *ipso facto* become part of Central Europe. For example, even if Serbia one day meets all these political criteria, it will not be part of Central Europe. It will still be in the Balkans.

The trouble is that, at the moment, these are not neutral statements. They are heavily charged: positively in the first case, negatively in the second. This is the danger in making any association of a geographical expression with a set of values or aspirations. It's a problem not just with 'Central Europe', but with 'Europe' (as in 'European values') and 'the West' (as in 'Western civilization', or 'Western values' contrasted with 'Asian values').

Yet the difficulty lies precisely in the fact that this association with Central Europe (as with Europe and the West) is *not* completely arbitrary. There is some truth in it. There was a core and a periphery in European historical development. The difference between western Christianity – with its seminal separation of Church and state – and eastern Christianity – with its legacy of 'Caesaro-Papism' – has deeply marked the political history of, say, France as opposed to Russia. And this truth is not just historical. It is also hard contemporary experience. As I was preparing to fly to Slovakia from Heathrow Airport, I met a banker of my acquaintance who travels extensively in CEE. He bluntly summed up his personal findings thus: 'The further east and south you go, the more corruption and chaos.'

The cardinal fault, it seems to me, is to turn probabilities into certainties, grey zones into lines between black and white, and, above all, working descriptions into self-fulfilling prophecies. We know, for example, that the following pairings will be difficult to achieve: Balkan tolerance, Ukrainian prosperity, Russian democracy, Turkish respect for human rights. But to suggest that these are contradictions in terms is not just to relativize our own values. It is also to betray the many, many people who are fighting for these things in these places, against the odds, and sometimes at the risk of their lives.

I have made the case for Central Europe over two decades. I believe it has been a good cause, which has helped to transform the central region of Europe for the better. But I am appalled at the way the idea has now been recruited into the service of these politics of relativism and exclusion. Whatever and wherever Central Europe is, it should never be part of that.

Helena's Kitchen

One gloomy autumn afternoon in 1980, a pale, short, slightly built woman, with untidy brown hair and intense grey-green eyes, greeted me at the door of her small apartment in one of the ugly new housing estates that the communist regime had thrown up around Warsaw. I was in Poland to witness the workers' revolution led by the Solidarity movement, the greatest challenge to the Soviet empire in Eastern Europe since its creation at the end of the Second World War, and I had been told that Helena Łuczywo would be a good source.

Her tiny kitchen, cloudy with cigarette smoke, was packed with people arguing, gesticulating and laughing, pausing only for rapid sips of tea, drunk from glass mugs. In the living room, someone was laying out the next edition of a samizdat magazine called *Robotnik* ('The Worker'), while a real, live worker from Gdańsk, birthplace of Solidarity, held forth in one corner. In another corner sat a pretty seven-year-old, Łucja, Helena's daughter. The phone was ringing – it seemed always to be ringing – and Helena picked it up, shouted into it, talked to me, took a drag on her cigarette and giggled, all at the same time. Life in this crowded apartment was being lived at a mad tempo. Partly this was because there was a revolution on, and at any minute Russian tanks might roll across Poland's eastern frontier. But mainly it was because this place was, well, Helena's.

I visited Helena's kitchen many times during the revolution, until, in December 1981, General Jaruzelski declared martial law to crush Solidarity. Then the authorities made it difficult for me to re-enter the country. But whenever I could get a visa, I headed straight for Helena's: not telephoning beforehand, for fear of alerting the secret police – just turning up at the door. Poland was a police state again, and

Helena was now running an underground paper covertly distributed among Solidarity members and supporters. Our conversations in the kitchen were interrupted by her colleagues – wan, intense women, dashing in with news of some crisis. But now, rather than shouting, they scribbled their messages on scraps of paper. Then they burned the paper in a candle while chattering loudly about something else, for the benefit of hidden police microphones.

Helena and I became firm friends, but I would never have imagined the development that has led me to write about her now. Today, she is the key figure behind the most successful newspaper in the whole of post-communist Europe. *Gazeta Wyborcza* ('The Electoral Paper'), of which she is deputy editor and an executive-board member, sells more than half a million copies on weekdays and an additional 200,000 at the weekend. On its own custom-built web offset presses, it prints a full-colour weekly magazine, a television guide, eighteen different local sections, and book, property, car, job and computer supplements, plus acres of highly lucrative advertising. It employs more than 2,400 people. Its parent company, Agora, has invested in radio stations and satellite television.

This is a multimedia giant in the making – a Polish multimedia giant. And a hugely profitable one: so profitable that it is about to go public. Advised by Credit Suisse First Boston, Agora will soon be making an initial public offering on the Warsaw and London stock exchanges. Its senior managers will be wooing institutional investors in a roadshow through Europe and the United States. Estimates put its value as high as $600 million. Suddenly, my old friend Helena is a very powerful woman. She is about to be a rich one too.

'The Electoral', as most people call it, has a distinctive style – sometimes abrasive, often sarcastic, always irreverent. The political line laid down by its editor-in-chief, Adam Michnik, is a source of constant and even venomous controversy. The nationalist right attacks the paper for being part of a conspiracy – a Jewish-ex-Bolshevik-capitalist conspiracy, you understand – that is sapping the moral fibre of a nation in which to be Polish should mean to be Catholic. Others, such as *Trybuna*, the paper of the former communists, denounce 'Adam Michnik's media cartel', screaming, 'Agora builds an empire!' *Trybuna* has called for the company's radio and television interests to be referred to Poland's Anti-Monopoly Office – an ironic demand from what was once the central organ of the communist party.

I don't like everything about the new paper. But I do like the way it perfectly upends so many Western clichés about Poland as a nation of tall, drunken, bragging, mustachioed, male-chauvinist, anti-Semitic noblemen, making doomed cavalry charges against tanks. Or the old German jibe about *polnische Wirtschaft*, implying that 'Polish economy' is a contradiction in terms. Or another cliché – meant to characterize the whole of post-communist Europe – which has former communist apparatchiks raking in the millions while embittered former dissidents sit in freezing attics, wrapped in nothing but a blanket of woolly memories.

The truth is that Poland is rapidly and quietly building a normal consumer democracy. It has a burgeoning middle class and one of the highest growth rates in Europe. It has started negotiations to enter the European Union, and will join Nato in the spring of 1999. And near the heart of the Polish miracle is this hugely successful paper run by ebullient former dissidents, several of them Jewish and many of them women.

How do you write about someone who has become a close friend? Helena and I had our first formal 'interview' seated in a quiet, modern conference room in the paper's Warsaw offices, talking over the Polish version of a light executive lunch – thick soup, then meat and potatoes. We both laughed at our predicament. There were so many basic things I didn't know. For example, when and where was she born?

During the first winter after the war, in Warsaw. Her father, Ferdynand Chaber, the son of wealthy Jewish wine merchants, had become a communist during the 1920s, spent the war in Russia, and returned after the Polish communists came to power on the back of Russian tanks. He worked in the propaganda department of the new ruling party. The detail suggests an obvious conceit: 'from the father's communist propaganda to the daughter's battle against communist propaganda'. But Helena resists this fiercely. Her mother, she says, had been the more influential figure in her life.

Dorota Guter, who came from a family of Jewish small traders, was a model of industry, discipline, commitment – and deep Polish patriotism. She earned a university degree in law; when the Germans invaded, she fled to Russia, where she took a second degree, in engineering, and was reunited with her husband. On their return, she raised two children, and held a position as a senior engineer at a car factory near Warsaw. At the same time – and this is so important – this determined Jewish mother was deeply immersed in the Polish Romantic tradition represented by poets such as Adam Mickiewicz, the Polish Byron.

Helena was brought up to think of herself as simply Polish. That proved to be difficult. In 1968, while she was studying economics at Warsaw University, she experienced a revolting anti-Semitic campaign orchestrated by communist leaders. Week after week, the communist press was full of tirades against rootless cosmopolitans, parasites on the Polish nation. Polish Jews were denounced as 'a gallery of traitors'. When Warsaw students protested, some were beaten up and others imprisoned, including Adam Michnik, one of their leaders. Most of Poland's surviving Jews – few enough already, after the Holocaust – left the country as a result, and those who stayed were marked for life. Yet the experience also shaped an extraordinarily dynamic generation of Polish '68ers, both Jewish and non-Jewish activists, so similar in some ways to Western '68ers (informal dress and lifestyle; much drink, sex), so different in other, more important, ways. Many came to revere an older generation of fighters against communism, whom their Western counterparts tended to abhor, and, while permanently immunized against utopian politics, they found ideals worth suffering and even dying for.

The year 1968 formed Helena's generation, but her own personal moment of truth came later. She went on to complete her degree in economics, worked in a bank for three years, got married to a bearded engineer called Witold, and gave birth to Łucja. Then she went back to Warsaw University to study English, intending to be a translator and interpreter. Set fair, it seemed, for an ordinary, unpolitical, life. But in the summer of 1976 a message reached her from an opposition leader, Jacek Kuroń. She had good English, so would she accompany a Swedish television team to interview persecuted workers in the industrial town of Ursus? She agonized for three days. She did not want to be a political activist. She was afraid of another anti-Semitic campaign. And what about her three-year-old daughter?

Finally, she decided to go. Why? She lights a cigarette, glances away for a second's thought, then says in her quick way, 'Oh, I don't know. Just a sense of decency.' Decency, Orwell's cardinal virtue. She doesn't stop to reconstruct the way she was then. Yet this was what in Poland is sometimes called 'the Conradian moment' – that single personal decision that makes or mars a whole life. Conrad's Lord Jim jumped the wrong way when he abandoned what he thought was the sinking ship. Helena jumped the right way.

A year later, in 1977, she joined a group of friends – '68ers all – to start the samizdat paper that I found her producing when I visited her three years later. The first issue of *Robotnik* – the title was taken from a famous paper edited by the Polish independence hero Józef Piłsudski before the First World War – appeared that September: four letter-size sheets of paper, with smudged print on one side only. Helena was among those who insisted that its opening editorial should express a clear commitment to the ultimate goal of Polish independence. With Leonid Brezhnev still in power in the Kremlin, that seemed like aiming your bicycle at Mars. But the romantic tradition taught that politics is the art of the impossible. As Byron put it, in lines memorably translated into Polish by Adam Mickiewicz:

> For Freedom's battle once begun,
> Bequeath'd by bleeding Sire to Son,
> Though baffled oft is ever won.

Or, in this case, bequeathed by reading mother to daughter.

More immediately, she discovered the first requirement of being an editor: saying no. She remembers one article which her colleagues thought they should print because it was by a friend. She read it. It was no good. She told the author so, and spiked it. *Basta* – an editor is born. The style they developed in this and other publications connected with KOR, the Workers' Defence Committee, was short, sharp, factual, colloquial. Friends jokingly referred to it as the 'popgun' style. (In Polish, a popgun is a 'corky', *korkowiec*, thus making a pun on KOR.) Partly this was a conscious reaction against the bloated Newspeak of the communist media. Partly it was because the magazine had so little space. Partly, I think, it was because they just wrote the way they spoke. Bang, bang, bang.

The 'printing' of that first issue was done on an ancient duplicator, 300 copies rolled from a revolving drum covered in blue ink. Later editions were produced by a home-made process involving a wooden frame and an inked silk-screen across which a squeegee was run by hand. Despite frequent harassment by the secret police, the paper's print run grew; by early 1980, they were distributing 20,000 copies. In August of that year came the Solidarity revolution, and for sixteen months the paper was produced without fear of immediate police action. Since she also ran a news agency for the movement, Helena scarcely slept.

Then, on 13 December 1981, everything changed with General Jaruzelski's declaration of a 'state of war'. That night, as army and police patrols arrested Solidarity members on Warsaw's snow-covered streets, Helena went into hiding. Within two months she and her colleagues had organized twenty hidden printing places – a small offset press in a cellar, a duplicator in an attic, an old silk-screen machine pressed back into service – and were publishing a new underground paper for the Warsaw region of Solidarity: *Tygodnik Mazowsze* ('The Mazovia Weekly'). Many of the staff were women. They puttered around the city in their tiny Fiat 126 cars, with samizdat in the boot, benefiting from the male chauvinism of the police. For how could a pale young woman, with a small child, in a little Fiat, be any threat to the manly police state? The publication, with the jumbly red Solidarity logo on its masthead (and a quotation from the union's leader, Lech Wałęsa, 'Solidarity will not allow itself to be divided or destroyed'), continued to appear regularly for seven years, until 1989, with print runs eventually as high as 60,000 copies.

Helena remembers this time as awful and exhausting. Although she no longer had to spend her whole life in hiding, everything to do with the paper had to be conspiratorial. The experience, she says, was 'insufferable' – especially with a young daughter to look after. Her marriage disintegrated. Most of her energy was spent on dodging the police. And there was 'no perspective': she did not know – none of us knew – that it would all end in 1989. As far as she could see, it would go on, and on, and on.

One spring day, she found herself walking past someone's allotment garden and looking at it almost longingly. What the hell was she doing with her life? Would she end up an isolated, fanatical activist, as her father had been as a communist before the war? After five years, she needed a break, and the communist authorities let her out to spend a year in the United States, as a 'peace fellow' at Radcliffe College in Harvard. It took an effort to return to Warsaw and go back to the endless grind of underground work. But she carried on producing *Tygodnik Mazowsze* out of cussed loyalty. Loyalty to the great idea of Solidarity. Loyalty to the readers who went on buying the weekly. Loyalty, above all, to her own underground team.

Then, in 1988, after a new wave of Solidarity strikes, the political ground began to move. The Jaruzelski regime, encouraged by Mikhail Gorbachev, sought dialogue with Solidarity, and, early the next year, all parties sat down to negotiate at a 'Round Table' – a model that would later be imitated in Hungary, East Germany and Czechoslovakia. By April 1989, they had agreed that elections should take place, that the opposition would participate, and that it should have a newspaper for the election campaign. Lech Wałęsa asked Adam Michnik to be its editor, and Michnik, in turn, asked Helena and her team from *Tygodnik Mazowsze* to run it. Michnik, that is, would be the public, political head of the paper; Helena would actually get the thing out.

There was very little time. The elections were set for 4 June 1989. With scarcely eight weeks to go, a limited company, Agora, was formed to publish the new paper (its founding shareholders – there were twenty-four – included the film director Andrzej Wajda and the Solidarity leader Zbigniew Bujak). A month later, the first issue appeared, with an editorial declaring that its editors wanted to produce a 'normal' newspaper. It seems now such a modest ambition, but the country had not known a normal newspaper for more than forty years. The newspaper, its editors promised, would be 'multifaced, quick, objective' – and, most important, it would clearly separate commentary from news.

Yet this first issue was openly partisan. In tabloid format, it carried a front-page appeal to its readers to vote for Lech Wałęsa, beneath a large photograph of him. On the masthead was the slogan that I had so often heard protesters chant in the streets: '*Nie ma wolności bez Solidarności.*' 'There's no liberty without Solidarity.' And six of the paper's eight pages were filled with potted biographies of what it called 'our candidates' for parliament. In fact, for the first couple of years, *Gazeta Wyborcza* was still a long way from its proclaimed ideal of a 'normal' newspaper: fact sacred, comment free. Its news stories could be selective and sarcastically partisan. Critics punned that the paper was not 'The Electoral' but 'The Selectoral' (*Wybiorcza* rather than *Wyborcza*).

In those early days, its poor-quality paper and print made it look very much like the old communist papers – not surprising, since it was actually printed on the same press as the communist party daily *Trybuna Ludu*. Adam Michnik had to wrangle with communist leaders to get the paper that was needed. The type was set up in lead, by hand; the typesetters drinking vodka by the litre and suffering from lead poisoning. Upstairs at the print shop sat the censor. Once, during the election campaign, I asked Helena if I could take a cartoon up for approval. I found a frumpy woman in a cheap floral dress, with a glass of tea and a cigarette hanging from her lip, who examined the cartoon carefully and then signed it on the back.

Its first editorial office, at 19 Iwicka Street, was a former nursery school. It still had low tables and child-size chairs. On warm days, editorial meetings were held round a sandpit in the garden. When I visited the office shortly before the elections, I found an atmosphere of creative chaos, with people dashing about amid plumes of cigarette smoke, shouts, laughter, crying and telephones ringing all over the place – Helena's apartment writ large. The underground veterans of *Tydognik Mazowsze*, who came to be known internally as 'the Mazovians', were joined by a few distinguished journalists from other camps, and by a rapidly growing band of the very young. Helena would sit with them at the nursery-school desks, like a schoolteacher, and show them how to write a news story.

'The Electoral Paper' was the organ of the Solidarity opposition in the first free election in Poland for more than fifty years. How much did it contribute to Solidarity's victory? It's an open question. The Poles had more than enough reasons to vote out the communists after so many years of unelected misrule. But the paper contributed decisively to the next step: the appointment of a non-communist prime minister – the first in Eastern Europe since 1948 – and the installation of General Jaruzelski as president, to reassure Moscow. It was the paper that first suggested this. In a characteristic division of labour, Michnik wrote the editorial advancing the radical proposal; Helena thought up the historic banner headline 'Your President, Our Premier'. His article, her headline. With interventions like this, *Gazeta Wyborcza* wrote itself into the history of Poland's negotiated revolution, rather as the Spanish newspaper *El País* had done during Spain's transition from dictatorship to democracy.

Like so many revolutionaries before them, Solidarity's leaders began fighting among themselves soon after their triumph. In the aftermath of this 'war at the top', as Wałęsa described it, the official Solidarity leadership told the paper to remove from its masthead the familiar red logo and the slogan 'There's no liberty without Solidarity.' There was not much solidarity left now that liberty had arrived. In an election in late 1990, Lech Wałęsa stood for president against his own former adviser, Tadeusz Mazowiecki. The paper backed Mazowiecki, but Wałęsa won.

It was high time to do what they said in the first issue they would do: make a 'normal' newspaper. The editors moved out of the nursery school and took over two floors of a nearby office building. Today, those offices do look, at first glance, much like those of a normal Western paper: modern, open-plan, highly computerized, with a cool aesthetic of pale blues and greys, so unlike the strident red, white and black of the years of struggle. And yet they aren't. Helena shares a cramped office at the end of the newsroom with another senior editor. Both have small modern desks rather like something you might buy for a teenage daughter. Casually dressed journalists crowd into this small room for the afternoon conference, standing in the doorway or sitting on the floor. No instructions are barked from the head of a long editorial conference table. Instead, people argue to and fro through the cigarette smoke, with Helena joining in from her little desk. If I half close my eyes I can almost imagine myself back in Helena's old kitchen.

But insiders warn me that appearances can deceive. When I use the word 'egalitarian' to describe the ethos of the paper, one of them exclaims, 'Egalitarian shmegalitarian! You should see the way Helena talks to an intern.' She can lose her cool and bawl out older colleagues.

There's a toughness there that I, as a friend, may not have seen. I ask Helena if she feels that her new power has changed the way people relate to her. She reflects for a moment and says, 'Well, perhaps a little, yes.' I'm afraid it may be a little more than she thinks. Another insider, who preferred not to be named (and that in itself was revealing), told me that younger members of the editorial staff go in fear of her. Several talented journalists have left after arguments. Most painfully, she has ceased to be friends with two of her closest associates from the underground resistance team – those pale, intense women I remember dashing into the old kitchen and burning messages in a candle flame. It's an old story: together under oppression, divided in freedom.

Everyone, but everyone, says that the whole editorial side of the paper revolves around Helena. The only person to dispute this is Helena herself. She is there from morning to night, and is renowned for going over pieces line by line. Even close friends sometimes don't have her private number, because you can always reach her at the office. And she likes other people to be there, too. I was told that one afternoon word got about that Helena had gone out for a few hours to the beautician. Within twenty minutes the office had emptied. Even if not literally true, the story expresses a deeper truth.

What is the paper like now? The offhand, mildly sarcastic tone persists. It's a tone that is impatient, even contemptuous, of an older, stuffier, conservative, Catholic, nationalist Poland, for which Warsaw slang has the delightful term 'bogoojczyźniany' – roughly 'god–fatherlandized'. ('Mrs Z is very nice, but a little god–fatherlandized.') The tabloid-format paper's front page still carries its short, lively, 'popgun-style' stories. Picking up a copy at random, I find the headline 'Fed tnie stopy' – that is, 'Fed Cuts Rates'. (Ten years ago, most Poles would not have known what the Fed was, let alone cared about its rates.) There are high-quality colour photographs – in this copy, the lead picture is of a new Renault car. And there are short items paging the longer stories inside. But these inside news stories are still written in a sharp, readable style. When I've been interviewed by journalists from the paper, I have found that my sentences get chopped up into short, snappy ones, so I started sounding like one of them: bang, bang,

bang. There is strong foreign coverage and – reflecting the country's rapid advance to capitalism – a growing amount of business news. And it has excellent reportage, often written by young journalists on the regional supplements, who track down stories of local corruption, mafias, the drug scene, and so on.

In the weekend edition, there are long essays – about history, the Polish Catholic Church, Polish–Jewish relations, developments in other post-communist countries – of the kind more usually found in intellectual monthlies and quarterlies. It's like having the *New York Review of Books* in the centre pages of a tabloid newspaper. Finally there is the personal contribution of the editor-in-chief, Adam Michnik, who sets the political line. His sharply written, signed commentaries have provoked fierce protest even from his own staff – as when, in the middle of the 1995 presidential campaign, he seemed implicitly to give his support to the post-communist (and ultimately successful) candidate Aleksander Kwaśniewski, against none other than Lech Wałęsa. He was also one of very few people in Poland to criticize, albeit from a position of profound respect, some of the statements made by the Pope on his last visit to his native land.

Wanda Rapaczynski explained to me the commercial strategy of what the rest of the Polish press enviously calls 'Agoraland'. Wanda is the paper's business supremo. She and Helena were childhood friends and attended the same secondary school. Wanda left Poland after the anti-Semitic campaign in 1968 and, at the age of twenty-one, moved to the United States, where she studied to be an academic psychologist, married, had a daughter, then went to the Yale School of Management and worked for Citibank in New York before Helena persuaded her to return.

The company had to grow and diversify, Wanda said – accounting for the business's expansion into radio and television. It needed to protect itself against a possible future recession, in which advertising revenues might slump. Advertising – which until 1989 rarely featured in any Polish periodical – now accounts for more than 70 per cent of the paper's revenue: the kind of healthy ratio that you'd expect to find in any British or American publication. Anyway, to diversify was simply 'the law of the market'. But where to find the capital? 'My borrowing capacity far exceeds the lending capacity of any Polish bank.' Hence the decision to go public. But, before doing so, they had to restructure the company.

The paper is no stranger to foreign investors. In the heroic early days, it had help from Western friends. The French newspaper *Libération* sold a special issue on the paper's behalf. *Le Monde* donated an old printing press, and a group of American supporters, including Robert Silvers and Rea Hederman of the *New York Review of Books*, lent money to transport the press from France. Although that press was never actually used, it served as useful collateral for loans from Polish banks. (So much have things changed that a couple of years ago the paper got a letter from *Le Monde* asking if *Gazeta* would now like to invest in it.) The editors found a substantial American private investor, Cox Enterprises, and they obtained an $8.5 million loan from the European Bank for Reconstruction and Development.

Until recently the company was a business anachronism, a financial world's wonder: worth millions of dollars, but without any clear owner. It had twenty-four founding shareholders but, true to the idealistic collective spirit in which it had begun, their shares had no financial value. What was to be done? Finally, they came up with a solution that creates two kinds of stock: special voters' shares, called A shares, which protect the company from hostile takeovers but cannot be traded, and B shares, which can be traded and will soon have substantial financial value. The three members of the executive board, Helena, Wanda, and the thirty-nine-year-old publisher, Piotr Niemczycki, together with one other editor and a senior manager, control the A shares. The five of them also own B shares, along with ninety-five others. In addition, there is a stock-purchase scheme for 1,700 employees, and an annual incentive plan will reward managers and journalists with further stock. 'Hardly a case of heartless, cold capitalism,' comments Wanda.

Yet, however liberal, meritocratic and broad-based they have tried to make the dividing of the cake, the fact is that in a few years some of those involved in the paper will be very much richer than the others. Seriously rich, by Polish standards. I'm told people already have plans to buy new apartments. 'I worry about the day when department heads start arriving in their new BMWs,' one younger journalist told me. What will happen then to the casual, informal, still outwardly egalitarian atmosphere of the paper? And, in this capitalist multimedia giant, what place is there for the trade-union movement whose organ 'The Electoral Paper' originally was? Not much, it would appear.

I ask Helena if there is a Solidarity branch in the paper. No, there isn't. And she is unapologetic: 'I'm not going to pretend to you that it's in my interest, as an employer, to have a Solidarity branch here.' But she says the paper is an exemplary employer, giving generous work conditions and benefits. The story is complicated by the fact that Solidarity has now become a movement of the political right. It led a coalition of right-wing parties called Solidarity Electoral Action that won the 1997 election, promising, among other things, more state help for workers. Helena, by contrast, is a vehement supporter of the free-market liberalism of the Freedom Union, itself born of the Solidarity movement of the 1980s.

When I first sent her a note about this essay, I recalled how years ago I had described her as 'the Rosa Luxemburg of Solidarity' – an allusion to the early-twentieth-century left-wing Polish-Jewish-German revolutionary. She wrote back, 'I am Thatcher now, not RL any more.' Later, as we talked in Helena's apartment, Adam Michnik teasingly remarked that what she likes about Margaret Thatcher is the 'strong woman'. She retorted that what she really admires is the way the 'Iron Lady' revived Britain's moribund economy by tough, neo-liberal economic policies. Just as she admires the way the Polish economy was transformed after 1989 by the neo-liberal 'shock therapy' of Leszek Balcerowicz, now leader of the Freedom Union. Nonetheless, she insists the paper is still true to the broader ethos of the original Solidarity, with its goals of democracy, civil liberties and human rights.

Meanwhile, one person who won't have the awful problem of deciding what to do with all the money is Adam Michnik. He has flatly declined to take any shares at all. In effect, he has just turned down a million dollars. He told me that his intellectual independence and editorial judgement might be jeoparized if he was always thinking, 'What might this do to the value of the shares?'

So no one can now credibly accuse Adam of heading the paper for personal gain – which doesn't mean they won't still try to. As people realize just how rich and powerful Agora has become, the Jewish theme may re-emerge in the right-wing press – since Adam, Helena and Wanda are all Jewish – with implicit, if not explicit, use of some classic stereotypes. Helena thinks this subject of Polish–Jewish tensions is often greatly overplayed in the West. But she is the first to accept that the relationship is still far from normal.

The continuing tensions are illustrated by one small regular feature in the paper. In a supplement called 'Supermarket', they publish a long list of helplines: Aids, drugs, suicide and so on. At the end of the alphabetical list appears 'Żydowski' ('Jewish') – 'telephone of the Jewish Forum for people who have problems with Jewish origins'. Ring 652 2144 on a Thursday evening.

Normal this isn't. But the new Poland for which the paper stands is precisely one in which people can be Jewish Poles, or Catholic Poles, or agnostic Poles, or Protestant Poles, or Ukrainian Poles; white, black or brown Poles. Here is the great battle that runs through the Polish – and the European – twentieth century: the battle between a narrowly ethnic nationalism and a broader civic patriotism. Even if *Gazeta Wyborcza* has not always managed to practise the tolerance that it preaches towards those who live or think differently, at least it has always preached it.

I find myself wondering where the paper, and Poland, will be in another ten years. Both have travelled such a vast distance towards a Western-style 'normality' over the last decade, and travelled it so exuberantly and so well. Yet still, at every turn, you find some Polish peculiarity. Will these peculiarities, too, gradually disappear? Will the editorial mix become more like that of any other Western paper, with more entertainment and fewer ideas? Perhaps in the new editorial building they are currently planning, to cost an estimated $25 million, there will be large offices and desks, and men in suits and ties barking orders from the end of long conference tables. But perhaps this new Poland will also be a place where, at long last, people can be Jewish Poles as they can be Jewish Americans.

Must the gains and losses always balance out, like entries in an accountant's ledger? More prosperity, less equality. More freedom, less intensity. More tolerance, less solidarity.

I would like to think that some positive singularities will remain. But, if I had to lay a wager, I would bet that they will go. The pressures of a Western consumerist, entertainment model of 'normality' may prove more difficult to resist than those of the Soviet-type communist 'normalization' that Solidarity so roundly and unexpectedly defeated. Perhaps this is the last irony of freedom's battle: the compulsory could be defied, but the voluntary may be irresistible.

Envoi

This book is a kaleidoscope. I hope a few truths about Europe emerge from these mirrored images of coloured fragments, constantly rearranged into different patterns as time's hand twists the tube. Perhaps one truth is that Europe is itself a kaleidoscope. The real Europe, I mean – a jagged, diverse continent of more than 600 million individual men and women, speaking more than fifty languages, living in more than thirty-five states, making food, love and politics in countless subtly different ways.

Such a book can no more end in a summary than a kaleidoscope can be turned into an organization chart. History of the present must acknowledge its own limitations. Systematic conclusions need a greater distance of time. Since the privilege of historians of the present is to record what we ourselves see and hear, our favoured tools are fine brushes and smaller canvasses.

Nonetheless, it is occasionally worth taking up the broad brush to paint what is called 'the big picture'. I have tried this at a couple of junctures, especially in the essays entitled 'Catching the Wrong Bus' and 'The Case for Liberal Order'. Let us revisit this big picture briefly at the end of both decade and book.

Throughout modern European history, periods of order have alternated with generally shorter ones of violent disorder, during which the political map is redrawn. The last decade of the twentieth century has been one of these formative times. A glance at the maps of Europe in 1989 and 1999 will remind you that the political face of Europe changed more between those dates than in any decade since the hellish one of 1939 to 1949. The disorder of the 1990s was not as violent as

413

its predecessors; still, in former Yugoslavia it was violent enough to puncture our Western European leaders' comforting platitude that 'war has been banished from our continent'.

There is no reason at all why order should descend neatly at the end of an arbitrary division of time. As it happens, the main elements of a new order do seem to be in place for the end of the decade – and the millennium. Most of the states of Western Europe, joined together in a slightly larger European Union, have taken the great leap to monetary union. For good or ill, this will determine the shape of West European development for years to come. Germany has absorbed the former East Germany without seriously upsetting its own political system. Its capital moves to Berlin shortly after the Federal Republic's first ever complete change of government through the ballot box. The core states of Central Europe have crossed the bottom of the valley on their journey from communist dictatorship to capitalist democracy, and from East to West. Poland, Hungary and the Czech Republic have become members of Nato. Even if joining the EU takes much longer, we know which slope they are climbing. In the Balkans, the former Yugoslavia has been dismembered into a patchwork of small nation states, together with one or two international protectorates. That process is almost complete.

There are still long ragged edges and large unanswered questions. Won't the effects of one interest rate for all create intolerable political strains between the countries participating in monetary union? How will the Berlin republic reconcile the two souls in its Faustian breast: sovereignty regained and sovereignty surrendered, restored Berlin and sacrificed Deutschmark? What about those states on the borderlines between Central Europe and the Balkans or eastern Europe? And all that unfinished business of Kosovo, Macedonia, Albania, Bosnia, Montenegro and Serbia itself? But only in the former Soviet Union is the shape of the new order still quite unclear. In these four major parts, Western Europe, Germany, Central Europe and the Balkans, the basic direction is apparent.

None of us knew that things would go this way. (Look at the fears expressed early in this book.) The changes for the better experienced by friends in Warsaw, Prague and Budapest have outstripped all our dreams. What happened to those in Belgrade, Sarajevo and Priština has been worse than our worst nightmares.

None of this was inevitable. At every stage, there were other possibilities, paths not taken. In extraordinary times, political leadership is more important than it is in ordinary ones. A large part of the responsibility for two of these four great castings of the die – European monetary union and the shape of German unification – lies with one man: Helmut Kohl. The personal leadership of a Havel or a Göncz was at moments decisive. In the opposite direction, so was that of Mečiar, Tudjman and Milošević. The received wisdom of the early 1990s suggested that the economy was the key in both Western Europe and the former Eastern Europe. Instead, we experienced the primacy of politics.

The new European order has no name as yet. Previous ones have often been known in shorthand by the name of a great international conference. Following the Thirty Years War and the Peace of Westphalia, there was 'Westphalia Europe'. After the Napoleonic Wars came the Congress of Vienna and 'Vienna Europe'; after the First World War, the Europe of 'Versailles'. Most recently we had 'Yalta Europe', which was a result of the Second World War but frozen in place for forty years by the Cold War. There was no single grand international conference to redraw the map of Europe at the end of the Cold War. German politicians, in negotiating their unification, deliberately set out to avoid that. The last thing they wanted was a new Versailles.

We might think of calling the new order 'Paris Europe', after the November 1990 Paris Charter for a New Europe, signed by all the states of the Conference for Security and Cooperation in Europe. But the Paris Charter bears as much resemblance to what happened afterwards, in the 'new Europe', as our personal new-year resolutions do to our subsequent behaviour. Contemplating the EU and monetary union, some might say 'Brussels Europe'. Those who overdramatize Germany's return as the great power in the centre of Europe would counter with 'Berlin Europe'. Then again, if I look at Central Europe or the Balkans I am tempted to suggest 'Washington Europe'. With the enlargement of Nato and the United States' leading role in the

Balkans, the Americans are as heavily involved in Europe at the end of the 1990s as they were at the beginning.

Whatever its name, this is not the order I hoped for. In this respect, I feel a painful contrast with the 1980s. In the 1980s, I argued that the Soviet empire in what was then called Eastern Europe was both illegitimate and fragile. Peaceful change could come only with pressure from below. The West had not just a moral but also a political interest in supporting the so-called dissidents. During the 'velvet revolutions' of 1989 I enjoyed a sense of triumph and vindication. I felt that I had contributed, in a very small way, to a great change for the better.

Since the beginning of the 1990s, I have argued (mainly in newspaper commentaries, lectures and conference talks not reprinted here) that the West's top priority should be to seize the opportunity offered by the peaceful ending of the Yalta division of Europe and build a liberal order for the whole of Europe – a 'Europe whole and free', as George Bush put it, in one of his few memorable phrases. So Nato should aim to embrace the new democracies. The European Union should concentrate on preparing for eastward enlargement and on the close coordination of its members' national foreign and security policies, to meet the challenges that would surely arise from the upheavals of post-communism. I have wanted Britain to take a lead in this direction.

The Nato argument has been won, mainly by the advocacy of others, especially in America and Germany. The argument about priorities for the European Union has been lost. We did not prevent war returning to our continent. We fiddled while former Yugoslavia burned. The United States had once again to step in to sort out Europe's mess. Preparations for eastward enlargement of the EU have been sluggish and niggardly, as if the EU's secret motto was what the French businessman said to me in January 1996: '*Il faut toujours en parler, et jamais y penser.*' If Central Europe is now joining the West, 90 per cent of the credit belongs to the Central Europeans themselves, scarcely 10 per cent to us. As I feared in my essay of July 1990, we have been Dr Johnson's patron: 'one who looks with unconcern on a man struggling for life in the water, and, when he has reached ground, encumbers him with help'. Britain has been too hobbled by its own 'European debate' to take much of a lead in the direction I had urged.

This failure of advocacy is hardly surprising. If you think you have influenced policy as a commentator, it is usually an illusion anyway. All commentary is a kind of blowing in the wind. When the wind is blowing in the same direction, as it was for me at the end of the 1980s, you may imagine that it is your breath that is bending those trees. When the wind is against you, the spit comes back in your face. Nonetheless, I still have a personal sense of failure.

Much more seriously, I think Europe is in worse shape than it might have been. In the end, something has happened along the two fronts upon which I concentrated. Enlargement negotiations have begun with Poland, Hungary, the Czech Republic, Estonia and Slovenia. In 1999 we are promised a single foreign policy representative of the EU. As I write, a conference jointly chaired by the French and British foreign ministers is trying to broker peace in Kosovo. However, the conference is organized not by the EU but by the Contact Group on former Yugoslavia, including Russia and the United States. The plan they are putting to Serbs and Kosovar Albanians is essentially the work of an American diplomat, and it will succeed only with Americans on the ground. Meanwhile, Poland, Hungary and the others seem unlikely to become members of the EU until the middle of the next decade. They will survive the wait, but the impact of delay on those behind them in the queue – countries like Romania and Bulgaria – may be more serious.

Instead of pressing ahead with enlargement of the EU, the leaders of Western Europe have concentrated their energies on the adventure of monetary union. I admire the efforts of statesmanship and political will that made this happen. Only a fool or a bigot could not see potential benefits. But I think it was simply the wrong priority for the 1990s. After the miraculously peaceful end of the Cold War, we should have concentrated our efforts on building that liberal order for the whole of Europe. And I am afraid that EMU is a bridge too far for Western Europe itself. Some of the countries now in the monetary union are not ready for it. I fear the resulting strains will make Western Europe a very bad-tempered place – perhaps even worse – at some point in the next ten years. The only consolation in making such a guess is that I would be glad to be proved wrong.

*

Most of the fragments in this kaleidoscope come from faraway countries of which most British readers know little – and I'm not thinking only of Ruthenia. Everyone can see the central importance of Germany, but most people in Britain still hardly know that country. (Perhaps this is because we tend not to go on holiday there, whereas we do go to France, Spain and Italy. The Bonn republic also had the reputation of being a little boring – this may even be accounted one of its great achievements.)

The political argument I have made in the 1990s, like that of the 1980s, has of course been influenced by my personal involvement in Germany, Central Europe and the Balkans. To be thus deeply engaged in the affairs of other countries brings the danger of being partisan and quixotic – and certainly of being seen as such. Yet to be judged on your arguments rather than your motives is a basic intellectual right, and I maintain that my argument is valid for the whole of Europe. Where does it leave the country in which I live and about which I care still more deeply?

Although Britain stands a little apart from Europe, the singularity of its apartness and ambivalence is often overstated. For example, it is said that Britain is one of only two European countries in which people talk about 'Europe' as being somewhere else ('Jim's just back from Europe'). The other, we are told, is Russia. Yet I have encountered this way of speaking about Europe in many other European countries, from Portugal to Poland and Sweden to Greece. Swedes, Poles and Greeks insist their countries are part of Europe, but also worry that there's a political, economic or cultural reality to which they may not fully belong.

In fact, about the only European countries that never question their own belonging to Europe are France, Germany, Belgium, the Netherlands and Luxembourg. Yet, even in those core countries of Western Europe, there is ambivalence about the shape that the political project known as 'Europe' has assumed in the 1990s. Remember that only a bare majority of French voters approved of the Maastricht Treaty in the referendum of September 1992. Until well into 1998, more than half the Germans asked in opinion polls said they were opposed to giving up the Deutschmark for the euro. One of the chronic British fallacies about 'Europe' is the notion that over there, on the

Continent, 300 million people are lined up behind a single grand design, like a Napoleonic army.

Britain also vibrates to some deeper European rhythms, often without knowing it. Take 'sleaze', for example – one of the big themes of British politics in the 1990s. If you look through the chronologies in this book, you will find that the exposure of political corruption was a feature of politics across Europe. In Italy, France, Spain and Greece, serving or former prime ministers were accused, indicted, imprisoned or committed suicide as a result. Why did political corruption become a major issue across Europe? Was it because the end of the Cold War meant that people felt free to expose corruption where previously this would have been seen as playing into the hands of the other side? Because more than forty years of the same system had encouraged the slow erosion of standards? Because, since elections are now won by television and advertising, politicians need ever more money to fund them? Whatever the reasons, Britain had a rather mild bout of an all-European disease.

Or take devolution. Is it pure accident that Scotland and Wales vote for their own new national assemblies at a time when smaller peoples all over Europe have been pressing for greater autonomy or seizing independence? Catalonia and the Basque country, Wallonia and Flanders, Slovakia, Croatia, Slovenia, Moldova, Ruthenia . . . Again, the local causes are diverse, but there is a deeper pattern, a dance to the music of Europe.

That said, in some respects Britain really is different. The most obvious of the differences include common law, the unwritten constitution and the sovereignty of Parliament, our deep affinities with what Churchill called 'the English-speaking peoples' (Americans, Canadians, Australians, New Zealanders) and having the Anglo-American version of capitalism, as opposed to the Franco-German or 'Rhenish' model that predominates in what is now popularly called 'Euroland'. While many European peoples doubt whether they fully belong to Europe, we are one of the few who also doubt whether we want fully to belong. (Who are the others? Russia, certainly. Perhaps Ukraine and Serbia. Denmark? Sweden?) So at the end of the 1990s we once again stand aside from a major continental development, as we agonize over whether or not to join Euroland.

Our choice will matter to Europe, since Britain is the fifth largest economy in the world, politically and militarily one of the EU's big three states, and home to its most important financial centre. If Russia is the great unknown in Europe's east, Britain is that in its west. Our choice coincides with the incremental disuniting of the United Kingdom, in Scotland, Wales and Northern Ireland. Together, these two developments pose fundamental questions about where and what we wish Britain to be. And, for us English, questions about England. As the historian Geoffrey Hosking has suggested, the English have this in common with the Russians: that our national identity has for centuries been bound up with an imperial one. So the Matter of England is set fair to be one of Europe's more interesting subjects over the next ten years.

The trouble with the choice about entering monetary union – shall we call it The Choice? – is that it hinges on economics, and on speculative assertions about the political consequences of economic actions. In this it differs from other great foreign-policy choices like the Suez crisis or Vietnam, where most ordinary citizens could easily grasp the main facts. This is more complex, impenetrable and imponderable. (Am I alone in feeling that it is also more boring?)

As a non-economist, there are only three things that I can say with any confidence about The Choice. First, if you care at all about the rest of Europe you must now hope for the existing monetary union of eleven states to succeed, even if you wish (as I do) that it had not been tried in this decade. Second, it is possible to be in favour of the European Union and opposed to Britain joining the monetary union. Some British opponents of monetary union really are 'anti-European', but it is quite wrong to dismiss all opponents with that tag. Third, and most important, don't believe anyone who tells you that the course they advocate – to go in, to stay out – is without large dangers.

Both courses are heavy with risk. If we go in, we risk sacrificing some of our hard-won flexibility and competitive advantages, joining an enterprise that is flawed, having an interest rate that may not fit our economic circumstances, and also diminishing democratic, parliamentary control over vital areas of national policy. If we stay out, we risk a loss of influence over European decisions that will directly affect us, long-term decline in the foreign direct investment that has created many jobs in Britain, discrimination against British exports to our largest market, and downgrading as a political partner of the United States. For us in Britain, the chief legacy of Europe's 1990s is this unenviable choice.

We can – and I think should – wait for another few turns of the European kaleidoscope. But we will have to decide, as the historian of the present has to write, before the long-term consequences are clear. Whichever way we finally jump, one thing we owe to ourselves, and to Europe, as we prepare to make The Choice. That is to see Europe plain and to see it whole.

1999

Asked what was his greatest problem as prime minister, Harold Macmillan is said to have replied, 'Events, dear boy, events.' The same is true of writing history of the present. This book went to press at the end of March, just a week after Nato went to war with Serbia over Kosovo. I list a few important entries in the European political diary for the rest of 1999, but I leave spaces for those unexpected events that are often more important.

11 March. Oskar Lafontaine resigns as German finance minister and leader of the SPD.

12 March. Poland, Hungary and the Czech Republic formally join Nato at a ceremony in Independence, Missouri.

15 March. Kosovo peace talks resume in Rambouillet.

16 March. The whole European Commission under Jacques Santer resigns after a damning independent report on corruption and mismanagement in the Commission.

19 March. Kosovo peace talks in Rambouillet end with Kosovar Albanian delegation signing but Serb side refusing to sign the agreement.

23 March. Nato gives order to bomb Serbian military targets after special envoy Richard Holbrooke fails to persuade Slobodan Milošević to accept the Rambouillet agreement.

24–25 March. A special EU summit in Berlin agrees budgets for 2000 to 2006 and nominates former Italian prime minister Romano Prodi as president of the European Commission.

24 March. Nato bombing campaign begins against military targets in Serbia, Kosovo and Montenegro. Serbian forces conduct a campaign of terror and 'ethnic cleansing' in Kosovo, resulting already by the end of March in the flight of perhaps as many as 200,000 Kosovar Albanians, in addition to the estimated quarter of a million already made homeless.

19 April. The first meeting of the Bundestag in the restored Reichstag building in Berlin.

23–25 April. Nato's fiftieth-anniversary summit in Washington.

6 May. Elections to new parliamentary assemblies in Scotland and Wales.

3–5 June. An EU summit under German presidency in Cologne.

June. Elections to the European parliament. General elections scheduled in Belgium and Luxembourg.

October. Presidential elections in Ukraine.

December. Parliamentary elections in Russia.

Notes

Introduction

1. See Reinhart Koselleck, 'Sprachwandel und Ereignisgeschichte', in *Merkur*, 8/43, August 1989.
2. E. J. Hobsbawm, 'The Historian between the Quest for the Universal and the Quest for Identity', in *Diogenes*, no. 168 (vol. 42/4), 1994.
3. Neal Ascherson, 'Fellow-Travelling', in *London Review of Books*, 8 February 1996.
4. On this, see my 'Orwell in 1998', in *New York Review of Books*, 22 October 1998.
5. The don was Harry Willetts – an otherwise lovable, wry and learned historian of Russia and Poland, and translator of both the Pope and Solzhenitsyn.

The Solution

1. Armin Mitter and Stefan Wolle, eds., *Ich liebe Euch doch alle! Befehle und Lageberichte des MfS January–November 1989* ['But I Love You All! Orders and Situation Reports of the Ministry for State Security January–November 1989'] (Berlin: BasisDruck Verlagsgesellschaft, 1990). But see note 3 below.
2. See the chapter on Germany in my *We the People: The Revolution of '89 Witnessed in Warsaw, Budapest, Berlin and Prague* (new edn, London: Penguin, 1999).
3. Like many of the most famous quotations in history, this is generally misquoted. It is usually given as *'Ich liebe Euch doch alle'*, as in the book title cited in note 1. But in the televised record of the People's Chamber session he says just, *'Ich liebe doch alle . . . alle Menschen.'*

After Solidarity

1. *Rok 1989: Bronisław Geremek Opowiada, Jacek Żakowski Pyta* ['The Year 1989: Bronisław Geremek Relates, Jacek Żakowski Asks'] (Warsaw: Plejada, 1990); Lech Wałęsa, *Droga do Wolności: 1985–1990 Decydujące Lata* ['The Path to Freedom: 1985–1990 The Decisive Years'] (Warsaw: Editions Spotkania, 1991); Jarosław Kurski, *Wódz* ['The Chief'] (Warsaw: Pomost, 1991).
2. Krzysztof Dubiński, *Magdalenka: Transakcja Epoki* ['Magdalenka: The Transaction of the Epoch'] (Warsaw: Sylwa, 1990). Besides the Father, the Son, and the Holy Ghost, there was also the Holy Father, whose close interest in Polish affairs is described in both the Geremek and the Wałęsa volumes. Geremek recalls the Pope telling him how he had asked President Reagan to help Poland economically. Solidarity also hoped to learn about Soviet attitudes to Poland through the Vatican's diplomatic service, which, however, could not tell them much more than they already knew.
3. This is one of many moving details in Jacek Kuroń, *Wiara i Wina: Do i od Komunizmu* ['Faith and Guilt: To and from Communism'] (Warsaw: Nowa, 1990).
4. The detail about the forger's plates comes from Maciej Łopiński, Marcin Moskit and Mariusz Wilk, *Konspira: Solidarity Underground*, trans. Jane Cave (Berkeley: University of California Press, 1990).

Intellectuals and Politicians

1. See my account in *We the People: The Revolution of '89 Witnessed in Warsaw, Budapest, Berlin and Prague* (new edn, London: Penguin, 1999).
2. Václav Klaus, *Proč jsem konzervativcem?* ['Why am I a conservative?'] (Prague: TOP Agency, 1992).
3. A very useful exploration of this subject, partly inspired by Havel's earlier writings, is Ian MacLean, Alan Montefiore and Peter Winch, eds., *The Political Responsibility of Intellectuals* (Cambridge: Cambridge University Press, 1990).
4. I first used this phrase in my essay '*Après le Déluge, Nous*', see above, p. 22.
5. Published in English as George Konrád and Ivan Szelényi, *The Intellectuals on the Road to Class Power* (New York: Harcourt Brace, 1979). Szelényi notes in his introduction that the manuscript was completed in 1974.

6. The full title of the English-language volume is *Toward a Civil Society: Selected Speeches and Writings 1990–1994* (Prague: Lidové Noviny, 1994). A note on the copyright page indicates that this volume is edited by Paul Wilson, with the translations by Paul Wilson and others. A slightly different edition has now been published as *The Art of the Impossible: Politics as Morality in Practice: Speeches and Writings, 1990–1996* (New York: Knopf, 1997). The Czech collections are Václav Havel, *Projevy leden–červen 1990* ['Speeches: January–June 1990'] (Prague: Vyšehrad, 1990), Václav Havel, *Vážení občané, Projevy červenec 1990–červenec 1992* ['Dear Citizens: Speeches, July 1990–July 1992'] (Prague: Lidové Noviny, 1992), and *Václav Havel 1992 & 1993* (Prague: Paseka, 1994).

7. The Czech original is even more emphatic, saying literally, 'All lie who tell us that politics is a dirty business.'

8. Václav Havel, *Vážení obcané*, pp. 198–9.

9. The sequel is amusing. After being instrumental in reactivating the PEN club, Klíma was summoned for interrogation by the security police. Their main concern was that Václav Havel should not become president of Czech PEN. Three months later he was president of Czechoslovakia.

Bosnia in Our Future

1. This and many other details come from the superb documentary series 'The Death of Yugoslavia' (made for BBC Television by Brian Lapping Associates, series producer Norma Percy) and the book that accompanies the series, Laura Silber and Alan Little, *The Death of Yugoslavia* (London: Penguin/BBC, 1995). See also Misha Glenny, *The Fall of Yugoslavia* (rev. edn, London: Penguin, 1993).

2. The decision to adopt the term 'Bosniak' as the name of the nation previously described as the 'Bosnian Muslims' was taken by the Second Bosnian Assembly in 1993 and reaffirmed in the Dayton agreement and constitution. (I am most grateful to Robert Donia for this information.) I use the term not only because it is the correct one, but also because, in my experience, many Bosnian 'muslims' are not at all muslim in the sense that, say, an Iranian or a Saudi would recognize.

3. In fact it was the linguist Max Weinreich who observed, in 1945, 'A language is a dialect with an army and a navy.' I am most grateful to Tim Snyder for this information. Perhaps one could also say that a state is a language with an army.

Forty Years On

1. The excellent English-language edition is György Litván, ed., *The Hungarian Revolution of 1956: Reform, Revolt and Repression 1953–1963*, ed. and trans. János M. Bak and Lyman H. Legters (London: Longman, 1996).

2. Entitled 'Hungary and the World 1956: The New Archival Evidence', the conference was organized by the Institute for the History of the 1956 Hungarian Revolution and the Hungarian Academy of Sciences, in Budapest, and the National Security Archive and the Cold War International History Project, both of Washington, DC.

3. The Malin notes are translated and expertly annotated by Mark Kramer, a Harvard specialist on Soviet–East European relations, in a compendium of declassified documents prepared for the conference by the 1956 Institute and the National Security Archive. A larger collection of documents is due to be published by Central European University Press.

4. The memorandum is included in the compendium of declassified documents mentioned in note 3.

5. See my review essay 'From World War to Cold War', *New York Review of Books*, 11 June 1987.

6. *Victoire d'une défaite* is the title of the original French edition, published by Fayard in 1968. The English edition is entitled *Budapest 1956. A History of the Hungarian Revolution* (London: Allen & Unwin, 1971).

7. Suitably enough, Miklós Haraszti's book on the position of artists under Kádárism was entitled *The Velvet Prison* (New York: Basic Books, 1987). See also my 'The Hungarian Lesson' in *The Uses of Adversity: Essays on the Fate of Central Europe* (new edn, London: Penguin, 1999).

8. See István Bibó, *Democracy, Revolution, Self-Determination. Selected Writings*, ed. Károly Nagy (Boulder, Colo.: Social Science Monographs, 1991).

9. 'Refolution in Hungary and Poland', *New York Review of Books*, 17 August 1989.

10. János Kenedi, *Kis Állambiztonsági Olvasókönyv a Kádár-korszakban* ['A Small Reader on the State Security Services in the Kádár Period'] (Budapest: Magvetö, 1996).

The Witness Wolf

1. Markus Wolf (with Anne McElvoy), *Man Without a Face: The Autobiography of Communism's Greatest Spymaster* (London: Jonathan Cape, 1997).

Trials, Purges and History Lessons

1. Priscilla Hayner is currently completing a book about truth commissions. I am grateful to her for confirming this tally.
2. I look at the work of the South African truth commission in 'True Confessions', *New York Review of Books*, 17 July 1997.

Cry, the Dismembered Country

1. I put 'muslims' in inverted commas in both cases, because Islamic observance seems to be even more lax in the Kosovar case – certainly in the towns – than in the Bosnian one. There is also a small but significant community of Kosovar Albanian Catholics.
2. 'Dervishes' is no mere figure of speech. Although the dervish orders were officially closed down in 1952, I was shown the mosque in Orahovac where the dervish rites are now again observed.
3. This and much other invaluable information is to be found in two excellent reports by the International Crisis Group, *Kosovo Spring*, and *Kosovo's Long Hot Summer*, both available from its web site: http://www.crisisweb.org.
4. See 'The Serbian Tragedy', above, p. 254.
5. It is striking that the few references to Kosovo in Richard Holbrooke's *To End a War* (New York: Random House, 1998) concern the time before or after he was active in the Bosnia negotiations. The only mention of Kosovo that I can find in his account of the actual Dayton negotiations is this: 'Once, as Milošević and I were taking a walk, about one hundred local Albanian Americans came to the outer fence of Wright-Patterson with megaphones to plead the case for Kosovo. I suggested we walk over to chat with them, but he refused, saying testily that they were obviously being paid by a foreign power.'
6. Mr Ademi told me has not seen a copy of this document, although 'Mr Rugova must have one in his drawer.' In her *Between Serb and Albanian: A*

History of Kosovo (London: Hurst, 1998), p. 253, Miranda Vickers quotes an October 1991 statement by the 'Coordinating Committee of Albanian Political Parties in Yugoslavia' – presumably the same body – which canvasses more radical options including an Albanian Republic embracing all the Albanian-settled parts of Kosovo, Macedonia, Montenegro and Serbia proper, or, in the event of a change to the external frontiers of former Yugoslavia, territorial unification with Albania 'within the boundaries proclaimed by the First Prizren League in 1878'. However, the only source she gives is a study by a Serb scholar in good standing with the Milošević regime, and one would wish to be sure that the text and context of the Albanian original are fairly given.

7. For a scholarly and acerbic dissection of these myths, see Noel Malcolm, *Kosovo: A Short History* (London: Macmillan, 1998).

8. The claim would be that, contrary to what President Kučan of Slovenia told me (see above, p. 333), Kosovo, as an 'autonomous province', was a constituent part of former Yugoslavia, and therefore has the same right to secede as all other constituent parts. Noel Malcolm, *Kosovo*, pp. 264–5, argues with fiendish ingenuity that, when Kosovo was taken from the Ottoman empire by the Serbs in 1912–13, it was never properly, legally incorporated into Serbia at all . . .

9. I owe this insight, like many others, to Pierre Hassner.

Where is Central Europe Now?

1. 'Does Central Europe Exist?', *New York Review of Books*, 9 October 1986. The essay is reprinted in my *The Uses of Adversity: Essays on the Fate of Central Europe* (new edn, London: Penguin, 1999).

2. 'Nato Enlargement: Build a Europe Whole and Free', *International Herald Tribune*, 30 April 1998.

3. Karl A. Sinnhuber, 'Central Europe – Mitteleuropa – Europe Centrale: An Analysis of a Geographical Term', *Institute of British Geographers Transactions and Papers*, 1954.

4. Milan Kundera, 'The Tragedy of Central Europe', *New York Review of Books*, 26 April 1984. The version of this essay published in *Granta*, no. 11, 1984, bore Kundera's own title: 'A Kidnapped West or Culture Bows Out'.

5. Vesna Goldsworthy explores the literary-political past and present of these negative images of the Balkans in her *Inventing Ruritania: The Imperialism of the Imagination* (New Haven and London: Yale University Press, 1998).

6. See his *The Clash of Civilizations and the Remaking of World Order*

(London: Touchstone Books, 1997). His original article on 'the clash of civilizations' was published in *Foreign Affairs* in summer 1993.

7. On Milošević's and Tudjman's *demokraturas*, see 'Cry, the Dismembered Country', above, p. 354.

8. See the forthcoming book by Milada Vachudova, *Revolution, Democracy and Integration: The Domestic and International Politics of East Central Europe since 1989* (Oxford: Oxford University Press). The argument in this essay is also indebted to the article by Tim Snyder and Milada Vachudova, 'Are Transitions Transitory? Two Types of Political Change in Eastern Europe since 1989', *East European Politics and Societies*, vol. 11, no. 1, and to comments by Tim Snyder, Vladimir Tismaneanu and Charles King.

Acknowledgements

I am most grateful to my outstanding editors: Robert Silvers of the *New York Review of Books*, Bill Buford, first at *Granta* and now at *The New Yorker*, Ian Birrell at the restored *Independent*, Ferdinand Mount at *The Times Literary Supplement*, Fareed Zakaria at *Foreign Affairs* and, last but not least, Stuart Proffitt at Penguin Books. They have improved these texts by asking the quintessential editor's question 'What do you really mean?'

My Oxford college, St Antony's, is a model of reaching out across the frontiers that I describe in the Introduction. I thank particularly its two Wardens of the 1990s, Lord Dahrendorf and Sir Marrack Goulding, and the many colleagues and students who have commented on, or garnered information for, the essays in this book.

Finally, there are the friends and acquaintances across Europe who contributed in so many different ways: sometimes unknowingly, but more often with deliberate generosity. This book would not merely have been impossible without them. It is, in a deeper sense, all about them.

PERMISSIONS

Methuen Publishing Ltd for 'The Solution' by Bertolt Brecht from *Poems 1913–1956*, edited by John Willett (1980); Shukat & Hafer (Attorneys) on behalf of Leonard Cohen for lyrics from 'Suzanne' from the LP *Songs of Leonard Cohen* (1968); The Ecco Press for an extract from 'The Envoy of Mr Cogito' from *Mr Cogito* by Zbigniew Herbert, translated by John Carpenter and Bogdana Carpenter (1993), translation © 1993 by John Carpenter and Bogdana Carpenter, © 1974 by Zbigniew Herbert; A. P. Watt Ltd on behalf of The National Trust for Places of Historic Interest or Natural Beauty for lines from 'The White Man's Burden' (1899) by Rudyard Kipling from *Selected Poems*, edited by Peter Keating (Penguin Twentieth Century

Classics, 1993); Sony/ATV Music for lyrics from 'Hey Jude' by Paul McCartney (Apple Records, 1968); Random House UK Ltd for 'Apologies for Being Human', quoted in *Man Without a Face: The Autobiography of Communism's Greatest Spymaster* by Markus Wolf and Anne McElvoy (Jonathan Cape, 1997).

Every effort has been made to trace or contact copyright holders to obtain their permission for use of copyright material. The publishers will gladly receive any information enabling them to rectify any errors or omissions at the earliest opportunity.

Index

This index lists only personal and place names

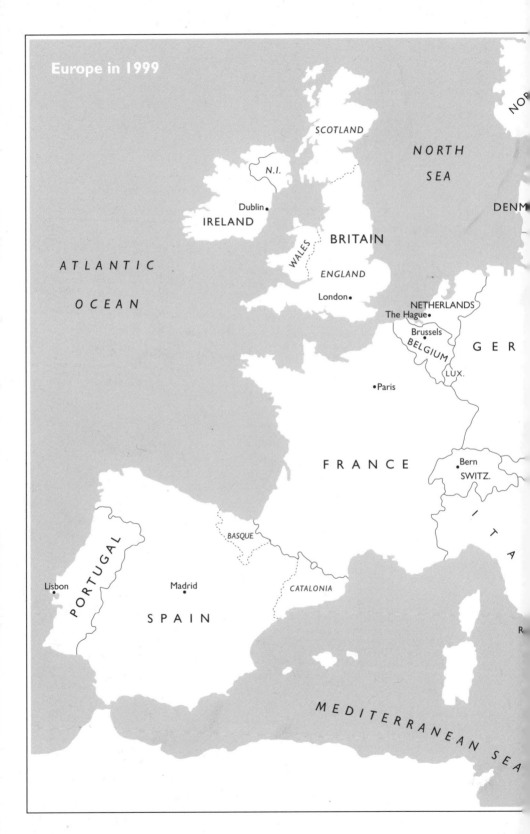

Europe in 1999